Kangchenjunga, a drawing by John Dugger

THE
ALPINE JOURNAL
2005

Roger Payne and Julie-Ann Clyma above the big dihedral on the Innominata Ridge, Mont Blanc, completing the route *From Dawn to Decadence*. (*John Harlin*)

THE
ALPINE JOURNAL

2005

The Journal of the Alpine Club

A record of mountain adventure
and scientific observation

Edited by Stephen Goodwin

Assistant Editors:
Paul Knott and Geoffrey Templeman

Production Editor: Johanna Merz

Volume 110

No 354

Supported by the
MOUNT EVEREST FOUNDATION

Published jointly by
THE ALPINE CLUB & THE ERNEST PRESS

THE ALPINE JOURNAL 2005
Volume 110 No 354

Address all editorial communications to the Hon Editor :
Stephen Goodwin, 1 Ivy Cottages, Edenhall, Penrith, CA11 8SN
e-mail : sg@stephengoodwin.demon.co.uk
Address all sales and distribution communications to:
Cordée, 3a De Montfort Street, Leicester, LE1 7HD

Back numbers:
Apply to the Alpine Club, 55 Charlotte Road, London, EC2A 3QF
or, for 1969 to date, apply to Cordée, as above.

© 2005 by the Alpine Club

First published in 2005 jointly by the Alpine Club and the Ernest Press
Typesetting by Johanna Merz
Printed in China

A CIP catalogue record for this book is
available from the British Library

ISBN 0 948153 79 2

'When Charles Evans first beheld Kangchenjunga, from Darjeeling in
1945, his feelings, he said, were deeper than he could have imagined.'
[Then I suggest] In an account of that wartime visit, published in this AJ
for the first time, he wrote,'I put my hands on an iron railing and looked
down at the brightly coloured bazaar below but my eyes went back to the
gigantic mountain vision.'

Foreword

When Charles Evans first beheld Kangchenjunga, from Darjeeling in 1945, his feelings, he said, were deeper than he could have imagined. In an account of that wartime visit, published in this *AJ* for the first time, he wrote, 'I put my hands on an iron railing and looked down at the brightly coloured bazaar below but my eyes went back to the gigantic mountain vision.'

Kangchenjunga entrances like no other 8000er, rising immense yet seemingly weightless above the cloud-shrouded foothills; tourists, painters, pilgrims and climbers have all caught their breath in wonder. In 1955, the young Joe Brown found it a 'truly incredible sight'. Weeks later, after leading the highest crack climb on the planet, there was still a note of reverential awe. Rather than triumph on the summit, he felt only relief at not having to step up yet again, 'and also a feeling of peace and tranquillity'.

Brown and George Band stopped 20 feet away and five feet below the sacred summit cone on 25 May; Tony Streather and Norman Hardie followed a day later. The so-called 'reconnaissance in force' led by Evans was an exemplar of exploratory mountaineering, modest in demeanour yet audacious in its negotiation of nearly 10,000 feet of untrodden ground, with pitches of rock and steep ice and a Crib Goch-like ridge.

This 110th volume of the *Alpine Journal* pays tribute to the 1955 team. Kangchenjunga was also the focus this year for Alan Hinkes, intent on becoming the first Brit to climb all 14 of the 8000m peaks. In a piece that publication schedules demanded he write *before* departure for Nepal, Alan looks forward to what was his third visit to Kangchenjunga and reflects on his 18-year marathon. Why does he do it? 'I suppose if you chop me in half…it doesn't say "Blackpool Rock", it says "Mountain Climber"…I just can't do anything else,' he told the BBC. It does not have quite the enigmatic ring of Mallory, but was a good northern riposte to the perennial question.

Kangchenjunga apart, there is little attention given to 8000-metre peaks in this volume – except through the brush of Howard Somervell whose paintings are the subject of a detailed survey by David Seddon. Somervell's hazy watercolours feature right through the book. The focus of leading alpinists in 2004 continued to be on bold but less time-consuming face routes – Ian Parnell and John Varco on Saf Minal, Jon Bracey and Rich Cross on Mt Kennedy's 'Arctic Discipline Wall', and Nick Bullock concluding his affair with Teng Kangpoche's north-west face, this time with Nick Carter. These and more are recorded here, perhaps illustrating Ken Wilson's belief, expressed on the dust jacket of Mick Fowler's new book *On Thin Ice*, that we are in the midst of a new 'golden age of super-alpinism'.

Outstanding in this extreme department was the first ascent of the south-west ridge of the Great Trango Tower by Americans Josh Wharton and Kelly Cordes. Flagged as one of the biggest rock routes in the world, it ran to 54 nerve-jangling pitches, taken over five days, the last two without water.

Cordes tells the story in one of a trio of articles spawned by renewed activity in Pakistan. Simon Yates recalls his hungry (most of the food was dropped) ascent of the south-west face of Hispar Sar with Andy Parkin, and David Hamilton describes traversing the Karakoram on skis, a 260km journey over high cols and crevasse fields in the grand tradition of Himalayan exploration.

This *AJ* also sees a new blossoming of the Anglo-US 'special relationship', a peaceable mountaineering one, that is, rather the military adventurism to which the term has been more recently applied. Along with the contribution by Cordes, deputy editor of the *American Alpine Journal*, this volume is enhanced by an account by his boss, *AAJ* editor John Harlin III, describing a new route on Mont Blanc's Innominata arête, and an essay by Royal Robbins on the American climbing authors who most influenced him.

One of the most influential climbing authors this side of the Atlantic in the last century has to be Heinrich Harrer. The author of *The White Spider* and confidant of the young Dalai Lama was busy finishing a photo book on Bhutan, when he telephoned from Carinthia earlier this year to say how pleased he would be to write an appreciation of his Eiger *Nordwand* rope mate Anderl Heckmair, who died in February. At 92 years old, Harrer must be oldest contributor to this *AJ*. Though it wasn't accorded due recognition in these pages at the time, the exploratory verve and tenacity shown by Heckmair, Harrer, Kasparek and Vorg in 1938 was of an order typified today by the likes of Bracey and Cross on *A Pair of Jacks* or Bullock on *Edge of Darkness*.

The *AJ* is very much a co-operative effort. Production editor Johanna Merz has again performed wonders, accommodating an ever greater number of illustrations; Paul Knott has expanded the Area Notes to more countries, Geoffrey Templeman has chased book reviewers (which this year include our president Stephen Venables, past president Doug Scott and writers Peter Gillman and Dennis Gray) while publisher Peter Hodgkiss at the Ernest Press has offered sage advice and waited patiently for the copy.

Leslie Stephen, perhaps the most erudite of *AJ* editors, was unlucky in holding the office during a brief fallow period in mountaineering, largely caused by the shock of the Matterhorn disaster in 1865. He remarked, somewhat gloomily, that the journal might 'perish for want of contributions'. Looking at the burgeoning Area Notes and the reports of many MEF-funded expeditions, there is clearly no lack of probing activity in ranges right across the globe. The raw material for journal contributions therefore hardly seems in short supply. Please do not let modesty hold you back.

Stephen Goodwin

Contents

Illustrations

Erratum:

Illustration No 103 facing page 259 in *AJ 109*, 2004 which was inadvertently credited to
the Alpine Club Photo Library was, in fact, reproduced by courtesy of the Wayfarers' Club.

Kangchenjunga Jubilee
1955 ~ 2005

T H Somervell *Kangchenjunga from below Darjeeling*
Presented to E F Norton and inscribed 'EFN from THS 1925'
Watercolour and bodycolour
Private collection

ALAN HINKES

Close Encounters with Kangch'

With luck, by the time you read this I will have climbed Kangchenjunga and my quest to climb all the world's 8000-metre peaks will be over. But, as they say, 'I've been here before,' and as I write this in March 2005, I think back to a previous close encounter with Kangch'.

My personal danger signals were moving into overload. I was absolutely alone near 8000m and pushing for the top. It was five years ago; a solo bid with only my support – a base camp crew of cook, cook-boy and sirdar – 2500m below. There were no other expeditions left on the mountain.

Spindrift was pouring down the avalanche-prone snow slopes and the weather was socking in. I was getting anxious, in fact scared, and knew I must retreat. I really wanted to push on to the summit. It would have been my 12th 8000er and I knew I was so close to the top. But it was not to be and I turned down. As I descended, the weather worsened to a near white-out with a metre of fresh snow aggravating the avalanche risk.

Reaching less steep ground around 6500m, I knew there were now several hidden crevasses to negotiate. At times I sank into waist-deep snow, sometimes I crawled over what I suspected were crevasses. Twice I sank to my chest as snow bridges settled. My racing heart just about burst out of my head each time it happened. Then I fell harder, up to my neck in a slot and banged my arm across on the hard-as-concrete wall of the crevasse. A bone in my elbow snapped with a metallic crack as if my ice axe pick had broken.

Still, I had another arm and two legs, so I just got on with getting out of the crevasse and struggling down to base camp. At least I could still walk and abseil with one arm. It could have been worse. I thought, if Doug (Scott) can crawl down the Ogre with a broken leg, what have I got to complain about? It was almost dark when I reached the old site of camp one at 6000m. There was no tent there now. From here, when uninjured, I had descended to base in 50 minutes. Now, in the dark with a head torch and broken arm, it took me more than three hours. I arrived in camp around midnight, feeling lucky to be alive, though I had not reached the summit. I would have to wait awhile to enter those Five Treasure Houses of the Snows.

That wait became prolonged when a second attempt on Kangchenjunga, in 2003, ended almost before it started. I contracted a SARS-like virus of the upper respiratory tract and that was that.

3. Kangchenjunga south-west face from Camp 1 in 2000, showing the crevasse field where Hinkes fell in and broke his arm. (*Alan Hinkes*)

'Why bother?' I am asked. After all, 12 people have climbed all 14 of the 8000ers already. 'Why not?' I reply. Or why bother indeed to climb any mountain? Eric Shipton thought it was impossible to provide an entirely satisfactory explanation for any recreation, especially mountaineering with its inherent danger. If climbing all 14 was easy or a straightforward succession of plods, then I would not bother. Maybe I would just head off collecting bolt routes in Spain, using uplift and huts in the Alps to enjoy a 4000m peak or an Alpine face route, or making just a short trip to a 6000m peak, all of which I enjoy.

Sometimes near the top of an 8000er I feel like I am on the moon. Perhaps it is the lack of oxygen fuzzing my brain and eyes and the thin, clear atmosphere which make the rock seem lunar in texture and colour. Strangely different to anything I have climbed on or examined as an amateur geologist at lower altitudes, it can be frost-shattered, sickeningly loose and horrible from a rock-climbing aspect. But it is more than that; it has a stark, ethereal quality.

It is common knowledge that humans can only survive at these extreme altitudes for a few days at most. If you become trapped by bad weather or immobile due to an accident, you will die. No helicopter can reach heights above 7000m. Some people think I must have a death wish to keep going above 8000m, but far from it.

4. Climbing the rock step below Camp 1. (*Alan Hinkes*)

5. Kangchenjunga base camp, south-west face, with track leading off to Camp 1. (*Alan Hinkes*)

I have always gravitated and aspired to the big hills. Even when I started rock climbing I always went for length. Bouldering was never for me. I served an apprenticeship in the Alps, lower Himalayan peaks and Scotland in winter, long before getting hooked on the big 14. Over the last 20 years I have been on 25 expeditions to 8000m peaks, as well as trips to mountains in the 5000-7000m range and plenty of rock climbing.

My first taste of a big hill was in 1984, when I attempted the north side of Everest with the Cumbrian Everest Expedition, but it was not until 1987 that I climbed my first 8000er, Shisha Pangma (8046m). Steve Untch (USA) and myself climbed a new route on the north face up the central couloir in alpine style. Messner had looked at this line but decided against it and went up the route of the first ascent. Steve and I were part of a Polish expedition led by Jerzy Kukuczka.

For 'Jurek', it was his 14th 8000er and he became the second person to climb the full set. I learnt a lot on that expedition, especially not to underestimate an 8000er and always to take a tent. Steve and I had bivouacked at 7800m on the ascent with no tent. We just dug two tiny coffin-sized ledges in the snow and ice, tied ourselves on and laid down in sleeping bags. Spindrift poured over us for most of the night and it was difficult to use a stove to melt snow. The next day we carried on to the top – the real top of Shisha Pangma – and descended part way to around 6900m. Steve had horribly frostbitten feet. Back in the USA he had several toes amputated.

I did not go home after Shisha Pangma but trekked in to Lhotse south face for an attempt with Krzysztof Wielicki. We were battered back down from high on the face by some of the worst October storms in the Himalaya. The logistics, level of commitment and danger on one of these 8000ers fascinated me. In '88 after climbing a hard new line on Menlungtse West (7013m) with Andy Fanshawe, I tried Makalu, alpine style, with Rick Allen on an expedition organised by Doug Scott. Disaster struck at 8200m when Rick was avalanched 400m. Miraculously he survived although badly cut up, disorientated and shocked. It was a minor epic to get Rick down. Unusually, but fortunately, the weather remained settled and lower down we were helped by a Catalan team. Any lesser mortal than Rick would have given up and died.

In late '88 I was telephoned by Benoît Chamoux who invited me on his *L'Esprit d'Equipe* expeditions. I flew over to Paris on Christmas Eve 1988 and agreed to climb Manaslu in '89 and Cho Oyo and Shisha Pangma (by a new route) in 1990. *L'Esprit* had fairly good sponsorship from French companies; there was a team of seven climbers from France, Italy, the Czech Republic, Netherlands and England (me), but it was really a Franco-Italian affair. Benoît had openly stated his aim to climb all the 8000ers and be the first Frenchman to do so. I still had no desire for this 'grand slam' and nor did I see the possibility of being able to achieve it had I wanted to. I was only interested in climbing and was enjoying the luxury of being involved in well-sponsored trips. I didn't have to worry about airfares, hotels, porters to base camp, food or anything other than climbing.

Benoît was easygoing, but very determined and fit. He was a mountain guide, like myself, and lived near Chamonix. We climbed Manaslu by the south face route. Hardly anyone had been on it for several years and we had to hack a path through the jungle to base camp. The first part of the route was steep rock followed by a high glacier valley, steepening again to the summit. It was the first British ascent of Manaslu (still the only British ascent). The following year we did Cho Oyu almost as an acclimatisation peak for Shisha Pangma where we climbed a steep couloir left of the one I climbed in '87. In 1995 Benoît disappeared on Kangchenjunga, his 13th 8000er.

In '91 I was on another big expedition, this time to Broad Peak where I was guiding for Himalayan Kingdoms, now Jagged Globe. Broad Peak belies its reputation and name and is neither an easy plod nor is it broad near the top. The summit ridge from the col at 7800m is narrow and steep. Broad Peak was my fourth 8000er. Whilst there I visited K2 base camp and met Sigi Haupfaur. It was like meeting one of the Gods. He had been on the Eiger in winter and climbed 10 of the 8000ers. I could not imagine climbing another six, let alone all 14, but K2 impressed me; it burnt itself into my psyche. I had to climb K2 but I still had no ambition to climb all 14.

In 1992 I went with Doug Scott to attempt the Mazeno ridge on Nanga Parbat. The following year I made my first attempt on K2 from the Pakistan side. It was thwarted by having to help down an exhausted climber from another team after his partner had fallen to his death. I realised that K2 had very short weather windows so you needed to set off in poor conditions and be high on the mountain for when a summit opportunity arose. Generally on any 8000er there are only a handful of days when it is possible to summit. The rest of the time it is too cold, too windy, too avalanche prone or generally just too inhospitable. I reckon K2 is the hardest of all the mountains, and for me it gets the gold medal. Kangchenjunga may well get the silver with Everest taking the bronze.

In 1994 I tried K2 from China. The north face is more difficult to approach than the south-east ridge. Technically, it is no more difficult when you are on it, but it does have worse objective dangers. The lower slopes are avalanche prone and the icefield around 6800m is raked by stonefall like the *Eigerwand*. Our expedition fixed double ropes across the icefield and regularly both would be cut by stones. The upper hanging snowfield is also avalanche prone. I decided to turn back here, possibly only five hours from the top. I just could not accept the avalanche danger.

I went straight back to the Abruzzi ridge route the following year. People had started to suggest I was obsessed with K2. 'What is wrong with that?' I would say. 'What about Mallory and Everest, Whymper and the Matterhorn or a rock climber working a route to redpoint it?' Anyway, K2 was not an obsession. I just wanted to climb it, so I reckoned I was showing true Yorkshire Grit, as fine a human quality as it is rock for climbing. Almscliffe has given me as much pleasure as K2.

Alison Hargreaves and I joined the 1995 American K2 expedition. We climbed together for two weeks before both teaming up with Americans. My partner dropped out around 6500m and I pushed on alone to the top on the same day as two Pakistanis and two Dutch climbers. Only five of us summiters survived that year; eight were killed, including Alison. K2 truly is a 'Savage Mountain' and I would never go back.

In the 12 months July '95 to July '96 I climbed four 8000ers: K2, Everest, Gasherbrum I and Gasherbrum II. That was the point, in late '96, when I decided I ought to climb all 14. I had done eight and only had six left to do. My grand plan was actually to climb all six in one year: Lhotse, Makalu, Kangchenjunga, Nanga Parbat, Annapurna and Dhaulagiri. It was not to be. Weather and injury conspired against me. It was well into May when I climbed Lhotse, leaving no time for Makalu before the monsoon hit. I cancelled Kangchenjunga and went to Nanga Parbat.

I was more burnt out than I realised and by the time I reached Nanga Parbat it was my seventh attempt on an 8000er in 24 months. I had pushed my body hard with no support or back-up team. Lifting heavy loads to gauge the weight for porters, I strained my back. The final straw came when I sneezed on some chapatti flour and prolapsed a disc – a bizarre and ignominious end to an expedition, but a salutary and painful lesson.

I got fit with physiotherapy and rock climbing and went back in '98 to climb Nanga Parbat; in 1999 I made a lightweight, two-man ascent of Makalu; and 2000 saw me nearly summit on Kangchenjunga (the broken arm trip).

Annapurna had always seemed a particularly dangerous mountain. Statistics can be misleading but on paper it seemed to have had around 100 ascents and 60 fatalities before I attempted it. My tactics changed from a slow acclimatisation to a relatively rapid push, non-stop Kathmandu-base camp-summit-base camp. Nineteen days after leaving Kathmandu I was on the summit via a new route. It was the first British ascent since Don Whillans and Dougal Haston some 32 years earlier.

I thought Dhaulagiri, in 2004, would not be too bad as far as big mountains go. But once again it was far more difficult than I had expected, with steep ice slopes and rockfall like incoming mortar fire. The summit of Dhaulagiri must be one of the most inhospitable, wind-blasted places on earth. Bare brown exposed slabs of rock, blown clear of snow by jet-stream winds, make it utterly uninviting. All I could think of when I literally 'touch-tagged' the highest point of shattered rock was getting down. I couldn't face filming, photographing or even savouring the moment.

Dhaulagiri left me burnt out mentally and physically. In June 2004 I returned to Britain and tried not to think of Kangchenjunga, my final 8000er. I needed mental rest from just the thought of extreme altitude, and that isn't easy when people want to know when you're going back or are asking for talks on the 8000er experience.

6. Alan Hinkes with the traditional family photo – daughter Fiona and grandson Jay –
   on the summit of Dhaulagiri in 2004. (*Alan Hinkes*)

7. Number 13 on the Hinkes hit list, Dhaulagiri from above the Kali Gandaki.
   (*Alan Hinkes*)

8. The summit ridge of Dhaulagiri at about 8100m. (*Alan Hinkes*)

But then you have to be able to suffer at this game, and I've always liked a bit of suffering. Kangchenjunga offers plenty of it and by 2005 I felt ready. It is a very, very big mountain, not much lower than K2 and perhaps just as difficult. Even getting to base camp is an arduous challenge, not a tea-house jaunt like the Khumbu approach to Everest. It may take 10 or 12 days just to reach base camp. The final glacier can be very tricky with a rock step requiring fixed rope just below base camp at around 5400m. If I had a bigger budget I would contemplate using a helicopter to ferry all my supplies to base camp rather than using porters.

The summit push will be a long, committing and dangerous, maybe over 15 hours. I am anxious about my attempt, but looking forward to it. Kangch' feels like an old friend waiting for me. And the timing seems auspicious, the chance to complete all 14 of the 8000ers on Kangchenjunga in this 50th anniversary year of the first ascent. The fantastic achievement of Joe Brown, George Band, Tony Streather and Norman Hardie will be in my thoughts. I just hope I can make it to the top this time, at least to just below the holy summit, and then, more importantly, get back down.

'Challenge 8000' has been my personal quest. Climbing all the 8000m peaks is a quantifiable achievement, like the four-minute mile. From a bagging point of view it is no better or worse than collecting all the Munros, VS routes on Stanage or 4000m peaks in the Alps. It is, however, somewhat more dangerous and it will be a British first. Only 12 people have climbed all 14 8000ers – that is the same number of people who have stood on the moon. When it is done I will feel a sense of freedom, ready to go and climb anywhere I want. There are still lots more challenges for me in the hills.

Postscript:

Bad weather beset Kangchenjunga for much of May 2005. But while other climbers departed, Alan Hinkes and his climbing partner Pasang hung on in the hope of a late attempt on the 8586m summit. As the AJ was going to the publishers, Alan sent the following account from base camp:

'The final summit push was without a doubt the hardest climb of my life. Pasang and I left base camp on Thursday 26 May and began to push up the mountain. The weather had not been good which meant there was an awful lot of fresh snow to break through. Risk of avalanche was incredibly high and every step of the way was a matter of physical and mental endurance. The snow was so deep that we were unable to make camp three and had to bivvi on the hillside at around 7400m. We tried for a summit attempt on the 29 May but we were beaten back by the weather.

'A second summit attempt saw us leave at about 1am next day. More snow had fallen but we made good time. Pasang had to stop around 15 minutes short of the summit due to exhaustion. I reached the summit on the 30 May at around 7pm in driving snow and wind. It was the worst summit conditions I can remember. I took the obligatory photo spent around 10 minutes on the summit and then began my descent.

'It was about 9pm when I caught up with Pasang but with no head torch it was difficult to locate him and I honestly thought he was dead. It was with great elation that I found him and we got back to the bivvi site around 27 hours after setting off. The next couple of days saw us descending through fresh snow with high risk of avalanche. Getting back to base camp was one of the best feelings of my life. I sat down in my tent and thought, "I've finally done it!"'

9. Showing the strain at the end of his Challenge 8000, Alan on Kangchenjunga, 30 May 2005, in wild weather. Only recently a father at the start of his marathon, he was a grandfather by the finish. (*Alan Hinkes*)

CHARLES EVANS

Darjeeling and Beyond

On leave from the Forgotten Army

*When Charles Evans died in 1995, he left a manuscript of his experiences as a
'Doctor in the XIVth Army – Burma 1944 -1945', the so called Forgotten Army.
In 1998 his wife Denise secured a publisher – Leo Cooper of Pen and Sword
Books – who wanted it shorter so some sections were cut, including this delightful
account of two weeks ' leave' over New Year 1945, to Darjeeling and beyond in
the shadow of Kangchenjunga. It is now published for the first time as a special
tribute to Charles Evans to commemorate the 50th Anniversary of the first ascent
of that majestic mountain on 25 May 1955 by the British team led by Charles
himself. In his own prophetic words at the age of 26, 'I was at the edge of what
I wanted to do and yet it seemed utterly unattainable.'*

There was a wide choice of places to go on leave. Some liked the bright
lights of the clubs and hotels of Calcutta; others chose to spend their
leave at one of several hill stations where the climate was good and limited
social amenities could be found. My idea was to go to a hill station and see
how close I could get to the big mountains. I chose Darjeeling partly because
it was nearest to Calcutta and partly because the name had magic
associations; it had been the starting point of the early expeditions to Everest
and Kangchenjunga and as far as I knew it was the only place outside
Nepal where the Sherpa people, of whom I had read a good deal, were to
be found.

Siliguri, where the mountains began, was the end of the main line and
the Darjeeling Mail from Calcutta went no farther. I crossed the station
platform to what at first looked like a toy train – the mountain railway to
Darjeeling. The squat little steam engines were driven by hillmen with
pillbox caps and Gurkha faces; they had two helpers, cheerful-looking
urchins who sat over the front wheels of the engine, one each side; their
job was to throw handfuls of sand on the line whenever the rails were
slippery on the climb of nearly 8,000 feet to Darjeeling.

Darjeeling was on the crest and western slope of a narrow ridge; only
the small bazaar some way below the ridge was on flat ground. At the
station a pale girl with slanting brown eyes and pleasant features lifted my
heavy kitbag on her back with an easy movement, at the same time arranging
a carrying strap across her forehead. I hesitated to let her add my rucksack
to her load but she made nothing of it and we set off to walk up The Mall,

the main street, to the Windamere Hotel. Before long I was breathing heavily and turned to see if she was falling back: not a bit of it. She was at my heels and showed no signs of breathing, heavily or otherwise. Clearly I had misjudged the situation. She was the first Sherpa, or rather Sherpani, that I had met. We passed a café in a square called the Chowrasta and I heard the voices of soldiers on leave. 'Ham an' eggs an' chips twice, please Miss.' And 'What's at the flicks tonight?'

The Windamere was high on a sharp ridge, and more like a boarding house than a hotel. The guests seemed much the same in Darjeeling as they would have been in a wartime English country hotel – Wantage, say, or Woodstock, or for all I knew even Windermere itself. There were old ladies, hook nosed and grey haired, some plump, some thin, dressed in lace and black fur; there were a few middle-aged and young women, rather flabby, busy feeders; and there was a sprinkling of hearty young soldiers on leave from the 5th Indian Division.

Next day I artlessly set about arranging my 10 or 12 days' trek. I went first to the Deputy Commissioner's office and tackled the Indian clerk at the reception desk. He was from Bihar and his name was Gopal Prusung.

'Have you any maps of the area?' I asked. He gave a sideways twitch of the head.

'O yes Sir, we have 500 maps.'

'All right. I should like to have a look and buy one or two.'

'Sir, they are not for sale.'

He told me there was no place where you could buy maps and when I explained that I was intending to go for a trek, and would be camping where I felt inclined he added that there was no place where you were allowed to camp. 'There are many wild animals about, Sir. They will eat you up.'

He went on to say that the rules were that any trek must be officially approved and places booked at dak bungalows. In the end I persuaded Gopal Prusung to book me in for a night at a bungalow near Tiger Hill above Ghum and also at a number of bungalows along the Singalila ridge to Phalut, a well-known viewpoint at about 12,000 feet.

I spent the next two days by myself, walking down the 3,000 feet to Batamtam one day and coming back the next. Batamtam had about it a deep calm; I had a bungalow to myself where a friendly old *chowkidar* anticipated my efforts to light a fire by doing it for me. The small garden was lent a dash of colour by the bright red leaves of poinsettia, a magnolia was just coming into flower and there were sweet-smelling roses, red and white, and ferns and many small flowers whose names I did not know. The Rungneet, a tributary of the Teesta, roared in the glen below, and all about the bungalow I could hear the subdued voices of children. I cooked a simple meal and looked at *Blackwood's Magazine*, of which there were old copies in the bungalow; after dark I went outside to enjoy the moonlight and listen to the chirping of crickets. The night was warm down there and I was tired, and content to be alone. As I climbed back to Darjeeling next day I was overtaken by a spindly-legged figure dressed in white; he held an umbrella as, I was sure, a badge of status. I was breathless and his insistence on entering into a long and one-sided conversation in English was irritating. 'Where are you going? What is your business? Why are you carrying your luggage?' My answer to the last question, 'Because I enjoy it' must have sounded hollow when anyone could see that I was not enjoying it at all, and his next question had about it a remorseless logic, 'In that case, why are you going so slowly?'

I decided that night to swallow my pride and find a porter for my next excursion. I went to see a Captain Kydd who could, I was told, engage porters for me. He was a plump man, a civilian, and wanted I think to be helpful. We fell out as soon as he exclaimed that I should on no account have been given dak bungalow passes without evidence that I had first booked Sherpa porters and a cook – 'and,' I retorted crossly, 'I suppose a sweeper and water carrier as well!' He countered by informing me that the local Area Commander, a General, had issued orders about not lowering British prestige by having too few servants. To my irritation he addressed me all the time as 'Sahib'.

Next morning I rang the Station Staff Officer and had no difficulty in obtaining authorisation for the trek to Phalut. I then borrowed a map of Darjeeling from another officer in the hotel and made a copy of it. He had bought it without trouble in Calcutta from the Survey of India, as I should have done if I had known better.

In the Darjeeling bazaar I encountered groups of Tibetans; their long hair was in pigtails and they wore earrings, embroidered hats with fur-trimmed flaps, and long cloth boots bound below the knee with colourful woven garters; they were wild and dirty-looking men who had come over the passes from Tibet for trade. As I walked up from the bazaar to the hotel the dank grey cloud which had covered Darjeeling since I got there parted; I turned to look north and saw Kangchenjunga before me, its whiteness against a pale blue sky making the white of the clouds below appear a dirty grey. My feelings were deeper than I could have imagined.

I put my hands on an iron railing and looked down at the brightly coloured bazaar below but my eyes went back again and again to the gigantic mountain vision. From the edge of the hill by the Windamere Hotel I sat down to gaze once more; after about 10 minutes the clouds closed the gap before me and that day I did not again see the vision. I had a feeling that I remembered from a first visit to the Alps, of being on the edge of going into new mountains: I was at the edge of what I wanted to do and yet it seemed utterly unattainable because of my lack of familiarity with local conditions and my dislike of some of the accepted ways of doing things there. All right, I thought, I will behave like a Sahib until I have found out all I need to know. I went back to Kydd and engaged a sturdy, smiling young Sherpa called Lobsang.

The Singalila Ridge, high and winding, ran west from Ghum, then north-west and finally north, over the high points of Tanglu (10,000ft) and Sandakphu (12,000ft) to Phalut, only slightly lower. North and east of the ridge was Sikkim, accessible to foreigners only by permission of the Government of India. To the west lay the closed and secret kingdom of Nepal, home of the Gurkhas, a land of great mountains in which lay the whole of the west side of Kangchenjunga and the south side of the main Himalayan range, which included Makalu, Everest, Lhotse and many other peaks. At that time Nepal was almost totally closed to foreign travellers whose eyes, from the Singalila ridge, could only gaze across the tangle of hills with yearning.

Lobsang bought rice at Sukhiapokhri bazaar and we carried on to Jorepokhri bungalow at 7,500 feet. Lobsang was a cheerful and colourful figure; he wore a grey Balaclava helmet with the peak pointing any old way; three shirts, a blue, a light red and a grey; a light grey jacket; bright blue pants; two pairs of stockings and large black boots. The boots were so big that he soon began to suffer from blisters which turned into ulcers; from that moment he carried the boots slung round his neck and walked barefoot whether there was snow on the ground or not. He walked at a steady three miles an hour with a rapid step, whistling as he went; sometimes he imitated bird calls and whenever he reached the crest of a rise he whistled shrilly through his teeth like a marmot. Jorepokhri bungalow was on a hillock covered with mossy lawns. There was a small lake and the plot was surrounded by fir trees. Lobsang lit a fire and we drank tea. I went outside and as I walked quietly by the lake I came on a deer; it stood about four feet high at the shoulder and showed its white tail as it bounded away through the trees.

Ten years later there was a jeepable military road to Sandakphu, but in 1945 and even in 1952, when I again walked that way, there was no more than a bridle path. As we climbed the 3,500 feet from Mani Banjyiang to our next night's stop at Tanglu, Lobsang began occasionally to converse, going uphill with only slightly slackened speed, and maintaining his quick step. He always had enough breath to talk and presently pointed out a tumbledown ruin of a bungalow, remarking with a grin, '*Achcha wala bangala, Sahib*' – 'Fine bungalow, Sir', betraying a sense of irony that quickly became the basis of our relationship. Five hundred feet short of Tanglu, when I was longing to sit down, he stopped and produced a bottle of the local beer, '*chang*', which we shared. It was a clear yellowish liquid tasting vaguely of wine, rather sour and yeasty. He made certain that I had more than half the bottle and either the last 500 feet were very steep or else the *chang* was hard on the wind, for long before we reached Tanglu I was going very slowly and feeling muzzy about the head. Our path was along a bare grassy ridge; the grass was short and yellow and below us on either side were rocky outcrops and stunted, moss-covered trees – dwarf oak, and holly. Farther down were jungle and the depths of a great valley. In one place we passed huts where there were dirty, ragged children and many chickens. The path was either stony or muddy and Lobsang stoutly ploughed his way up in bare feet through mud or snow. I liked his straightforwardness:

'How old are you, Lobsang?'

'Me?'

'Yes'

'20 years,' pause, 'What about you?'

'26'

After a rest I went to the top of a rise 200 feet above the post at Tanglu. There was a dusting of snow everywhere. The west side of the sharp peak fell quickly to dense jungle and I heard the murmur of a distant river; beyond a succession of sunlit valleys I could see terraces and clusters of houses.

I sat sheltering from the wind behind a small stone tower on which white flags fluttered from bamboos: Lobsang called it a *daza*. Here at over 10,000 feet were only barren stones, moss and stunted vegetation. On the hills to the north was a patchy covering of snow, streaks of cloud lay in the valleys and parts of the steep hillsides far below were terraced. They recalled the Chin hills except that those were rarely high enough to lose the jungle altogether. Three thousand feet below and only 10 miles away in a direct line the windows of Darjeeling reflected the setting sun and later, after dark, I could see the lights of street lamps. After I had cooked some of what Captain Kydd ('for prestige, you understand') had called 'the Doctor Sahib's special experimental food' – and what was it but wheat flour, curry, rice and dal? – the local police visited me.

'Where have you come from, Sahib? Where are you going? What is purpose of journey?' He was a nice sergeant, but what a fuss!

'You will not be entering Nepal, Sahib?'

'I would not dream of it.'

The rice, bought at Sukhiapokhri and carried wrapped in an old handkerchief, was the best I had ever eaten, and so was the rest of the meal. Lobsang carried a large *kukri* in his belt and used it indifferently to spread butter, to chop firewood and to pare his toenails. The ordinary *kukri* has as one of its attachments a small blunt blade about whose use I was curious – it was shaped like the main blade – he explained that it was for striking a light.

Alone by the fire I fell to wondering what I wanted in life. I admired the strong and gentle, those who were masters of themselves; I wanted to be like that. I wanted to know more of mankind, how he lives, how he thinks; I wanted experience of the mountains and the sea, of my own power, and of life in different places, city and wilderness. As to work, I did not know.

On 5 January 1945 sunrise came very rapidly and lit everything in the west with a bright clear light which made rocks and trees and grassy hillocks stand out with startling clarity against a grey-blue background. My feet had grown cold in the night and as we left Tanglu a little snow was falling, greeted by Lobsang with cries of affected dismay belied by a cheerful grin.

We walked over open scrubland patchily covered with snow through which showed clumps of red moss. Soon we lost the way, went too far down on the Nepal side, and had to climb strenuously back to regain the ridge. Snow began to fall more thickly and a chill wind sprang up which lasted for the rest of the day. On the ridge were lengths of wall, the stones carved with figures of Buddha and writing in Tibetan script – *Om mani padme hum*. We passed to the left and I asked Lobsang his religion.

'Lama,' he said, which I took to mean Buddhist.

We now lost height and went down and down to a narrow saddle where there were huts. Lobsang found more *chang* and stood me a drink; profiting by experience I drank only half a mugful – we still had a long way to go. The cold was bitter. We climbed steeply and steadily for four miles to Kalipokhri at 10,000 feet. Kalipokhri means 'black lake' and near some wattle huts I could see a dark stagnant pond. The climb of 2,000 feet in four more miles to Sandakphu was simple misery in wind and blizzard. I was carrying only some 20 lbs and Lobsang had three times as much. I arrived about 15 minutes behind him, icy cold, sheeted with snow and trembling all over.

At Sandakphu there were several buildings. Lobsang and I entered the first, a tin-roofed shack with two rooms; in the blizzard conditions we had failed to see either the main bungalow or a building occupied by the caretaker or *chowkidar*. Lobsang soon had a roaring blaze going and over tea and chapattis and a small bottle of *chang* we settled down to a pleasant late afternoon. Outside the hut the blizzard continued to blow and when Lobsang brought in a pail of water there was ice on it.

I liked his rough humour. When he slipped on the snow he cried out 'Very good snow', and if I then said 'Well done', he roared with laughter. He told me that his home was in Nepal and that he meant to go back there the next year after earning more money.

I do not think I ever spent a more wretched night or longed so heartily for the dawn. First we got in two mattresses from the bedroom and put them down before the fire. I gave Lobsang a spare sweater and my groundsheet to add to his one blanket but even so he must have been terribly cold. I had two blankets and spent my time trying to ease aching limbs and at the same time lose as little heat as possible. About four in the morning Lobsang blew up the fire and we sat round it for half an hour while I made tea, then we tried again to sleep; this time I put my feet in my rucksack and was warmer. I found too that the mere act of turning over, and the puffing and blowing that followed, warmed me up enough to make me comfortable for a quarter of an hour. All night I had a sore nose, the prelude to a bad cold. In the morning I looked at the mess: dirty dishes, frozen water, snow on the table and over some of the chairs, snow piled 18 inches high inside the door, a gusty gale outside rattling the shutters and piling up more snow. I shaved painfully. I was extremely breathless.

After a look outside and a talk with Lobsang I went to see who was in the main bungalow. I found three army officers and half a dozen Sherpas.

10. Charles Evans thanking hospitable villagers at the first hamlet on return from the first ascent of Kangchenjunga, June 1955. (*George Band collection*)

They were going no farther and were about to start back to Tanglu. Lobsang and I decided to follow their tracks and 400 feet down overtook them. They were ploughing slowly through two feet of new snow in the blizzard. The going was very heavy for the leader and the four of us who had no loads took it in turn to break a trail.

To reach Kalipokhri took four hours. We entered one of the huts and shared out some food before going on. My contribution of cold chapattis seemed as welcome to my new friends as their tinned butter and jam were to me. We struggled on down to the saddle where Lobsang and I had had *chang* the day before. We entered one of the huts there too and the Sherpas made tea for everyone. Since leaving Sandakphu we had been on the go for six hours.

Before going on, the Sherpas tore from the roof of the hut some long bamboo poles with which to test the depth of the snow on the track: the occupants were quite indifferent to this pilfering. All day I had had an unpleasant cold but I now began to feel better. The surface of the snow was sometimes firmer than it had been and I thought that I was beginning to recover. All the same, to plough ahead, spurred by conscience to take a turn at making the track for a 50-yard stretch, was heart-bursting. At 5.50pm the blizzard was blowing as hard as ever; we were in deep soft snow on the crest of the ridge and the light was beginning to fail. Everywhere was silence except for our grunts and groans and the noise of the wind. We had a short rest and then tried again but after 100 yards we all came to a stop and held a consultation. We turned back to a cluster of wattle huts that we had just passed and stumbled into the first one we reached; inside, except for a faint light from the glowing embers of a smoky fire, all was dark; the roof dripped melting snow and round the fire a family squatted, huddled together, looking up at us. We stood, breathing fiercely as cold and tired people do, stamping the snow from our boots and brushing it off our clothing.

Many years later I became used to the way in which Sherpas will enter the house of a stranger and take it over. They did so now. They carried embers from the fire to another part of the floor, breathed on them with those bellows Sherpas have for lungs, and soon we were sitting on low circular cane stools holding out our hands to a blaze and trying not to put our feet in the puddles on the floor. Slowly we undressed, drank tea out of china and copper bowls and warmed up; it was a strange scene – dim, blanketed figures, much coughing and spluttering, drips from the roof.

Lobsang merged in with the other Sherpas whose *sirdar* Ang Purba later fed us on army meat and vegetable stew followed by coffee. We ate in semi-darkness and retired into a wet corner of the room. The Sherpas carried on with their chatter (they will talk all night) and devoured huge bowls of rice while we looked on. Warm and fed, we were comfortable in spite of the stinging smoke and drips of water.

I slept on and off until a cock in the shack began to crow and I could dimly see the fowls, dogs, cats and children that shared our lodging. Gradually we came to and found on going outside a glorious sunny dawn which I hardly appreciated as my cold was worse again and affected my chest. There was not a cloud in the sky and Kangchenjunga was clear before us; we tried in vain to accustom our eyes to the glare of the bright sun on new snow. After a large breakfast we assembled outside the hut and were required to take photographs of everyone who had been there, especially of one I took to be the lady of the house and who now appeared for the first time and politely proposed some recognition of her hospitality. She wore Sherpa style clothes, a dark blouse and a heavy striped woollen apron held in place by a pink cloth about the waist; she had knee-length woollen boots with leather soles and a long, thick, heavy necklace of alternating coral and a variegated stone that the Sherpas call *Zi*. She had two long pigtails and her earrings were gold-coloured metal discs four or five inches in diameter. Over everything she wore a purplish woollen coat or cloak which reached from the top of her head to her ankles. Like many Sherpa ladies she had the look of a woman on no account to be trifled with.

For four hours we plodded wearily in hot sunshine through deep soft snow and reached Tanglu exhausted. The sun on the new snow had been hot on our faces all the way, burning the eyeballs in spite of our efforts to shield them with pieces of cloth.

On the way from Sandakphu we had simply taken each other as comrades, sharing discomforts, food, drink, trail-breaking and the making of decisions; during the afternoon at Tanglu, as we rested, ate, and dried our sodden clothing we found out about each other, and I discovered that my three chance companions were as friendly, interesting and good-natured as I could have wished. They were a captain, a lieutenant and a corporal, gunners from 5th Indian Division.

Outside the bungalow the light was brilliant, the snow at our level was a smooth, fresh white and Kangchenjunga in this light looked whiter than ever. When I looked at it, pencil in hand to make a sketch, it was so bright that when I looked back to the paper I could for about 15 seconds see nothing of the sketch I was trying to draw.

In the valley was dense white cloud; Darjeeling in the distance was covered with snow. The arc of the northern horizon was a jagged line of rock, snow and ice. The sky beyond was a clear pale blue; far in north Sikkim the heads of one or two solitary peaks showed above the rest. Each peak alone would have been striking were it not that Kangchenjunga, knocking one off balance by its height, mass and nearness, made others look by comparison insignificant.

There was no wind and the sun was warm. Close at hand I heard the tinkle of a pony's bell, the drip of melting snow and the sound of icicles falling from the eaves. Lobsang pottered about all day barefoot in the snow, sometimes sitting beside me on the warm doorstep, watching me write and wondering, I supposed, what it was all about. We shared out the rice that was left and he began to cook his half while tuning and playing a four stringed instrument like a primitive guitar. I handed him my binoculars and he at once turned them to look from the big end to the small, clicking his tongue against his teeth, 'tck, 'tck with pleasure and repeating

'How small! How small!' Sherpas have distant vision which is so good as to be past belief and back to front was the only way I ever saw them use binoculars – a favourite pastime was to look at one's feet through the wrong end and try to walk like that over rough ground.

In the evening I sat on one side of the wood fire, Lobsang squatting on the other – clean, attractive little beggar. I gave him a dish of stewed prunes and afterwards he carefully pushed the stones through a hole between the floorboards and then neatly put a matchstick across the hole as though to complete the act; he would hold up a light for me to read, tend the fire or look quietly at a map of India. I had grown fond of him.

Two days' leisurely walking brought us back to Darjeeling. When we came to an awkward frozen bit of path he exclaimed 'Oho, ho, ho' and when I slipped and went to the bottom on my behind, burst into outright laughter. At Jorepokhri the lawns and trees were covered in new snow and the lake was hard frozen. We had bought rice on the way and I wondered how on earth Lobsang could eat so much: he told me that a pound of uncooked rice and two pounds of wheat flour were a proper day's ration; I could eat no more for a meal than the equivalent of a handful of uncooked rice.

He described how *kukris* were fashioned in the furnace and on the anvil in the villages. He claimed that in Nepal there were no '*chiddar*', the wattle huts in which we spent a night, and if by 'Nepal' he meant, as was customary with Nepalese, the capital Kathmandu, then he was right, but I came to know later that there were plenty of such huts up and down the country. Nothing had prepared me for the sort of life I saw led by the family in that hut: we could not make out where they slept nor how in spite of the drips and mud and smoke and damp they turned out for their photographs in the morning – apparently dry and fairly clean.

Back at the Windamere, I thought about my leave; measured in one way I had achieved nothing, but I had seen mountains of a size and splendour that no amount of reading, no photographs could have made real to me. I had found a closeness that makes relationships with Sherpas easy; I had found that I could live in this country on what I could find in villages by the way; and I had learnt something that I could not describe but which I knew would make future expeditions easier.

Lobsang came to see me off and brought his young wife; she was a pretty girl; she had a wide brilliant smile, her cheeks were like red apples and were framed by a fur-trimmed hat. She held a small brown puppy in the crook of her arm. Lobsang went with a party to the Zemu glacier within 12 months and all were lost in a heavy snowstorm.

When I left Darjeeling the mist was thick. Snow lay on the ground and small boys ran alongside the train offering Nepalese coins for sale and throwing in snowballs at anyone silly enough to open a window.

JOHN JACKSON

Kangchenjunga Jubilee ~ Indian Style

The Himalayan Club was founded on 17 February 1928 and despite the radical changes following the partition of India in 1947 it has continued to flourish, with honorary local secretaries in 11 locations in India and in 14 other countries around the globe. In 2003 it celebrated its 75th Anniversary.

Nanda Devi was the highest peak in the British Empire, but when in 1975 Sikkim became India's 22nd province, Kangchenjunga, so wonderfully visible from the popular hill resort of Darjeeling, became India's highest peak. Well ahead of time, the Himalayan Club resolved to celebrate the 50th Anniversary of its first ascent on 25th May 1955 by Charles Evans' Expedition. Several surviving members of the team received letters of invitation from the Club to attend seminars in February 2005 in Mumbai and Kolkata (formerly Bombay and Calcutta) followed by a few days in Darjeeling.

The moving spirit behind this generous invitation was our friend and honorary AC member Harish Kapadia. In the event, three of the 1955 team were able to accept, accompanied by their wives: George and Susan Band, Norman and Enid Hardie, John and Eileen Jackson. John Jackson wrote this account of the visit just a few months before he died on 2 July 2005. An obituary of 'Jacko' will apper in the next AJ.

Early morning Mumbai – temperature rising to 85 degrees. Quickly we were transported to Panchgani (Five Hills), a cooler hill resort at 1200m in the Western Ghats. Harish Kapadia had written the guidebook to the area, *Trek the Sahyadris*. This revealed that the rugged scenery, eroded over millions of years, was made up of some of the oldest rocks in the world capped by basalt lava flows. It was a trekking and rock-climbing playground for the Mumbai section of the Himalayan Club.

This time it was the hill fort of Kenjalgad (1302m) that was the focus of attention, with an ascent designed to celebrate the 50 years since Kangchenjunga was first climbed. Well planned. One group, including George and Susan Band, made the two-hour walk to the top, whilst the halt and the lame, Norman Hardie and myself on sticks, plus our wives Enid and Eileen, stayed down below. Chaperoned by Veneeta Muni, we were able to visit a huge earthen dam enclosing a lake supplying water to many towns and cities in the area of Pune (Poona). Below the dam was an ancient Shiva temple; peaceful and with little eagles, weaver birds, long-tailed drongos and a small minivet adding interest to the scene.

We returned to Mumbai the following day refreshed and ready for the three days of seminars to follow. The British Council provided the first day's evening venue at the Mittal Tower. Tanil Kilachand opened proceedings and I gave the Kaivan Mistry Memorial lecture. Kaivan was a young and enthusiastic mountaineer, a member of many expeditions. In 2000, he was drowned in the ice-cold river issuing from the Siachen glacier. Eileen and I were in Nubra in Ladakh at the time but didn't know of the tragedy. Back in Leh we met a distraught Harish Kapadia and his team. This then was the memorial talk for Kaivan. For me it was a touching experience, the more so when Kaivan's mother spoke from the platform and expressed the hope that more young people would go out and experience the wonderful environment of the Himalaya.

The second day opened with an address by the Governor of Maharashtra, Shri S M Krishna. George Band then gave a splendidly illustrated talk, 'Kangchenjunga Revisited', describing the 1955 climb as well as later excursions in Sikkim including an abortive attempt to emulate Douglas Freshfield's 1899 circumnavigation of the Kangchenjunga massif. After tea, the film *The Elusive Mountain Gya* was shown, featuring an ascent led by Motup Chewang when the discovery of a piton driven into the summit rock revealed an earlier first ascent. In the final talk of the day, Harish gave a survey of the history and politics of Sikkim, backed up by many fine photos.

All three of us 1955 veterans contributed to the final day of seminars. When a film was cancelled, George Band stepped in with a beautifully illustrated talk of trekking and climbing in Bhutan in 1991. He neglected to say that Susan had also been on the trip, whereupon all three ladies were called to the platform to speak briefly about their experiences and were then given a standing ovation. Norman Hardie's slides, showing the construction of the Silver Hut below the Mingbo La at 5800m, were out-standing. He went on to illustrate early attempts on Makalu and ended with dramatic slides taken on the first ascent of Ama Dablam in 1961.

Col Ashok Abbey, Principal of the Himalayan Mountaineering Institute in Uttar Kashi, revealed a keen interest in history as well as mountain train-ing, with an overview of K2 from its early exploration to present day attempts on many different routes. I gave the final illustrated talk, de-scribing a journey from Everest to Kangchenjunga in 1954, partly through Tibet. The closing vote of thanks was by the Vice President of the Club, Tanil Kilachand.

The reception in Kolkata on 8 February was as enthusiastic as in Mumbai. An 80-page souvenir booklet celebrating the first ascent of Kangchenjunga was presented to each of us. The Himalayan Club is to be congratulated on this fine publication, which includes reprints of *Himalayan Journal* articles from the 1920s through to the present day. It opens with a message of support from A P J Kalam, President of the Republic of India, stressing the benefits of adventure tourism in schools so that young people may become aware of the Himalaya and its varied environment. The value of this type of experience was evident when Apurba Battacharya gave a splendid account

11. Sherpas of Darjeeling host Kangch climbers and their wives on Observatory Hill, 2005. (*George Band collection*)

of the first ascent in 2004 of Tingchen Kang, a 6000m peak near Pandim in Sikkim. All nine of the team were young and enthusiastic members of the Kolkata section of the Club. They showed what could be achieved with good leadership and teamwork.

A very full programme for the Kolkata day included talks by Harish and myself and a joint presentation by George and Norman entitled 'Kangchenjunga Climbed, 1955'. Col Narinder Kumar showed slides of only the second ascent of Kangchenjunga, made in 1977 by the Indian Army via the north-east spur. These were very revealing of the difficulties faced by the historic German expeditions of 1929 and 1931. Another highlight of the day was the talk by Dorjee Lhatoo, 'Round Kangchenjunga', describing the fourth circuit of the massif, completed in November 1992. His description of the move across the Nepalese border into India when the expedition was nearly fired upon by their own Indian troops was most dramatic. Meher Mehta, who, with his two committees, had worked so hard organising the event, gave the final vote of thanks.

Moving on to Darjeeling, we stayed at the old Windamere Hotel owned by the Tenduf La family. Very little had changed throughout the 50 years we have known the hotel. Sadly, Mrs Tenduf La, who would have been 100 years old in March 2005, died in November 2004. But it was good to see the old values are being kept up and that the family is still going to celebrate her birthday.

Gloomy cloud cover did not auger well for our hopes of seeing Kangchenjunga, so off we went to the Himalayan Mountaineering Institute. Major Dhillon, the Principal, made us welcome and showed us round the impressive exhibits of the early Everest mountaineers and their equipment. Our next visit was to the home of ever hospitable Nawang Gombu and his wife Sita. The room filled quickly and soon it seemed as if the whole Tenzing family was present. Talking to Eileen, Susan and Enid was Jamling Tenzing, Tenzing Norgay's eldest son, who in 1996 reached the summit of Everest and described his experience in *Touching My Father's Soul.* It was also good to see the youngest son, Dhami, who with his wife and other children was enjoying Jamling's visit to Darjeeling. Dorjee Lhatoo joined in the conversation along with Gombu and his daughter Yangdu. There was a general 'buzz' all round and the hours sped away.

The following day was clear for rest and shopping but in the afternoon a visit from Pem Pem, Tenzing's daughter, proved very entertaining. She described a trek she had made with her son, Tashi Tenzing, through the Karta Valley to her father's birthplace. She pinpointed every stopping place on the route, by dotting the air in front of her, thus producing a 'map' which we could follow well to the east and south of Everest's northern base camp. It was a magical performance by a delightful lady.

The final morning of 13 February was clear with a blue sky. Would we see the Kangchenjunga massif at last? We did! Jannu and Rathong stood out boldly, then the summits of Kabru began to show. Further east, Pandim and Tingchenkang were impressive. But the 'Five Treasures' were playing hide and seek so that only fleetingly did they show themselves. It was enough. In the early morning, streams of people were making the ascent of Observatory Hill for a special puja. For the Hindus, it was to Durga, a consort of Shiva, and for the Sherpas, a celebration of the Buddhist New Year. Dorjee Lhatoo, Gombu and Sita with their daughter Yangdu, led us up the long flight of steps. The reception there was overwhelming. A huge parachute tent had been erected and at one end a banner proclaimed:

1ˢᵗ Ascent of Kanchanjunga
"50ᵗʰ Anniversary"
Sherpas of Darjeeling Felicitate the Climbers

Here was the whole Sherpa community expressing their appreciation of all mountaineers with whom they had shared days of endeavour, hardship and friendship on the mountains. We three represented thousands from countries far and wide. It was a touching moment and the Sherpas had got it just right.

'Have some chang!' Cups full to the brim were handed to us and quickly refilled, if we were not careful, or followed by chasers of rakshi. A never-ending stream of Sherpas and Sherpanis came to offer more, and to place gold and silver threaded katas around our necks. Ominously, a 20 gallon drum of chang stood nearby, already filled to overflowing. Somebody was going to do some serious drinking on this, the Sherpas' New Year's Day.

Dorjee and Gombu began to bring Sherpas and Sherpanis to meet us. Here was the youngest sister of Ang Tsering who chuckled happily when I told her he had been my sirdar in 1954. Now who was this with such a familiar face? 'He is the son of Gyalgen Mikjun ,' (Big Eyes) said Dorjee. He was a foot shorter, but the face was identical to his father's who had been with me on Nilkanth in 1952. Where was Ang Nima, we asked. Sadly he died some years ago and his family had gone away. It was the same answer for Ang Dawa V, son of Ang Tsering III. But Kanche is still living in Namche Bazar, said Gombu, and Ang Norbu, who had carried to Camp VI on Kangchenjunga in 1955, is still living in Pangboche.

At last the greetings came to an end and we strolled through the main area, where the pujas were still being celebrated. There was a riot of colour and a great feeling of happiness. Thousands of varied-coloured prayer flags were strung up high into the sky. These Lung-Ta 'Wind Horses' fluttering in the breeze were sending their messages of peace and goodwill around the world.

The kindness and enthusiasm of all Himalayan Club members was exceptional. We who were invited to take part in the Indian celebrations of the 50th anniversary of the first ascent of Kangchenjunga will remember with gratitude the friendship and the exceptional generosity of our fellow Club members who were our hosts.

Kangchenjunga 8586m: Chronology of Ascensionists 1955 ~ 2004

	NAME	NATIONALITY	DATE	ROUTE	EXPEDITION	LEADER
1	George C Band	UK	25.05.55	SW Face	UK	Charles Evans
2	Joe Brown	UK	25.05.55	SW Face	UK	Charles Evans
3	Norman D Hardie	NZ	26.05.55	SW Face	UK	Charles Evans
4	Antony H R Streather	UK	26.05.55	SW Face	UK	Charles Evans
5	Prem Chand	India	31.05.77	NE Spur	India	Narinder Kumar
6	Naik Nima Dorje	India	31.05.77	NE Spur	India	Narinder Kumar
7	Peter Boardman	UK	16.05.79	NW Face	UK	Doug Scott
8	Douglas Keith Scott	UK	16.05.79	NW Face	UK	Doug Scott
9	Joe Tasker	UK	16.05.79	NW Face	UK	Doug Scott
10	Ryoichi Fukada	Japan	14.05.80	NW Face	Japan	Masatsugu Konishi
11	Haruichi Kawamura	Japan	14.05.80	NW Face	Japan	Masatsugu Konishi
12	Ang Phurba II	Nepal	14.05.80	NW Face	Japan	Masatsugu Konishi
13	Naoe Sakashita	Japan	14.05.80	NW Face	Japan	Masatsugu Konishi
14	Shomi Suzuki	Japan	14.05.80	NW Face	Japan	Masatsugu Konishi
15	Nima Dorjee II	Nepal	15.05.80	SW Face	Germany	Karl Herrligkoffer
16	Lhakpa Gyalu	Nepal	15.05.80	SW Face	Germany	Karl Herrligkoffer
17	Georg Ritter	Germany	15.05.80	SW Face	Germany	Karl Herrligkoffer
18	Dawa Norbu	Nepal	17.05.80	NW Face	Japan	Masatsugu Konishi
19	Motomu Ohmiya	Japan	17.05.80	NW Face	Japan	Masatsugu Konishi
20	Toshitaka Sakano	Japan	17.05.80	NW Face	Japan	Masatsugu Konishi
21	Pemba Tshering	Nepal	17.05.80	NW Face	Japan	Masatsugu Konishi

	NAME	NATIONALITY	DATE	ROUTE	EXPEDITION	LEADER
22	Kazumi Fujukura	Japan	09.05.81	SW Face	Japan	Kinichi Yamamori
23	Akinori Hosaka	Japan	09.05.81	SW Face	Japan	Kinichi Yamamori
24	Kunio Kataoka	Japan	09.05.81	SW Face	Japan	Kinichi Yamamori
25	Shigeru Suzuki	Japan	09.05.81	SW Face	Japan	Kinichi Yamamori
26	Noboru Yamada	Japan	09.05.81	SW Face	Japan	Kinichi Yamamori
27	Nima Temba	Nepal	09.05.81	SW Face	Japan	Kinichi Yamamori
28	Jozef Psotka	Slovakia	20.05.81	NW Face	CSSR	Ivan Galfy
29	Ludovit Zahoransky	Czech	20.05.81	NW Face	CSSR	Ivan Galfy
30	Michel Parmentier	France	15.10.81	SW Face	France	Jean-Jacques Ricouard
31	Jean-Jacques Ricouard	France	15.10.81	SW Face	France	Jean-Jacques Ricouard
32	Innocenzo Menabreaz	Italy	02.05.82	SW Face	Italy	Renato Moro
33	Oreste Squinobal	Italy	02.05.82	SW Face	Italy	Renato Moro
34	Nga Temba	Nepal	02.05.82	SW Face	Italy	Renato Moro
35	Reinhold Messner	Italy	06.05.82	NW Face	Italy	Reinhold Messner
36	Gottfried Mutschlechner	Italy	06.05.82	NW Face	Italy	Reinhold Messner
37	Ang Dorjee	Nepal	06.05.82	NW Face	Italy	Reinhold Messner
38	Georg Bachler	Austria	28.05.83	SW Face	Austria	Hanns Schell
39	Pierre Beghin	France	17.10.83	SW Face	France	Pierre Beghin
40	Marc Bruchez	Swiss	21.10.83	NW Face	Swiss	Denis Bertholet
41	Vincent May	Swiss	21.10.83	NW Face	Swiss	Denis Bertholet
42	Takashi Ozaki	Japan	19.05.84	SW Face	Japan	Katsuhiko Kano
43	Ang Tshering	Nepal	19.05.84	SW Face	Japan	Katsuhiko Kano

	NAME	NATIONALITY	DATE	ROUTE	EXPEDITION	LEADER
44	Toichiro Mitani	Japan	20.05.84	SE Ridge – SW Face	Japan	Katsuhiko Kano
45	Seishi Wada	Japan	20.05.84	SE Ridge – SW Face	Japan	Katsuhiko Kano
46	Roger Marshall	Canada	18.10.84	SW Face	Canada	Roger Marshall
47	Krzysztof Wielicki	Poland	11.01.86	SW Face	Poland	Andrzej Machnik
48	Jerzy Kukuczka	Poland	11.01.86	SW Face	Poland	Andrzej Machnik
49	Josep Permanye	Spain	24.10.86	SW Face	Spain	Joan Hugas
50	Ang Rita	Nepal	24.10.86	SW Face	Spain	Joan Hugas
51	Phu Dorjee II	India	25.05.87	NE Spur	India	Prem Lal Kukrety
52	Phu Pu Bhutia	India	25.05.87	NE Spur	India	Prem Lal Kukrety
53	Naik Chorten Tshering	India	25.05.87	NE Spur	India	Prem Lal Kukrety
54	Rifleman Subhas Limbhoo	India	31.05.87	NE Spur	India	Prem Lal Kukrety
55	Lance Naik Bhawan Singh	India	31.05.87	NE Spur	India	Prem Lal Kukrety
56	Naik Chander Singh	India	31.05.87	NE Spur	India	Prem Lal Kukrety
57	John Coulton	Australia	10.10.87	SW Face	Australia	Michael Groom
58	Michael Groom	Australia	10.10.87	SW Face	Australia	Michael Groom
59	Jeong-Chel Lee	S Korea	02.01.88	SW Face	S. Korea	Jung Sang-Moo
60	Peter Habeler	Austria	03.05.88	NW Face	International	Carlos Buhler
61	Carlos P Buhler	USA	03.05.88	NW Face	International	Carlos Buhler
62	Martin Zabaleta	Spain	03.05.88	NW Face	International	Carlos Buhler
63	Masayuki Unno	Japan	17.10.88	SW Face	Japan	Masaaki Fukushima
64	Nima Temba	Nepal	17.10.88	SW Face	Japan	Masaaki Fukushima

	NAME	NATIONALITY	DATE	ROUTE	EXPEDITION	LEADER
65	Vasili Yelagin	Russia	09.04.89	SW Face	USSR	Eduard Myslovsky
66	Vladimir Koroteev	Russia	09.04.89	SW Face	USSR	Eduard Myslovsky
67	Yevgeni Klinezky	Russia	09.04.89	SW Face	USSR	Eduard Myslovsky
68	Aleksandr Sheinov	Russia	09.04.89	SW Face	USSR	Eduard Myslovsky
69	Kazbek Valiev	Kazakhstan	16.04.89	SW Face	USSR	Eduard Myslovsky
70	Viktor Dedy	Kazakhstan	16.04.89	SW Face	USSR	Eduard Myslovsky
71	Grigory Lunyakov	Kazakhstan	16.04.89	SW Face	USSR	Eduard Myslovsky
72	Vladimir Suviga	Kazakhstan	16.04.89	SW Face	USSR	Eduard Myslovsky
73	Zijnur Khalitov	Kazakhstan	16.04.89	SW Face	USSR	Eduard Myslovsky
74	Aleksandr Glushkovski	Russia	16.04.89	SW Face	USSR	Eduard Myslovsky
75	Yuri Moiseev	Kazakhstan	16.04.89	SW Face	USSR	Eduard Myslovsky
76	Leonid Troshchinenko	Russia	16.04.89	SW Face	USSR	Eduard Myslovsky
77	Viktor Pastuk	Ukraine	29.04.89	SW Face	USSR	Eduard Myslovsky
78	Mikhail Mozhaev	Russia	29.04.89	SW Face	USSR	Eduard Myslovsky
79	Vladimir Karatayev	Russia	29.04.89	SW Face	USSR	Eduard Myslovsky
80	Rinat Khaibullin	Kazakhstan	29.04.89	SW Face	USSR	Eduard Myslovsky
81	Sergei Bogomolov	Russia	29.04.89	SW Face	USSR	Eduard Myslovsky
82	Sergei Bershov	Ukraine	01.05.89	W Ridge Traverse	USSR	Eduard Myslovsky
83	Anatoli Boukreev	Kazakhstan	01.05.89	W Ridge Traverse	USSR	Eduard Myslovsky
84	Yevgeni Vinogradsky	Russia	01.05.89	W Ridge Traverse	USSR	Eduard Myslovsky
85	Aleksandr Pogorelov	Russia	01.05.89	W Ridge Traverse	USSR	Eduard Myslovsky
86	Mikhail Turkevich	Ukraine	01.05.89	W Ridge Traverse	USSR	Eduard Myslovsky
87	Sergei Arsentiev	Russia	01.05.89	SW Face	USSR	Eduard Myslovsky

	NAME	NATIONALITY	DATE	ROUTE	EXPEDITION	LEADER
88	Valeri Khrishchaty	Kazakhstan	01.05.89	SW Face	USSR	Eduard Myslovsky
89	Yevgeni Klinezky	Russia	01.05.89	SW Face	USSR	Eduard Myslovsky
90	Vladimir Suviga	Kazakhstan	01.05.89	SW Face	USSR	Eduard Myslovsky
91	Vasili Yelagin	Russia	02.05.89	SE Ridge Traverse	USSR	Eduard Myslovsky
92	Grigory Lunyakov	Kazakhstan	02.05.89	SE Ridge Traverse	USSR	Eduard Myslovsky
93	Zijnur Khalitov	Kazakhstan	02.05.89	SE Ridge Traverse	USSR	Eduard Myslovsky
94	Vladimir Balyberdin	Russia	02.05.89	SE Ridge Traverse	USSR	Eduard Myslovsky
95	Vladimir Koroteev	Russia	02.05.89	SE Ridge Traverse	USSR	Eduard Myslovsky
96	Nikolai Cherni	Russia	03.05.89	SW Face	USSR	Eduard Myslovsky
97	Sergei Yefimov	Russia	03.05.89	SW Face	USSR	Eduard Myslovsky
98	Babu Chiri	Nepal	03.05.89	SW Face	USSR	Eduard Myslovsky
99	Philip Ershler	USA	18.05.89	NW Face	USA	Lou Whitaker
100	Craig Van Hoy	USA	18.05.89	NW Face	USA	Lou Whitaker
101	Edmund Viesturs	USA	18.05.89	NW Face	USA	Lou Whitaker
102	Robert Link	USA	21.05.89	NW Face	USA	Lou Whitaker
103	Larry Nielson	USA	21.05.89	NW Face	USA	Lou Whitaker
104	Gregory Wilson	USA	21.05.89	NW Face	USA	Lou Whitaker
105	Mark Udall	USA	14.05.90	SW Face	USA	Rob Gustke
106	Stipe Bozic	Croatia	01.05.91	SW Face	Slovenia	Tone Skarja
107	Viktor Groselj	Slovenia	01.05.91	SW Face	Slovenia	Tone Skarja
108	Hideji Nazuka	Japan	24.05.91	NE Spur	India/Japan	Hukam Singh/Y. Ogata
109	Hirotaka Imamura	Japan	24.05.91	NE Spur	India/Japan	Hukam Singh/Y. Ogata

	NAME	NATIONALITY	DATE	ROUTE	EXPEDITION	LEADER
110	Ryuzo Oda	Japan	24.05.91	NE Spur	India/Japan	Hukam Singh/Y. Ogata
111	Kanhaiya Lal (Pokhriyal)	India	25.05.91	NE Spur	India/Japan	Hukam Singh/Y. Ogata
112	Sunil Dutt Sharma	India	25.05.91	NE Spur	India/Japan	Hukam Singh/Y. Ogata
113	Tsewang Smanlia	India	25.05.91	NE Spur	India/Japan	Hukam Singh/Y. Ogata
114	Carlos Carsolio	Mexico	12.05.92	NW Face	Mexico	Carlos Carsolio
115	Mikhail Sitnik	Ukraine	23.05.93	NE Spur	India/Ukraine	Prajapati Bodhane/ Vadim Sviridenko
116	Aleksei Kharaldin	Ukraine	23.05.93	NE Spur	India/Ukraine	Prajapati Bodhane/ Vadim Sviridenko
117	Aleksandr Serpak	Ukraine	23.05.93	NE Spur	India/Ukraine	Prajapati Bodhane/ Vadim Sviridenko
118	Valentin Boiko	Ukraine	23.05.93	NE Spur	India/Ukraine	Prajapati Bodhane/ Vadim Sviridenko
119	Vladislav Terzeoul	Ukraine	23.05.93	NE Spur	India/Ukraine	Prajapati Bodhane/ Vadim Sviridenko
120	Aleksandr Perkhomenko	Ukraine	26.05.93	NE Spur	India/Ukraine	Prajapati Bodhane/ Vadim Sviridenko
121	Dmitri Ibragimzade	Ukraine	26.05.93	NE Spur	India/Ukraine	Prajapati Bodhane/ Vadim Sviridenko
122	Viktor Kulbachenko	Bulgaria	23.10.94	SW Face	Bulgaria	Sergei Novikov
123	Erhard Loretan	Swiss	05.10.95	SW Face	Swiss	Erhard Loretan
124	Jean Troillet	Swiss	05.10.95	SW Face	Swiss	Erhard Loretan
125	Abele Blanc	Italy	14.10.95	SW Face	Italy	Sergio Martini

	NAME	NATIONALITY	DATE	ROUTE	EXPEDITION	LEADER
126	Sergio Martini	Italy	14.10.95	SW Face	Italy	Sergio Martini
127	Alberto Inurrategi	Spain	06.05.96	NW Face	Spain	Felix Inurrategi
128	Felix Inurrategi	Spain	06.05.96	NW Face	Spain	Felix Inurrategi
129	Juan Eusebio Oiarzabal	Spain	06.05.96	NW Face	Spain	Felix Inurrategi
130	Scott Mckee	USA	24.05.97	NW Face	USA	Daniel Mazur
131	Akbu	China	09.05.98	SW Face	China	Samdrup
132	Bianba Zaxi	China	09.05.98	SW Face	China	Samdrup
133	Cering Doje	China	09.05.98	SW Face	China	Samdrup
134	Daqiong	China	09.05.98	SW Face	China	Samdrup
135	Jiabu	China	09.05.98	SW Face	China	Samdrup
136	Luoze	China	09.05.98	SW Face	China	Samdrup
137	Rena	China	09.05.98	SW Face	China	Samdrup
138	Fausto De Stefani	Italy	15.05.98	SW Face	Italy	Fausto De Stefani
139	Gyalzen III	Nepal	15.05.98	SW Face	Italy	Fausto De Stefani
140	Kenzo Akasaka	Japan	15.05.98	NW Face	Japan	Taro Tanigawa
141	Kenta Hirose	Japan	15.05.98	NW Face	Japan	Taro Tanigawa
142	Masakazu Okuda	Japan	15.05.98	NW Face	Japan	Taro Tanigawa
143	Atsushi Shiina	Japan	15.05.98	NW Face	Japan	Taro Tanigawa
144	Taro Tanigawa	Japan	15.05.98	NW Face	Japan	Taro Tanigawa
145	Konrad Auer	Italy	17.05.98	SW Face	Italy	Hans Kammerlander
146	Hans Kammerlander	Italy	17.05.98	SW Face	Italy	Hans Kammerlander
147	Ginette Harrison	UK	18.05.98	NW Face	International	Gary Pfisterer (American)

	NAME	NATIONALITY	DATE	ROUTE	EXPEDITION	LEADER
148	Timothy Horvath	USA	18.05.98	NW Face	International	Gary Pfisterer
149	Jonathan Pratt	UK	18.05.98	NW Face	International	Gary Pfisterer
150	Christopher Shaw	USA	18.05.98	NW Face	International	Gary Pfisterer
151	Young-Seok Park	S Korea	12.05.99	SW Face	S Korea	Young-Seok Park
152	Sherap Jangbu	Nepal	12.05.99	SW Face	S Korea	Young-Seok Park
153	Sange	Nepal	12.05.99	SW Face	S Korea	Young-Seok Park
154	John Doyle	UK	13.05.00	SW Face	UK	Stephan Jackson
155	Adrian Cole	UK	13.05.00	SW Face	UK	Stephan Jackson
156	Nima Dorjee	Nepal	13.05.00	SW Face	UK	Stephan Jackson
157	Pemba Norbu (Nuru) IV	Nepal	13.05.00	SW Face	UK	Stephan Jackson
158	Hong-Gil Um	S Korea	19.05.00	SW Face	S Korea	Hong-Gil Um
159	Mu-Taek Park	S Korea	19.05.00	SW Face	S Korea	Hong-Gil Um
160	Wangchuk Sherpa	India	20.05.00	SW Face	India	Sunil Dutt Sharma
161	Pasang Narbu	India	20.05.00	SW Face	India	Sunil Dutt Sharma
162	Dawa Wangchuk	Nepal	20.05.00	SW Face	India	Sunil Dutt Sharma
163	Brian Duthiers	Swiss	15.05.01	SW Face	International	Piotr Pustelnik (Polish)
164	Piotr Pustelnik	Poland	15.05.01	SW Face	International	Piotr Pustelnik
165	Martin Schmidz	USA	15.05.01	SW Face	International	Piotr Pustelnik
166	Goncalo Velez	Portugal	15.05.01	SW Face	International	Piotr Pustelnik
167	Wang-Yong Han	S Korea	13.05.02	SW Face	S Korea	Wang-Yong Han
168	Woong-Sik Kim	S Korea	13.05.02	SW Face	S Korea	Wang-Yong Han
169	Dawa Wangchuk	Nepal	13.05.02	SW Face	S Korea	Wang-Yong Han

	NAME	NATIONALITY	DATE	ROUTE	EXPEDITION	LEADER
170	Martin Minarik	Czechoslovakia	13.05.02	SW Face	Czechoslovakia	Zdenek Hruby
171	Sergei Brodski	Kazakhstan	13.05.02	SW Face	Kazakhstan	Yervand Ilinski
172	Vassili Pivtsov	Kazakhstan	13.05.02	SW Face	Kazakhstan	Yervand Ilinski
173	Denis Urobko	Kazakhstan	13.05.02	SW Face	Kazakhstan	Yervand Ilinski
174	Maxut Zhumayev	Kazakhstan	13.05.02	SW Face	Kazakhstan	Yervand Ilinski
175	Radek Jaros	Czechoslovakia	14.05.02	SW Face	Czechoslovakia	Zdenek Hruby
176	Sergei Lavrov	Kazakhstan	14.05.02	SW Face	Kazakhstan	Yervand Ilinski
177	Damir Molgochev	Kazakhstan	14.05.02	SW Face	Kazakhstan	Yervand Ilinski
178	Aleksei Raspopov	Kazakhstan	14.05.02	SW Face	Kazakhstan	Yervand Ilinski
179	Stuart Findlay	UK	24.05.02	NW Face	International	Daniel Mazur
180	Christopher Hugh Grasswick	Canada	24.05.02	NW Face	International	Daniel Mazur
181	Christian Kuntner	Italy	20.05.03	SW Face	International	Christian Kuntner
182	Mario Merelli	Italy	20.05.03	SW Face	International	Christian Kuntner
183	Silvio Mondinelli	Italy	20.05.03	SW Face	International	Christian Kuntner
184	Carlos Pauner	Spanish	20.05.03	SW Face	International	Christian Kuntner
185	Kobi Reichen	Swiss	20.05.03	SW Face	Swiss	Norbert Joos
186	Maj M S Chauhan	India	10.10.04	SW Face	India	Lt Col S C Sharma
187	Nb/Sub Mohinder Singh	India	10.10.04	SW Face	India	Lt Col S C Sharma
188	Nb/Sub Chhering Norbu Bodh	India	10.10.04	SW Face	India	Lt Col S C Sharma
189	Nb/Sub Neel Chand SC	India	10.10.04	SW Face	India	Lt Col S C Sharma

	NAME	NATIONALITY	DATE	ROUTE	EXPEDITION	LEADER
190	Nk Surender Singh	India	10.10.04	SW Face	India	Lt Col S C Sharma
191	Lnk Ashok Kumar	India	10.10.04	SW Face	India	Lt Col S C Sharma
192	Pemba Rinji Sherpa	Nepal	10.10.04	SW Face	India	Lt Col S C Sharma
193	Damai Chhiri Sherpa	Nepal	10.10.04	SW Face	India	Lt Col S C Sharma
194	Dawa Wongju Sherpa	Nepal	10.10.04	SW Face	India	Lt Col S C Sharma
195	Ngima Ongdeki Sherpa	Nepal	10.10.04	SW Face	India	Lt Col S C Sharma

SUMMARY OF ASCENTS

1955-1964	4
1965-1974	0
1975-1984	42
1985-1994	76
1995-2004	73
Total	**195**

Climbs

T H Somervell
Aiguille Noire de Peutery and the Dames Anglaises from the Col de Géant
1913. Watercolour.
Painted while Somervell was a medical student
at University College Hospital, London.
Lakeland Arts Trust

JON BRACEY

'The Arctic Discipline Wall'

What's all that about?

I am told that the north-west face of Mount Kennedy was regarded as one of the great unclimbed lines in the Yukon. Dubbed the 'Arctic Discipline Wall' by that pair of Jacks, Roberts and Tackle, after several concerted efforts, it all sounded rather glamorous and a bit scary. Mountaineering is about being lucky, so in May Rich Cross and I went to see what it was all about.

As the distinct drone of the 1973 Cessna faded into the distance, all I could do was concentrate on not being sick. Due to a gusty northerly wind it had been quite a hairy flight into the heart of the Saint Elias range. Just as we were about to part company with the dirt airstrip at Kluane Lake a sharp crosswind caught the tail, leaving bush pilot Andy Williams fighting at the controls. This was only the start of the excitement. As we gained height and turned the mountains, the winds became more ferocious and occasionally we entered vicious patches of turbulence. With no warning a sudden drop of about 20 feet left our stomachs way above our spinning heads. Seeing Andy almost jumping out of his skin and grasping for the cockpit strut did little to reassure us.

It had all started in the usual fashion down at our grotty local, The Broadfield, in Sheffield. 'Where we gonna go next year, the Moose's Tooth, the Ruth, or how about India?' asked Rich, mid-pint. 'Yeah brilliant, let's go to them all,' I replied with blithe over-optimism.

A few weeks later Rich showed me a photo of a mountain in Canada. Some American hotshots had been two-thirds of the way up, climbing big-wall style, and Andy Cave and Mick Fowler had been there so it must be good.

And there it was in front of us – Mount Kennedy. Thankfully we had somehow landed in one piece and as my nausea slowly subsided the utter remoteness of our location became more and more apparent. Looking all about us, we struggled to get a grasp on the scale of our surroundings and were awestruck at the majestic beauty of the vast glaciers and stunning peaks breaking the horizon.

The final rays of the evening sun cast a golden light on Kennedy's north spur and the north-west face beyond. However, the warm glow did little to help make our climb look less daunting. At about 2000m high, the face is on a Himalayan scale. It was far longer than any route either of us had previously attempted and filled us with fear. The face had been attempted a couple of times by the Americans Jack Tackle and Jack Roberts.

13. Rich Cross skinning in to the north-west face of Mount Kennedy. (*Jon Bracey*)

14. Jon Bracey on mixed ground on Kennedy's north-west face. (*Rich Cross*)

Their efforts culminated in the spring of 1996 in the 36-pitch route *Pair of Jacks* (VI, M6, WI5+), a 10-day effort, enduring atrocious weather and a dropped crampon. Finishing some 450m short of the summit, it stood as the most technically difficult route undertaken in the St Elias range.

So far our typically small, under-organised British expedition was running smoothly bar the slight inconvenience of some lost skis. This had given Rich and I plenty of time in Whitehorse to do all our shopping and gather supplies for the next three weeks. The Yukon is certainly one of the remoter parts of the world; twice as big as Great Britain and with a population of only 30,000 people. Even half the Canadians we spoke to elsewhere didn't know where it was. Whitehorse is the biggest town in the Yukon, with wide dusty streets and bars full of rednecks. It was like being on the set of a Western.

Operating on a tight budget, we had searched hard for the cheapest transport from Whitehorse to the airstrip at Kluane Lake. The best option turned out to be a lad called Woody at 'Royal Limo'. On the dot of 12.30pm, as arranged, we heard a large vehicle pull up outside our hostel, then watched in awe as a gigantic 300lb man with a long grey ponytail struggled out of his gleaming black stretched limousine. The colossal Woody had been a trapper for 20 years, then a Hell's Angel, and was now, allegedly, on the run from a bank job. After stashing our beer in the refrigerated drinks cabinet, we sat back as Woody steered the limo up the Alaskan Highway and told us the whole story.

Thanks to those poor flying conditions, Andy had not been able to drop us at our proposed location beneath the face and we were left a good 10km away. With dinner stewing on the stove, we took stock of the situation and discussed our options. With no chance of any kind of forecast, we knew that we'd just have to go climbing and battle against whatever the Yukon weather had in store for us. And having been warned about this coastal range's reputation for dismal weather we went prepared for the worst.

We woke early to bright sunshine. After a quick breakfast Rich suggested that we get straight over to Mount Kennedy. We meticulously packed our rucksacks with six days' food and a load of good luck. A morning ski tour brought us to the base of the north spur. We'd brought along a telescope to get a close look at the face and trace the exact line we would try to follow, limiting route-finding errors later. Conditions looked good and icy, but the first 1000m of the face is very steep and with few bivouac options we decided to camp for the night and make an early start in the morning if the weather was still good. To help speed our progress in the early hours we broke a trail up the steep lower snow slopes and scoured the bergschrund for a way through. Overhanging ice cliffs loomed above us, but we spied a possibility and trudged back down through the thigh-deep snow for dinner.

At 3am the alarm woke me from a deep sleep. This was brutal. Rich, who sleeps like a dead man, showed no sign of life despite my efforts to make as much noise as possible while I lit the stove. We began the daily ritual of alpine climbing – always on the go, no time to relax, and always in a heightened state of awareness. After all the preparation it was a relief to get going. Rich's arms were rudely awakened by a section of vertical rotten ice made worse by a weighty rucksack pulling down on his shoulders. But we were over the bergschrund.

'Woosh!'

I instantly tensed and cowered against the ice as a rock the size of a small television set hurtled past us at terminal velocity. It was a fast-moving reminder that we were back in the big mountains and far from being completely in control of our destiny.

Good ice runnels allowed us to make steady progress through the steep blank cliffs of granite and by early afternoon we reached the first of the major difficulties. The ice thinned out and steep rock loomed grimly above with no easy options. Rich led rightwards across thin patches of ice without which we would have to resort to hard aid. This is what makes this kind of climbing so special, unlikely blobs of icy névé plastered onto steep rock. Upward progress is only just possible.

As the rock reared up the ice disappeared, leaving snow lying at the back of a faint groove. We hoped to find a crack that would allow us to gain access to easier ground above. But with one swing of his axe Rich cleared all the snow to reveal a blank seam. We both cast our eyes around searching for an alternative way through and soon Rich was teetering out across a steep slab desperate to find a solution. The lack of any protection and the prospect of further hard climbing forced him back. We had one alternative, a steep corner directly above us. It was only VS or so, but plastered in loose snow it proved a real test and the crux of the route.

Sensing that I could be belaying for a while yet, I pulled my duvet jacket from my rucksack and shouted words of encouragement to Rich, who was busy removing his sack in preparation for a bout of steep climbing. Over the next two hours he fought a desperate struggle, whilst I fidgeted about every couple of minutes trying to get comfortable and stay warm on my hanging stance. Finally the rope came tight and I prepared to follow the pitch, tying Rich's rucksack onto one of the ropes a metre above my head so that he could haul it as I climbed.

Desperately hanging off my axes I struggled to make upward progress. Thanks to the slack, Rich's rucksack was now dangling from my waist. My shouts and curses were lost in the wind, along with white flurries of goose feathers as my down jacket tore against the rough granite. Eventually the fight was over and I pulled up to find Rich straddled over a small rock edge attached to two tied-off ice screws in a tiny blob of ice and a loop of rope draped around a rounded spike. Tired and weary from our struggle we decided to get the stove out and have a brew to try and regain some strength. Watching the stove struggle to melt ice into water, I rested my head against the rock and slumped in my harness. Our bodies were already dry and the water was quickly gone.

15.   Jon Bracey above the northern vastness on Mount Kennedy. (*Rich Cross*)

16.   Bracey (*left*) and Cross in their 'Mark III Coffin' bivvi tent on Kennedy's
north-west face. (*Rich Cross*)

Traversing out from the belay I contemplated the idea of several more pitches before finding any kind of bivouac for the night ahead. But poking my head around a corner I was shocked to find a sun-bleached blue bag and the remains of a portaledge protruding from the ice. I had struck upon Tackle's and Roberts' abandoned camp and, more importantly, some easier-angled ice that had potential for transforming into a bivvi ledge. We hacked away at the iron-hard ice, hands numb and cramped from the effort, until, after nearly two hours of tedious effort, we had sculpted a pair of fine bucket seats. Then we erected 'The Mark III Coffin', a multi-purpose bivvi shelter designed by that infamous sufferer Al Powell. Pulling it over our heads and zipping up the doors, we sat back to relax in relative comfort, pleased with our day's progress. But clouds were building outside, making us apprehensive of incoming bad weather. There was nothing to do but slump forward like a pair of drunks and try to grab some sleep. It was here that Jack Tackle had dropped a crampon back in 1996. At only a third of the way up the face it was truly remarkable that they had carried on.

The next day came and went quickly. The clouds dispersed and we were even graced with some late afternoon sunshine. After another 15 pitches we failed to find any kind of rock ledge for the night ahead. Rocky outcrops kept luring me on in the hope of finding a tent-sized ledge, but in the end I wasted too much time. Abseiling back down to Rich, we set to work chipping out two more buckets to sleep in.

Day three on the face dawned with a spectacular cloud inversion giving us breathtaking views. But they came at a price. Bitter north winds frayed at our nerves. After the relentless front-pointing up grey ice over the last two days, five pitches of mixed climbing through the final rock band offered relief to our sore toes and weary calves.

The ground above eased, and with little hope of any protection we tied both ropes together in the hope of finding belays. A series of backbreaking 120m pitches began, our faces blasted by ice particles whipped up by the fierce winds. Moving together up the final summit slopes, it was now only a matter of time before we reached the top, but it didn't make progress any easier. Eventually I was sat on the summit pulling in the rope as Rich came to join me. I didn't feel any great ecstatic emotion. I just said a few words in my head for friends lost but not forgotten.

We had originally planned to abseil back down the face and return to our well-stocked base camp. We didn't want to rely on a pick-up from the far side of the mountain with so few supplies. But contemplating the 50 or so stressful abseils spread, quite probably, over two days, we chose the slightly more attractive option of a walk down the Cathedral glacier, and prayed for good weather. Heads tucked in against the wind, we struggled to stand up in the worst of the gusts. We even resorted to walking backwards at times to protect our faces from the relentless ice shards. Finally we came to a small hollow off the ridge sheltered from the worst of the winds and lay down, delighted to be back on flat ground again.

The next day we set off down the glacier, happy to have completed our route and confident about getting picked up. The sun beamed down on our burnt faces. We had been warned about monstrous crevasses on the glacier, but found a fortuitous path through the most treacherous icefalls and by lunchtime reached what we thought was a suitable landing spot. Without delay I pulled the satellite phone from its case and called Kluane Lake.

'Hi Andy, it's Jon on the Cathedral glacier. Any chance of getting picked up today?'

'Afraid not guys, we're clagged in here but will try tomorrow.'

Our hearts sank. We mulled over the reality of our predicament and considered how long it might be possible to survive without food. Our three remaining gas cylinders might last a week, but after that the chances of surviving would decrease quite rapidly. We woke up next day in thick cloud feeling sorry for ourselves. I dozed off hoping the sun might burn through and – miracle! – this actually happened and we sat back enjoying the warmth, certain of getting out that day. It was just after midday when Rich first said he could hear a plane. I couldn't hear a thing and told him he was losing it. But in about 20 minutes, lo and behold, we could both absolutely hear the buzz of a small prop' plane getting louder and louder. Disturbingly, a small, evil cloud was rapidly shrouding us. The plane came in low but at the last minute banked away. It tried again, but the same thing happened and then we could see the plane disappearing into the distance. We couldn't believe it.

It was the seventh day since setting off. We shared our final fig roll for breakfast and pondered how long our greyhound-like bodies might survive. It was decided that I, being the scrawnier of us, would eventually have to kill and devour Rich in order that one of us might survive. A sing-along was suggested to pass the time, but quickly dismissed. We are both tone-deaf. The frustration of our situation was getting to us. As a mountaineer, one is always taught to be self-reliant and here we were, sitting around with our lives completely in the hands of a Welsh pilot and his little aircraft. It looked like we'd be stuck on the glacier forever ... But hang on. What's that sound?

Summary: An account of the first complete ascent of *A Pair of Jacks* (VI, M6, WI5+, Roberts-Tackle 1996) on the north-west face of Mt Kennedy, Yukon, Canada, by Rich Cross and Jon Bracey in May 2004. Variations on the 1996 line included the mixed crux at hard Scottish 7. The final 450m, above the Roberts-Tackle high point, cut through the second rock band, then straight to the summit via the upper icefield/north spur.

Acknowledgements: Cross and Bracey would like to thank the Mount Everest Foundation, UK Sport, British Mountaineering Council, DMM, Rab, Outdoor Designs and Sprayway for their support.

DAVE WILKINSON & DES RUBENS

Unfinished Business in the Andes

Snow mushrooms, heavily corniced ridges, fluted faces and other bizarre formations are what spring to mind about the Peruvian Andes, especially the well-known cordilleras Blanca and Huayhuash. At the other end of the country from these honeypot areas is another range with similar character, the more tranquil and secluded Cordillera Vilcanota.

I had been there in 1982 and again in 1983, but an attack by robbers at the 1983 base camp caused that year's trip to end prematurely and dampened my enthusiasm for future visits. The subsequent rise of the Sendero Luminoso terrorist organisation then caused the Peruvian Andes to be avoided by climbers for a decade. Recently, however, as the perceived threat from terrorists has shifted elsewhere in the world, there has been renewed interest in the Andes. And nowhere has better scope for pioneering routes of a high-Andean character than the Vilcanota.

In a fairly casual email, Geoff Cohen mentioned that he was considering an Andean visit with Des Rubens, but they had limited knowledge. I suggested I knew a good part of the Andes, Steve Kennedy was also enlisted, and so the trip was born.

The vast majority of Peruvian people are extremely friendly and helpful, but a minority are kleptomaniacs. The risk of robbery is one of the least attractive features of Andean trips and it is worth spending a bit of extra trouble and money to reduce the risk. The 1983 robbery was partly caused by our staying at a base camp on our own. Having local men accompany us would act as a deterrent.

Organising one's own transport is also risky – one is vulnerable hanging around with piles of luggage waiting for buses. Transport organised in advance with trusted locals is far safer. Having only four weeks to spare, we contacted Angelina Laiso, a woman of Irish descent who lives in Cusco and runs a trekking company. She organised everything for us in Peru apart from the actual climbing.

We decided to stay at the idyllic base campsite near the small lake of Yanacocha, as used in 1983 and a suitable starting point for a host of good objectives. Our main objective was a first ascent from the south-west side of Colque Cruz I (6102m), one of the principal 6000m peaks in the Vilcanota. It had been climbed from the other side but not from this.

We flew Edinburgh-Newark-Lima, then straight on to Cusco, heart of the old Inca realm and the nearest city to our mountains. Being at 3400m, our acclimatisation started immediately. Cusco is also ideal for visits to Spanish colonial churches and Inca ruins, or simply soaking up the charm of the old city.

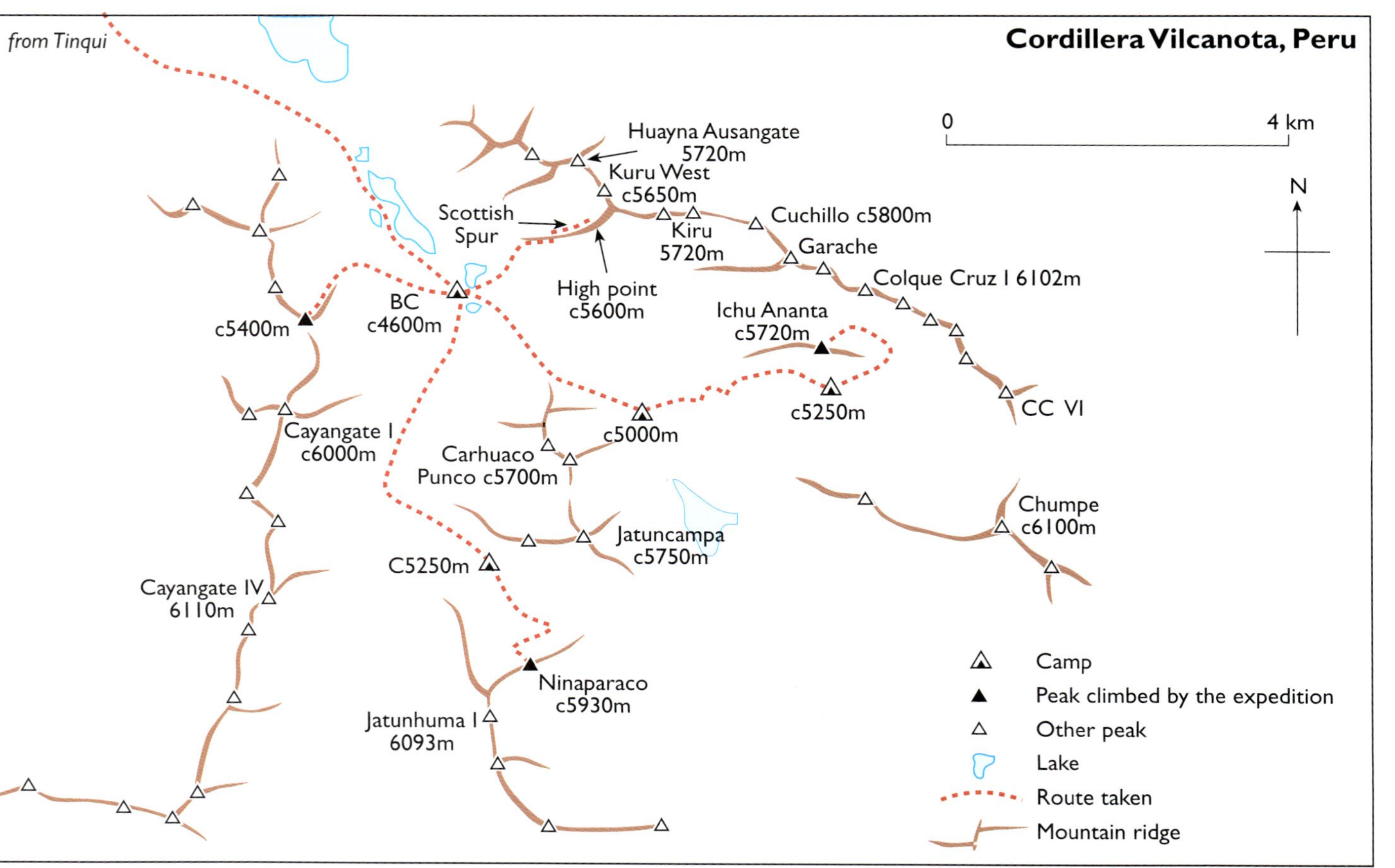

Cordillera Vilcanota, Peru
from Tinqui
0   4 km
N
Huayna Ausangate 5720m
Kuru West c5650m
Scottish Spur
Kiru 5720m
High point c5600m
Cuchillo c5800m
Garache
Colque Cruz I 6102m
Ichu Ananta c5720m
c5250m
CC VI
BC c4600m
c5400m
c5000m
Carhuaco Punco c5700m
Cayangate I c6000m
Jatuncampa c5750m
Chumpe c6100m
C5250m
Cayangate IV 6110m
Ninaparaco c5930m
Jatunhuma I 6093m
Camp
Peak climbed by the expedition
Other peak
Lake
Route taken
Mountain ridge

Two days later, we met our cook Domingo and his assistant Quintino, then set off in a well-loaded minibus on a seven-hour journey, mostly on twisting gravel roads, to the village of Tinqui, where our walk-in would start next morning. At the halfway point of this drive, we got a taste of the luxury catering we had semi-inadvertently subscribed to. The minibus stopped at a stream bank where we were treated to a fish salad lunch, hamper and tablecloth on the grass, reminiscent of a Victorian country picnic, with Domingo and Quintino as cook and butler.

Andean approaches have much less rugged terrain than the Himalaya or Karakoram, so pack animals take the place of porters. We left Tinqui well before our horses, leaving our *arriero* Leonides to complete the packing, and knowing that being unacclimatised we would be overtaken all too soon. We were. A short pull-up from the village led onto the grassy altiplano that slopes up gently towards the dazzling contrast of the snowy mountains. This undulating plain has a deceptive scale, a fascinating monotony, and gave me a treadmill illusion. Easy strolling over short-cropped, sun-bleached grass had an endless feel to it. Herds of alpacas grazed placidly, drifting past in the cool breeze. The ground moved under my feet but in the background, the mountains seemed to stay fixed.

Lunch was another alfresco Victorian picnic and eventually, within sight of a col at the altiplano's top, we stopped for the night. A couple of hours next morning took us to the col and a sudden change of scenery. On the other side was a steep-sided valley occupied by a string of glittering lakes. The way continued with a descending traverse into the valley, a sharply undulating path avoiding craggy lake-side obstacles, and a final rise between rocky bluffs to the campsite, a hidden grassy meadow surrounded by old moraines.

Surprise! Another party was already in residence. This was quite unexpected in a range so little frequented. The nine Slovenian climbers seemed to have a tent each, plus communal ones. However there was still a little room for us, and the Slovenes seemed friendly enough. Slovenes are not generally teetotal but this team seemed to have run out of alcohol. Thus during our first evening we jointly disposed of one of our bottles of good malt whisky, further warming British-Slovenian friendships. They had some bad news. A big unseasonal dump of snow had fallen in June, creating poor conditions on the hills, especially on south-facing slopes. In fact, we had had advanced warning of this. Angelina had told us of heavy snow right down to the streets of Cusco, something never seen before. But there was also good news: the Slovenes had not climbed the south-west face of Colque Cruz. And they were leaving in two days' time. No matter how amiable another party might be, one does like to have remote mountains to oneself.

We bid the Slovenians a fond farewell, moved our tents into prime positions, and the expedition started in earnest. With the base camp at 4600m, the first three days were spent in further acclimatisation and reconnaissance, particularly of the glacier leading eastwards, gateway to our main objective. In spite of the Slovenian warnings, hope persisted (vainly as it turned out) that a week or two would see sufficient consolidation of the soft snow.

The path leading to the moraines of the glacier, while still not passable by horses, has been much improved in recent years, with flat rocks laid in steps, like a Peruvian equivalent of a job creation scheme in the Highlands. We learned later that the work had been done by porters employed on a newly popular trek over to the large lake of Sibinacocha, several days' walk to the south-east. It certainly made for easier walking over this rocky ground, and led in a couple of hours to a camp site in a sandy hollow on the glacier's south flank.

We moved up with small tents and enough food and gear for a proper look at the approaches to Colque Cruz. However this advanced base proved to be on the wrong side of the glacier. The Colque Cruz peaks are mostly unclimbed from this side and we were about to discover one reason why. Next morning we left the engineered path and spent three hours crossing the rubble-covered glacier. The tedium was made worse by patches of recent snow covering bouldery ground, causing no end of expletives as feet plunged through the soft snow to jar on rocks below. The crossing completed, we continued up an icy corridor on the north side of the subsidiary glacier descending SSE from Colque Cruz I. This corridor led past a big crevassed area onto a flatter section we hoped would give access to the mountain. We left a small dump of gear, and returned to base camp.

A few days later we were back with big sacks for a closer look. A camp was made on the side glacier ready to continue to the foot of the mountain in the morning. The glacier above was covered in recent snow, its softness varying markedly with the slope's angle and orientation. South-facing slopes, especially steep ones, get little sun during this season. Level ground or east or west-facing slopes were quite firm, but as soon as the angle steepened or the direction changed to south, we were up to our crotches. A more broken part of the glacier gave interesting ice pitches as a relief from the floundering; then easier ground led back west to the broad col below the main peak of Colque Cruz, and it was time to take stock.

A broad spur led from the col to the summit. This looked climbable ground but the recent snow had stayed put. There were no striation marks to indicate sliding, nor avalanche debris below. The fresh snow was poised, waiting to slide off, onto us or with us. Thoughts of persisting with our main objective vanished. However, having travelled halfway round the world we had no intention of returning empty-handed. And we even had an alternative objective ready and close at hand. Immediately south of the col was a peak called Ichu Ananta (c5720m). It seemed that it was unclimbed ... but not for much longer.

Above the col, moderate snow slopes led to a mixed ridge, sideways-on to the col, with several summits. It was not clear which of these was the highest. There were two main candidates, and in a spirit of idleness we chose to try the nearer one first. A snow slope of about 40° faced north and got plenty of sun, so the snow was well consolidated. In fact it showed serious signs of too much sun, being eroded into 'snow fences', parallel plates of snow, at right-angles to the slope, hard but thin and fragile, with air gaps between. These demanded care, but were inconvenient rather than dangerous. Above, were rocks on the ridge and then our peak, which proved to be the lower one. Peruvian ridges are often harder than faces. Rather than traverse the heavily corniced ridge to the main summit, we descended part way and crossed the snow-fenced face, reascending for the final section of ridge. This gave pleasant moving together, mixed climbing with cornices and short rock and ice steps. We stumbled back down to our top camp in the gathering darkness, using head torches for the last hour. In these tropical latitudes, one has to be aware of the short days and rapid sunsets.

As if to make up for its June misbehaviour, the weather had treated us kindly, with only one morning of light snow showers at base camp and otherwise wall-to-wall blue skies and night frosts. This near-perfect pattern continued throughout the whole trip, the best weather we had ever experienced in big mountains.

After a good rest, we felt another route coming on. However, there was disagreement over route choice. This did not cause any problems as we were equipped to climb as two pairs and it also increased our 'productivity'. Close to base camp, a prominent spur rose to the north-east, leading towards the main Colque Cruz ridge well west of the summit. Des and Steve were keen to try this, while I felt it could harbour some of the same poor snow conditions observed elsewhere. Instead, Geoff and I opted for the rubble-strewn glacier to the east of base camp, intending to climb one of several possible routes in the Jatunhuma and Cayangate groups.

The Cayangate peaks have a number of challenging unclimbed east faces. But those closer to our base camp showed problematical approaches off the glacier. In the Jatunhuma group, the main peak, Jatunhuma I, has been previously climbed from most sides, but on its long curving north-east ridge is an unclimbed peak called Ninaparaco (c5930m), an obvious challenge. Ascending a seemingly unvisited side glacier between Jatuncampa and Ninaparaco, we made camp just above its lower icefall. Next morning, travelling light, we continued up the glacier towards the north face of Ninaparaco. At a levelling, a surprise was in store. The glacier visible below the face was a shelf, detached from the main glacier, necessitating a long deviation left, then back right along the shelf to the foot of the face proper. This misjudgement used up valuable time and contributed to our subsequent benightment.

Above the shelf, the north face of Ninaparaco started with wet slabby rocks which would have been time-consuming. Without bivouac equipment, more rapid terrain was preferable. Over to the right, a hanging glacier under the col between our mountain and Jatunhuma I gave easier climbing, but exposed to sérac fall. We climbed this as quickly as possible, with some sections of Scottish III ice, and a short rock slab at Severe. Unroped climbing led to a sheltered spot in a big ice cave that gave our lungs and nerves a brief rest while we roped up. I led up a gully on gradually steepening ice to further respite at a stance under a welcome rock overhang. Geoff led left and up the rock slab to an easier couloir and held his breath at an exposed stance. I led on up another ice pitch, then leftwards on a ledge system to gain a snowy spur above the lower slabby rocks and out of the firing line of the seracs. We could relax a bit now yet felt a sense of total commitment. Time was pressing but we were determined to complete the climb.

Ridges on Peruvian mountains are often scary and time-consuming, with convoluted cornices and snow mushrooms, making it preferable to reach the top directly, rather than emerge some way down a summit ridge. On the previous day's approach, while still well back from the face, we had taken careful note of the summit's location in relation to other features. This enabled a good line to be taken. Now unroped, a left traverse was made from the spur into a gully leading directly to the highest point. We reached the summit at 4pm; not much time to linger. We roped up to descend the top pitch, then unroped again, following our ascent route. I had belatedly got my second wind and pressed ahead to locate the right traverse line before darkness. Unfortunately, this led to our becoming separated and by the time contact was remade (by voice and head torch), Geoff had taken too high a traverse line, but found an adequate ledge and settled down to bivouac. Then the full moon emerged and shone so brightly that a night-time descent would have been possible had we been together. Spare clothing was donned, feet put in rucksacks and teeth clenched for a long cold vigil. During the night, the sky clouded over and snow started to fall, but mercifully this was only light and intermittent.

Even long Andean nights eventually end, and a very chilled pair were reunited, shook limbs back to life and continued the descent, reaching our advance camp in mid-afternoon for much needed food and re-hydration. With only four full days remaining before our scheduled departure from base camp, there was insufficient time for further routes. The fine weather had re-established itself, food and fuel were plentiful, so we indulged in a complete rest day, and then set off down again. Back at the ranch, the cooks were fretting over our continued absence, and Domingo even came up to meet us an hour above base camp – an unnecessary but kind show of concern. Meanwhile, Des and Steve had not been idle.

Des Rubens writes:
The prominent spur we coveted was a clear objective, leading up to the peak Kiru west (c5650m) on the ridge that connects all the main Colque Cruz summits. The spur looked rocky for about half of its length, after which it turned to snow and ice, decked in part by flutings, cornices and

honeycombs. We had all studied it closely from various angles. While Dave, with his greater experience of Andean ridges, was pessimistic about the outcome, we felt it might go. Adventure lay in the uncertainty. We would have to rub our noses in the ice to find out.

Setting out early, we climbed tedious scree and a steep snow gully to gain the spur at a tiny col. Though we had hoped the snow might have consolidated, we endured much thigh-depth wallowing. Once on the rocky crest, there was little in the way of route-finding problems and no roping up required. The rock was generally loose and required a lot of care. We also took care to memorise the descent and built the odd cairn for guidance.

Abruptly, and pleasingly soon, a large cornice loomed over us. We roped up and I moved out left and up good snow-ice onto a fine crest. The views had really opened up with a magnificent Matterhorn-like peak to the left and the Colque Cruz group and the peaks on the other side of the valley to the right. Steve went on and almost immediately discovered a good bivvi site about 30m down. It was the first reasonable site we'd seen, six hours from base camp, and gave us a beautiful sunset and a good night's sleep.

Next morning, we roped up almost immediately and Steve began traversing under the crest. The climbing was demanding and time-consuming, being mixed and with unconsolidated snow. After about 60m, a way beckoned to the crest and I took it. The ice was good and bypassing a threatening overhang without difficulty led us onto the crest. The only line was sharply defined. Swinging curvy modern axes with gusto, we tackled another two long pitches of beautiful, steep, exposed but not too difficult climbing that led to a short levelling off.

Crossing over to the south side, I found a fine, if chilly, lunch spot overhung by a honeycombed cornice. Then we were forced back onto deep, soft granulated snow. Ahead loomed an intimidating-looking ice wall with an icy chimney. The spur here took on a fantastical form, with mushrooms, massive icicles and plunging voids. We were forced onto the south side where the snow was horrendous. Progress slowed dramatically. Initially Steve found a route down a short icy chimney and ploughed along just below the crest; I ascended more steep unconsolidated horrors but eventually, with relief, struck more solid ground.

This led to the final obstacle on the ridge, the bottomless icy chimney spotted days before as a possible way to the easier-angled ground above. So it proved, but only after a struggle with wide bridging and good ice gave way to several feet of truly dreadful snow, leaving us panting at the top in the thin air. The crux of the route had been overcome. We estimated the two difficult pitches at a maybe soft-touch Scottish Grade V.

Although the spur was now broad and exposed to the sun the snow was as awful as ever. Steve, heroically floundering up to his waist, led up to below a rise, just left of a prominent crevasse well seen from base camp. Had the snow been good, we might well have continued for another hour or so, but on level ground and on the south side of the spur, it was, without exception, very deep and unconsolidated. Unfortunately the clouds had been drifting across for a while and we had no views.

Retreat went easily with some down-climbing and our use, for the first time, of Abalakov threads and, for the descent of the icy chimney, Geoff's snow stake. We were content at the bivvi. We had enjoyed a first-rate tussle and some superb technical climbing. Although the amount of unconsolidated snow was disappointing, we felt we had achieved our objective.

With our departure imminent, we were served an even more lavish than usual 'final dinner', complete with a bottle of Peruvian red wine. We finished this, then asked why it had come a day early – departure was not till the next morning but one. Domingo hadn't realised that July has 31 days. Next evening there was still a little whisky left to go with the second final dinner. Leonides arrived with the horses and a long walk saw us all back at Tinqui by evening for a third final dinner. Tinqui is not an especially well-appointed village, but we managed to find enough beer for a rowdy session with all and sundry. The minibus arrived the following day, taking us back to Cusco for a fourth final dinner, this one in a proper restaurant. Sadly, the trip was now ending – next day we flew home, enjoying a fifth and final dinner at Lima airport.

The terrorist threat no longer exists in Peru, but 'ordinary' robbery seems as likely as ever. Employing an agent was certainly effective as an anti-thieving measure and we got home with all possessions intact. The cooks may not have realised it, but they were really employed as camp guards. From the climbing point of view, the conditions this year did not enable full advantage to be taken, but the Vilcanota still has some of the best scope for 'high-Andean' style new routes in the whole Andes. There's certainly unfinished business in this little-known range.

Summary: Climbing in the Vilcanota range, Peru, including first ascents of Ichu Ananta (c5720m) and Ninaparaco (c5930m) by its north face.

PAUL KNOTT

The Great White Mountains of the St Elias

The St Elias range is a vast icy wilderness straddling the Alaska-Yukon border and extending more than 200km in each direction. Its best-known mountains are St Elias and Logan, whose scale is among the largest anywhere in terms of height and bulk above the surrounding glacier. Other than the two standard routes on Mount Logan, the range is still travelled very little in spite of ready access by ski plane. This may be because the scale, combined with challenging snow conditions and prolonged storms, make it a serious place to visit. Typically, the summits are buttressed by soaring ridges and guarded by complex broken glaciers and sérac-torn faces. Climbing here is a distinctive adventure that has attracted a dedicated few to make repeated exploratory trips. I hope to provide some insight into this adventure by reflecting on the four visits I have enjoyed so far to the range.

In 1993 Ade Miller and I were inspired by pictures of Mount Augusta (4288m), which not only looked stunning but also had obvious unclimbed ridges. Arriving in Yakutat (permanent population 600) we were struck by the enthusiasm and friendliness of our glacier pilot, Kurt Gloyer. There were few other climbers and we prepared our equipment amongst bits of plane in the hangar. Landing on the huge Seward glacier, we stepped out of the plane into knee-deep snow. It took some digging to find a firm base for the tents.

Our first attempt to move anywhere was thwarted when Ade fell into an unseen crevasse 150m from the tents. The deep unconsolidated snow and flat light made it impossible to see the faint lines that can conceal even huge caverns. Ade's fall caused the rope to cut in several metres, pulled out my hastily placed stake and pulled me some distance towards the crevasse. It was hard to get a firm stance in snowshoes. The other pair who were with us approached to help, but unfortunately one of them fell down the same slot. We pulled out both victims using the dropped loop and pulley system, since it would have been almost impossible to prusik beyond where the rope had knifed in.

The crevasse problem was exacerbated by the low mist that often blanketed the glacier, causing near whiteout despite the sun burning just above. To avoid getting lost on the 15km-wide icefield we took frequent back bearings and placed plenty of glacier wands (these were pre-GPS days). When it cleared we could see across to the vast south side of Mount Logan. Best known for the 10km Hummingbird Ridge, this has a number of other existing routes, all very long and committing, and continues to attract exploratory interest.

18. Mount Augusta from the north. The 1953 north ridge route slants up from the right to the shoulder below the summit. The 1987 north rib route divides sunlight and shadow towards the right. The area from which Jack Tackle was rescued in 2002 lies in the hidden area between these two routes. (*Paul Knott*)

19. Ade Miller at 10,000ft camp on the north ridge of Mount Augusta. Behind is the south side of Mount Logan, with the Hummingbird ridge dividing light and shadow. (*Paul Knott*)

During our reconnoitre we met four German climbers – the only people I have met on any of the four trips to the range. They intended to climb a direct and rather avalanche-threatened route up Augusta's north face. The same area was the scene for Jack Tackle's dramatic helicopter rescue in 2002. The foursome later switched to the Early Bird Buttress on Logan, where one unfortunately was killed in an avalanche.

We first attempted Augusta's east ridge, which we approached via a northern spur. After wading through wet, unconsolidated snow to a small 3050m summit we found ourselves faced with 2km of steeply corniced ridge on the spur and over 4km of east ridge, including rock steps and a sizeable fluted peak. In such conditions, it was too serious for us and we descended. To date, the ridge remains unclimbed.

After this we made the fourth ascent of the 1953 North Ridge route, approaching it from the east. Although mostly straightforward, this involved strenuous trail-breaking through deep snow and was punctuated by major crevasses all the way from base camp to summit. On the final slopes we collapsed a huge snow bridge and were lucky to avoid injury. The summit view was of a great white wilderness, with Mount St Elias nearby, Mount Vancouver across the glacier and the Fairweather massif 200km down the coast. At the same time, we later discovered, Bill Pilling was crawling and being lowered down Mount Vancouver, having been injured in a crevasse fall after making the first ascent of the south rib.

On the descent we nervously sat out poor weather. Our seventh day heralded the end of our supplies, and it was a relief when the morning was perfect with well frozen snow. We hurried down, passing over new debris in the avalanche-prone approach valley. At base camp the radio worked, and by 3pm we were back in Yakutat surrounded by the sights, sounds and smells of spring.

That evening we sat among the hunting and fishing trophies accumulating a large bar bill. We were satisfied with our ascent and had enjoyed the sense of adventure provided by the sheer scale of the landscape. I still have vivid memories of the pastel colours of the night and the sharp contrasts of the low morning sun. Even the glacier life was a distinctive experience. The tents were bright and warm as we sat reading in sunglasses, drank Red Zinger and listened alternately to the silence of the glacier and the roar of the X-GK stove.

Ade and I returned three years later, this time with our eyes on Mount King George (3741m), an impressive peak 35km east of Mount Logan. Its 1500m north face in particular was remarked upon in 1961 as an objective for future climbers. The mountain was not climbed until 1966, and had only seen two successful ascents before we arrived to attempt the unclimbed north-east ridge.

Prior to the trip our main concern was glacial break-up on the approach. In the event, Kurt solved this problem by confidently landing on a small flat area in the glacier bowl north of the mountain. Our new concerns were the alarming-looking séracs on the upper part of our route and the absence of radio reception. We simply had to trust that Kurt would pick us up in five weeks. As a team of two, we took extra precautions in case of crevasse incidents. On the glacier we always carried separate rescue ropes so that we could travel far apart (in case of large crevasses) and still perform a dropped-loop rescue. We also carried two 75cm snow stakes each and enough equipment for a full 6:1 haul system.

The start of the route was but a short walk away. The climb was in the lee of the usual storm winds and involved weaving around séracs on steep windslab. The snow collapsed so badly that sometimes the only way to progress was to plunge a snow stake and pull up on it. Several times the séracs forced us down and left onto the face. After two camps on the ridge we reached just over 3100m on one of these diversions before turning back at a steep section of hard ice covered with a layer of crystalline snow under yet more windslab. Our disappointment was tempered by a sense of relief once we had safely descended the avalanche slopes below.

This side of King George remains unclimbed, with some reason. Beyond our high point several more séracs interrupted the ridge and would force lengthy traverses onto the scoured-looking face. As consolation, we made the first ascent of Peak 3089m between King George and Queen Mary. On the descent an oncoming blizzard forced us to camp on the ridge. Fortunately the 16-hour snow-blast cleared early next morning and we literally trenched our way down.

For a larger objective we looked to Mount Queen Mary (3928m), a peak that has straightforward routes from the north and west, one of which has even been climbed by a dog. Our new route from the south involved 11km of winding ridge starting with the north-west ridge of Peak 3118m. Anticipating poor snow conditions we set off with seven days' food and fuel. In the event the going was good (we were on the south side with better freeze-thaw and more wind exposure) and we reached the summit early on the third day. It was a beautiful morning, the extensive view producing the cover photograph for *AJ102*. We had a forecast for five more settled days, but less than five hours later were enveloped in blizzard. The radio that had given us the forecast also failed to make contact from the summit.

By morning we had partial visibility to continue, but our footprints had been obscured and we repeatedly lost the route or were grounded by whiteout. Our few marker wands were useless; even if they hadn't melted out, we couldn't see them in the mist. I joked about trying to procure radio-wands. On one stretch we persisted through whiteout by throwing snowballs to create texture and get some idea of the terrain ahead. We reached the glacier exasperated, but rapidly became grateful for our escape as heavy snow fell for another two days.

Having had our fill of climbing, we tried to leave by stamping GET US OUT in the snow. We knew that this would be spotted by Andy Williams,

20. The east rib of Mount Vancouver with the icefall blocking access. The photo was taken in 1999. The smooth area on the left side of the icefall was much more broken in 2003. (*Paul Knott*)

the Yukon pilot who had flown over us regularly. However, during the sunny days that followed, Andy did not fly over; instead our ears created low rumbling noises that sounded like an approaching aircraft. Partly to stave off possible madness we walked out to the Hubbard glacier to try our luck with the radio. We eventually reached 50km from base camp, but still failed to make contact. We were wearily plodding back, resigned to another week of tedium, when Kurt landed next to us. He had been told of our message and had conducted something of a search.

In 1999 we returned to the Hubbard glacier with the objective of climbing a rib we had seen on the east side of Mount Vancouver. The only routes to have been climbed on this side of the mountain were the north-east ridge in 1975 and the south-east ridge in 1979. In between is a vast amount of ground and several major ridges. Fred Beckey had looked at the most southerly of these in 1979 but found the approach 'nearly hopeless'. Like other mountains in the area, Mount Vancouver has two main summits, of which the north summit is the higher at 4812m. Our route led directly to this summit.

The winter had shown a La Niña weather pattern with south-east Alaska experiencing unusually heavy snowfall. Patches of snow remained in Yakutat, despite our arrival in late May. In the mountains the weather still seemed unsettled and it was five days before we left base camp, prepared for 10 days on the mountain. We spent some hours finding a line through the icefall, climbing around and over blocks using the generous snow cover.

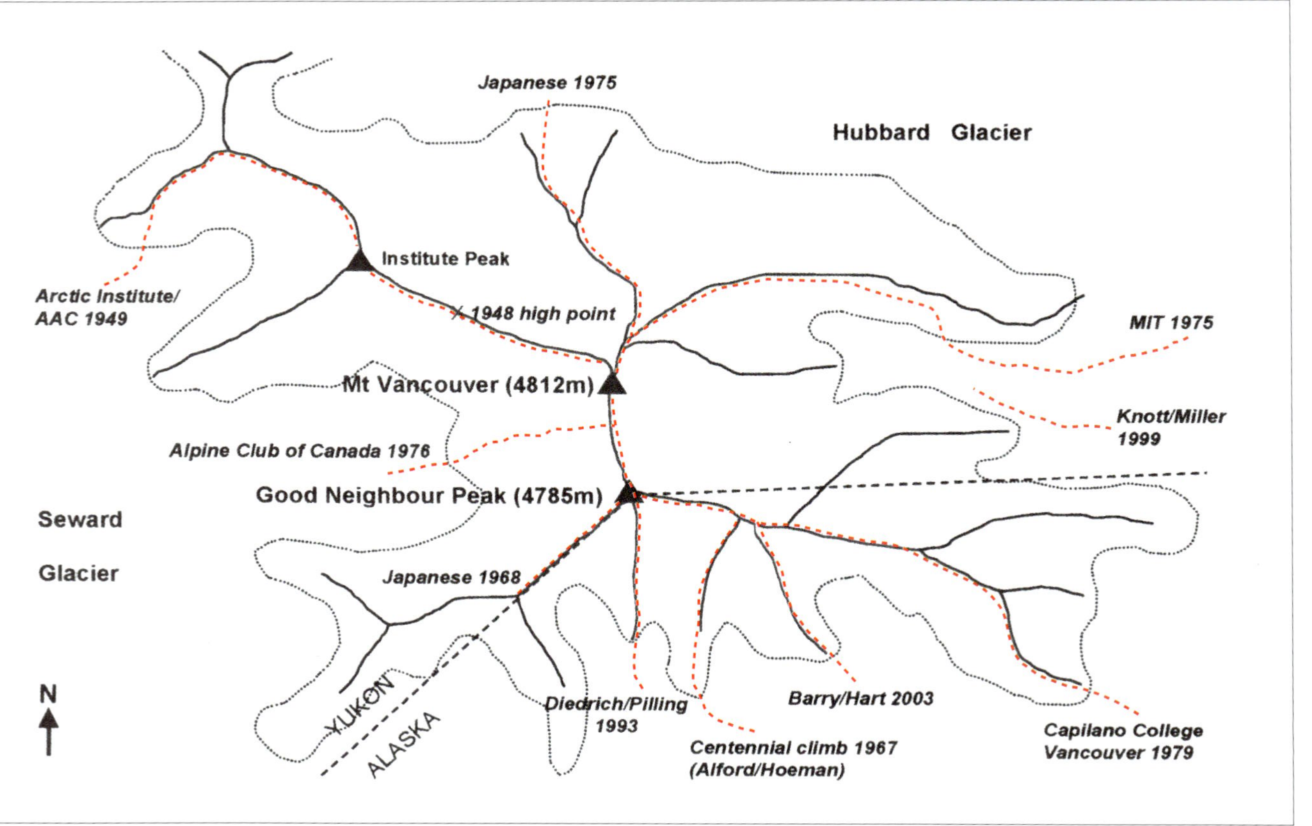

21. Routes on Mount Vancouver 1948-2004. Only the Diedrich/Pilling route has been repeated.

Above, we had to traverse north-facing avalanche slopes to avoid crevasses. As the day warmed up the hazard seemed too great, so we walked out between two crevasses and pitched the tent. That night the weather changed and we were trapped: near-whiteout and unfrozen snow prevented all movement. Our third morning at this rather dismal camp dawned clear enough for us to move — downwards. On the lower section the mist came down again, and the GPS waypoints proved crucial to our escape. My desire for a 'radio-wand' had been fulfilled.

In the perennially unsettled weather we felt we would have a better chance on Mount Seattle (3069m), which had no icefall approach. The only previous ascent of this mountain was of the south summit by Fred Beckey's party in 1966. They had climbed it from the Russell fjord, despite sinking their boat on the approach, and found it to be the higher summit. We snow-shoed the 30km down the glacier at the first available clearance, dragging our packs behind us on plastic sleds. During this interminable plod we weighed up the possible routes to the unclimbed north summit, marked as higher on the map. The north ridge was an option, but we selected the east ridge as offering a more direct line. There was a sérac band guarding the summit ridge, but we convinced ourselves using the 500ft contours on our 1:250.000-map that we would be able to traverse left onto easier ground.

The scale of the mountain, 2000m above the glacier, was compounded by the early-June conditions. Because our route faced the rising sun, the snow became dangerously slushy after about 8am and only consolidated after 1am. To cope with this our tactics allowed for many days on the mountain despite modest loads. We used a small single-skin tent and light sleeping bags, wore Buffalo gear with no shell and no spare clothing, kept fuel burn to 100ml per person-day by melting snow in a dark bag, and kept the rations under 400g per person-day.

The first two days involved wading in soft snow, shovelling our way over snow mushrooms and using the snow-stake aid technique on exposed windslab-laden slopes. Parts of the face poured constantly with avalanche and rockfall. The summit séracs did not look stable, and, given the poor freeze, it was with trepidation that we traversed the steep mixed ground below them. Crossing a spur we were horrified to be confronted with a scoured rock and ice couloir barring our escape. Luckily, after an intimidating pitch the slopes we had hoped for materialised and we escaped, as the sun gained in strength, to the safety of the summit ridge.

The north summit was noticeably lower than the south, but we rejected the intervening 3km traverse as too time-consuming in the rapidly softening snow. Our overriding concern was for a safe retreat below the séracs. When we finally made radio contact with Yakutat from our camp on the summit ridge, the congratulations felt disturbingly premature.

We reversed the route without mishap, finding snow-bridges weakened and many features altered due to melting. Back at base camp, the tents

22. Mount Foresta from the Hubbard glacier side. The pointed summit on the right is the North Peak. The left-most summit is the South Peak. The ridge facing the camera is unclimbed. (*Paul Knott*)

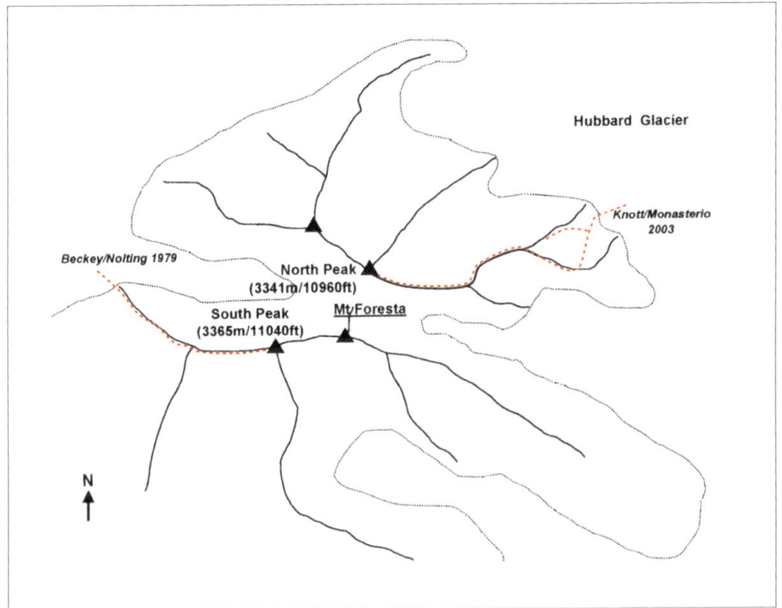

23. Routes and summit topography on Mount Foresta.
    (*Sketch map by Paul Knott*)

stood on pedestals and cracks had opened up in the glacier. Luckily when Kurt arrived we convinced him these were inconsequential. In Yakutat we found there had been few successful ascents that season, the poor weather in May having prevented almost all activity.

I returned in early May 2003 to try again on the east rib of Vancouver, this time with Erik Monasterio. Tragically Kurt Gloyer, whose dedication and tolerance had been pivotal to my previous trips, had been killed while trying to rescue climbers high on Mount Kennedy. Selecting from several more distant airfields, we chose to fly with Paul Swanstrom from Haines. For communication we used a satellite phone. Lamenting this loss of commitment, I consoled myself with the thought that Bradford Washburn had full communication in the mountains even in 1934.

It had been a strong El Niño winter with half the average precipitation. Paul circled, eyeing suspiciously the crevasse lines extending into the flat Hubbard glacier. He was concerned it might not be safe to pick us up if the melt continued. When we stepped out of the plane it was onto firm melt-freeze crust.

From the landing site, Mount Foresta was such a striking sight we decided to tackle it first. This highly attractive massif has multiple pointed summits lying along two main ridges. We were looking at the North Peak, marked as the highest summit at 11,960ft (3645m) and completely unclimbed. The potential routes all involved 5km or more of ridge and 2100m of ascent. The only previous ascent of any point in the massif was of the distinctly separate South Peak (3365m), climbed by Fred Beckey's party in 1979. As on Mount Seattle, they had found this to be the highest summit.

We approached the mountain in low cloud, picking routes as best we could. After a false start that cost us a day, we took a steep north-facing snow rib that joined the east branch of the east ridge at 1950m. Under normal conditions it would probably be too dangerous to contemplate, but our confidence had been boosted by the firm snow. As we might have predicted, it turned out to consist of unconsolidated wind deposits with a sliding surface layer. On the ridge, easy slopes soon turned to a steep, corniced crest. The climbing felt insecure, as the cornice was large and partially detached from the sharp underlying ridge. We felt progressively more committed as we overcame one hidden obstacle after another - sometimes steep rock steps, sometimes poorly bridged gaps in the cornice.

After six hours the going finally eased, and we made good progress on hard névé to a camp at 2635m. The conditions were in stark contrast to those we had endured on Mount Seattle. Similarly firm snow above led us surprisingly quickly to the summit, where GPS and altimeter readings gave 10,960ft (3341m), exactly 1000ft below the map height. Visually, the South Peak was very much separate and a little higher, consistent with the 80ft difference between its map height and our measured height. The Geological Survey later acknowledged that the spot height of 11,960ft was likely a typo error for 10,960ft.

The following day, in warmer conditions, our descent of the corniced ridge was distinctly unnerving. Our old footprints were now over hollow ground and we were forced to choose between the awkward rock crest, the detached cornice, or the gap between the two. The only belays were snow-stakes or detached spikes. Concerned about conditions on the rib we camped, hoping for a freeze. We ignored the lenticular clouds that had so often come to nothing, but overnight the weather deteriorated, bringing mist and light snow. Finding the rib was a challenge, even with the GPS, and felt like stepping onto the cornice over an unseen void. Below, the snow was wet and poorly bonded. We descended without incident, but had to rely entirely on GPS waypoints to navigate back to base camp in what were rapidly becoming full storm conditions. A metre of snow fell on the glacier during the next 48 hours, practically burying the tents.

After four days the weather finally cleared and we skied to the 1999 base camp to attempt Mount Vancouver. Conditions had changed so radically that we found ourselves navigating around large crevasses where the ski plane had landed four years earlier. The icefall above was also dramatically transformed, leaving only the most tenuous of possible lines through an impenetrable jumble of blocks. The next morning we found ourselves entering a labyrinth before even reaching that tenuous line. The difficulties and danger ahead were too sustained – later reflection suggested 2km to the end of the icefall – and we aborted the attempt.

Thus ended what will surely not be my last visit. The range has great potential, and not only for climbs of the type I have described. A few harder face climbs have been done, including the route on Mount Kennedy by Jon Bracey and Rich Cross, and there is potential for more, where access is not blocked by séracs and icefalls. In recent years Mount St Elias has seen a winter ascent, a ski descent and a paraglider descent. There are also hundreds of smaller but pretty-looking unclimbed peaks, and there is huge scope for extended ski traverses. But most importantly, this great white wilderness remains just that, a wilderness.

Notes

A summary of peaks and routes appears in an article by Roger Wallis in 1992 *Canadian Alpine Journal* (although many of the suggested new climbs have been taken). The range is included in *Alaska: A Climbing Guide* by Michael Wood and Colby Coombs. Historical information is found in articles by Terris Moore and Kenneth Andrasko in *AJ81* and *AJ83*, and in *Fifty Classic Climbs in North America* by Steve Roper and Allen Steck.

All four trips described were supported by the MEF and BMC.

DICK ISHERWOOD

King of Mountains

Haizi Shan 5833m, Sichuan

> The good mountaineer is never separated from his pit.
> Ken Wilson, c1966

In case you haven't heard, Western Sichuan is the 'in' place. Tamotsu Nakamura publicises it at every opportunity, and very generously gives out his beautifully produced *East of the Himalayas* to all comers. Young hard men and old soft men alike are flocking there.

Geoff Cohen and Martin Scott got a hold of this and recruited two others in the latter category – Bill Thurston and myself. With a mean age of 59 we had a bit of trouble finding anything in Tom's book that we thought we could climb, but we settled for Haizi Shan, a little over 19,000ft and not too far from the road. It had a bit of a history – the survey expedition of the Baron Szechenyi in 1877 determined its height at 7774m, in a region where there was thought to be at least one peak over 30,000ft. The Tibetan name, Ja-Ra, apparently translates as 'King of Mountains' and there is a story that the Tibetan King's eldest son preferred to live up there for ever more, despite offers of palaces and concubines down below. He must have had good circulation.

Haizi Shan is a fine peak, mostly snow on the north and rock on the south, well separated from everything else, and looking over the big plain of the Tagong grasslands to the west. We had some pictures from the north, which seemed the way to go, and were pleased to find we could drive to the base camp in a day and a half from Chengdu. We established ourselves in a meadow, with two cooks and two huge propane cylinders to look after the catering and tons of fresh vegetables, noodles and Sichuan red peppers, and immediately found ourselves surrounded by a Tibetan horde. There was a seasonal camp just up the trail, with at least 200 people in it devoted to the collection of worm grass, also known as caterpillar fungus. This slightly mysterious substance is variously described as a worm, a fungus and a grass, and has remarkable properties, in common with most Chinese medicines.

'Make you strong. Make you strong at night.'

'What does it do to women?' Geoff asked.

'Make your woman hot inside.'

25. Gatherers of the sought-after 'worm grass' below Haizi Shan. 'Make
     you strong at night,' the mature alpinists were told. (*Dick Isherwood*)

Personally, when I saw my first one, I thought it was just a little weed, but at least one website tells me it is in fact a dead caterpillar with a fungal fruiting body growing out of its head. Yet another miracle of the Orient.

The energy expended on the collection of these small things was astonishing – young ladies in bright red headdresses adorned with silver were all over the hillsides, 2000ft above the trail. Maybe you need to eat some just to get you going. Perhaps, we thought later, we should have taken a few up the hill.

We had driven to 3800m so we had an excuse for a fester. We walked for two hours to a very fine hot spring and lounged in the pool watching some hyped-up snails moving much faster than you would expect, and speculating about the west face of Haizi Shan which would make a good route for someone a little younger. On another day we encountered a yak caravan and I got into the wrong place at the wrong time. A small boy was leading them, waving a little whip in a very photogenic fashion. I pointed the camera at him but he didn't want any, so I put it away. While doing this I was suddenly attacked by a classic Tibetan dog, mustard and black and rather determined. It just popped out from between the legs of the yaks and before I could find a rock to throw it had made a big hole in my jeans and two deep gashes in me. I washed them out as best I could and hoped the dog wasn't rabid. Xiao Mei, our interpreter/minder, was reassuring:

'I was once bitten by a dog too,' she said, 'but the public health man in Kangding says rabies is very rare here.' I decided to believe her. No frothing at the mouth so far.

Eventually we had to address the hill. It was necessary to move about 60lbs per head of gear and food to a camp about 4000ft higher up if we were to have any real chance of getting to the top. In the good old days we would just have put it on our backs and headed up. Now, however, a debate began over whether we should do it in two carries of 30lbs or three of 20lbs. Since most of us weighed around 180lbs with boots and other stuff before even lifting a load, I argued strongly for the former.

I felt that the condition of the lower mountain justified me. Steep rhododendron forest with a metre of soft snow on it, and disintegrating steps of ice with bad snow on top and gurgling water below left us totally exhausted and rather short of our planned camp site, despite a good combined effort in which we all shared the trail breaking. Bill led one of the wettest ice pitches I can remember. The fewer times one did this the better. A moraine crest above was the obvious route and we kept looking at it to see how much snow had thawed off it. Not enough, unfortunately. It was still a soggy mess when we left in early May. If I come back here it will be post-monsoon – though maybe a couple of weeks later in the pre-monsoon season might work well enough.

With much effort we established a camp at around 4900m, in a slightly fraught spot on a cone of old avalanche debris, below a couloir that seemed

26. North face of Haizi Shan (5833m), western Sichuan, showing the Isherwood-Cohen route and high point. (*Dick Isherwood*)

to have shot its load for the season. A Hong Kong party had climbed the ridge above here as far as the north summit, so we knew it was feasible. We carried a dump of food, gear and fuel another 300m up the hill to a jolly little spot on the bottom lip of a crevasse but lack of acclimatisation prevented us going further that day. The weather now became less than perfect, though far from bad, and by consensus but with some reluctance we went down to the valley for another fester. The theory was that we would return reinvigorated and feeling wonderful.

Three days of beer-drinking and nine hours of serious effort later we were back, and I felt awful. The rhododendron forests and soggy ice had got worse, if anything, and we had been forced to do what Geoff called 'real Scottish climbing' – pick in the heather and pulling up on half-attached vegetation. We were all pretty exhausted. However, trying to display the character of Englishmen, we set the alarms early and packed everything up for a shot to carry a camp to the north summit, from which we thought we could surely get there and back.

We were very slow indeed that morning. When we had battled our way up to the dump by the crevasse it was clear that we weren't going to make the north summit even on the best scenario. Geoff then came up with a new plan. Camp here and go for it with minimal gear. Only 600m of vertical to go. Everyone bought in to avoid further load carrying.

The weather was now good, removing our only excuse. Geoff, who had mostly so far been lingering near the back, moaning about his lack of fitness, suddenly sprang to the front, got out of the tent first and beat a mighty trail up the hill in the dark while the rest of us were still grappling with our porridge. We followed him to the ridge crest and a stunning view of Minya Konka and adjacent peaks to the south and enormous plains to the north.

The ridge was of course a bit steeper than we had anticipated and the cornice needed watching. Here and there were nasty cracks going down rather a long way. I had a theory that there was so much tonnage of nice flat frozen cornice that you could walk on it without your weight making any real difference, but I wasn't quite bold enough to put this to the test. We all agreed we would have been uncomfortable soloing this with full camping gear. After a bit Martin and Bill decided to go down and Geoff and I continued, unroped, to the north summit.

We got there around eleven o'clock and thought we had lots of time. We went on easily to the big saddle before the rise to the main summit where a 30m sérac cuts across the ridge. Geoff led off round its right side and took a while, though protesting that it was all straightforward. When I followed I was impressed by the view – you stepped a long way to the right, across a big hole, and then found yourself looking straight down a good 6000 ft to the hot spring valley. The rest of the pitch was steep and distinctly exposed.

Somehow this one pitch took us almost two hours and it was now 2pm. The remainder of the ridge was steep on the north side, very steep on the south, and corniced. It was definitely climbable but a bit hard to solo, we thought, and would take four to six more pitches. We had no bivvi gear, having failed to follow Ken's dictum, and didn't fancy a cold night out. Therefore we chickened. We both agreed that 20 years ago we'd have pissed on up it, but what's the use of that?

We returned to the north summit and descended the big glacier below it, which was rather crevassed. Geoff introduced me to snow mushrooms as abseil anchors. The first one worked fine – the second disintegrated when I was two metres above a friendly snow bank. I landed flat on my back and made what I thought was an impressive crater. We saved a sling and I felt no pain – it was probably worth six visits to the chiropractor. We got back to the tent just as dark was falling. I don't wish to tell you about the descent next day through the rhododendron forest.

We had a bit of time left, though not enough for another attempt on the mountain, so we went touring to the north and west through this interesting part of culturally Tibetan China. The villages were all Tibetan, the bigger towns at least half populated by Han Chinese. We visited several monasteries all of which, except the one in Tagong, had been destroyed during the Cultural Revolution and completely rebuilt. They seemed to be flourishing; lots of monks wandered the streets and the official Chinese presence was certainly low profile, apart from a couple of very long PLA convoys on the road which were probably heading for Tibet proper. The only thing you mustn't do, we were told, was display a picture of the Dalai Lama. Construction was going on everywhere – the Tibetan villages looked very prosperous, the roads were being worked on after a fashion and the shops were full of stuff. I replaced my dog-eaten jeans with a far more fashionable pair in Garze. We ate exceptionally well everywhere, though we did leave a few red chillies and pigs' intestines on the table. I never thought I could tire of Sichuan food. Mr Ka, who drove our car (no kidding), stuck to tea during the day but in the evening introduced us to serious 'Chinese Alcohol' in quantity. The old tea-trading town of Kangding, deep in a spectacular gorge, now has a six-figure population and apart from its setting is just like Kowloon, with ten-storey buildings being demolished to make way for thirty-storey ones. See it all soon before the hordes arrive.

Summary: An attempt on Haizi Shan (5833m) in the Daxueshan of Western Sichuan, April 2004. Geoff Cohen and Dick Isherwood reached around 5800m on the north ridge. Grade AD, as far as we got.

Acknowledgements: The trip was supported by very generous grants from the Mount Everest Foundation and from the UK Sports Council via the British Mountaineering Council, to all of whom we would like to express our thanks and appreciation.

JOHN TOWN

Nganglong: Walking on the Moon

Nganglong Kangri lies in the north-west of the Tibetan Plateau at 81°00'E 32°49'N, too far from the routes of the classic explorers to feature in the literature, yet standing out on the map as a compact group, the highest peak for a hundred miles in any direction. Too far, I thought, and probably too expensive – someone else would get there first.

Time passed, and a few pieces started to fit together. The mountain is only 45km north of Tibet's northern highway, which crosses the country from Nagchu in the west to Ali in the east. It was plain from the *Lonely Planet* that plenty of backpackers and Kailash tours passed that way, despite the appalling roads. The area might be remote, but getting there was no mystery – the book said four or five hard days from the Nepalese border.

The mountain was a complete unknown – no visitors, so no photographs and no descriptions. Nonetheless, if it were there, the satellites would have seen it and the Soviet military have mapped it. Identify the appropriate image or sheet, pay your money and make what you can of what is revealed. Declassified Intelligence Satellite Photography (DISP) images, taken in the sixties and seventies as part of the Corona programme, have a particular beauty. The black-and-white photos were taken on film, not video, reflecting the subtle play of light on rocks and water. They showed a mountain range holding around 35 glaciers, with over 40 peaks above 6000m. The 24 x16km area was split by a deep valley into a smaller southern group and the main northern group. The main group ran east to west, falling very steeply on the northern side into a series of narrow valleys, but sloping gradually to the south and south-east in a number of high snowfields and broad glaciers. The Chinese give the highest peak as 6596m. The Soviet map showed a peak, Aling Kangri 6542m, in about the same location (NK5 on the attached map) but also a number of other unnamed peaks of over 6600m.

The Ngo Sang valley, which leads into the south-eastern face of the massif, seemed to be the key to our attempt. Relatively gentle slopes appeared to provide access to a number of the highest peaks. This aspect of the mountain was also closest to civilisation, though we would have to find some way of crossing the 36 kilometres of country between the nearest minor road and a suitable base for the mountain.

Our team consisted of Derek Buckle, Martin Scott and myself, who had climbed together on our successful trip to Beutse in 2003, and Toto Grönlund, an Anglo-Australian Finn whose enthusiasm was a valuable antidote to us grumpy old men. First stop was Kathmandu, which, as so often these days, was in a state of turmoil. As we arrived on 29 August

Nganglong Kangri
0   4   8
km
5810
5898
5618
5531
4961
Amkabdzhur
5762
5582
5430
5165
5570
5680
6001
5961
5967
5841
NK8
6435
NK5
6542
NK2
c6600
NK6 c6480
NK4
6582
NK3
c6600
6125
5491
NK7
c6480
Kang Ngolok E
Pk 6330
NK1
6595
Kang Ngolok
6710
Ngo Sang Chu
5487
6074
Naglung La
5615
6220
5813
6095
Southern Valley
5282
6260
5925
6430
5604
5465
6013
5845
6386
5375
5822
5495

2004, the Maoist guerrillas had just called off a blockade of all the roads in and out of Kathmandu. On the night before we set out for Tibet, terrorists in Iraq murdered 12 Nepalese hostages, sparking spontaneous uproar in the streets. Advertising British citizenship became unwise. As we drove towards the border, enraged crowds burnt down Muslim buildings and the offices of Qatar Airways. (Guess whom we had flown in with?)

The Maoists had called off their blockade but for Mother Nature it was still business as usual. Just before Barabise a landslide barred our way and we waited an hour before a bulldozer cleared a way round a half-buried lorry. In town the locals were commemorating their dead in Iraq – burning tyres in the road indicated that we should also pay our respects, so we retired to a nearby teahouse. At midday we set off again, swerving round more burning tyres and enduring a series of military checkpoints. The Nepalese border office at Kodari, by contrast, had retained its quaint charm despite the pouring rain. The usual gaggle of young boys and women carried our gear across the Friendship Bridge while their 12-year-old boss pointed out all the sights on the 250m trek. Here we met Ming Ma, our agent, Dawa, a friend from 2002, Lhakpa, our Land Cruiser driver, Pasang, our guide, Kusang, our roly-poly cook and our gangling lorry driver. The lorry's main purpose was to carry our fuel supplies. The fuel in the north, when it could be obtained, was high quality spirit from Sinjiang – too pricey for our needs, I was told. No wonder we were to have trouble with the stoves.

I had always been wary about the next part of the trip, despite it being done by thousands every year. The border is at about 1700m and from here the road rises continuously up the Matsang Tsangpo gorge to the 5120m Tong La, a five to six hour journey with a height gain of 3400m. To avoid mountain sickness, medical advice is to limit altitude gain to no more than 300m a day above a 2800m threshold. This route involves a permanent gain of 1600m in just a few hours, and a temporary gain of 2300m at each of three 5000m passes later in the day. We spent the night in Zhangmu, the Tibetan town closest to the border, which is perched precariously on the side of the gorge and, at 2300m, is too low for any acclimatisation. I had planned a two-night acclimatisation stop at Nyalam (3750m), about three hours' journey from Zhangmu. We arrived there in the morning of the following day and Derek and Toto went for a walk in the direction of Shishapangma, while Martin and I went for a short walk to confirm that there is no more to Nyalam than meets the eye. We had lost a day by our unplanned night in Zhangmu and were going to lose another because the ferry at Saga was out of action, which necessitated a diversion. By late afternoon, since everybody felt fine, the acclimatisation plan was ditched

Left
27. Nganglong Kangri, the highest mountain in Ngari Province, western Tibet. Of the two summits, the 'map height' of the highest is 6595m, though two separate GPS readings of 6710m were recorded. (*Sketch map by John Town*)

and the next morning we set off over the Tong La and La Lung to Tingri. From here we continued to Shekar and on to the dreadful road leading to the 5220m Gyatso La, where one member of the party began to suffer badly. In retrospect it was not a good idea to ask Lhakpa to lose altitude as fast as possible, as his performance on the hairpins possibly did for a second team member. Martin denied suffering from mountain sickness but remained uncharacteristically silent for the next 36 hours.

Our desire to make progress was understandable – the road journey from Kathmandu to Base Camp was just over 1500km. From Lhatse we travelled west for a day to the depressing hamlet of Raka. The rubbish dump was spectacular even by Tibetan standards and, as it doubled as hotel toilet, we all went to have a look. The next day we turned north on Route 22, the remote and beautiful road which runs 408km from Raka to meet the Northern Highway near Dong Tso. The county town of Tsochen offers the only accommodation on this stretch – otherwise you must camp. Beyond Raka we started to see groups of gazelle and, after an hour, passed the hot springs and geysers at Tagyel Chutse. The road then runs over a low pass and along the eastern shore of the turquoise Tagyel Tso, beyond which runs a series of snow-clad 6000m peaks. We stopped to drop off supplies of brick tea for a nomad family camped at the lake edge. The road then begins to climb and eventually reaches 5500m at the Song Ma La, a place of lonely views and utter desolation. A Land Cruiser had broken down at the summit and a Chinese lady was running about in panic, frightened of dying of mountain sickness before she could get down. I had never been in a place of such cruel beauty.

The road descended, then hopped from one valley to another until I lost all track of where we were. We lunched at a truck stop whose name we wrote down but then lost, and finally recognised the wide river valley which leads to Tsochen. Dreams of cans of Sprite faded as Lhakpa drove straight through, but after crossing yet another pass, we eventually made camp by the shores of the shining Dawa Tso. Five days on the road were beginning to take their toll. Toto deserved a medal for staying squeezed in the back seat between men twice her length and weight. Despite the sun the windows had to remain closed to keep out the dust. Day six took us along the eastern flank of the 6800m Shahkangsham range with spectacular views of a line of icy peaks, before we finally reached the Northern Highway – a grand name for another set of ruts in the dust. Camp that night was at Oma, following a long search for a site with drinking water.

The next day's travel was the last and as we passed through Tsaka and onto the back road to Gegye, excitement mounted. We snaked over a low pass near Chaktsaka and the sight of some snowy mountains prompted a flurry of photography, despite their being in the wrong place. A few miles further and a wide valley opened to the north-east. A salt lake filled the middle distance and a line of snow peaks stretched across the horizon. However much you study maps and satellite images, seeing is believing.

The other mountains we had seen ran to the south of the valley. A well used but unmarked road ran past distant workings and 'Keep Out' signs. We had stumbled on a sizeable working gold mine but there was no time to visit. Beyond the lake was a village – deserted apart from three beautifully dressed ladies of great age. They had never seen anything like us before but they struggled gamely to understand what we were up to and tried their best to direct us on our way. Two miles down the road, at a village on the map that didn't exist, we feebly scanned the horizon for a possible track to the mountains. Lhakpa was made of sterner stuff. 'Did we want to cross the (big) river?' Without waiting for an answer, he plunged the vehicle in and roared across. 'Where now?' he gestured. I had had a satellite photo, and a series of waypoints from the map, programmed into my GPS back in the UK. I had also spotted a low pass on the photos, leading from a nearby valley system into the Ngo Sang valley – who needed a track ? We set off across country and into the side valley. As the valley narrowed we found tyre tracks. We followed them and then navigated by GPS towards the pass. More tyre marks. A track gradually appeared and led us to the top of the pass, the Naglung La. I know what Moses felt like looking down at the promised land.

Unlike Moses we had a job to finish and it was getting late in the day. We descended the pass, continued for a couple of miles up the valley and then waited for hours for the lorry to catch up after a delay refuelling. The going had been easy along a raised terrace above the river but then the struggle started. It was vital that we should get far enough up the river to make a useful base camp. The vehicles crossed and re-crossed the river, lurching at crazy angles over moraine and boulders as the evening sun shone straight in the drivers' eyes. There was a limit to how much of this punishment the vehicles could take. From the satellite photos it appeared that the valley narrowed to a final section of gorge that we didn't believe was motorable, but Lhakpa was in no mood to give up until he had given it a try. As he finally turned the Land Cruiser round, a shadowy creature loped across the valley from right to left. The Tibetans were ecstatic – a black wolf had crossed our path. 'What if it had gone the other way?' I asked Dawa. 'Bad time' he smiled.

Base Camp was a dusty slope at 5000m, with little protection from the sun or the wind funnelling up the valley. The next morning the Tibetans were further excited to find a herd of wild yak grazing the subsidiary valley north of the camp and Dawa followed them with his telephoto lens. We set off up the gorge and, after a couple of hours, reached the point where it opened out to the north. Broad easy slopes stretched away to an amphi-theatre of peaks set back about 10km. Nearest and most prominent was a large double peak that offered an obvious route up a number of snow terraces. The other peaks were more difficult to assess, the distance and subsidiary ridges making it difficult to gauge their height or topography.

28. Nganglong Kangri from the south. (*John Town*)

29. Advance Base Camp. (*John Town*)

30.   Panorama from Peak 6253 saddle: *L to R* Upper Ngo Sang glacier, NK2,
NK6 subsidiary peak, NK3, NK6, NK5 and 'Block Peak' c6400m. (*John Town*)

31.   Nganglong Kangri I from Peak 6153. (*John Town*)

When we compared notes back at Base Camp it was difficult to reconcile what we had seen with the map or satellite photos. The preliminary view was that the big peak must be the 'Aling Kangri' of the Russian and Chinese maps (NK5) but that meant the map would have to be wrong, since the peak was clearly not on the watershed. Our problems did not end there. We had also hoped to find villagers or animals to ferry loads, but the area was deserted. Apart from a couple of sheep-herding families below the Naglung La, there was nobody within 30km. We were saved by our three, brave Tibetan partners who volunteered to carry for us. Over the next two days they made two overloaded carries up the gorge.

The next day, 9 September, we retraced our steps up the gorge and established ABC on a broad glacial plain at 5400m, about 6 km south of Nganglong Kangri I, or Kang Ngolok as the big peak was known by the sheep herders. By now we had been on the go for nine consecutive days and Martin and I took a rest day. Derek and Toto, who were still full of beans, headed up to reconnoitre the route onto Kang Ngolok and to cache gear for the next camp. I was becoming increasingly concerned that we could not relate our mountain to what we could see on the map or satellite photos and, since the team was going well and the route seemed well within our capabilities, I decided that this was a problem we needed to solve. There was a 5900m col just to the north of nearby Peak 6125 that would give a grandstand view of the area in question. On the 11th I descended to Base Camp with the aim of reaching it.

Meanwhile, Derek, Martin and Toto set off upwards, establishing a site for Camp 1 on a rocky promontory at 5775m. Their route then climbed over the lateral moraine and made an easy rising traverse of the south-east glacier to Camp 2 at 6200m, which they occupied on 13 September.

On the 12th, loaded with cameras and a bivouac bag, I had set off from Base Camp, north and then north-west into the steep valley leading behind Peak 6125. After bivouacking at 5400m I continued upwards to the 5900m col and on to Peak 6125. This viewpoint provided great views of Kang Ngolok and also allowed me to reconcile what we had seen on the ground with the map and satellite photos. Kang Ngolok (NK1) was not the 'Aling Kangri' of the Russian and Chinese maps, but an unnamed peak south of the watershed with a map height of between 6640m and 6680m. I was also able to see all the other big peaks on the watershed except NK4 (6582m) and these appeared lower than our peak, which accorded with the map.

While I descended, Derek, Martin and Toto were at Camp 2 preparing for their summit bid. The next day, 14 September, they aborted a pre-dawn start because of cold and stove problems, but eventually departed just before 10am. Their route lay over a snow dome and up the SE face towards a rightward slanting snow ramp at 6600m. This proved unattractive on closer acquaintance and they took a more direct route up the steep face to its left, which led easily to the summit ridge and on to the summit. Readings from two GPS units both gave the height as 6710m. On the 15th the party descended to the lateral moraine, where Martin continued the descent to ABC while Derek and Toto climbed the striking but easy south-east ridge of the 6595m east summit.

Curiosity, and a concern at not having been able to see the hidden NK4, led me to a further solo trip. On 15 September I set off west from Base Camp to try and cross into the Southern valley, which splits the northern and southern parts of the range. If I could get into a suitable position on the far side of the valley, I would be able to see NK4 and the Southern glacier, the biggest in the range. A long day took me up across gravel uplands towards the divide and a bivouac at 5500m. The ground showed no evidence that man had ever been this way before – only the occasional tracks of solitary wild yak or kyang. Vegetation was almost completely absent. My footprints would stay here unaltered for many years and I was therefore, in a sense, walking on sacred ground. Perhaps the astronauts had felt like this, walking on the moon.

I reached the divide the next day, photographed the 6000m peaks of the southern part of the range, and descended into the remote Southern valley. Time ran out before I could climb far enough up the other side to see NK4 and it was 9pm before I got back to the bivouac bag. I regained Base Camp the next day and, after a day's rest, we set out on the return journey to Kathmandu, which we accomplished this time in five days, via the ferry at Saga.

Most climbers pursue their sport blessedly free from ethical conflict. Mountain explorers rarely go where no man has gone before, until they set foot above the snowline – hunters and nomads were there long before. We suppose that we pose no risk if we 'Take only pictures, Leave only footsteps'. Nganglong was different – leaving footsteps, taking photos, writing accounts which may encourage others' explorations, adding these peaks to the notches on one's ice axe – all of this was to fundamentally alter the place. What is known cannot be unknown, but I realise now there is a cost to all our explorations, our naming of parts, our ceaseless need to know and to document.

Summary: In August-September 2004 John Town with Derek Buckle, Toto Grönlund and Martin Scott travelled from Kathmandu 1500km by road to Rutok County (Ngari Province) in far west Tibet, where there are some 35 glaciers (two over 6km in length) and more than 40 peaks over 6000m. They were successful in making the first ascent of both summits of the highest mountain, Nganglong Kangri, by routes graded PD and F. Although the 'map height' of the highest is 6596m, they recorded two separate GPS readings of 6710m.

ANNE ARRAN

Big Walls of China

Giant pandas and Chinese acrobats swung the balance for this trip. Inspired by Tamotsu Nakamura's splendid photographs of blank-looking granite and unclimbed walls, featured in the *Japanese Alpine Journal*, we headed off in search of an oriental adventure in the Suang Qiao Gou valley, close to Mount Siguniang. It was a gamble, with a limited three weeks of climbing set against a July forecast of frequent showers.

Mick Fowler helped out with much useful information, as did Tanja and Andrej Grmovsek from Slovenia who provided a superb collection of images of their climbs in the same valley. Lenny, our Chinese helper and chef extraordinaire, was enthusiastic as we shopped for provisions, playing 'Guess what's in the packet?' with incomprehensibly labelled packages.

The coach to Rilong called and we set off on the six to seven hour journey through wooded, panda-inhabited valleys. After visiting the Tourist Service Centre for our permissions and paying an environmental protection tax and park entrance fee, we set off on the tourist bus up the Suang Qiao Gou valley. It was clear that the east side of the valley held more promise in terms of rock quality for summer ascents with big walls and spires extending into the distance. There was also a feast of unclimbed peaks in the 5200m-5900m range.

Once beneath our objective we waded the valley stream to establish a camp away from habitation and out of easy reach of the feisty and curious yaks. John had to sprint off at one point for daring to tread too close to a bull. We moved on to set up advanced base camp at around 4100m and stashed equipment higher still at the base of our chosen route near a stunning aquamarine lake. We were tempted by a superb, but hard, three-pitch climb leading to the shoulder of the nearby Putala Shan. However, we weren't yet acclimatised and in no fit condition for such a tricky line.

John was sick that evening and we both found it hard to sleep and eat before starting up our objective at 6am. The granite intermittently formed rubble-strewn ledges as we weaved our way up, excited to be under way. Behind us, a snow-flushed cirque beckoned for another day. In the morning light these grey, smooth faces looked harder than walls we had seen in the Ak Su valley of Kyrgyzstan. There appeared to be little between 'broken alpine' and full-on aid or free climbing desperates. The fine array of mixed objectives here are probably best tackled between January and March but were out of the question for us in wet July.

Our wall was above the lake opposite Putala Shan. We ascended right of a spur for nine pitches (350m at E3/E4 5c) to reach a sub-peak we called Mi Mi Shan (5018m). Should you be feeling particularly brave it may be possible to descend into a notch and then ascend a long, tricky, loose and extremely narrow ridge from here to reach the main unclimbed summit at 5400m.

Our next objective was the unclimbed 'Heart of Cow', a fine rocky peak of almost 5000m which occupies a very prominent position at the head of the Suang Qiao Gou valley. According to Lenny, a Japanese team had attempted it in 2003 and reached approximately halfway. Rhododendrons repelled us from attempting the longest face, as swimming and wriggling through them proved unbearable without a machete. Advancing even 20 metres seemed to take an eternity so we opted for a change of plan. Finally escaping the dense foliage, we set up ABC at 4400m in a bivvi cave at the foot of the face and spent a day of incessant rain hanging out, huddled, freezing and surrounded by low lying mist. During the second night we recycled our last tea bag three times and shuffled around, unable to sleep without sleeping-bags. Rain thrashed down while a little way above it fell quietly as snow. Our only comfort was Coeheli's *Eleven Minutes*.

The weather at this time of year is not kind. However, come morning, glimmers of sunshine banished the swirls of thick-hanging mist – an extremely welcome sight as I got up, struggling to stand straight after the night's torment; or is that just age? After initial slabs, the wall reared steeply, promising at least some work for the arms. We both made jokes about this being far too much like mountaineering as we carefully ascended a snowfield, front pointing in trainers, cutting steps and using carefully selected stone daggers to make upward progress.

A sportingly damp 6a traverse led to a section of beautiful rock. The unclimbed Mount Hunter and its rotten dark rock lay behind, still shrouded with stubborn cloud, while beyond other unclimbed peaks winked at us. The climb was confirming our belief that this was the right side of the valley for good quality rock. Just another couple of pitches and we emerged at 6pm on the easy, but occasionally narrow, summit ridge. We had climbed the north-east face and north ridge to reach the summit in 10 pitches with climbing up to UK 6a plus sections of moving unroped.

Heart of Cow (4942m) became our peak for a few minutes and we realised, looking at our proposed descent line, why the mountain had not been easily climbed before. As darkness encroached, I left a wire in memory of our friend Jules Cartwright. While this was hardly a challenge worthy of his attention, I knew he would have liked the evening moment up there. We abseiled off a few pitches and by the time we reached the base of the wall it was fully dark.

The adventure, unfortunately, was far from over and it took until one o'clock the following morning to relocate the bivvi site. We descended into ravines where distant gurgles indicated water in the darkness and as the ground steepened began a series of roped lowers over grassy humps and finally off a sturdy rhododendron bush. After the waist belays the bush was a winner and we were at last established on easier ground, no longer faced with a night out on the vertiginous bank.

32. Beautiful climbing on the lower reaches of 'Heart of Cow'. (*John Arran*)

33. On the final ridge to the summit of 'Heart of Cow'. (*John Arran*)

34.   Magnificent views from the summit of 'Heart of Cow'. (*John Arran*)

The descent had become tedious. At around midnight, feeling the effects of the day's exertions, I was keen just to descend all the way to the valley and return for the gear at our bivvi site the next day. John, however, was convinced that we were close and was keen to continue our search. Sensing he could be right, and with legs and back becoming ever more weary, I set a deadline of another 45 minutes to find it. We began to hurry so as to make the time last longer and maximise the chances of finding our target.

As we strained to identify any useful feature in the blackness, the ground beneath our feet suddenly began to feel more familiar. Then with a few seconds to go to my deadline, we simultaneously recognised the shape of a boulder above our bivvi. After tweaking the basher sheet, a waterproof cover held in place by strategically placed wires and stones, we settled down for a few hours of sleep feeling relieved and extremely happy to come away with anything.

There are many walls worth climbing here, the harder ones requiring a dedicated big wall approach rather than alpine style. Pandas can be seen at the Wolong nature reserve or Chengdu zoo, however it is unlikely you will spot one hanging out in the wild.

Summary: First ascents of new subsidiary peak 'Mi Mi Shan' (5018m) and main peak 'Heart of Cow' (4942m) in China's Suang Qiao Gou valley by Anne and John Arran in July 2004.

Many thanks to the Mount Everest Foundation, BMC and UK Sport for providing some expedition funding and also to Petzl, Beal and Boreal for equipment.

IAN PARNELL

Saf Minal North-west Face

I tried to time my bouts of shivering with those of the form crushed next to me. I doubted that its Gore-Tex clad bulk could actually be sleeping but, just in case it had managed a brief moment of escape, how cruel to wrench it back to this cold dark place. Maybe if I could just find a glimmer of comfort I too might step sideways from the refrigerator into a warm golden room… I shifted my hips to release a blood-starved limb… the room would be filled with heat radiating from a huge fire… my arm was coming back to life and I could now wiggle the fingers… in front of the fire she was there welcoming me down onto the soft rug… I moved my arm round and pulled close to snuggle up. 'Dude!' John's voice dragged me back to reality, the golden fire was gone and I was back in our tiny frozen tent five days up Saf Minal's north-west face. 'You know what you need?' She was gone too. And in her place I was squeezing my irate climbing partner closer to me. 'You need a girlfriend. Big time!'

It's a popular theory that today's self-styled über-mountaineers are merely emotionally retarded lonely men still playing at being boys. And that the attentions of a good woman would deflect their misguided energies back to normality. But such simple theories always have flaws. Take John Varco, the rather disturbed American alpinist I was now mistakenly clutching in my arms in search of solace. He had found Sue who catered for his every bizarre whim, even tolerating his rather narrow taste in music. (John disputes it is 'bizarre', claiming he likes both kinds of music, Ozzy Osbourne *and* Black Sabbath.) Anyway what better picture of domestic bliss could there be for the alpine male than Sue cooking up a lumberjack slam breakfast, a weight-watcher's favourite involving lots of steak, as the strains of *Iron Man* mingle with the morning bird song?

Unfortunately Sue shared John's unusual taste in holidays; in fact her own high-altitude perversions more than matched his own. In 2003 she dragged the poor man away from the fireside on to Kalanka, a rarely ascended beast of a north Indian mountain with a beauty of an unclimbed spur on its north face. They spent over two weeks romancing the thing until, 300m below the summit, the dream slowly turned to nightmare. Trapped by the weather within a day of success, the pair cut meagre rations to a mere 400 calories a day. After four days even these starvation supplies ran out and they spent another four with no food before stumbling back to civilisation.

John lost 20 pounds in weight, but at least the eight days marooned high on his Kalanka honeymoon had given him plenty of opportunity to spy on the beautiful pile of ice and rubble where I now clung to him. Saf Minal (6911m) dominates the approach to the north side of the Nanda Devi Sanctuary. Surprisingly, despite this prominent position it had only been climbed once, from its softer southern side. Its untouched north face presents a dramatic sweep, almost 2500m of gradually steepening snow and ice topped by a rocky summit headwall. And here lay the reason for the peak's unpopularity; for while its glamorous sisters Kalanka and Changabang are dressed in fine white granite, Saf Minal broods under dark shale. But beauty is a subjective thing and while the sisters were undeniably pretty, it was Saf Minal's perfect outline, sheer scale and dark mystery that set my heart racing.

Lifting the veil on such a mystery was not easy. The mountain was not on the Indian Mountaineering Federation's list of climbable peaks, and then there was the issue of the Sanctuary and the elusive Inner Line. We knew that despite being home to India's highest and arguably most coveted peak, the Nanda Devi Sanctuary had been closed for years. Officially, access is restricted for conservation reasons. However, there is also said to be radiation leaking from a spying device 'lost' on Nanda Devi following a series of CIA-sponsored expeditions in the 1960s. The abortive mission to spy on the Chinese with a nuclear-powered monitor became one of the agency's least well-kept secrets. Maybe Indian irritation over this poisoning of a source of the Ganges lay behind the bureaucrat's reluctance to grant Varco the special X permit needed to approach even the outer edge of the Sanctuary. I had managed to acquire the said papers the day before departure, but for the American it became an ill-tempered five-day struggle in Delhi. Finally the mandarin relented and hand wrote the precious document. We ran from the government buildings before officialdom changed its mind, knowing we'd cracked the crux of the route.

For me, alpinism has a lot in common with 'drum and bass', that Anglo take on hip-hop music distinctive for its frantic 'edge of chaos' beats and dark, driving bass lines. For a start there is the relentless rhythm and unforgiving pace. Couple that with the apocalyptic atmospherics; there is nothing that gets the heart racing more than teetering on the edge of the storm, sonically or geographically. And then there is that darkness, the willingness to stray from the beaten path, to explore difficult landscapes, fractured and insecure; and crucially the ability to discover beauty where others only see noise and discomfort.

Most drum and bass tunes start with a lengthy intro, building anticipation. Ours had been building throughout the X visa debacle and now, with precious time lost, the tick of the clock rang loud over our trek to advanced base camp as we rushed through 10 days of acclimatisation. Frequent snow and lethargy meant we only managed to stagger up the slopes of the smallest of fore peaks, spending barely 30 minutes at 5500m, hardly textbook preparation for a near-7000m mountain. But it would need a lot more than

Right
36. Ian Parnell on day 4
     above the rock band.
     (*John Varco*)

this to put us off. We had been thinking about this ascent for the past year, momentum building as we rehearsed each step of the climb in our dreams; acclimatised or not, now was the time to act.

We packed light and fast for something we both knew could take us much longer than our planned five days' rations. But if both of us were good at anything, it was the ability to keep going no matter how low the fuel. After goodbyes to Razzu, our liaison officer, and Chander, our cook, we managed three days of steady progress over moderate ground, plodding through thigh-deep snow, cresting ridges and weaving through mixed terrain as the rock changed from light, sound granite to dark, disintegrating shale. It was the kind of climbing that non-mountaineers dismiss as boring and uninvolved, but it is exactly this ground that makes mountains such a challenge, ratcheting up the commitment many notches above that of, say, the Alps.

On day four things got particularly interesting. A poorly protected traverse picked its way through stacked useless blocks of yellow decaying shale. The rope ran out with nothing worth belaying on so we continued simul-climbing. Deflected away from the safety of the ridge we were forced into the open of the great ice bowl that forms the north-west face. Here the pitches flew by but there would now be few places to hide and a direct retreat looked horrific. We had little choice if we wanted to climb the thing, but I couldn't banish the thought that we were being drawn into a trap of our own making. As if to confirm my suspicions, snowflakes began to fall and by the time we skirted the edge of the ice to reach the upper rock band spindrift avalanches were pouring down the face. We frantically searched for some kind of tent site, any spot that would hold our tiny two-person shelter. All we could manage was a patch of 50-degree black ice that took three hours of hard labour to chop into a two-foot wide sloping scoop. It would have to do; John and I only had to shiver through one night here.

Well that was how it was supposed to work, but we were not the ones driving. That night, the following day and through another interminable night we clung on as snow continued to fall. Avalanches darkened the air and spindrift accumulated inexorably behind our little tent. We gradually slipped off the edge of the ledge where we hung, two damp fish squashed together at the bottom of the net, until the inevitable happened and the poles began to give.

The key point in any drum and bass tune is the drop. Often preceded by a moody build-up, the drop is a moment of sudden silence at the top of a gathering crescendo of beats before the track is finally fully let loose. This second of silence represents a pause for breath, a brief space to gather your wits, anticipating the onslaught about to be unleashed. It's an emotional pressure point, the moment of commitment.

Squashed in our tent, one pole broken and the other threatening to snap at any minute, we were faced with our moment. A decision had to be made. Racked with cramps, low on gas and almost out of food, staying put wasn't on the menu. It was either down (at 1700m up the face, not a trivial option) or bite the bullet, zip up our hoods and head up into the storm. We chose the latter. I guess that's the thing about the drop. You're poised at the top of the roller coaster and theoretically you could inch your way back down. But I can rarely resist when the big adventure calls. We are humans after all and a driven species if ever there was one. John and I had talked through this scenario continuously during our 36-hour confinement and now, faced with our call to action, momentum took us and we burst out into the maelstrom.

To describe the crux of a route as 45-degree snow might sound a little tame. But factor in that rotting dark shale lies six inches below the slush, that night has fallen on a 14-hour push and you're about to ask your partner to unclip from his belay and start simul-climbing with no protection worth talking about, then you begin to get the measure of it. In terms of numbers this might have been the technically easiest climbing either of us had done but it was definitely the most committing. Strangely, despite the obvious consequences of a mistake, this type of situation is panic free. Instead, the intense concentration brings detachment. It was what I call 'calm clawing', dragging axes through the slush until they snag on unseen placements, equalising four minimal points of contact and improvising with anything that gains upward movement. I dragged John further into the darkness; I knew the ridge was close. The bivvi prospects so far amounted to little more than standing where we were with the tent fly draped over our heads, but if we could make it to the ridge there was a good chance of deep enough snow to dig a tent platform.

The light blinded me and I realised I'd just woken from a deep sleep. I remembered the battle with the storm to get the tent up at 1 o'clock this morning when we had finally made it to the ridge. It had been worth it though – a chance to lie down properly and my first shut-eye for three days. The light really was bright, it couldn't mean... could it? We whooped for joy as John ripped open the tent to prove the storm really had blown itself out. Not only that, but blue sky topped the most flawless alpine vista either of us had seen. We peered out incredulously. Our gamble had paid off and, as if in confirmation, the incredible face of Nanda Devi reared up in front of us; perhaps the least-sighted aspect of India's highest mountain.

Much of top-flight alpinism is spent heads down, struggling for progress. Despite the fact that the high mountains offer some of the most incredible sights in the world, you get little time to take it in. It is only later, leafing through your holiday snaps, that you can really comprehend the sheer beauty. Now John and I had been given the perfect summit day and what looked to be only a few hours of moderate plodding to our summit. The fact that we were now out of food, isolated beyond rescue and with only a day's gas left, just added to our sense of appreciation. We were like gawping tourists stopping at every rise and false summit to snap ourselves against the dream backdrop. We dallied for half an hour on the summit, John producing a small frog given to him by Sue to take there. As he held it out,

37. Ian Parnell on the summit ridge of Saf Minal. (*John Varco*)

beaming with pride, Kalanka's north face was there behind him, their high point painfully close from this vantage. Saf Minal's summit seemed only fair consolation.

Writing this, I look back on those beautiful, frantic days and feel a warm glow inside. I have to restrain the urge to laugh out loud in celebration of what we did, what we got away with. I also smile because I've had a good go at proving that theory right. Four weeks after my return from India I met a beautiful Texan lady who swept me off my feet. She's not an alpinist and I'm not going on a big Himalayan trip this year. Instead I'm going to enjoy the simple things in life. So the theorists were right? Well, maybe. On my office wall just left of the computer screen a creased postcard winks back at me. I trace imaginary lines on the west face of Gasherbrum IV and feel my heart race with plans for next year.

Summary: An account of the first ascent of the north-west face of Saf Minal (6911m) in the Garhwal Himalaya, India, by Ian Parnell and John Varco, in October 2004.

(What was that about no big Himalayan trips this year? A likely story! Shortly after this article was edited, Ian was on his way east for 10 weeks filming on Everest. Of course it is not the first such expedition-denying resolution to crumble. SG)

NICK BULLOCK

Shadows on Teng Kangpoche

The plane touched down with a screech of tyres. The warm humid air hit us like a blast furnace and here I was once again in Kathmandu. This time it was different. This time Cartwright wasn't with me. His memory was, though. His ghost lingered. I saw him in the airport. I saw him as I met friends from last year who were compassionate and inquisitive. I saw him and felt him in the streets, the cafes and the bars. I missed my friend who was no longer with us. I vowed to do his memory justice and hoped I could live up to the standard he set on the hill.

Nick Carter was my partner for round two on Teng Kangpoche's north-west face. Carter was no Cartwright. He was easygoing, driven in a quiet kind of way. He was even willing to listen and compromise. He was happy to let me make the decisions and would be content with a successful ascent by whatever line. Mostly, though, I would not have to keep a close eye on the expedition funds whenever we were near a bar.

The weather was unseasonable. 2003 had given one day of snow. So far in 2004 there had been storms in Kathmandu, delays at Lukla and frustration for me. Carter and I had attempted my solo line from the previous year, *Love and Hate* (*AJ* 2004) on the north-east face of Teng Kangpoche, hoping to bag the summit. We were lucky to escape with our lives. My high point from the year before was still a long way up when we turned. The snow slid past on more than one occasion, hunting, searching… Fortunately we avoided the white-sliding harbinger of misery and cautiously ran to the valley.

Eventually the waiting and reading, the eating, sitting and sleeping drove us to the chosen line on the north-west face, where Cartwright, Powell and I had struggled in 2003.

'We will just take a look.'

There was no doubt that the snow would be treacherous, and with nerves scorched like the fresh growth on a flower caught in a late spring frost, we made our way to the end of the moraine.

The snow on the edge of the initial snow cone tumbled away in blocks with each plunge of the boot. Carter was ready to turn. I could see it in those haunted eyes.

'I'll take a look in the middle.'

Out into no-man's-land the powder had pummelled and pressed, cut a furrow as deep as a storm drain and given us a consolidated way up. Up into the massive void of white nothing, up into the very heart of the mile-high hell of the loose, the soft, and the uncertain.

38. North-west face of Teng Kangpoche, above Thame in the Khumbu, Nepal.
(*Nick Bullock*)

39. Nick Bullock on the upper section of *Edge of Darkness* on the north-west
face of Teng Kangpoche. (*Nick Carter*)

We followed a toboggan run; curves and twists carved by spindrift made the going good and took us deep into the depths of the north-west face. We soloed, as the climbing was not difficult and speed was safety. The dawn lit our awe-inspiring position like a floodlight on a football pitch. Snow crept across the miles of the vertical desert. Hunting cracks and fissures, it whispered to me in a mesmerising melancholy: 'What are you doing here? You don't belong here. Turn back.'

The snow slapped my face, it woke me from my dark-lonely thoughts, it whipped and snaked, cutting cleaves as clean and as sharp as the edge of a tile. Midday found us high and committed. 1300 metres opened out beneath our feet. Fins and crests of ice and snow surrounded our lonely position. Folds sharp, sagging and random like the points of a jester's hat made for a mad moon-like maelstrom. The cold gnawed into flesh; hands and feet had long given up the struggle for feeling. We decided to stop and re-warm. Recovery was required if the final 300 metres was to be successfully tackled tomorrow.

The second day of the climb started and finished in the dark and in bone-numbing cold. The final 300 metres were more technical than any of the climbing below. Vertical and hard-plated ice peeled from rock. Out in the middle of nowhere, 1500 metres high, fighting the fight in the dark, in a deep unconsolidated runnel of powder, I wondered why? By 7pm, with 11 hours already done, deep lines etched and creased a face that had seen too many years and lost too many friends. Wet with sweat and melting snow, I sprinted for the summit ridge. This torture was finally coming to an end and with it I hoped for peace and recovery from the ghosts.

Carter joined me beneath a mushroom of snow balanced on the summit ridge. It was 8pm and we would go no further. The ridge to the summit shone in the light of the crescent moon. Gargoyles of snow, hideous, sagging monstrosities, clung to a tenuous existence, struggling to remain in touch with the reality of the ridge. Having walked the tightrope once already this year along a ridge of insanity in Peru, I was not prepared to repeat it. Tomorrow would see us heading down and I was sure that would be no easy ride.

Sweat froze. I sat shivering waiting for Carter at the side of the initial snow cone and took comfort in feeling the cold, knowing soon I would return to life and living. Sensations, feelings and emotions coursed through my body. Waiting for Carter, the dark moved in for my last time on Teng Kangpoche.

I replayed a conversation with a friend. We talked about loss and about my climbs. 'You think it'll never happen to you, don't you? You think it will always be the other person?'

'No, I actually do think I'll kill myself.' She looked shocked.

I continued, 'It's a matter of time and percentages. If you place yourself in a dangerous situation repeatedly and push, the chances are something will happen at some point. I just hope it's not for a long time, I still have a lot of living to do.'

40. Nick Carter on *Edge of Darkness*, north-west face of Teng Kangpoche, with Everest in the distance. (*Nick Bullock*)

Ice tinkled from the dark. Carter was near and the worry I had experienced waiting for him now subsided. I wasn't ready to lose more friends. I will always have pain and I will never forget. I will continually question and try to understand. Pain is appreciation.

Summary: Nick Bullock and Nick Carter. The first ascent of the north-west face of Teng Kangpoche, Khumbu, Nepal. *Edge of Darkness*. TD+/ED1 Scottish IV 1600m. 23-25 October 2004.

Nick Bullock and Nick Carter would like to thank the following for their continual support: the MEF, the BMC's Alpinist *magazine, Mammut and DMM. Without their help this trip would not have happened and for that we are very appreciative.*

Nought but Noodles on Hispar Sar

'You come and meet Osama,' the porter said mockingly as we reached the collection of shepherds' huts called Bitanmal marking the sight of the evening camp. Andy and I looked at each other puzzled as the man dived into the nearest hovel. He reappeared moments later to great peals of laughter, followed not by the world's most wanted terrorist, but a 14-year-old yak herder. It was a comic end to what had been a long and tiring day.

In the company of Andy Parkin, 12 Hispar porters and a cook I was back in my old stomping ground of the Pakistani Karakoram, after a four-year absence. Personal circumstances and the events of 11 September 2001 had conspired to make the region a no-go area in the intervening period. It felt good to be back.

A day and a half later, having crossed a further glacier, negotiated cliffs of tottering moraine, forded several rivers and walked across the intervening rubble, we arrived at our base camp. Jutmal, a small grassy ablation valley high above the Hispar glacier, is a magical spot. Further up the valley and in direct line of sight on the eastern side of the Yutmaru glacier lay our objective – Hispar Sar (6400m). Fifteen years earlier, with my regular climbing partner of the time Sean Smith, I had made a thwarted attempt to climb it. A three-day approach followed by two nights of storms on the route had stopped us, but the memory of a perfect line and the quality of the climbing had made me return.

A rather farcical argument then developed as we came to pay off the porters. We offered to pay the five and a half stages as agreed in Hispar village plus a tip. The porters demanded six. Tempers frayed. Just as it looked like the matter was going to be referred to the Nagar magistrate, a timely piece of arithmetic revealed that our offer amounted to more than what was being demanded anyway. With the crisis over, the smiles returned. We handed over the cash, said our goodbyes, and were left to the solitude and vastness that characterises the great Karakoram glaciers.

Over the next week we made a variety of excursions to scope out the mountain, move up food and equipment to an advanced base camp and to acclimatise. However, the combination of two days of storm, which confined us to base camp, and a tight schedule meant we were not as well prepared for climbing as we both would have wished.

On 25 September we took a rest day. It was Andy's fiftieth birthday. I presented him with a water bottle filled with whisky, brought along to mark the occasion. He examined the bottle cautiously.

'It's not piss you know,' I said jokingly.

41. The Yates-Parkin objective – the south-west face of Hispar Sar, Karakoram. (*Simon Yates*)

Andy smiled and opened the bottle. The idea of a bottle of liquor in Muslim Pakistan had obviously thrown him, but over the following few hours he warmed to it.

By the next evening we were encamped at our advanced base and ready to go. In the early morning we crossed the remaining short section of glacier. The snow cone at the base of the couloir soon led into steep icy runnels, giving some superb climbing before the angle eased off. Route-finding was not a problem. We followed the great gully for pitch after pitch until, with darkness approaching, we moved right into a small snow basin, hoping to excavate a bivouac ledge below a rock wall. The shelf we managed to dig was small but with no alternative it would have to suffice. In the twilight Andy fumbled with a karabiner clipped into a loop of rope. Mishap. The 'biner along with three stuff sacks slid off down the route as Andy swore loud and long in his naturalised French. The bags contained most of our food, the brewing kit and a spare can of gas.

'We could always go down,' I offered, but the look on his face told me Andy was made of sterner stuff and that the thought had not even entered his head. A quick search revealed that some gas, noodles and a few chocolate bars remained. We settled down to what was to become our set evening meal – a bowl of instant noodles washed down with several cups of warm water.

The night passed slowly and uncomfortably, made even more unpleasant by sporadic spindrift avalanches. It was a relief to begin moving again in the morning. The day passed uneventfully as we continued, in fine weather, up the more gently-angled central section of the couloir. A two-tiered bivouac in soft snow provided a much more comfortable night and a better place to begin the day from. The early start proved fortuitous. As I led the first pitch it started snowing, bombarding Andy with regular avalanches. By late afternoon a steep icefall gave access to the uppermost basin of the couloir, which blanked out above. As nightfall approached Andy led a difficult mixed pitch to gain a knife-edge ridge to the right.

The bivvi was sensational – a small shelf hacked into the crest of the ridge. I sat uncomfortably, while Andy lay out precariously. Luckily he did not roll over in the night, which passed slowly with persistent wind, snow showers and biting cold.

In the morning Andy led the hardest pitch of the climb, clearing rotten snow to climb runnels of steep ice to reach the south ridge proper. A further exposed pitch along waves of corniced ridge led to a flat spot below easy-angled slopes leading to the summit. It was mid-afternoon. With the weather set fair we decided to spend the rest of the day drying damp sleeping bags and to make a push for the top and back the following day. We went to sleep happy, with the alarm set for midnight.

During the evening the wind got up, cloud moved in and we were soon enveloped by a storm. The weather was no better by morning. With only vapour left in our remaining gas cylinder there was only one choice open to us. At first light we packed our rucksacks and started a series of abseils.

2. Hispar Sar – Andy Parkin climbing steep ice runnels on the first day on the face. (*Simon Yates*)

43. The Upper Hispar glacier, the Hispar La and the Ogre in the distance viewed from the ridge above the couloir on Hispar Sar. (*Simon Yates*)

44. Andy Parkin cresting the ridge above Hispar Sar's south-west face on the fourth day of climbing, with Spantik in the distance behind. (*Simon Yates*)

It was a long day. The storm intensified sending ever-larger powder avalanches down the couloir. Towards the bottom it was only possible to descend at carefully timed moments between the deluges. Finally we ploughed down the snow slope at the base of the route. The food bags lay on the glacier, almost jeering at us. One had been pecked at by choughs, but the Tang they had discovered was obviously not to their taste.

It snowed heavily during the night, but we ate well and savoured the shelter of the tent. After a leisurely breakfast we loaded our rucksacks and staggered off down the glacier. The snow-covered moraine proved tiresome, but by midday only the crossing of the Yutmaru glacier separated us from the luxury of base camp. As we started across, the storm intensified. Soon we were lost. We weaved around on the glacier trying and failing to recognise features in the driving snow and wind. The hours slipped by. This was the last thing we needed.

Finally, with dusk approaching, a brief lull in the storm provided some visibility. We were on the Hispar glacier having already walked below its junction with the Yutmaru and the point where we needed to climb the moraine wall to return to Jutmal. We had to go back. The rest of the walk was exhausting, but at least we had found our way. With great relief we reached base camp and the comfort of the kitchen tent. Nazir Ali, our cook, kindly kept the stove roaring well into the night.

The blizzard was still raging in the morning. Amazingly the porters arrived in the early afternoon having walked up through it. The weather cleared that evening, allowing us to leave the mountains in an orderly fashion the following day.

In keeping with modern tradition we will certainly claim the first ascent of the south-west face of Hispar Sar, but being an old-fashioned sort I am still disappointed we were not granted the weather window to top out, bag the first ascent of the mountain and get our views of the great mountains to the north.

Both Andy and I found this the most trouble-free expedition we have ever undertaken in Pakistan. The travel logistics all worked seamlessly, aided in no small measure by the people of the northern areas of Pakistan being as hospitable as ever. At no time did we feel even remotely threatened. Word on the streets of Islamabad is that the concession granted in 2002, lifting the height at which peak fees must be paid to 6500m, will be raised further to 7000m. This will free a great number of potential mountaineering objectives from the bureaucratic hassle and extra cost of obtaining a permit and dealing with the Ministry of Tourism. Hopefully this will encourage climbers and other tourists to return to the Pakistani Karakoram and enable the region to regain the popularity it so richly deserves.

Summary: An account of the first ascent of the south-west face of Hispar Sar, Hispar, Pakistani Karakoram, by Andy Parkin and Simon Yates in September-October 2004. The route is 1100m and alpine grade ED VI.

Acknowledgements: *Andy Parkin and Simon Yates would like to thank the Mount Everest Foundation, UK Sport and the British Mountaineering Council for their financial support of the expedition.*

KELLY CORDES

Just Climbing

It seems to me that there are times and events in life – too few and too far between – that a person never forgets; a time when everything you've been looking for, dreamt of, worked towards and wanted to be, finally connects with an inexplicable depth, and you realise it might never work that way again. It's the sort of thing that leaves you gazing off later, at random times in public places, seemingly spaced-out like some druggie burnout, except that the memories replaying are vivid and real, more real than anything you've known. That's what four and a half days in Pakistan were for me, July 2004, when Josh Wharton and I were free.

We'd gone to Pakistan for the south-west ridge of Great Trango Tower, 2250 vertical metres from base to summit and unclimbed, though not unattempted and not unknown. Some have called it the biggest rock route in the world, though I don't know if that's true, nor does it matter. What I do know is that we wanted to climb it, and we didn't care what others thought. Not the paranoid US populous, too afraid to travel, who bought into the hype and were busy wrapping their homes in plastic wrap and duct tape, watching the terror alert level rise every time Bush needed a boost in the polls. Not the super-famous, A-Team pair of climbers who called me when they heard of our plans, wondering if we were really going, because, well, they were too and, well, the one calling me had seen that route years ago (along with every other climber who's ever walked along the Baltoro or Trango glaciers) and had really, really wanted to climb it for a really, really long time and, well, are we really going? (Yes, we're really going, good luck to you, see you there, I said. They bailed.) And certainly not the many people who, clearly, gave us little chance of pulling it off, certainly not in the style we'd envisioned.

Style – some people don't care, but I do, because I love climbing and I love the mountains. 'Hey man, it's just climbing,' goes the cliché. I know. It's worthless. Like managing high-end investments, slaving away to buy more unnecessary crap, or most things that most people do with their lives when you really think about it. Style is indisputably a personal choice – climb how you want, so long as you don't wreck the place and are honest about what you do. But for me, it is deeper than just climbing; for better or for worse, I can't separate how I approach the things I value from the person I want to be. Yes, to me, it matters.

In retrospect, our 'Disaster Style' plan (to use the correct nomenclature) bordered on the absurd. Fuelled with delusional optimism, we figured we could climb the route with a single 28-pound pack and a relatively basic rack. And, of course, alpine-style. We had a double set of cams, a bunch of wires, a few pitons and no snow or ice pro. From a mile and a half below, the glacier descent and the mixed climbing up high looked easy, so for 'ice gear' we had Gore-Tex sneakers, ultra-light aluminium strap-on crampons, and one and a half ice axes between us (the 'half' was an axe that Josh and his father had made even lighter by chopping the already diminutive shaft down; I brought a real, but lightweight, axe). We brought just one fuel canister because we counted on finding water flowing down the rock (we went thirsty). Food comprised a couple of soup packets (useless without water) and, mostly, bars and gels (hard to choke down without water). We also brought two summer-weight down sleeping bags, one pad, one ultra-light emergency tarp' and an aluminised emergency blanket (no bivvi sacks or tent). Not much else.

Far more than our strategy, gear or intense pre-trip training, the single most crucial element to our ascent happened early, without discussion and not while climbing. At our second bivvi, our only fuel canister sputtered empty. We had climbed some 1200m of broken terrain, mostly moderate (lots of 5.8, some scrambling, and some 5.10/11, including a 5.11 R/X pitch that Josh fired) and not terribly dangerous, just one pitch of death blocks. Most of the huge, loose boulders were perched on ledges. We were feeling strong, and were halfway up the route, albeit the easy half. The skies were clear and we'd melted enough snow and ice for water to last through noon the next day. Continuing upward without fuel might have been illogical, but as we settled onto our sloping rocks to bivvi, we said nothing. 'Nothing' because something stronger, something rooted deep in our subconscious, had taken hold. It was, in retrospect, reflected for us both in the closing words of my journal entry the night before starting up the biggest route of our lives: 'Be mentally strong. Suffer well, it'll be worth it.'

Day three started cold, and I leapfrogged our biggest cam up a crack until it turned to hands. Before long, we had reached the headwall, and Josh took over, masterfully piecing it together. (On the second pitch of the first day, our jury-rigged gear sling had come undone and we had lost one-quarter of our cams, all key sizes for the headwall.) Above, I took us up more moderate terrain to a bivvi and day four continued into steep rock blended with sketchy sugar snow.

Late in the day came the technical climbing highlight. Were it not such a spectacular lead, it might seem silly to single out one pitch on such an overwhelming total package. We were close to the top, near 6250m and a day above the previous high points and the relative comfort of their proven retreat paths. It'd been 30 hours since we'd drunk the last of our water. Rappelling down the overhanging big-wall faces on either side of the often knife-edged ridge wasn't an option, given our meagre rack and lack of bolt kit. Reversing our course, with the multiple tension traverses, pendulums, and run-outs, would have been problematic at best, and we knew the summit, and therefore our descent route, had to be close. Our plan was to

45. Azeem Ridge (right syline) on Great Trango Tower (west summit), seen from high up the Trango glacier. Wharton-Cordes route begins lower right. Red arrows mark the line of ascent to west summit. (*Kelly Cordes*)

46. Kelly Cordes leading splinter cracks on day 2 of the Azeem Ridge climb. (*Josh Wharton*)

47. Josh Wharton on 'easy' terrain, relatively low on Azeem Ridge, day 3. (*Kelly Cord*

rappel from the top and connect to the sérac-riddled, avalanche-swept hanging glacier to the north-west.

It was Josh's block, and he'd just punched it, for 20 unprotected feet above a ledge, through a 5.10+ off-width. Above, he led left around the corner onto the smooth big-wall face (home to the famous American and Russian routes of 1999), linking together 5.11 free climbing, dubious aid moves and pendulums to reach the only passage possible without a serious aid rack: a verglas smear in a right-facing corner, down and left. He strapped one of his crampons to his left rock shoe, put his pint-sized kiddie-toy of an ice axe in his left hand and tapped his way upward, climbing verglas with his left side while crimping and smearing 5.11 granite with his right. Twelve metres above his last pro, an equalized knife-blade and beak, he gained a perfect bivvi ledge. Following, I lowered out multiple times, pulled his scant gear under body weight, and jugged vertical to overhanging granite 2200m above the Trango glacier in awe. It was the finest lead I've ever seen.

On the ledge, I cultivated a tiny pile of ice chunks by my head – my ritual throat-wetting – and curled into a ball for another night of something resembling sleep.

As storm clouds crept close on our fifth morning, I took over leading and, wearing every piece of clothing I had, grunted up a vertical, mixed off-width capped by an overhanging cornice. Three more mixed pitches brought us to the west summit, where I didn't stop or even pause, missing out on what must be one of the grandest views on earth. I scratched over the top of the snow-covered slab and down the other side, to where I could get an anchor and we could descend. After several rappels, the wall grew increasingly blank, forcing one rappel from a single RP in a seam, backed by two horrible knife-blades. Our relief – if that's what a virtually emotion-less state could be called – at reaching the glacier was short-lived as, after 20 metres of pulling and with the other rope end midway up the smooth wall, our ropes became stuck. We both yarded with all our remaining strength. Nothing. Jugging on the mystery jam, with the other end unsecured, was a roulette spin we were unwilling to take, so we cut off what was left – just 20 metres of our tag line. We had no snow or ice pro, and our decimated rock rack was useless. Ahead lay 800 vertical metres of crevassed and sérac-riddled glacier. We'd traverse, punch-through slots thigh-deep, down-climb ice up to 60-degrees and make one short rappel from an ice bollard. But before starting down and just after tying in, I said to Josh, simply, 'No mistakes.' Our thousand-yard stares met, he nodded and we began down-climbing.

A couple of tense hours later we reached the toe of the glacier and fell upon a stream of melt-water, gorging ourselves. We soon scrambled down to the Nameless gully and unroped. Josh's words of congratulations and our embrace momentarily snapped me out of my trance, and I felt a surge of emotion. It seemed fitting that it was only us, no hype, no web reports to send or sat-phone calls to make (especially since we had no 'phone).

There was, however, one spectator. As we stumbled down the rubble-strewn gully, a lone figure scrambled rapidly up toward us, wearing tattered clothes and sandals. It was Ghafoor, our good friend and cook, coming with the biggest smile I've ever seen and a huge hug for us both. I felt tears, like I was crying, but my body spared no moisture. Ghafoor placed glittery ribbons around our necks and grabbed our pack – he refused to let us take it down, 'No-no, Sir,' (no matter what we said, he insisted on calling us 'Sir') 'I carry, I carry!' and set off at high speed, hopping over boulders, to prepare one helluva hot meal. Ghafoor told us that he'd be watching from camp through our binoculars, though we doubted he'd be able to see us. Once we were high on the ridge, he hustled out to the nearest 'village' (a very loose term), bought some Coca-Cola and, somehow, got some cheesy party favours. He and his little brother Karim, our assistant cook, had strung the camp with banners and home-made congratulatory signs, spelled in wonderfully broken English, and built stone-lined walkways from our tents to the cook-tent.

We staggered down to base camp just hours ahead of the storm, and for the next week I lay around camp sleeping, resting, eating, drinking; trying to hydrate and recover, though I couldn't seem to regain my energy. We had gone the final 48 hours on Great Trango without water. I didn't care as much as I might have about the mysterious health funk I'd developed, reeking of ammonia on any physical exertion and having unprecedented, erratic swings in blood sugar. It continued on the trek out, and for months I'd be tired, napping, sleeping late, unable – or maybe just lazily uninterested – in doing anything demanding. Regardless, my reflections on where we'd been and what we'd done were purely introspective, but this is no place for the clever omissions or misleading details that seem all too common in climbing accounts today. Here's what we did:

We had two ropes: a 9.1mm lead line and a 7.9mm tag line. We did no fixing. We carried no bolt kit. We started climbing around 9am on 24 July and summitted around noon on 28 July. The second jugged with the pack where it was steep, which was probably half of the route. We clipped fixed gear when we saw it – mostly belay bolts, and perhaps a half-dozen protection bolts – but did not use any of the fixed ropes we saw abandoned from prior attempts. (We later scrambled up and cleaned one that someone had fixed and abandoned at the start.) We carried off all of our garbage (empty fuel canister and food wrappers) but left a few pieces fixed along with five (or six?) rap anchors (many cams) and, unfortunately – my only regret of the climb – our ropes (save for 20 metres of the tag line that we'd salvaged for the remaining descent).

Our route starts on the lower right of the broad south-west buttress, at just under 4000m and climbs to the west summit (c6237-6250m, depending on the map) of Great Trango Tower, which was 17 pitches (including the hardest climbing) beyond the highest anchors, or any trace of passage, that we found from previous attempts. (The highest was from a team of four

48. Josh Wharton 'jugging high' on a steep section of the Azeem Ridge, day 4.
    (*Kelly Cordes*)

Spaniards, who climbed 61 pitches, with fixed ropes and camps, over three weeks in 1990 while making a movie – they claimed to be just a few pitches of easy terrain from the top…) Josh led the hardest pitches, including five that were 5.11 (one included M6). My hardest leads were 5.10+ (and M5), though not as serious as Josh's. With 60m ropes and some simul-climbing on a handful of pitches on the lower half, we climbed 54 pitches. Twenty-five of the pitches were 5.10 or harder. I led 30 and Josh 24, but Josh was indisputably the ropegun, leading the hardest and most dangerous pitches. We named the route *Azeem Ridge* and rated it 5.11R/X M6 A2. Azeem is an Urdu word we learned from our cook and good friend Ghafoor and his assistant (and little brother), Karim. It means 'great', both in terms of stature/size but more importantly as a greeting of fondness and respect between friends. That, in a word, describes our feelings about the wonderful people we met in the Northern Areas of Pakistan. Our friends in the Charakusa (and later, Nanga Parbat), one of only two other American groups climbing in Pakistan in 2004 to my knowledge, were met with the same warmth. The widespread, sweeping nature of fear and propaganda at home is absurd and carries an ugliness disturbingly similar to racism in its de facto portrayal of all people in one entire region of the world as 'bad'. People need to quit listening to the Fox News and Bush regime drivel and do a little thinking for themselves.

A week later we tried to make the first alpine-style ascent of the Slovenian Route on Trango (Nameless) Tower. We bailed about two-thirds up on the second day, because of all the normal excuses: weather, icy cracks, etc, etc. And because right then - since wanting it is part of being good - we weren't good enough. But that's okay, because for four and a half days on Great Trango we lived everything I've always dreamed of. I know it might seem worthless, even silly, to everyone else – after all, it's just climbing – but it meant everything to me.

Summary: An account of the first successful ascent of the south-west ridge of Great Trango Tower, Pakistan, in July 2004 by Josh Wharton and Kelly Cordes. They named the 54-pitch route *Azeem Ridge* and graded it 5.11 R/X M6 A2.

Journeys

T H Somervell *Camp at Kampa Dzong* 1922
Watercolour and bodycolour
Lakeland Arts Trust

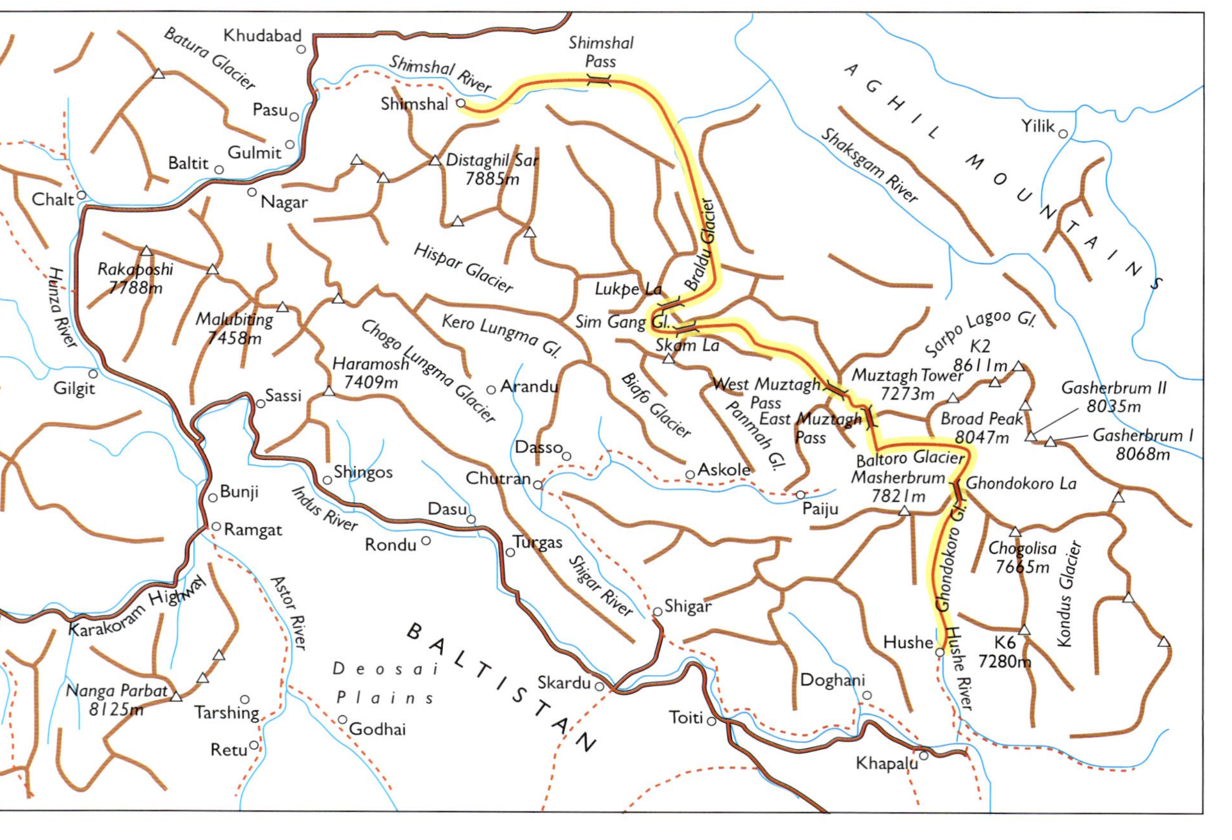

The Great Karakoram Ski Traverse, 2004

DAVID HAMILTON

The Great Karakoram Ski Traverse

On 4 May 2004 I stood on the top of the East Muztagh pass (5393m) looking at the steep drop to the Muztagh glacier 250 metres below. I wondered what Francis Younghusband must have thought surveying the same scene in 1887. It was day 30 of my endeavour to force a ski route through the high glaciers along the spine of the Karakoram, crossing six high passes close to the Pakistan-China frontier. The East Muztagh was the fifth pass, and it looked the most difficult yet. For a team of ski mountaineers carrying 350m of rope and a full range of modern climbing equipment, the descent was going to be quite a challenge.

It is little wonder that Younghusband's crossing 117 years ago won him considerable fame and became one of the defining moments of the 'Great Game' phase of mountain exploration in the Karakoram. My aims in repeating the feat were more modest. The golden age of exploration has passed, and today's mountain adventures increasingly take place on a diminishing number of high-profile peaks. However, there are still mountain areas that, for reasons of politics or geography, have seldom been visited since the days of pioneering exploration. With a little research and planning, these are the places where the spirit of exploration and adventure can still be enjoyed today.

The idea for a springtime ski expedition following the Karakoram watershed first occurred to me in 1997 when I completed the classic Hispar-Biafo ski journey for the second time. After a great trip several members of the team were keen to try a similar but more ambitious project. I studied maps to see if it would be possible to link little-known glaciers and high passes, creating a ski route through the wildest and most remote parts of the range. There was one obviously exciting option. The 260km route from Shimshal in Upper Hunza to Hushe in eastern Baltistan was clearly the longest continuous ski journey that could be attempted in the Pakistan Karakoram. Almost the whole route would be above 4000m, and the main challenge would be the six passes at heights up to 5700m.

Little did I realise that it would be seven years before I would have the chance to make this journey. Each summer as I guided expeditions on the 8000m peaks of the Karakoram my eyes would drift westwards and I would pick out the peaks, passes and ridges between the Baltoro and Shimshal imagining how my planned ski route would snake between them. There was always a list of potential companions for this expedition, mostly friends impressed with my enthusiasm to take a break from the predictable world of commercial guiding and take a risk on a project with a very uncertain outcome. Plans to make the journey in 2002 collapsed when I suffered a back injury in South America. Then in 2003 the project was postponed again when I was invited to lead an Everest expedition.

Of the six companions who assembled in Skardu on 4 April 2004, I was the only remaining member of the 1997 team, and few of the dozen other people who had been committed to the project in the intervening years were present. Ashley Hardwell (with me on Masherbrum in 1991) and Grant Dixon (from Chogolisa in 1993 and Tirich Mir in 1995) were the familiar faces. Robert West, Dave Cowell and Annette Dean were friends of friends. The team contained an interesting mix of ages, skills and experiences. Between us we had climbed and skied in almost every major mountain range on Earth.

The history of ski expeditions in the Karakoram is a short one. The initial explorations of the range were all summer projects, from the expeditions of Godwin Austen in 1861 and Conway in 1892, to the Italian and British cartographic and scientific expeditions in the 1930s. In the second half of the 20th Century the number of expeditions grew steadily to their current level of more than 50 each year. Today several thousand climbers and trekkers visit the Karakoram each summer. It took the American party of Rowell, Gillette, Schmitz and Asay in 1980 to recognise the potential of the huge glaciers for springtime ski expeditions, with their pioneering journey from the Bilafond glacier to Hispar, broken only by six days of porterage to join the Baltoro and Biafo glaciers via Askole. The second half of their journey, the 120km system of the Biafo and Hispar glaciers, linked by the 5151m Hispar pass, has become the classic Karakoram ski itinerary and has been repeated by about a dozen groups. In the 24 years since Rowell's expedition only two groups have completed new ski routes in the Karakoram. Bernard Odier's French group in 1990 completed a technically difficult circuit of the Biafo, Sim Gang, Nobabde Sobande, Chiring, Lakhmo and Muztagh glaciers, crossing three high passes in the process. Five years later a five-person American group made the ski crossing from Shimshal to Askole via the Lukpe La. My 2004 route would join together sections of these previous routes and also cover some new ground, creating a high-altitude west-to-east ski route through the heart of the Karakoram. This would be a longer continuous journey than any of the previous ski expeditions had achieved. It would probably also rank as the longest journey ever attempted in the Karakoram (summer or winter) unaccompanied by local porters.

At Skardu, we gathered together the expedition food and the new 1.4m plastic sleds that had been brought from the UK. The remaining equipment was collected from my Skardu store and packed for the journey to Hunza. We then spent a pleasant afternoon in the garden of the K2 Hotel studying maps and discussing the details of our proposed route. This was the first time that the team had met and we began to appreciate the scale of the seven-week project that we were about to embark upon.

The weather was dreary on the drive to Karimabad where we visited the recently renovated fort before spending the night in a deserted hotel. The new road to Shimshal removed the need for the long three-day walk from Passu that I had made on previous visits in 1989 and 1990. My Shimshali cook from these visits, Baktawar Shah, is now a guide and organised the 20 porters that would be needed for the seven-day trek to the Braldu glacier. The landscape of the northern Karakoram can look bleak at the best of times, and the area around Shimshal is very dry and barren. In summer sunshine it has a dramatic beauty, but in April mist and drizzle it had a dark and foreboding aspect.

I had foolishly assumed that the trip would not really start until we unpacked the skis at the snowline. I had underestimated the difficulty of the trek along the gorge of the Pamir-I-Tang river and over the Shimshal pass. The heavily laden porters made light work of the faint paths crossing steep cliffs and unstable scree slopes. The experienced mountaineers in the party found the trek among the hardest they had encountered anywhere in the Himalaya. The top of the 4758m Shimshal pass is a broad, open, grassy plateau used as summer grazing by the Shimshalis. Winter snow lay thick as we reached the cairn commemorating Younghusband's visit in 1889. This was the first of four crossings of the Karakoram watershed that we planned to make. As we descended to Chikar in the Braldu valley the waters ahead of us drained towards the Taklamakan desert to the north, while those behind flowed south through the entire length of Pakistan to reach the Arabian Sea at Karachi.

The broad Braldu river presents a major obstacle to summer travel in this area but we crossed the frozen stream of ice with little difficulty. Seven days after leaving Shimshal we reached the terminal moraine of the Braldu glacier and prepared to say farewell to the Shimshal porters who had worked hard and remained cheerful despite the poor weather and cold conditions. Their final act was to carry our 240kg of equipment a further 10km towards the snowline across the unstable rocks and rubble of the lower glacier. Ibrahim and Abdullah, my two Hushe cooks who had accompanied us from Skardu, were asked to meet us on the Ghondokoro glacier 20km north of their village in 30 days' time. If they were sceptical of our chances of success they did not show it as they bade their farewells and walked off into the mist.

The sun appeared for the first time in many days and we found ourselves surrounded by jagged granite spires with steep faces covered in fresh snow. It took two days of hard effort to carry the equipment to the first usable snow at 4445m. The expedition almost ended before it had really got going. Robert had been acclimatising slowly and appeared to have developed a chest infection. Following long discussions we were all on the verge of returning to Shimshal before he recovered sufficiently to continue. Over the next few days we gained height slowly as the wide, snow-covered glacier led southwards towards our next goal, the Lukpe La. The daily distance

50. Porters about to leave the Hamilton group at the snowline on the Braldu glacier. (*David Hamilton*)

51. Making progress on the way to the Skam La, the Ogre in the distance. (*David Hamilton*)

covered was less than we had anticipated. The effects of altitude, the weight of the sleds, the soft snow and the poor weather meant that our daily target of 10km was rarely reached.

After a stormbound day a few kilometres short of the pass we eventually reached the top at 9.30am on 21 April and measured the height as 5634m. To the south we had excellent views down the Sim Gang glacier. The snow-covered mass of the Ogre's north face was the most prominent peak visible. The first crossing of this pass was by Bill Tilman in 1937. It lies far from the regular trekking routes and has probably not seen many repeat crossings. We were only the second group to make a ski crossing. The ascent had been problem-free, but the descent involved broken and crevassed ground. The heavy sleds that had performed admirably on the flat proved to be more of a handful on descents. Had we not been blessed with good weather the descent to the Sim Gang glacier would have been unacceptably dangerous.

Our next goal, the Skam La, was visible a mere 5km to the east. The climb to the short 200m headwall was very gentle, but deep soft snow made progress infuriatingly slow. It would be three days before we were able to establish the expedition's 14th camp on top of the 5657m pass. During these days the fate of the expedition would once again hang in the balance. Just 3km on 22 April, followed by a stormbound day on the 23rd, created a grave problem with supplies. The Skam La was the most difficult climb of the trip, for which we needed good weather. Our re-supply depot was 25km distant on the other side of the pass. If we were unable to cross and reach these supplies our only retreat lay down the Biafo glacier. The journey to Askole might take about eight days. We had supplies of food and fuel for only three-four days.

Yet again our luck held when it mattered most. We climbed the steep snow face of the Skam La on 24 April. It took 12 hours of backbreaking effort under the glare of a merciless sun to drag the six sleds to the top of the pass using pulleys and more than 200m of rope. We were rewarded with the best views of the expedition: an unbroken panorama of peaks to east and west, and our first view of K2 in the distance. Eric Shipton made the first crossing of this pass during his 1939 expedition. Camped on top of the pass, the temperature dropped overnight to minus 25°C, the lowest recorded on our trip. Annette's hand froze to the snow spade as she collected snow for cooking.

The ski descent of the Nobande Sobande glacier was the best of the entire expedition. After a few kilometres of polling across level but slightly soft snow the gradient increased and the snow became firmer. For the first time since putting on skis 10 days before, we glided effortlessly over a smooth level surface covering almost 20km to a campsite with running water close to the junction with the Chiring glacier. The perfect weather and snow conditions continued into the following day and we covered 5km in an hour to reach our re-supply point. This had been placed a few days earlier by Musa Khan and his team of Tisar porters. Our spirits soared as we saw three large red flags flying in the breeze indicating 100kg of food and fuel stored in five large kit bags. At 4221m this was one of the lowest altitude points on the route.

Our jubilation was short-lived. The 15km ascent to the West Muztagh pass was to take six days and be the most exhausting and frustrating of the entire journey. Efforts to reach this pass by the early explorers (Schlagintweit 1856, Godwin Austen 1861, Younghusband 1887) all failed due to the difficulty of negotiating the junction of the Panmah, Chiring and South Chiring glaciers. It was not until 1939 that Eadric Fountaine (a member of Shipton's expedition) made the first recorded ascent of this pass in modern times, although it is believed to have been a traditional trade route prior to European exploration of the region.

It took most of a day to drag and carry the heavily laden sleds over the moraine band separating the Chiring from the Nobande Sobande glacier. The novelty of stepping on our first rocks for several weeks soon wore thin. A far bigger obstacle lay ahead. The outflow of the South Chiring glacier entered the Chiring in a chaotic jumble of broken ice blocks and deep unstable crevasses. A full day of porterage on the lateral moraine was required to pass this obstacle that was no more than 400m in length. Poor weather, difficult snow conditions and complex terrain added to the nightmare of the Chiring glacier. We had reached the re-supply point only one day behind our projected schedule. By the time we reached the West Muztagh pass we were running five days late.

The first signs of despondency began to show in the team. The prospect of reduced rations had to be considered and it looked as if we might have to choose between completing our journey and missing our flights home. GPS readings gave the height of the pass as 5720m. Of the six passes crossed during the course of the expedition, this was not only the highest but the only one we could claim as a 'first ski crossing' (although Bernard Odier came this way in 1990, they failed to find the West Muztagh pass in poor weather and crossed another pass a few kilometres to the north-east). We descended without difficulty into the upper branch of the Sarpo Lago glacier, passing close to the Sarpo Lago pass used by Shipton to gain access to the north side of the range in 1937. Lack of time forced us to turn from our preferred route over the Moni pass leading north of Muztagh Tower towards the more famous East Muztagh pass.

The climb to the top of the East (or Old) Muztagh pass (5400m) was straightforward, but by now we were all showing signs of cumulative fatigue. This was the 28th day since we had left Shimshal and the meagre diet of 900g of food per day was beginning to have an effect as our strength and energy levels began to drop. Each of us felt an increasing sense of fatigue as the days passed and clothing which had been tight at the start of the trip began to feel loose as the signs of weight loss began to show. Our camp on top of the pass (measured as 5393m) gave great views over the Chinese side

52. Nearing the top of the West Mustagh pass (5720m). View north towards the
Skarmi peaks (c6730m). (*David Hamilton*)

53. Team photo on the Baltoro glacier. *Left to right*: Grant Dixon, Robert West,
Ashley Hardwell, Annette Dean and Dave Cowell. (*David Hamilton*)

of the range with the Chantok and Chiring peaks prominent. The huge north face of Biale dominated the view to the south. Descending from the pass took an entire day, plus an extensive reconnaissance the previous afternoon. This was arguably the most difficult part of the journey, and certainly the most dangerous. We used more than 250m of fixed rope to prepare a route down steep slopes of snow and ice constantly threatened by massive overhanging ice cliffs above. The glacier below was strewn with thousands of tons of blue and green ice blocks that had fallen across our descent route in the previous days. I held my breath as one by one the rest of the team abseiled down the frighteningly dangerous slopes encumbered by 30kg sleds dangling from their harnesses.

When we were all standing safely on the level ground of the Muztagh glacier, well back from the threat of falling ice, we could contemplate the magnitude of Younghusband's efforts in 1887. It certainly was a remarkable achievement to lead a group of untrained and ill-equipped locals down such a feature using only a single pick axe, a few yards of pony tack and the unravelled turban of Wali, his faithful servant. There would be no second crossing of this pass until 1929 when Ardito Desio (later famous as the leader of the successful 1954 Italian K2 expedition) made a crossing as part of the Duke of Spoleto's large scientific expedition. Bernard Odier's 1990 team claimed the first crossing by a ski expedition.

The ski descent of the Muztagh glacier mirrored that of the Nobande Sobande 10 days previously. Firm snow gave easy skiing conditions and we sped towards the snow-free Baltoro glacier, 10km ahead and 1000m lower. By noon we were camped on the north side of the Baltoro, below Lobsang Spire and opposite the Pakistan Army camp at Urdokas. It was 29 days since we had left Shimshal. Time and supplies were now a consideration. By reducing our daily rations it would be possible for the entire team to reach Hushe, given good weather and snow conditions. But poor weather leading to slow progress might leave us a little hungry. It was also looking unlikely that we would complete the journey in time to get our scheduled return flights home. After a short discussion Robert, Dave and Ashley decided to take the shortest route home via Askole, while the remaining three would push on towards the expedition's original goal. Before departing they helped to carry loads over the rocks of the Baltoro glacier to the south side where we hoped to find better snow.

On the morning of 7 May, Grant, Annette and myself set off along the Baltoro, our sleds weighed down with the extra supplies donated by our departed companions. We searched for a strand of continuous snow that would lead eastwards to Concordia. At an altitude of only 4160m the ice was patchy and the glacier surface covered with rocks. Crossing a small frozen lake in the lead, I broke through the ice and was soaked to my waist until Grant and Annette arrived to pull me free. Two frustrating days followed, with only 4.6km covered in 10 hours, and 2.4km covered in 8.5 hours. We spent more time carrying the sleds than pulling them and the experience was deeply depressing. Then on the morning of 10 May we reached good snow. Two days of 10km saw us speed eastwards along the Baltoro glacier and southwards into the Vigne glacier. Concordia, which I know well from years of expeditions in the area, lay under a thick blanket of snow and the high peaks were similarly covered. Many people have seen K2, Broad Peak and the Gasherbrums from this spot, but few have stood here at the end of spring when the glaciers are covered in many metres of snow and ice.

Before leaving Concordia I looked east to the snow-covered slopes of Sia Kangri and the Conway saddle. This will be the route of my next ski journey. If India and Pakistan ever settle their border dispute and the high glaciers of the Karakoram become demilitarised, it should be possible to ski from the Baltoro glacier over the Conway Saddle and down to the Siachen glacier and the mountain valleys of Ladakh. But that project would have to wait for another year, perhaps even another decade. Now only the sixth and final pass, the Ghondokoro La, blocked our path to the Hushe valley. Of all the passes on our route this one is the most frequently crossed. It is used by hundreds of climbers, trekkers and porters each summer. It was only discovered in 1989 by Ali Jangjungpa, a local Balti porter from one of the villages in the lower Hushe valley. The first foreigners, including myself, crossed it the following year. In summer the route is equipped with fixed ropes maintained (for a fee!) by the 'Hushe Rescue Team'. In mid-May it presented a formidable obstacle to three weary skiers encumbered with almost 100kg of equipment.

We abandoned all spare food into a deep crevasse and started the 600m climb at dawn. The slope was too steep for skis and sleds, so we fought our way up through the deep snow on foot, carrying everything in very large rucksacks. The snow varied between knee deep and waist deep, and the angle became steeper than 45°. The weather worsened until visibility was little more than 10m. Above our heads towered an enormous unstable cornice dripping menacing icicles. By early afternoon we were cold, wet and tired. Only a final 10m of near-vertical snow separated us from the top. Leaving my heavy pack behind, in a place judged to be acceptably safe from avalanche and cornice collapse, I led up this final section to secure a fixed rope. A little over one hour later the three of us crawled into a hastily erected tent on the flat surface of the pass. As the storm raged outside we lay exhausted in the tent, too tired to remove our frozen clothes.

By evening the storm had passed. Clouds parted to the south revealing the familiar shapes of Trinity, Leila and Masherbrum: peaks I recognised from 18 years of climbing in the Hushe valley. We threw dozens of large rocks down the snow slopes to release the unstable layers of snow. The 800m descent the following morning passed without incident despite our weakened state. On the level ground of the Ghondokoro glacier we were able to reassemble the sleds and put on our skis for a final time. The ski down the glacier offered everything that I could have wished from a ski

54. Gasherbrum IV (7993m) dominates the skyline, en route to Concordia. (*David Hamilton*)

55. View south-west from the Ghondokoro La (c4600m) with Trinity and Leila peaks on the left. (*David Hamilton*)

descent in the Karakoram: a firm surface, offering easy turning for a skier pulling a sled, terrain that was interesting without being difficult or dangerous and spectacular scenery. My only regret was that in our 37-day expedition we had experienced only three such days. Within a few hours we reached the place where the glacier takes a sharp left turn and is joined by the icefall that flows down from that of the Masherbrum La. At this point there were too many surface rocks for us to ski any further. As we stopped to remove our skis familiar voices called from the slope a few hundred metres ahead. True to their word Ibrahim, Abdullah and three other men from Hushe had come to meet us as planned. We were two days overdue, but they had waited for us. In fact they had seen us climbing down from the pass through binoculars several hours earlier and had a pot of hot tea and a plate of biscuits waiting for us.

I cannot say if we were more pleased to see them or if they were more relieved to see us. They have been my friends for many years and have worked with me on many expeditions in the Karakoram. They have seen me set off for five 8000m summits, and they have seen that I always return safely. However this time they thought that I had chosen a project with far more dangers and uncertainties. They cried with happiness to see the three thin, dishevelled travellers arrive out of the mountains. Later they told me that prayers had been said in the Hushe village mosque for our safe arrival.

We were in a daze as we walked the familiar trekkers' trail past the herder settlements of Dalsan and Gondoro to Saitcho. We were able to exchange ski boots for comfortable shoes and walk through a landscape of grass, bushes, trees and flowers. The 'shop' at Saitcho (possibly the only 'tea house' in the Karakoram) had been opened specially in expectation of our arrival and served up fried eggs, chips and fizzy drinks. The next day we were welcomed as heroes as we walked through the fields into the village of Hushe. These simple hardworking people know the high mountains of the Karakoram better than anyone. To receive such a welcome from them was a humbling tribute to a journey of exploration that had pushed us to our physical limits.

Summary: An account of the first, full ski traverse of the Pakistan Karakoram, a journey of 260km from Shimshal to Hushe taking 37 days in spring 2004. Team: Dave Cowell (UK), Annette Dean (Aus), Grant Dixon (Aus), David Hamilton (UK: Leader), Ashley Hardwell (UK), Robert West (UK).

GEOFF HORNBY

Coast to Coast in Arabia

After four years of rock climbing and exploration along the spine of the limestone mountains of Oman, I had a growing collection of new routes but a diminishing return in terms of a sense of adventure and achievement. As a student of the life of one of the greatest travel writers ever, Sir Wilfred Thesiger, I became increasingly interested in his camel traverses of the Empty Quarter and his journeys below the mountains of the Western Hajar.

Thesiger was able to throw his dice just before the game became automated and he has written movingly about the demise of the nomadic life of the Omani bedu. To travel once-classic routes by jeep, Thesiger regarded as a mere stunt. He despised the world of GPSs, satellite phones and rescue helicopters as having diminished the commitment required for long distance desert travel. It is very difficult to construct an opposing argument. I desperately wanted to experience Thesiger's world, however tenuously; to climb and travel, and better understand the Omani people.

Mike Searle provided the spark. Dining with Thesiger at the RGS, following a lecture on the geology of Oman, Mike was told by Sir Wilfred that one of his only regrets in life was 'failing to reach the summits of the Western Hajar mountains'. On several occasions Thesiger had been turned away from near the base of the mountains by the local sheikhs and imams. He had been chased, ambushed and forced to hide in wadi beds to avoid what could well have been a fatal encounter with the tribesmen of Ibri, Niswa and Birk al Mauz.

Thesiger's Oman has changed beyond recognition in the last 50 years. Where once he crossed arid gravel plains there are now black top roads. In fact the only two areas of the country that he knew that have not been sanitised are the sand desert of the Wahiba and the dolomitic mountains of the Western Hajar.

Our plan was to complete Thesiger's dream from the interior side of the range. Given our rock climbing skills and experience in these mountains, I thought we could traverse the entire central section of the range via a succession of new routes. If we added to that Thesiger's camel traverse of the Wahiba Sands and a bike traverse to connect the sands to the mountains (modern camels don't cross gravel plains under load) then we could travel from coast to coast under our own steam.

Standing outside Thesiger's home in Coulsden I felt quite nervous at the prospect of meeting the great man. We were on time but he had been

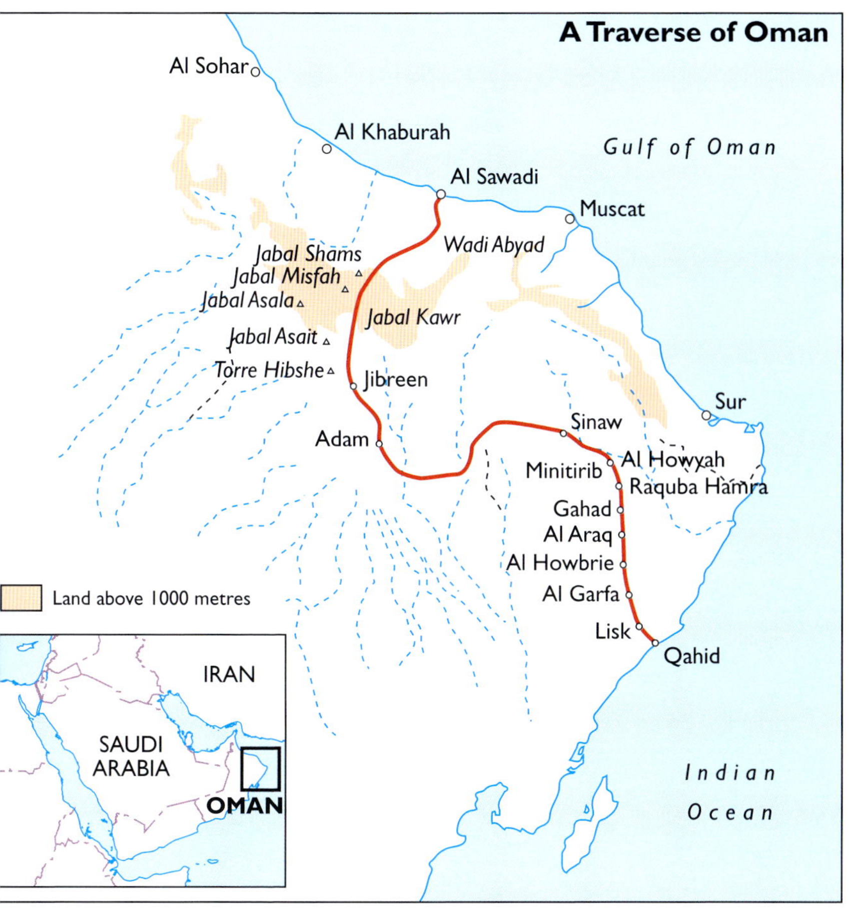

waiting for over an hour. He received few visitors and anyone who knew the wild places of Oman was always going to be welcome. We walked slowly to the Golf Club and lunched at a quiet table in the corner. The menu was irrelevant; whatever I ordered was good for him as well. His face was leathery and tired but his eyes were amazingly clear. It felt as if he could see right through you.

Despite his frailty, he could not hide his enthusiasm for our venture. There was no doubt that our camel trip and bike ride were going to be exactly the type of stunt he disapproved of, but our climbing traverse of the mountains via new routes would be, in his words, in 'one of the last environments where human endeavour cannot be replaced with technology'.

Boxed in by 28-day tourist visas, our trip was going to be little more than a headlong rush across country. Starting out in Muscat, our stack of climbing gear, food and bikes was strapped onto a jeep and we met our driver Masood for the first time. His experience of tourists consisted of driving slowly around the country with the air-conditioning on, trying to entertain his passengers between meals. He had never met four scruffs with attitude

57. The team for the Oman traverse. *Left to right*: driver Masood, Mark Turnbull, Geoff Hornby, Dave Wallis, Susie Sammut. (*Mark Turnbull*)

58. The bedu meet a stranger on foot in the Wahiba Sands and exchange news. (*Geoff Hornby*)

59. Geoff Hornby leading a new route on the north face of Torre Hibshe. (*Mark Turnbull*)

before and was to spend most of the next month worrying endlessly over the antics and continuous disappearances of his gang.

The jeep bumped and slewed through the soft sand down the coast from Sur. We were looking for the tiny coastal fishing village of Qahid where we had an appointment with the bedu. I had arranged for six camels and two bedu to guide us through the sands. 'Meet us at two in the afternoon under the big tree' was the instruction. The entire plan, arranged via a German friend who lives with the bedu, started to seem somewhat tenuous as we failed to identify any of the villages and did not see a single tree. Apparently there is only one tree on the entire coastline for 200km but when we asked directions, no one seemed to know what we were referring to.

Tension in the team was growing as we turned yet another dune strip and saw a solitary tree in amongst some fishermen's tin shacks. Rotting nets and worn boats lay on the beach and sitting in the shade was a small group of elderly men. We pulled up more in hope than confidence. My poor Arabic did not seem to impress but eventually a slightly-built bedu stood up and told me he had been awaiting our arrival since morning. Salvation! We introduced ourselves to Mohammed and Nasar whose company we would be keeping for the next week.

We said goodbye to Masood and the jeep, asking him to meet us with the bikes a week later, 175km further north. We took a last look at the Indian Ocean, and started staggering up through the soft sand to find our camels. The next seven days were wonderful; long days riding the undulating dunes and northward-running wadis, linking water wells and sheltering in the minimal shade through the midday heat. Eating the bedu fodder of rice, dried shark, dates and fire-baked honey-bread was fantastic.

In the first four days we met only one other person – an old bedu out searching for a long-lost camel. Mohammed and Nasar kept their distance before approaching him slowly and with caution, then, after 10 minutes of sparring, we all squatted down in the sand and the bird-like chatter commenced. This was exactly the scenario that Thesiger had so often described – gossip, news, camels and water.

Wild camels would encircle our camp at night having come to inspect the intruders. The morning dew and fog would quickly burn off and we would jump up onto the saddles and start the process of grinding our backsides into weeping and bleeding sores. First 'tape up the butt' was the preferred option for two of the party, but the foolhardy saw the journey through without assistance and suffered for their obstinacy. Ideas of only drinking the same amount of water as the bedu lasted about half a day.

Our slow but steady progress allowed for continuous observation of the desert floor. Every lizard and snake track, and bird foot imprint was carefully considered. The slightest change in camel temperament was monitored. To the bedu this was the coolest time of the year; to us it was an oven. At midday the bedu lay face down in the sand for a snooze while we searched for shade.

Nasar entertained us with a master class in camel riding. Standing free on the top of a camel, he would turn around to talk with us. I discovered that Mohammed's saddle was five times more comfortable than ours. He had made us suffer to see how tough we were. Davie Wallis demonstrated the subtle art of camel riding by dropping his camel stick, and to avoid being mocked by the bedu for his carelessness he just ignored the camel for the rest of the day. Needless to say the camel just followed on regardless. Losing your camel stick is, apparently, a sign that your wife is cheating on you. Our last camp overlooked a long wadi running down to the town of Mintirib. The camp was at the foot of a slope, too steep for riding, so we staggered down calf-deep in soft sand, pulling the camels behind us. The beasts were excited; they had plainly enjoyed their trip but now were almost home. Next day they came into camp at dawn, keen to be up and off. The morning found us following jeep tracks and passing tented homesteads with the first traces of barbed-wire fencing. It seemed dull after the pristine territory of the southern desert.

Close to town, the dunes bore the scars of four-wheel drive vehicles. The sport of wadi bashing in powerful jeeps is about as far from environmental sensitivity as you can get. In the entire week I never saw the bedu produce a single item of packaging waste. Every hessian sack, bag or strip of material would be reused until it was worn out and then sewn into a camel saddle.

We were all apprehensive about ending this stage of the journey, conscious of returning to a world of shoes, fast-moving objects and rapid decision-making. I was beginning to understand Thesiger's love of camel trips. We shook hands with the boys and rewarded our camels with date mulch. As if by magic, Masood pulled up in the jeep and off-loaded four mountain bikes for the next stage of the journey. He looked bemused as the crazy gringos set off down the road in the heat of the day.

The bike journey was a curious mixture of the modern world with roads, traffic, electricity pylons and petrol stations mixed with the unchanged world of bedu towns and rough camping in wadis and riverbeds. We cycled for four days, covering 275km. As the man who made the plan, I guess I bear the responsibility for picking a route directly into the prevailing wind for most of each day.

The market town of Sinaw lies on the gravel plain between the Wahiba Sands and the Empty Quarter and is used by the desert bedu to pick up supplies of dried shark, tuna and veggies, and to sell their goats. They observed us with narrow-eyed suspicion. Their world was still one of bandits from the Yemen and endless water management issues while ours was of discussion as to the relative merits of digital cameras versus slide film.

We rested up in Wadi Andam, where Thesiger had hidden whilst his men went into Sinaw for provisions, and then cycled hard into the desert wind to reach Adam. On our last day on the bikes, a view of the Western Hajar slowly unfolded, the southern wall of Jabal Kawr and the bulk of

60. Crossing the summits of Jabal Misfah with Jabal Misht in the distance. *(Geoff Hornby)*

61. Geoff Hornby new routing on the west face of Jabal Misfah.
(*Hornby collection*)

Jabal Shams appearing from a shimmering haze. I felt a bond with Thesiger who had watched this same vista unfold as he rode slowly on his camel. We, however, had ridden hard on our bikes, looking up to measure our progress against the size of the mountains.

Passing the ancient desert castle of Jibreen, for a while we became an object of amusement for tourist buses. We passed the point in the foothills where Thesiger was forced to retreat and eventually camped at M'Seeba, home to just one family, below the great wall of Jabal Kawr. It was New Year's Eve and the posse needed to rest. Over the next three days we were blitzed by high winds and there were rainstorms in the mountains. Jabal Kawr means the mountain of the waterfalls. Our neighbour the goatherd said that the previous year he had lost 30 goats in a flash flood down the gully system we were planning to use for our approach to an unclimbed pillar on the Rigma buttress of Jabal Kawr.

Time was running away from us and we needed to get on. We were on the move at dawn with some trepidation. The barrel-shaped buttress looked too hard to tackle directly so we moved to the east and climbed a spur leading to a short headwall. We hit the summit ridge after an 800m-approach climb and a 400m D Sup route we named the *Umbarak Pillar*. Success was tempered by a fast approaching storm and we bailed off the back for a long and strenuous descent. Nerves jangled as we tore down narrow wadis in the failing light, praying that it was not raining further up the drainage system. Our plan of traversing the summit ridge was ditched in favour of a northern route around to the oasis of Hibshe.

Kawr is a mammoth mountain, 10km long and with dozens of outlying peaks. Hibshe is an ancient palm grove fed by spring water from the eastern end of the Kawr massif. It lies between Torre Hibshe and Jabal Asait. Eastwards from the oasis is a succession of rocky peaks between 1700m and 2000m in height and we traversed them over five days, climbing new routes wherever possible. Torre Hibshe's north face provided an excellent water-worn slabby wall for *Assilla* (350m, TD inf). The crux was a seriously run-out slab pitch at about UK 5a. We were hoping that this would be a first ascent of the face but subsequently found that we had been pipped by Albert Precht and his Austrian friends.

On Jabal Asait's east face we climbed *Shamsa* (445m, D Sup) to finish close to the fantastic rock arch on the mountain's north ridge. The descent dropped us directly into the village of K'Saw and an invitation to the campfire for coffee and dates.

The west face of Jabal Asala, another Kawr outlier, yielded *Armina* (500m, D Sup), followed by a long and grinding descent to the Sint road. Jabal Misfah's west face provided a long approach and short-lived but very sharp difficulties on *Salmana* (300m, D). A triangular buttress led to a short pillar and a notch before a slabby finish. From the top of *Salmana* we traversed eastwards over the three summits of Misfah before getting lost and having to make a difficult abseil descent, in the dark, direct into the small village below the col with Jabal Shams. I should have known better, having climbed Misfah before, but my memory was thrown into disarray by the two communications towers built since my last visit.

Oman is changing fast. Black-top roads are replacing desert tracks and isolated mountain summits sprout ugly monuments to the god of text messaging. Every village has electricity and every family aspires to have a vehicle. Health care has improved dramatically. All the kids go to school.

A casual day in the sun allowed a long walk up the whale-back slabs approaching the lip of the Nakl canyon. We camped close to the rim and were treated to a glorious sunset. From this point to the summit of Jabal Shams (c3000m) the route follows further slabs to reach Wadi Bir Rumayn then traverses beneath the real summit of Shams to reach Ruweys al Kelb (the horn of the scabbard), a secondary peak and the only one accessible due to the presence of military installations on the main summit. Ridiculously, the tourist maps attempt to make you believe that you are on the highest point, but with a quick glance up at the security fencing you know that someone is looking down on you.

The route is only a strenuous hike, but our planned descent of the north face of Jabal Shams became the mother of all horror shows. We were unable to find the scrambling route leading down to the remote village of Wimjah and instead made the 2000m descent by traversing further west, necessitating an additional bivouac in an unknown wadi. The biting wind saved us from dehydration, but our moods were turning ugly. Mid-morning on the third day of the Shams traverse found us staggering down the road at the interior entrance to Wadi Abyad. This beautiful wadi consists of interconnecting water pools in groves of palms and ancient falajs (irrigation channels).

One of the best short walks in Oman, the wadi was a pleasant conclusion to three days of arduous work. We met up with Masood on the coastal plain and jumped onto the bikes again for the short cycle to the coast at Al Sawadi. We cycled slowly down the paved highway, almost resisting the end of the journey, before throwing the bikes down onto the shingle beach after 25 days on the move. It was a highly emotional moment. Peculiarly, we each wandered off in a different direction looking for peace and quiet. There was no collective sense of achievement. I picked up my old baseball cap and read the tacky message on the back, 'The journey is the destination'. I guess that said it all.

Unfortunately, Sir Wilfred Thesiger passed away before our trip set out. It would have been nice to have had lunch again at the Golf Club.

Summary: An account of a continuous traverse of Oman, by camel, mountain bike and new rock routes, over the Wahiba Sands, the edge of the Empty Quarter and the mountains of the Western Hajar, by Geoff Hornby, Susie Sammut, Mark Turnbull and David Wallis.

JIM LOWTHER, GRAHAM LITTLE & KEVIN KELLY

Miyar Nala 2004 ~
Exploring the Hidden Himalaya

Surprisingly, the first recorded climbing in the Miyar Nala area was not until 1992 by an Italian team. The Italians paid other visits during the 1990s and then the Slovenians became active in 2002. The *Alpine Journal* and a number of climbing magazines recently publicised the state of play and whetted our appetite for this area. It obviously had a wealth of unclimbed rock.

An Indian friend, Satyabrata Dam, who had trekked right up the Miyar glacier to the Kangla Jot (a high pass at the head of the glacier that gives access into Zanskar), confirmed the attractiveness of the area and recommended May as the month with the best weather. Although he was right about the weather, we soon discovered that there is normally too much snow about in May to allow rock climbing on the higher peaks.

Our expedition was the first to penetrate, explore and climb in the Jangpar glacier area to the east of the Miyar glacier, situated in the Lahul-Pangi region of Himachal Pradesh.

The team comprised Graham Little (55) as leader, Jim Lowther (39), Kevin Kelly (30) and Brian Davison (42), six Kumaoni porters, Dan Singh (23), Naresh Singh (24), Chamu Singh (22), Puran Singh (25), Hayat Singh (30) and Tara Singh (27), plus Dorje (Urgus), with his two horses, and our agent Sonam Tashi Negi (Manali).

The journey from Delhi to the roadhead in the Miyar Nala is often straightforward. However, pre-monsoon snowfall can block the Rohtang La and rainfall during the monsoon and post-monsoon can cause road-blocking mud and rock slides anywhere between Tandi, Udaipur and the roadhead.

Although the Rohtang La had been open for most of April 2004, late that month it had been blocked by the heaviest snowfall in the area for 25 years. Under normal circumstances, the pass would have remained blocked for weeks but the impending Indian elections added some urgency to opening it as the ballot papers for the remote valleys in Lahul were, like us, stuck in Manali. It soon became obvious that even when the road was opened, it would be one-way traffic only and, given the build-up on either side of the pass, would almost certainly result in chaos. We took pre-emptive action by going to see the officer in charge of the snow-clearing. Our meeting with Mahindra Kumar was bizarre – he lay in bed in a darkened room as we impressed upon him the criticality of our expedition crossing the Rohtang La. He agreed to help and was as good as his word.

After two snow blowers and two snowploughs had been working on the pass for five days, we were allowed to tag on behind the election convoy. We skidded, slithered and pushed our way through a snow trench, with walls up to 3m high, to descend into Lahul. Thank God for Indian democracy!

The walk from Chaling to base camp at Dali Got was an easy two and a half days with a height gain of only 700m (c3200m to c3900m) and many good campsites en route. We camped at Khanjar, the last habitation on the east side of the valley (the best site is well above the village), and by the shallow lake at Gumba Got. We were spoiled for choice at Dali Got where flat ground and fresh water abounds. The site selected was next to the first and lowest of the deep pools that are a feature of the Miyar glacier's terminal moraine. All the expedition's equipment was carried up to base camp by our Kumaoni porters (we'd only requested three but six met us at Manali) and two horses hired at Chaling. This was completed in a series of ferries with all the gear arriving at base camp by 12 May.

Other than a trip to the junction of the Miyar and Jangpar glaciers together on 11 May, we operated as two separate teams for all the time out from base camp – Little with Lowther and Davison with Kelly.

Graham's and Jim's mountain experience by Graham Little

13 May: We head up the north side of the Miyar glacier by a vague path above and sometimes on the lateral moraine, crossing side valleys choked with snow. Four porters carry our climbing gear and food. I'm out ahead keeping my eyes open for wildlife. I spot a marmot and a pair of Himalayan snowcock. We re-group at the edge of the Jangpar glacier and Jim breaks trail, under a hot sun, to Jangpar Got on the other side of the glacier. The porters unload and head back to BC.

14 May: We breakfast to birdsong and amazingly get going at 6.15 up the snow-slopes immediately behind camp. We move (too) quickly taking a line over rocks to the left of the obvious straight gully. Soon we need to don crampons as the ground steepens. Jim climbs a rather tenuous little rock step and on we go up steeper snow. We reach the summit, via a delightful little snow arête, at 10am.

It is a first ascent: Christina Peak by the south face, PD, but possibly easier without snow. We spend nearly an hour on top, surveying the magnificent mountain panorama. The sky is cloudless and windless. The bulk of Menthosa (6443m) dominates the view to the south-west, Shiva (6142m) and other peaks to the west, whilst the peaks of Kishtwar serrate the horizon to the north-west. However, our real interest lies to the east in the complex of unexplored peaks including the daunting Triple Towers.

15 May: A great mountain day although we do no climbing. Taking all that we can carry, we move up the glacier and pitch the Gemini just below

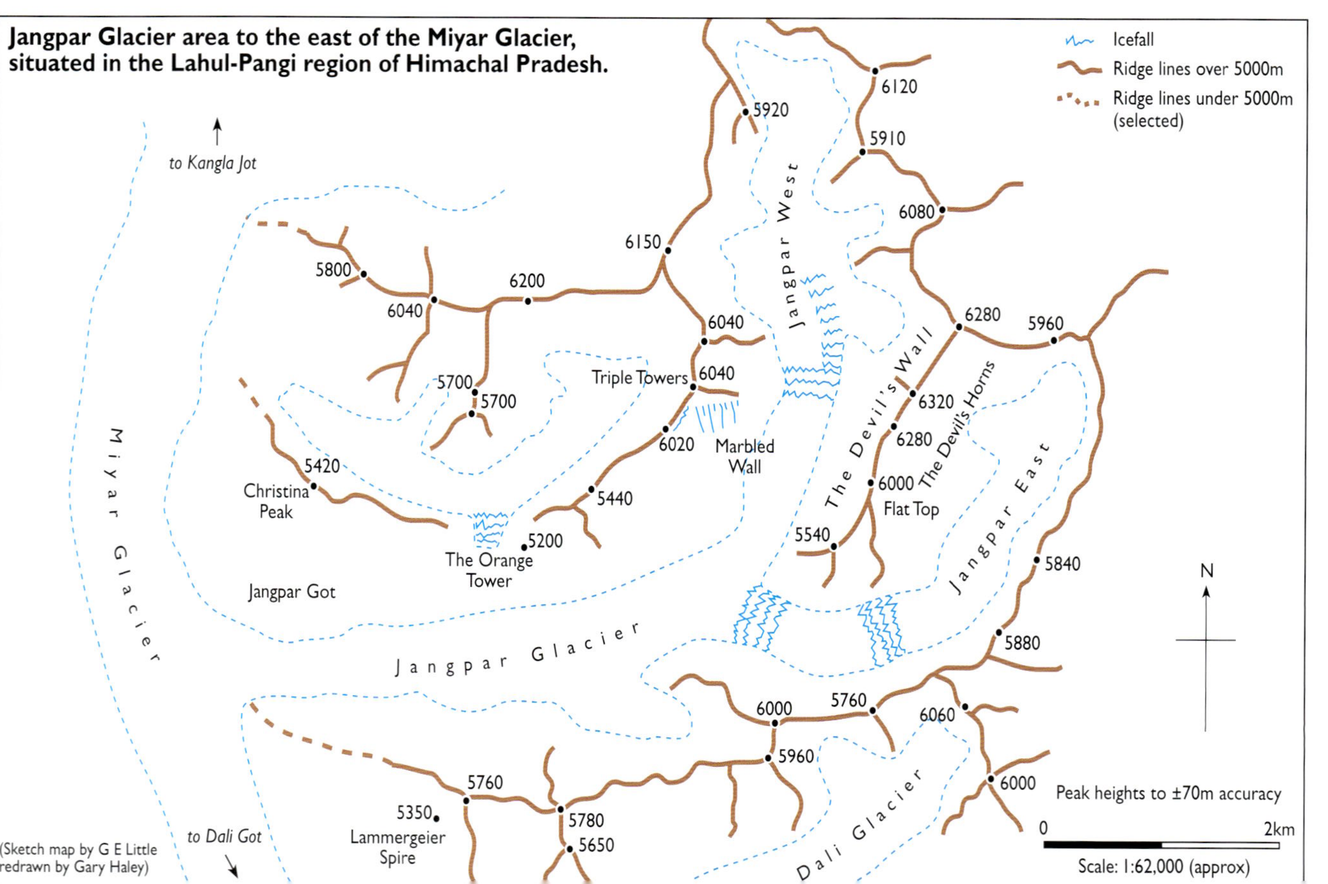

Jangpar Glacier area to the east of the Miyar Glacier, situated in the Lahul-Pangi region of Himachal Pradesh.
Icefall
Ridge lines over 5000m
Ridge lines under 5000m (selected)
to Kangla Jot
Jangpar West
5920
6120
5910
6080
6150
5800
6040
6200
6040
5700
5700
Triple Towers
6040
6280
5960
The Devil's Wall
6320
The Devil's Horns
6280
6020
Marbled Wall
5420
Christina Peak
5440
6000
Flat Top
Jangpar East
5540
5840
The Orange Tower
5200
Jangpar Got
Miyar Glacier
Jangpar Glacier
5880
6000
5760
6060
5960
6000
Dali Glacier
5760
5350
Lammergeier Spire
5780
5650
to Dali Got
(Sketch map by G E Little redrawn by Gary Haley)
N
Peak heights to ±70m accuracy
0
2km
Scale: 1:62,000 (approx)

63. The Devil's Wall, Jangpar glacier; plenty of big wall potential. (*Jim Lowther*)

the junction of the Jangpar East and West glaciers. Travelling light, we head up the Jangpar West between vast flanking cliffs (the entrance being immediately dubbed the Gates of Mordor). Massive buttresses foot the east flank, merging into the vast headwall of two distinctive horn-like peaks. The Devil's Horns is the obvious name for these peaks and it therefore follows that the 1300m-high flanking wall should be named The Devil's Wall. Although not as high, the west flank is the real jewel of the Jangpar, an awesome 800m high 'blank' wall dropping from the south-east flank of central peak of the Triple Towers. Hanging seracs define its left side and a wild overhanging edge its right. It is scribbled with mineral veins and so we name it the Marbled Wall – a mega objective for a very strong big wall team. We push on up to an altitude of 4950m by some blue pools below the icefall and call it a day.

17 May From a camp directly below The Orange Tower, we climb the tower's superstructure (250m to V Diff), establish a bivvi site and then try several lines near the edge of the upper tower (170m to 4c) in cloudy conditions with frequent snow flurries.

18 May We try another line to the left of yesterday's attempt (to 5a) but back off due to the obviously much more difficult rock ahead and a lack of confidence that we can get up the upper tower without using a lot of aid. We are happy to leave it to the choughs and wallcreepers who are clearly more at home in this vertical world than we are. On our return to base camp, we are privileged to see six bharal (blue sheep) high on the crags above the Miyar glacier.

21 May Assisted by Dan Singh, we carry our kit up towards the Lammergeier Spire. As no easy access to the base is available, we establish a bivvi just below the east side of a rock ridge that is roughly in the same alignment as the spire above. A late afternoon recce confirms that the ascent of a tricky, pinnacled rock ridge will be required to give access to the broad snow spur footing the spire. As we return, a lammergeier glides majestically past.

22 May We get moving by 7am and climb the ridge, with pitches up to Severe, and on up the hard snow slopes above to the foot of the Spire. 85m of climbing leads to a gap holding a squat pinnacle. The rock is immaculate and covered in 'chicken-heads' with the climbing much easier than anticipated (up to Severe). We gain the obvious long corner as the sky dulls and a biting wind rises. A short pitch above the top of the corner and we are on the wildly undercut summit block. The situation is spectacular but the views to the north are swallowed by a fast approaching storm. We make a hasty descent, with long abseils, through driving snow, intuition guiding us down alternative routes from the ascent. Again the great lammergeier sails past. We end up in the snow gully to the west of the lower ridge and have to climb up onto it by an interesting mixed pitch (Scottish III). This takes us to exactly the right point for the descent down the gully to the east and back to the bivvi site. A hasty packing of sacks and we head down into the gloom, over snow-covered boulders, arriving at BC at 6pm.

Kevin's and Brian's mountain experience by Kevin Kelly

Attempt at a route on Peak 5960m bordering the Jangpar and Dali glaciers:
13th May With the aid of two porters we climb the moraines directly above base camp to gain the lower extent of the Dali glacier. Here we establish a food cache, with a view to trying one of the ice and rock lines on the flanking walls of the hanging valley after an attempt on Peak 5960m (referred to in a Slovak text as Peak 7). We take advantage of the cold early morning conditions and continue quickly with our porters as far as the rock band that bars access to the upper glacier system. This rock band had been

4. A first view up the Jangpar glacier, Pt 5960m on the right. (*Jim Lowther*)

described as having pitches on rock slabs of grade UIAA IV. We find them to be almost entirely covered by snow and ice, although, as the day starts to warm, the thaw turns the lower and slightly steeper rock ramp into a waterfall.

Brian leads the first pitch which although wet is technically easy and gains the snowfield towards the left of the band which continues over steep scree and rocks for several hundred metres to the last short rock step, Scottish I, and the upper glacier. By the time that we start the long slog up the snow slope, the sun is full upon us and the snow turns to sugary mush. By early afternoon we gain the snout of the upper glacier, which has ablated considerably and appears to be stable. We dump our gear by a rock protrusion near the top of the band and head back down to the foot of the steepening to repeat the process with the gear deposited by our porters. Quite exhausted, we pitch our tent c4800m and set the alarm for 2am.

14 May We wake up to find the tent being buffeted by a moderate, but terribly cold wind coming down the valley. The pan of water in the porch, as with everything bar ourselves, is frozen solid. It is still very much winter here. We strip the camp with frozen fingers and manage to load all of yesterday's loads into or onto our rucksacks. The sky is clear and moonless. We move very slowly in the thin air and under our Himalayan loads. Our target is to camp below the south ridge of our peak. The wind drops and just as the sun is coming round onto our corner of the glacier we drop our rucksacks at the foot of the west flank of the south ridge c5200m. I rush to get my boots off, as I can't feel the toes of my right foot. Brian makes a brew. I enjoy tea and the hot aches as the temperature swings wildly from freezing to scorching in the unhindered sunshine.

15 May It is another cold night with the inside of the tent thick with frost. We start 30 minutes after midnight and our initial progress is slow. These higher snow slopes do not seem to have been affected by the warming of the sun and given the continuing cold air temperatures, have not thawed to any depth. Several hours of step plunging in steep snow, consisting of a thin crust on deep powder, deliver us to a notch on the south ridge. The unseen east flank drops steeply to the glacier below and the cornice is substantial. The lower section of the ridge is sharply defined and consists of a soft flaky rock.

I lead a mixed pitch across a narrow foot rail, outflanking the wall that blocks access from the notch to the ridge proper – 60m of Scottish IV with poor gear and belay. On the way across my head torch battery runs out. By the time Brian joins me and leads past to the easier ridge crest, it is daylight. We climb the ridge for a while then traverse across the south face to gain a gully that we had seen from the tent. The snow conditions are not very good, with large amounts of unconsolidated powder sitting on what appear to be steep granite slabs. We move as quickly as possible, but with few runners, to gain the foot of the gully. The next pitch rears up from the gully bed and constricts to form a Point 5 chimney on ice and rock. Brian leads this difficult pitch – Scottish V. Runners are poor and spaced, as are belays.

The next pitch is Scottish II on rotten ice. I lead through quickly as Brian's stance is no more than a foot ledge on a ramp in the gully wall. The route continues in this manner for pitch after pitch. We begin to tire, as we can find no place to rest or at the very least take food or water. As the sun melts the snow and ice in the gully bed, the 'easy' pitches become more and more demanding as they are transformed to bottomless wet sugar. Brian climbs one more mixed pitch up a rib protruding from the gully bed and finally belays a short way below a ledge near the top of the granite tower that defines the west ridge of the peak. From here we should be able to brew up and recover.

Brian is moving very slowly now and I am producing a competent display of slurred speech and mild confusion. The terrain to the summit ridge consists of several pitches of easy angled, but soft snow. The gully as a route is over. As I am following the last technical section, there is a shout and obligatory crash from above. I duck my head tight into my ice tools, but the sound is a bit different to the usual 'fridge-size blocks'. I pop my head up as Brian's rucksack, holding his spare clothes, all of our gas, the pan and most of the food spins out into space. I'm too tired to care and as I struggle over the last bulge, I see an apologetic Brian on the first decent belay since the start of the gully. Without food or fuel we cannot risk a night on the face and begin the first abseil after reaching a high point of 5800m.

16 May Our aim is to gain the col at the foot of the west ridge of the peak that we'd just failed on. As I climb out of the tent I notice that there is quite a lot of cloud build-up that has appeared overnight, moving in from the west. We make our way over the glacier and up to the 5300m col on still firm snow – Scottish I. From this vantage point we gain excellent views of the whole Jangpar glacier system. Even in the poor and flat light the massive walls and numerous complex and jagged towers cannot fail to impress. We linger only to take a few photos and as the weather gives every indication of breaking, descend to camp.

New routes on a large area of granite slabs on the east side of the Miyar valley, 5km south of BC.
21 May Today we moved our tent from BC, just over an hour down the valley, to a pitch below a sweep of granite slabs. We pitch the tent and climb steeply up the mountainside to gain the right hand end of the slabs c4400m. From here we follow the fine arête through its entirety. This gives us a fine line, *Time after Thyme* 360m UIAA IV.

   22 May An early start in fine weather sees us tackling a line up the main body of slabs. We follow a vague line of grooves, ramps and cracks more or less straight up, aiming for a large V-shaped break in the skyline at the top of the slabs. We make quick progress, spurred on by the appearance of a large amount of dark blue-grey cloud that is moving steadily down the valley. *Bent Fork of Acceptance* 750m UIAA , terminates a considerable way up the mountain affording excellent views of the surrounding objectives in the neighbouring tributary valleys. Once again we descend with haste, getting to the tent as the snow starts in earnest.

Future Objectives
Where to start! The whole Miyar Nala/glacier area has vast potential, some of it already identified by Slovenian and Italian expeditions. There is an absolute wealth of unclimbed peaks, mixed faces and rock walls surrounding the Jangpar glaciers and we will confine our comments to these.

- **Peak 5760m** big, mixed north face with an obvious line up a wide fan narrowing to a gully leading to a high notch on the north-west ridge.
- **Peak 5780m** beautiful snow-fluted north face.
- **Peak 5960m** a gob-smacking rock pyramid of a peak when viewed from the Jangpar glacier. The west ridge would be a good, challenging line and the col at its foot can be accessed from either the north (steep with objective danger) or the south (easy).
- **Peak 6000m** the neighbour of Peak 5960m and carrying a lot more snow. A serac wall sits below the connecting col, threatening the narrow snow/ice face below – no obvious safe route.
- **Flat Top, 6000m** at the junction of the east and west arms of the Jangpar glacier with a monstrous rock wall to the west.

65.
The Orange Tower (5200m),
Jangpar glacier. The nose was
attempted by Graham Little
and Jim Lowther. (*Jim Lowther*)

66. Looking up the Miyar glacier from base camp. (*Jim Lowther*)

- **The Devil's Horns, 6280m and 6320m** the vast and complex 1300m high **Devil's Wall** falls to the west – serious stuff.
- **Peak 6280m** a big retiring peak at the head of East Jangpar glacier.
- **Peak 6150m** a hidden snowy peak at the junction of ridges. East face looks formidable, south face easier.
- **Triple Towers** all just over 6000m and pretty formidable. **The North Tower** is the most distinctive and looks climbable from the east via a 1000m buttress. **The Middle Tower** is the proud owner of the **Marbled Wall** on its south-east flank, at a sheer 800m, the best looking bit of rock in the area – the ultimate objective for a serious big wall team. **The South Tower** is the least attractive of the three, with no obvious line. Séracs hang over the east flank of the col between the Middle and South Towers (but don't threaten the main section of the Marbled Wall).
- **Peak 6200m** an obscure snowy peak. Between it and Peak 6040m, to the west, a wide spur juts to the south with a truncated rock tower at its termination (5700m).
- **Peak 6040m** could be climbed by a reasonable looking route on the south face from the glacier to the north and above the Jangpar glacier.
- **Christina Peak, 5420m** the baby of the area but a superb viewpoint. The only peak yet climbed! A long, corniced, ridge runs east from the summit and terminates in an impressive vertical rock wall.
- **The Orange Tower, 5200m** a very impressive tower of grey and orange coloured granite. The nose is the most obvious line. A good and easier alternative would be round to the left where a ramp up a buttress of grey rock (which is the best quality) leads to the top of the tower that sits behind the Orange Tower.

Although we did not explore the area to the east of the upper Miyar glacier, it is obvious that there is a network of untouched glaciers flanked by many fine unclimbed peaks up to 6300m.

Mapping, Names and Heights
Available mapping of the Miyar Nala/glacier area is generally small scale and of poor quality. Sketch maps produced by Slovenian and Italian expeditions are useful although not topographically very accurate. Some of the heights claimed for peaks climbed by these expeditions are exaggerated. Graham's outline map (page 150) of the Jangpar glacier area is more accurate although peak heights are only accurate to +/– 70m.

Summary A British team reveals the possibilities for big routes on unclimbed peaks in a previously untouched part of the Indian Himalaya.

Acknowledgements The team would like to thank the MEF and BMC for their support.

TAMOTSU NAKAMURA

Hidden valleys, Permit problems

Our initial plan for further exploration of the Nyenchentangla East range in the autumn of 2004 was vetoed by the Chinese authorities. We, in common with several other foreign groups who had hoped to visit and climb in hitherto unopened areas, were refused entry because westerners had entered closed areas and attempted mountains without official permits.

I negotiated with the Tibetan Mountaineering Association (TMA) and, finally, we were allowed to enter the unexplored Bena valley east of Lake Basong. But our time was limited to only one week. So after Bena valley we trekked along the Old Peking-Lhasa road from Gyamda and later that same month, October, we moved to Yunnan via Chengdu.

Bena valley

This was my fifth visit to Nyenchentangla East since June 2001. On 3 October, our elderly party (myself, aged 69, and Tsuyoshi Nagai, 72) left Lhasa for Lake Basong with Tashi, a Tibetan guide. We spent the night at Bayizhen, third largest city in Tibet, where we obtained a special permit from the public security police to enter an unopened area. On 4 October, we were able to arrange for our caravan at Juba village (3500m), an administration centre of Zhonggo District on the southern bank of Lake Basong. It is a scenic area which the local government of Gongpojiangda (or Gongbo'gyamda) county places regards as importance for developing tourism.

Four sizeable valleys extend from Lake Basong:
1. North from Zhonggo village at the north-eastern end of Lake Basong.
2. North-east from Zhonggo village, an approach to climb the west ridge of Jieqinnalagabu (Namla Karpo) 6316m.
3. Bena valley to the east of Lake Basong entered only by a NZ party in 1999. They turned back less than halfway and did not reach the moraine lake, Pukalo Tso, in the valley headwaters.
4. A valley with a large lake called New Lake (Xintso), further east of Lake Basong. The main stream from New Lake flows into Lake Basong from south-east near Juba village. A stream from Bena valley joins the stream from New Lake about one hour's distance from Juba.

The headwaters of all four valleys are encircled by fascinating 6000-6600m snow peaks with glaciers and are located along a mountain range that shares the watershed with Yigong Tsangpo (*see map on opposite page*). Three out of the four valleys have been explored and visited by foreigners, but the Bena valley has remained unknown to outsiders.

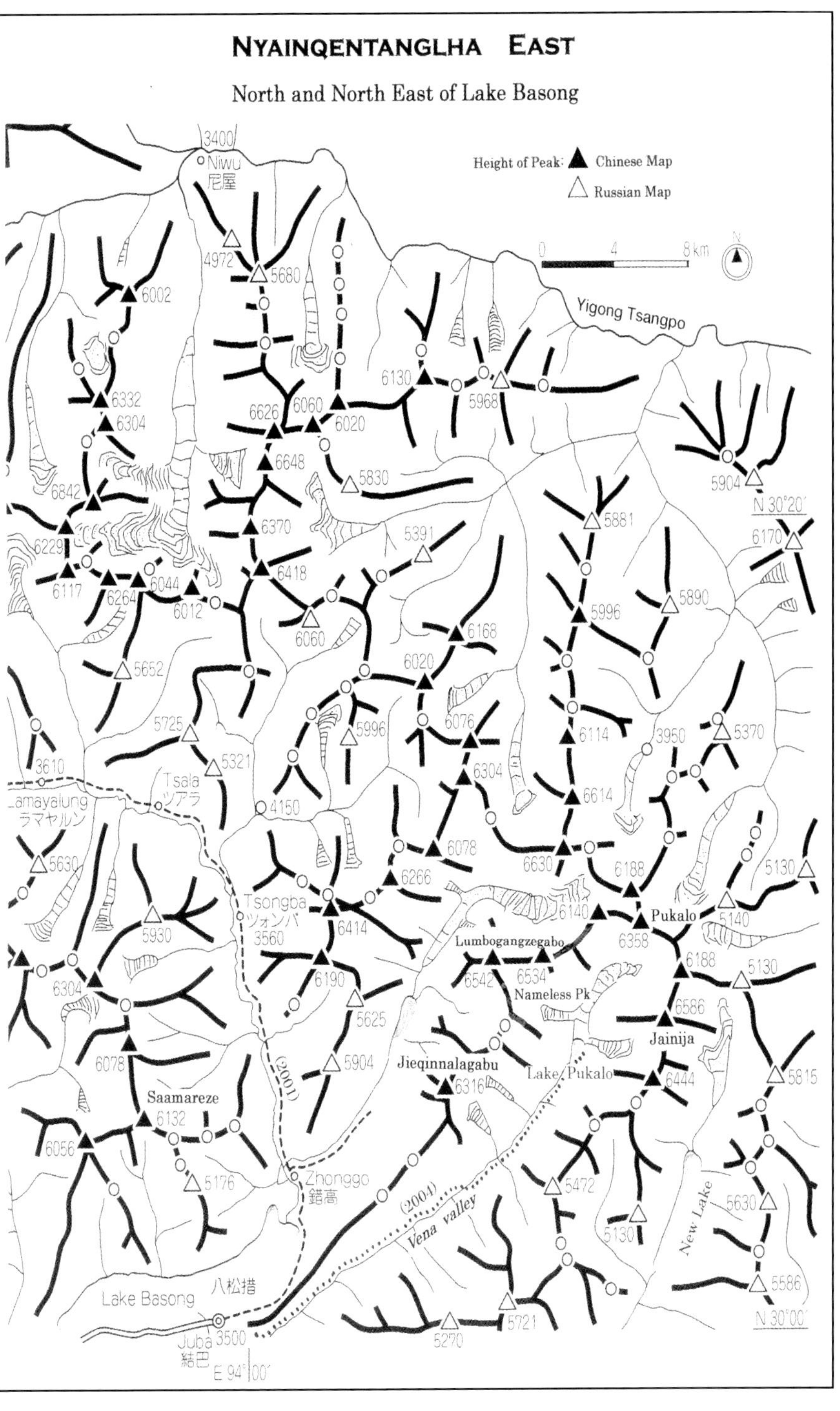

NYAINQENTANGLHA EAST
North and North East of Lake Basong
Height of Peak:
Chinese Map
Russian Map
0 4 8 km
N
3400
Niwu
尼屋
4972
5680
6002
6130
5968
Yigong Tsangpo
6332
6304
6626
6060
6020
6648
6842
6370
5830
5391
5881
5904
N 30°20'
6170
6229
6418
6117
6264 6044
6012
6060
6168
5996
5890
5652
6020
5725
5996
6076
6114
3950
5370
3610
5321
6304
6614
Tsala
ツアラ
Lamayalung
ラマヤルン
4150
6078
6630
6188
5130
5630
6266
6140
Pukalo
Tsongba
ツォンバ
3560
6414
Lumbogangzegabo
6358
5140
5930
6542 6534
6188
5130
6190
Nameless Pk
6586
6304
5625
Jainija
6078
5904
Jieqinnalagabu
Lake Pukalo
6444
5815
Saamareze
6132
6316
6056
5176
Zhonggo
錯高
(2004)
Vena valley
5472
5630
5130
八松措
Lake Basong
5721
New Lake
5586
Juba 3500
結巴
E 94°00'
5270
N 30°00'

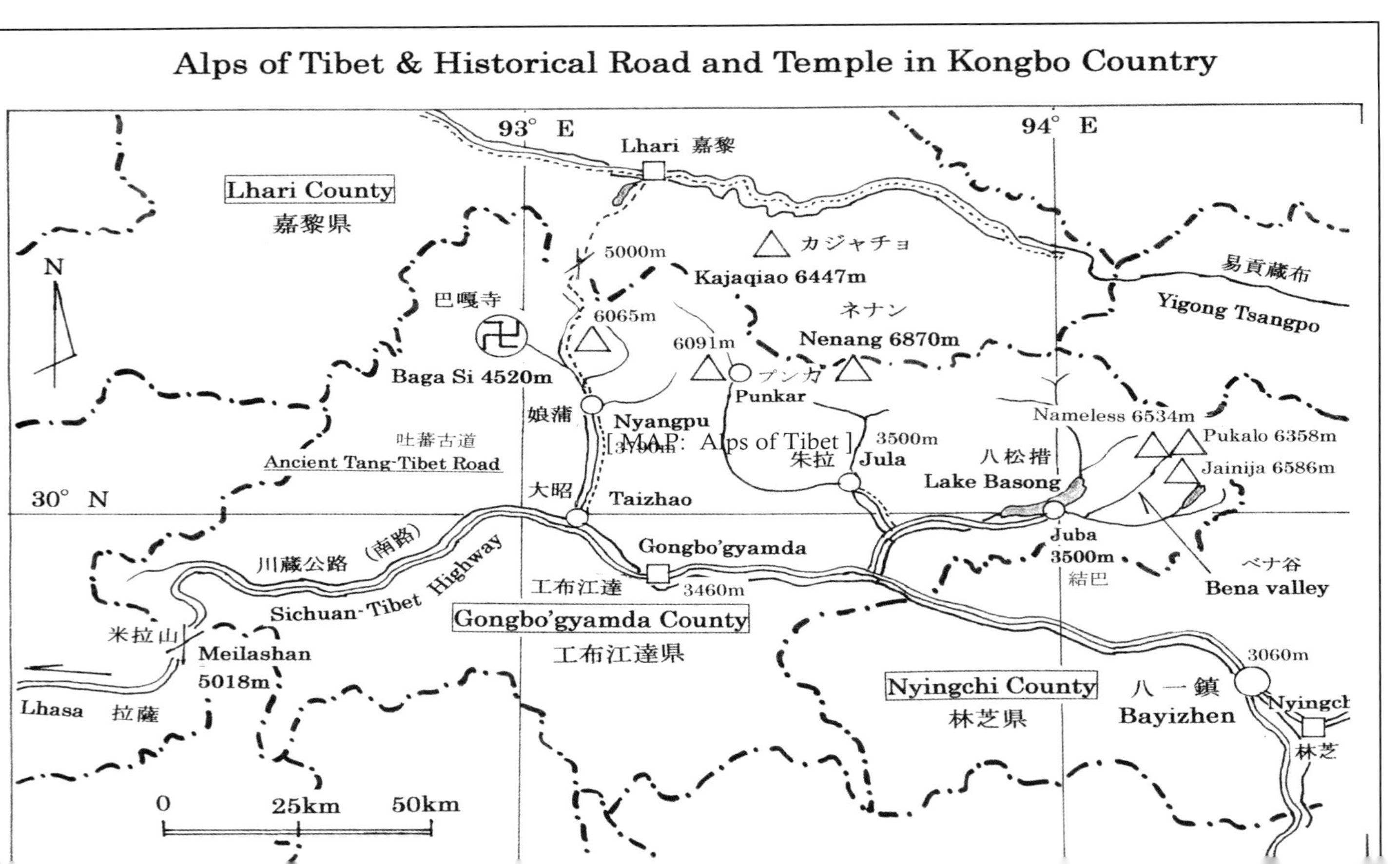

Alps of Tibet & Historical Road and Temple in Kongbo Country

5 October At 8am, while it was raining, we started our caravan with six horses and three Tibetan muleteers. First we followed a vehicle road to New Lake, then after one hour the caravan left the road at the confluence of two streams and entered the Bena valley. The valley is narrow at its entrance but becomes wider and open. Fertile grasses promise that the valley is a good pasture for grazing animals. Both sides are precipitous and covered with conifers and shrubs. At intervals small V-shaped valleys descend to the main valley. It rained all day. We got wet to the skin. We stayed at a grazier's hut (3790m) owned by one of our muleteers who has several yaks in this valley. Fortunately wood for fuel was abundant.

6 October At 8am we marched up the valley. As the sky was showing signs of improvement in the weather, we halted at a place called Lebong (3820m). Magnificent snow peaks and glaciers in the headwaters were gradually being unveiled in front of us to the north-east: from east to west, Jainija (6586m), Pukalo (6358m) in the centre, and a nameless peak (6534m) with a breathtaking south-west face adorned with beautiful Himalayan fluted ice. We spent two nights at a similar hut in Lebong.

7 October At 8am we went to a glacier lake, called Pukalo Tso (3900m) in the headwaters. Three glaciers flow into Pukalo lake from separate directions. The weather soon became unstable and again it rained. Next day we returned to Juba village, moving on to Nyangpu on the 9th.

A hidden valley along the Old Peking-Lhasa Road (Gya Lam)
The old Peking-Lhasa road is said to be the 'Tang-Tibet ancient road' that passes through Gongpojiangda county. It comes from the north to join the current Sichuan-Tibet Highway (South route) at 'The Ancient City of Taizhao', 274km east of Lhasa. A relay station was built here in the Yuang Dynasty after which the city began to take shape. The Tang-Tibet road behind the city was built in AD617. History tells that the king of Tibet, Songzangabu, welcomed the princess Wencheng of the Tang Dynasty who came by this road. In the late years of the Qing Dynasty, Taizhao was renamed Jiangda. Early explorers such as Pundit A-K, George Pereira and Frank Kingdon-Ward crossed a high pass of more than 5000m on the ancient road from the Lhari in the north to Nyangpu and Jiangda. In 1922 Pereira became the first westerner to reach Lhasa from the east.

Two hours' drive to the north from Jiangda, along the ancient road, took us to Nyangpu District. Nyangpu (3790m) is a base for visiting the historical Baga monastery in its fertile valley and exploring the unknown westernmost massif of Kongbo country. Imposing rocks and pinnacles soar behind the monastery.

10 October With the rainy season over, we enjoyed an excursion in fine weather to Baga monastery (Baga Si, 4520m). A half-day's horse-riding along a trail following the Baga valley took us to the monastery. The valley is wide with good soil and barley fields. In some villages there are remains of ruined stone towers. The monastery was built by a high Lama in the

69. An ancient monastery set on the turquoise water of Lake Basong, Nyenchentangla East. (*Tamotsu Nakamura*)

70. The west face of unclimbed Lumbogangzegabo (6542m) (*left*) and nameless 6534m peak (*right*) viewed from Lake Basong. (*Tamotsu Nakamura*)

71. Baga monastery at 4520m in Nyangpu district, East Tibet. (*Tamotsu Nakamura*)

11th century and is now worshiped by local Tibetans as a holy temple. It commands a splendid panorama of lofty 6000m peaks to the east beyond the Baga valley. These peaks are located very close to Punkar, north of Jula. In particular, the west face of a nameless peak (6091m) indicated on a map 1:100,000 of the People's Liberation Army looked outstanding and challenging.

11 October We entered a valley to the north of Nyangpu to explore two 6000m peaks indicated on a Russian topographical map of 1:200,000. We got to a point at 4330m three hours' distant from the headwaters but could see no actual summits in front as we were too near to the mountains themselves. Although, finally, on the way back, the south buttress of rock and ice of a 6065m peak came into sight from a village near Nyangpu, more than 12 hours' hard horse-riding without rest had resulted in a lean outcome.

12 October We visited Lungru monastery at Nyangpu, an historical site dating to the 15th century. The Fifth Dalai Lama came here in the 17th century, however the temple was thoroughly destroyed by the Red Army during the Cultural Revolution (1966 -1976). This monastery keeps Tibetan dogs. It is said that Tibetan dogs of pure stock are on the way to extinction. One of the monks told us that they would never sell the best dog among them even if five million RMB were offered [Almost £500,000]. On the same day we returned to Lhasa and flew to Chengdu on 14 October.

Permit problems

As the sudden cancellation of permits in autumn 2004 became an issue among mountaineers, perhaps it would be useful if I detailed the 'special reasons' for this decision as explained to me by Dou Changshen of the TMA.

1. Two Germans and two Americans entered Tsangpo Great Bend and crossed Doshong-La to the south-east. This was reported to the public security police by local people. For this illegal arrangement, a travel agency that had taken care of the foreigners was fined US$5,000 and ordered to suspend its business activity for a period of five years.
2. Two British climbers ascended peaks in an unopened area.
3. A Swiss mountain guide, Gabriel Voide, ascended Jieqinnalagabu (Namla Karpo) east of Lake Basong. This is the first ascent of the most famous and prominent peak in the region. A Kathmandu-based travel agent arranged for his travel.
4. An agent at Lhasa used by the Kathmandu-based travel agent for Mick Fowler's party intended to let their client climb the Matterhorn of Tibet – Kajaqiao – without the correct permit. Finally the agent asked Mr Dou of TMA to help in obtaining a permit for Mick's party, but this request was rejected.

These cases stiffened the Lhasa authorities' attitude and resulted in prohibiting foreigners from entering unopened areas and from climbing the mountains in East Tibet. A New Zealand party's application to climb Birutaso (6691m) and Chuchepo (6550m) in the Lawa valley east of Punkar was rejected along with our plan to march up the Yigong Tsangpo from Tongmai to Niwu and beyond to the north, crossing Shargung La. The NZ team of Sean Waters changed their objective and headed to the satellite peaks of Minya Konka in Sichuan.

Mr. Dou said, however, that as this measure would be a temporary one lasting about five months, the situation would improve before too long and the ban would be lifted perhaps in February or March 2005. It was hinted to me that my plan to visit Yigong Tsangpo and beyond would surely be given a permit in 2005. But frankly speaking, there always exists difficulty in communication with the Chinese people, since their information is insufficient in most cases.

Alps

T H Somervell *Zinal Rothorn*
circa 1971. Oil on board.
Private collection

JOHN HARLIN III

From Dawn to Decadence

Exploring new ground on Mont Blanc's Innominata Arête

Is there still unclaimed territory in Old Europe? That was the question Mark Jenkins and I struggled with while planning our rendezvous in the Alps. Mark is from Wyoming, where the buffalo roam, and I from Oregon, where the trees grow; we get together when schedules allow in order to climb something new – preferably new to the world, not just to us. Alas, our visits are infrequent, and our climbing skills modest at best. So the Alps didn't seem promising for new routing. After all, this continent of über-alpinists has a climbing history that pre-dates our national identity.

Fortunately, the previous year I had lured a Brit by the name of Roger Payne onto an unclimbed ridge deep in America's Grand Canyon, where very little has been climbed. Our crumbling 1000-metre arête was the desert-equivalent of an alpine outing, with precarious piles of choss standing in for corniced snow. I asked Roger about the chances for mortal-scale new routes in the Alps, and he volunteered that the Italian side of Mont Blanc still presented opportunities. This facet of the mountain seems relatively uninteresting to the Euro crowd because of the difficulty of access – or, to quote my favourite Diemberger maxim, 'the barrier of effort'. No problem there: wobbling under the influence of oversized packs is an American speciality, and what's more, Mark and I both had been staff writers for the monthly bible of the beast-of-burden set, *Backpacker* magazine. But to me the best thing about Mont Blanc was that my father had climbed new routes on its Frêney and Brouillard faces. To follow Dad's lead would be a dream come true, especially if I could be guided not by his handholds but by his spirit of new routing.

And that's why late August 2003 found Mark and me grunting up to the Eccles bivouac hut (4050m) via the lower Innominata Ridge and Punta Innominata (only ignorance kept us off the easier glacier approach to the left). Rucksacks overstuffed with 10 days of food and fuel and a big-wall rack aggravated the dangerous loose-rock scrambling and rappels. The weather forecast called for a storm, but our ambition was set. At the archives of Chamonix's Office de Haute Montagne we'd learned where the existing lines had been drawn, which allowed us to begin reading between them. Our objective was to reach the hut, have a look at the Frêney and Brouillard faces to see what ground we might stake for ourselves, acclimatise on our backsides while waiting out the weather, then go over the top and down the French side of the mountain. It seemed a cunning plan.

73. 1963 Chamonix campground scene, 'That's our drying laundry in the background, much to my mother's embarrassment.' *Adults*: Tom Frost, Gary Hemming, Stuart Fulton, John Harlin II. *Kids*: Brown's son, Andréa Harlin, Johnny Harlin III. (*Marilyn Harlin*)

Scrambling up the lower Innominata Ridge gave me plenty of time to reflect on Dad's experience with the mountain. In one of his many articles in the *American Alpine Journal* (the *AAJ* happens to be my current employer), he baldly stated that his 1963 route on the Hidden Pillar of Frêney, with Tom Frost, was the hardest route on Mont Blanc. Despite this claim, the Hidden Pillar has remained eclipsed in history by Dad's climb earlier that summer on the south face of the Fou, also with Frost, along with Gary Hemming and Stuart Fulton. Details of the Fou are familiar from many published photos and descriptions in various books. I remember it for more personal reasons. I was seven years old back then, living in a Chamonix campground for the summer, and Dad and Stuart took me for one of my earliest multi-pitch climbs behind the Envers des Aiguilles hut. This alpine palace was their staging ground for the Fou, and it became my home for several days. The climb with Dad and Stuart was memorable for me, but less so than the night I spent without parents during a raging storm. My mother had gone to see Dad off on the Fou and was supposed to be back before dark. Instead she and her companions huddled in the shelter of a crevasse while I tossed in my bunk listening to the screaming wind outside. She showed up the next day.

From what I gather, storms and the Alps go together like peanut butter and jelly, as we say in the States. Dad went so far as to call his story about his late-August 1965 ascent of the right-hand of the Brouillard Pillars, 'Thumbing a Nose at the Weather'. He teamed up with Chris Bonington, Rustie Baillie, and Brian Robertson, and they all left the low Monzino hut at midnight. He reported that on the way to the Eccles bivouac hut, where they would have breakfast, they had 'seen every known bad-weather sign…. We had been warned!' But they 'decided to go on, regardless of the weather. An unusual experience it was, going against one's better judgment in defiance of weather…. I hoped for the sake of the younger members of the team that it was not foolhardiness.' Dad was a ripe old man of 29 at the time. As it turned out, the weather increased in severity all day, but they climbed their route nevertheless and bivouacked on top before rappelling back down. He concluded, 'We were in our element.'

The morning after Mark and I reached the Eccles huts we eagerly scrambled up the Punta Eccles for a view before the predicted storm rolled in. Immediately it became clear that setting foot on either the Frêney or the Brouillard faces would be suicidal. The glaciers below both walls were covered in a black blanket of fallen stones, and every few minutes another cascade of boulders or a house-sized block tumbled down. Neither of us had witnessed a mountain decomposing like this. (Three weeks later we would interview climatologists in Zurich for Mark's article about how global warming is changing the Alps. (*Outside* magazine, December 2003, http://outside.away.com/news/200312/200312_fire_ice_1.html.) But all was not lost. A safe, seemingly virgin line rose out of the wreckage like a vision. Not only was it beautiful, it was the only rockfall-free space on the entire visible sweep of granite and ice. The line was the crest of the Innominata Arête.

As any Mont Blanc climber knows, there is already a route called the Innominata Arête – the first route on this flank of the mountain, and still the most popular. This line does indeed begin on the arête, but after a bit it wanders left across what used to be a snowfield and continues up a different ridge. In August of 2003, the 'snowfield' was just another river of tumbling rocks. And then there is the *Innominata Direct* route. But this quickly slips to the right-hand side of the ridge and climbs hidden gullies before rejoining the crest to ascend the upper buttress with the help of some aid climbing. Between these two 'Innominata' routes lies the actual ridge.

Where the Innominata route moves left and the Direct route cuts right, a perfect 70m dihedral splits the solid granite. Mark and I could scarcely believe this had not been climbed. The only trouble we foresaw was a three-metre icicle that hung from the first of two roofs.

74. *Left*
Mark Jenkins at the upper Eccles bivouac before the storm, 2003. The garbage is being collected for burning. (*John Harlin*)

75. *Right*
Mark Jenkins in the relatively spacious lower Eccles hut, 2003. (*John Harlin*)

76. Mark Jenkins on the Punta Eccles on the afternoon after the storm during the 2003 Harlin-Jenkins attempt on the Innominata Ridge. (*John Harlin*)

That afternoon we had with us a rack, one pair of rock shoes between us, and time to kill, so we decided to have a go at the dihedral. It begins at about 4300m. Mark led up to the roof's icicle while I cowered under a shallow overhang waiting for the dagger to drop. Under-clinging the roof, Mark knocked the icicle with his shoulder and sent it shattering over my shelter. Then he powered free through the suddenly exposed jam crack to a belay above the roof (5.11-). I followed in boots and had to rest on the rope in the icy roof crack. Mark led through the next roof (5.10+) and belayed on top of the buttress. I followed free, and while I was setting up the rappel Mark wandered up the easy blocky ridge to have a look at the next little buttress. We rappelled, left most of our gear and one rope below the dihedral, and continued down to the hut to enjoy the blow.

The storm hit around midnight. The little hut shook so violently we feared it would be blown off the mountain. We actually debated leaving the dwelling and anchoring ourselves directly to the rock. The stronger gusts sent spindrift between the roof's metal panels, coating us with a couple of centimetres of rime. In the afternoon during a lull we rappelled to the lower hut, which was drier and better anchored to granite. Three days later nearly a metre of snow had fallen. During these days we read a good chunk of *From Dawn to Decadence* (hence the route's name) and, as the food and fuel dwindled, we fretted that we'd never again see our stashed equipment.

Finally the sun came out and in the afternoon we climbed up to Punta Eccles to survey the new world. It looked perfect: All the loose rock was now anchored by fresh snow, and the dihedral's icicle had not returned. We left the hut again at 3am. By 6am we had reached the gear near the base of the dihedral. As dawn lightened the sky we noticed a sheet of thin grey clouds and a wind that snatched our breaths away. We screamed at each other about this being the front of another storm, and recalled our various conversations in the last days about how glad we were not to be trapped in bivouac sacks on one of Mont Blanc's summit ridges. Then we clicked off the headlamps and rappelled toward a building layer of clouds below. That afternoon, when we reached the car 3000m below our highpoint, the sky turned a brilliant blue, the summit glittered in the sun, and we felt disgusted. I have an expression for this sort of thing: Retreating in the face of imminent good weather. We drove to the Val di Mello, and then the Dolomites, to climb off our frustrations.

My next window of opportunity arrived in September 2004. Mark was busy with other travels, but Roger Payne was kind enough to join me, and we persuaded his wife, Julie-Ann Clyma, that traversing Mont Blanc yet again would be worth the effort. They had climbed the standard Innominata route and also the Central Pillar of Frêney, which made them far more qualified than I to wrap up *From Dawn to Decadence*. On 17 September we reached the Eccles hut via the more sensible glacier access, rather than the ridge Mark and I had scrambled. On the 18th we arrived at the dihedral shortly after the sun had warmed its jam-crack. Instead of one long icicle, this time two short icicles hung from the first roof 40m up. I climbed to them with an ice tool in my holster, hung from gear to knock the icicles off and chip out the crack, and then lowered to a belay stance. After Julie-Ann and Roger came up, I tried to free the roof but ran out of courage and therefore strength, so I rested on the rope before freeing to the belay (5.10+ A0). The next pitch had ice in the crack, and we all pulled on stoppers to pass the crux (5.10 A0). Hauling three packs individually up the dihedral had wasted so much time that instead of taking the next little buttress head-on as we should have, we skirted it on its lower left to reach the tight col at the base of the upper buttress. Here we found fixed pins and a narrow ledge from which we chopped ice to create a bivouac space. As we prepared the ledge, two climbers were helicoptered off the Frêney; we worried that maybe they'd heard a bad weather forecast and were taking the quick way out.

Around 2am, during a little brew to warm us up and pass the time, we discussed the sensual pleasures of middle-ageing bodies in cramped open bivvies. An eternity later, once the morning sun had warmed us, a semblance of youthful spirit returned, and soon we were locking jams with the buttress. The *Innominata Direct* route appears to take the icy cracks directly over our bivouac at the fixed pins. Instead, we moved 10m right to a sumptuous (and virgin) left-facing dihedral/crack (50m, 5.10-). A couple of easier rock pitches led up the ridge; then we switched to snow, which took us to the

77. Julie-Ann Clyma and Roger Payne on the upper buttress, 2004.
     (*John Harlin*)

78.   John Harlin on Innominata's crest above the upper buttress, 2004.
(*Roger Payne*)

79. Julie-Ann Clyma on the big dihedral, 2004. (*John Harlin*)

80. Julie-Ann Clyma and Roger Payne enjoying a cosy bivvi on the Innominata Ridge. 'We discussed the sensual pleasures of middle-ageing bodies in cramped open bivvies.' (*John Harlin*)

summit of the Innominata Arête proper. From there endless traversing and scrambling brought us to Mont Blanc's empty summit at 6pm, which was followed by more endlessness punctuated by a Brocken spectre and a fiery sunset before we arrived at the Cosmique hut well after dark but in the nick of time for bread, soup, and wine. Aren't the Alps the best? You can leave that tent-and-kit-carrying nonsense to the Yanks, who know not what they're missing. Wonders continued the next day as a gondola took us from the Aiguille du Midi back to Italy while I gawked at the finest and most historic climbing in our solar system.

Could there possibly be yet more untouched territory sandwiched between the lines? If not, who cares. There's so much beauty there to climb that I could hardly bear to leave. I even caught a view over to the Envers des Aiguilles hut, and remembered where my obsession began. As the lift dropped us into the Courmayeur Valley, I quietly cursed the shortness of life.

Summary: A new route on the Innominata Arête, on the Italian side of Mont Blanc: *From Dawn To Decadence*, 770m, TD, 5.10+ A0 (or 5.11-) 55°, September 17-20, 2004. Julie-Ann Clyma (NZ), John Harlin III (US), and Roger Payne (UK) completed the 2003 efforts of Mark Jenkins (US) and Harlin.

JERRY GORE

Alpine Turmoil

Consider the following dramatic headlines: 'Eiger Nordwand receives its first 8a rock route', 'Scottish Grade 8 climbed on the Grandes Jorasses', 'Alex Huber free climbs at French 8c on trad' gear in the Dolomites'. They are a regular occurrence, testifying to a huge rise in climbing standards across the Alps. Yet other changes, arguably with greater impact, have been taking place in the western Alps for almost a decade now. Most notable of these is the fact that our summers have been getting warmer for many years making traditional alpine mixed routes unsafe in the summer months of June, July and August.

This process has actually been going on for many years but reached a pinnacle during the 2003 summer. According to environmental historians, June 2003 was the hottest June in 250 years – six to seven degrees above the average. The result was that the heat melted the permafrost that acts like bonding glue on rock fissures within the mountain. As the adhesive lost its strength, cracks and joints simply fell apart. Even a general increase in ambient temperatures can have an effect, as temperatures do not have to rise above freezing to make a rock face become unstable. Because the alpine rock is now generally very dry in summer this has led to the massive rockfall that we have seen over the last few years.

The Petit Dru and the west face of the Blaitière have gradually been collapsing for up to 15 years now. The Petit Dru in particular is a good example of huge rockfall on a mountain the summit of which was once all snow and ice, holding the peak together. When the summit cone 'dried out' two summers ago, large sections of the peak fell down, including the Bonatti Pillar and many of the rock routes on the west face. Because there was no unusual snowfall or rainfall to trigger these incidents, geologists suspected that a thawing of the permanently frozen interior of the rocks was to blame.

Other dramatic changes over the last few years include the collapse of snow bridges on large and popular alpine glaciers such as the Mer de Glace and Glacier Blanc, making snow access to routes problematic. This general glacial recession and movement has in turn created more rockfall, as in some areas the glacier can no longer support the rock above it. The hot summers have seen an increase in accidents as a number of the classic mixed faces have not been in condition; climbers have been forced out to the sides and have fallen on the hard rocky sections they have encountered.

In 1977 I was involved in a BSES expedition to south-east Iceland where we gathered conclusive evidence of glacial recession that had been gathering pace over more than a quarter of a century. However, the processes at work in glaciers are well documented elsewhere in this *AJ*. So I will concentrate on what climbers more immediately want to know, and that is quite simply what's in and what's out! What routes or mountains in the Alps have been affected long term and are now considered too dangerous to attempt in summer, and those climbs that are still safe, fun and retain their 'must do' status.

The Mont Blanc Massif

Without doubt the biggest problems in the Alps in the summer of 2003 occurred in the Mont Blanc massif, with at least 50 deaths attributable to rockfall. It was the first year that the mountains of the Haute Savoie really dried out and in many cases all that was left was dry, crumbly gravel. On 17 October 2003, in Saint Gervais, French researchers reported that Mont Blanc had shrunk by 2m over the preceding two years due to the unusually warm weather. Utilising the latest GPS measurements, it was stated that the peak, which had a recorded altitude of 4810.4m in September 2001 now stands at 4808.45m. This represents a loss of 1.95 metres (6.4 feet), according to the topographic readings taken that month, which had a margin of error of 10cm. A spokesman for the 19-member research team, Pierre Bibollet, told journalists that the difference could be explained by 'the combined effect of the wind, which has worn down the peak, and the temperature, because the snow was warmer and it got compressed faster'.

So what actually happened that fateful summer of 2003? In the Chamonix Valley, from May to June, things were pretty much as per most summer seasons. The mixed snow and ice conditions were actually very good. But by mid-July the mountain conditions had so altered that the Walker Spur on the Grandes Jorasses, for instance, had changed to a pure rock route. Climbers were able to leave their rock shoes on for the entire route. On the glaciers in the 'Valley' fast travel was possible everywhere as they were in a totally 'dry' state.

But from 10 August things started to go wrong. It had been 0 degrees or warmer on the summit of Mont Blanc since mid-June and big rockfalls could be heard up and down the valley. In a normal summer season, temperatures at the summit, even in August, are between –5 and –15 degrees C. As for the Jorasses, nobody ventured onto the Walker Spur from approximately 14 August for the remainder of the season because of the incessant stonefall.

The mayor of Chamonix installed policemen on the glacier above the Les Houches train station and before the couloir leading to the Goûter hut, warning people off, as it was very dangerous below the hut. If you ignored the warning and insisted on proceeding, the policemen took your details so that an easy identification could be made in the eventuality of death. Mont Blanc was never officially shut as the authorities shied away from such a course. Many accidents continued throughout the summer, including the evacuation of 50 mountaineers by helicopter from the Goûter hut in July, when the stranded climbers could not safely retreat down to the glacier. It was estimated that there were 20 deaths in 2003 from stonefall just around the Goûter couloir.

The situation does not seem to have altered much in 2004. I spoke to a British climber who attempted the Goûter route in July that year who said that within a three-day period on the mountain he personally witnessed 12 helicopter rescues. He described the situation as a 'war zone', with injured alpinists constantly retreating from the route with cut or injured limbs due to the ever-present rockfall.

The Office De Haute Montagne (OHM) in Chamonix displayed a series of photographs from the middle of the summer showing wild images of large rockfalls on the Petit Dru (falls from the Bonatti to the couloir below and glacier), the Grand Charmoz, and the top of the Aiguille du Midi téléphérique. Here the usually prominent snow cave at the entrance to the station disappeared in August, and the arête ridge issuing from the tunnel was reduced to rock and scree rubble. The death of three members of the Equipe Jeunesse close to the Grand Mulets refuge, a day after competing in the World Cup championships in Chamonix, was also widely publicised across the French media. The accident was attributed to sérac collapse caused by the very hot summer temperatures.

Other noteworthy routes in the Chamonix Valley that were affected in 2003 included the north-west side of the Grand Charmoz. It is still unstable at the top and throughout the 2004 summer, climbers reported seeing rockfall on or from the route. The Cordier Pillar is not in the direct line of fire but the base is threatened, and rock dust was visible on the route at the end of the 2003 summer season. In 2004 the rock on the route clearly settled down and the pillar was climbed many times that summer.

Any route using the Nantillons glacier should still be treated with caution as this was one of the worst affected areas in 2003, with many tons of rock coming down it in July and August. Nikki Wallis, a North Wales activist who sent me a full report on her alpine season that year, said that during her mid-August trip she saw two mountaineers nervously making their way down the glacier around 7pm at speed, unroped and running. They collapsed on the moraine once safe, probably from nervous tension and relief. She thinks they may have come over from the other side not realising what it was like.

The Mont Blanc du Tacul glacier underwent the greatest change during 2003, necessitating the use of fixed ropes across crevasses so that guides could take clients up it. The largest recorded slot was more than 6m wide, forcing climbers onto the rock ridges to its side to avoid the glacier. It was the same story on the Tour Ronde. Heavy snowfall in October and November 2003 seemed to fill the crevasses and in 2004 no fixed ropes were necessary.

The Petit Dru has been badly affected by rockfall for at least the last two years. Really the only safe line in summer now is the American Direct,

81. Les Drus, collapsing for the last 15 years. *(Rogier Van Rijn)*

Robbins and Hemming 1962 classic. In the summer months there is now almost daily rockfall to the left and right of the route. Even the American Direct was affected in 2003 when a large piece came off on the 90m corner, above the 'jammed block'. The Bonatti Pillar has mostly fallen down and many were the tales of epic descents down the other side to the Charpoua hut. The tourist path below the Charpoua also received a large fall of rock and ice across it in 2003, so much so that much of the 'fixed' gear is either in a bad state or has gone completely. The general advice if attempting the American Direct is to abseil back down the route. A recent ascensionist told me that there were falls imminent on the upper part of the American Direct, but I have no confirmation of this.

Just to give an idea how bad the rock now is, a guide told me that when he first took clients on the normal traverse of the Drus in June 2003 he was able to put a piton into a crack half way up the route. By the middle of the season he was able to put himself into the same crack!

Over on the north face of the Petit Dru all the snow disappeared from the niche in 2003, and conditions did not greatly change in 2004. The general advice is only to attempt routes such as the *Guides Route* or the classic *North Face* route when it is dry. If not the melting snow can cause dangerous objective hazards, and the face remains a serious alpine objective.

On the Aiguille de Moine the ice has retreated quite a bit, making the negotiation of the bergschrund a difficult undertaking, as is the case with many bergschrunds on traditionally easy (PD, AD) routes. This is due to the fact that the crevasses have really changed following the heatwave and have not been restored during the winter snows. The base of the Nonne-Eveque-Cardinal ridge is a typical example of this, while the Boissons glacier had big signs up in 2003 saying don't use for ice work, use the Mer de Glace instead. These signs disappeared in 2004. Although the Mer de Glace is now the main sector for ice training, the Boissons is out simply because it is more dangerous and the approach to the Mer de Glace is really easy.

A number of climbers alerted me to the potential for a huge sérac/ice fall from the north-west side of the Aiguille Verte. There is a large crack opening up not far from the summit and if it went would carry with it a massive volume of rock and ice. One to be aware of at least! The Dent du Requin approach was also very dangerous in 2003 and the Requin hut was closed accordingly. This does not appear to have been the case in 2004. The Envers hut was also very quiet in 2003 because of the dangerous approach and the huge bergschrund up to the Aiguille Du Roc. Again after the 03/04 winter the situation reversed itself.

And finally, on the French side of the Valley, rockfall continues to be a problem on Mont Blanc's Brenva face. The old Trident hut is now definitely gone, with the nearest bivouac on the Col de la Fourche. The Dent du Géant also suffered bad stonefall on the approach route in 2003 and the base of the mountain is still very unstable. It needed its teeth filling with a lot of snow!

Over on the Italian side of Mont Blanc a big rockfall has made the east ridge of the Aiguille Noire suspect. The 2003 heatwave also had a big effect on the local economy of the area. Most of the outdoor shops in Courmayeur reported an upsurge in sport-climbing gear and a noticeable reduction in alpine equipment by the end of the summer, due to the wholesale change in climbing activity in the area.

So if that is the bad news, what is the good? One of the largest unaffected areas around Mont Blanc was the Aiguilles Rouges. Unfortunately, this popular area is always crowded because it is safe, and often dry in summer when other alpine rock routes are not. The busiest venues are always the Index and Glière areas. The west face of the Red Pillar on the Aiguille de Blaitière has suffered a lot of rockfall over the last 10 years and is still fairly unstable. But the rock routes *Majorette Thatcher* and *Fidel Fiasco* remain popular. Not all routes on this face are bolted and some are very hard, so be aware. I remember rescuing a couple of Brits who had got their ropes caught abseiling in a storm after an aborted attempt on *Thatcher*. Going lightweight does not always work, and certainly in this case the pair's T-shirts did not offer much protection from the driving sleet that had enveloped the face.

The Frendo Spur on the Aiguille du Midi has been in good condition over the last few years, but is not as described in the guidebooks. With that caveat, I think it is a good one to do as long as you are happy to tackle the long ice section at the top (the ice can be of an unpredictable quality).

Over on the Central Pillar of Freney three people were killed in 2003 by stonefall whilst traversing across to the base. Basically they were too late. They were hit around 6am-7am and should have been there by midnight. The route is fine in summer, and is often dry, but make sure you set out much earlier than normal, and avoid a retreat at all costs, as the approach is tricky and is not nice to reverse.

Finally, in Chamonix the rock climbs on the Aiguille du Chamonix and the east face of the Tacul are all unaffected and offer good quality climbing. I am not sure about the rock routes on the Petites Jorasses and the satellites around Les Drus as I have heard conflicting reports about the nature of the rock post-2003.

The Swiss Valais Alps

Throughout summer 2003 the Matterhorn certainly had its fair share of media coverage. It was actually shut twice, first in July after 70 people were evacuated from the Solvay emergency refuge high up on the Hörnli ridge. Climbers watched in horror as continuous massive rockfalls exploded below them at 3400m. The mountain was shut from the Swiss side shortly afterwards by officials in the Valais Canton to allow time for repairs to the fixed ropes and to clear debris from the ridge.

No one was injured in the rockslide, which was surprising as up to 150 climbers attempt an ascent every day during the summer. 'It's only down to luck that it wasn't more serious,' said Bruno Jelk, who co-ordinated the evacuation. Victor Saunders was one of those airlifted off, recording the experience in the 2004 *AJ*. 'I have never seen so much rock falling at one time,' Victor said. And he used to climb with Mick Fowler!

On a second occasion, the Matterhorn was shut for three weeks from both the Swiss and Italian sides. The cause of the rockfall was attributed by climate specialists to high temperatures throughout the summer, which they said had probably caused a melting of the permafrost that binds the rocks together. Rockfalls are not uncommon on the Matterhorn. I soloed the Hörnli back in 1983 and remember the large amount of loose 'choss' on the hill, some of which nearly wiped me out on the descent, having been dislodged by climbers above.

Over in Grindelwald, in mid-July 2003, the heat was also blamed for causing massive chunks of ice to break away from a glacier. The ice fell into a river, causing a 2m-high swell of water to barrel down the mountain. Police banned access to the Lütschine river and told holidaymakers and locals to stand clear as the wave carrying a mass of mud and rocks made its way towards Lake Brienz. A second, smaller wave followed two hours later after water trapped behind the fallen ice broke through. No damage was reported and no more movement detected on the glacier. 'It could be two weeks, two months or two years before we have this kind of situation again,' said Christian Anderegg of the Grindelwald fire department.

On the Eiger it was the same story. The icefields on the north face were reduced to gravel, and the White Spider section of the 1938 route disappeared by the end of July, making the climb more dangerous than normal. These days, March seems the preferred month for ascents of this route. Probably as a result of the changes the Eiger's east and west ridge routes are even more popular than normal, and offer a good excuse for avoiding the face!

The Swiss authorities have been wary of glacier movement in the Alps for many years. Ice collapses have caused major damage and deaths. In 1965 part of the Allalin glacier came down on the construction site of the Mattmark dam in the Saas valley killing 88 workers in less than a minute.

Wilfried Haeberli, a glaciologist at Zurich University, said it was not just climbers who were threatened by the permafrost meltdown. Mountain installations such as cable cars or huts could also suffer damage. 'We've known about this phenomenon for a long time, but people have not taken it seriously enough,' he said, describing the process as akin to leaving a fridge door open. 'Water starts to flow, and large chunks of rock begin to break away from the mountain.'

The Ecrins Massif

And so to the Ecrins Massif, the most southerly of the alpine climbing areas and my own 'local' patch. Basically the 2003 summer was pretty much business as usual. We always have low precipitation, a fact confirmed by the 300 days of sunshine the region enjoys every year. So the massif has dried out many times before. I guess the other thing to say is that the Ecrins Massif (or L'Oisans) is big – 30 times larger than the Chamonix Valley and comprises four different rock types: granite, limestone, quartzite and conglomerate. So a review of this area in terms of what is 'in' and what is 'out' is not a simple matter.

There was not one cloudy day in March 2003 in the Hautes Alpes – unheard of – and yet in terms of actual route change there very little was affected despite this prolonged dry, sunny period. The few exceptions include the north faces of the Pic Sans Nom, Pelvoux and Ailefroide which are now considered dangerous in August due to increased rockfall. The obvious routes here which are now slightly more affected by rockfall are the classics *Voie Chapoutot* (TD) and *Aurore Nucleaire* (ED) on the central pillar on the north face of the Pic Sans Nom.

Over on the south pillar of the Barre des Ecrins things have changed. Now only the classic 1944 route (TD) is still safe, but climb quickly in the lower part especially. Summer ascensionists report hearing and seeing rock fall throughout the day. However, the regular route *Voie Normale* to the summit of the Barre Des Ecrins (at 4102m the most southerly four-thousander in Europe) remains unaffected other than an increase in snow bridge collapse on the Glacier Blanc in the height of summer – one for the aspiring alpinist in search of AD grand voies.

Approaches to a number of the routes on the south face of the Meije have difficult starts these days due to glacial recession, leaving a tricky (poor rock) section to overcome in order to reach the first piton or bolt. Otherwise the two obvious classics, the *Traverse*, and the *Allain* route on the south face remain very popular. The *Allain* is a little difficult to follow exactly but has good rock and a great summit – probably VS/HVS depending on the line followed.

If you want to be super-cautious and yet enjoy big alpine objectives, the rock routes on the Aiguille de Sialouze, and on Pointe Louise (Glacier Blanc) offer easy access and sound alpine rock. For big wall/multi-pitch alpine rock without a glacial approach you have many objectives including the 600m south face of the Tête d'Aval (30+ routes), and the sub-alpine range of the Massif des Cerces. The Cerces itself is big with six distinct areas, over 100 routes from Facile to Abominable + and up to 400m in length. All of the climbs in the Cerces are unaffected by the permafrost reduction seen elsewhere.

So what is the general advice for summer alpine climbing these days? I think firstly, if climbing in July and August, try and choose alpine bolted rock climbs. The north-east pillar on the Pic Sans Nom here in Les Ecrins is a good example of a safe alpine climb, possible even in the middle of the summer heat – 25 pitches with no danger from rockfall above as the top is an independent summit, away from and not below the main summit.

If you want to get amongst the mixed stuff, try and go for snow and ice

grande courses like the *Voie Normale* on the Barre des Ecrins, which is possible from mid-June to mid-September without snowshoes. Another
example is the north-east slope of the Courtes which usually stays safe
throughout the summer. As for high mountain goulottes or ice routes, which
are becoming increasingly popular, go in late spring or at the very start of
summer. But if you do decide to go early be prepared to hire snowshoes or
short skis. April to early May are the ski-touring months in the high mountains, and you will need more than just leg power to get around the hills.

Avoid the peak summer months of July and August if at all possible.
Remember the French take their holidays between the 15 July and 15
August. Early season from say early June to mid July is often preferable
because there are fewer people, cheaper accommodation, safer glacier
crossings and better snow conditions up high.

Remember to stay off glaciers and glacier approaches in high summer
(July/August), and scout out routes in advance if possible (ie bivvi nearby
or ask people who have done the route recently). Do stick to rock routes
that follow solid lines or snow/ice routes that have traditionally stable slopes,
and do practise crevasse rescue at the start of your alpine season.

Avoid icy/snowy tops and look for solid rock ridges or pillars leading to
a saddle or col so there is no danger from falling ice or rock higher up.
Look for compact rock and peaks that have a good reputation as regards
rockfall, such as the Grand Capucin. And finally, always seek advice and
network around for up-to-date, reliable information. Route info can go out
of date very quickly – the mountains of the world are in constant change –
and now we all have access to the web there really is no excuse. A few
hours surfing the net just might save your life and ensure that you have a
really great alpine trip.

The good news is that we got what we all wanted at the end of 2003 – a
really good autumn-winter with a lot of precipitation above 2000m. Here
in the Ecrins we were ski-touring in deep powder as early as the end of
October that year, and our local ski resorts of Serre Chevalier and
Montgenèvre opened a full month earlier than normal. The mountain 'glue'
was replaced as the snow filled the fissures both on the mountains and on
the glaciers.

That's about it, other than to say Jackie, my wife, and I hire out chalets
and apartments for climbers and walkers via our website www.alpbase.com
We live here in the Ecrins Massif year round, and so if you need any
information on what is in condition in the Hautes Alpes, do contact us
via our site or email me at jerry@alpbase.com (tel: +33 4 92 23 45 69).
Safe climbing!

JOHN McM MOORE

Understanding Mountain Glaciers

Glacier retreat is regularly cited as one of the more obvious symptoms of global warming. Most of us will have seen examples in the mountains ourselves and perhaps been surprised to be traversing smoothed rock and debris where a not-so-old map suggests we should be on a glacier. The flights of ladders necessary to reach the Konkordia Hut from the ice highlight the reduction in size of the Grosser Aletsch glacier during the last 150 years. However, the implications may not be quite as apocalyptic as the more sensational reports would have us believe.

Understanding glacial behaviour requires an appreciation of physics, crystal chemistry and meteorology but, most importantly, of time scales much greater than human history. It is unrealistic to view any particular moment as 'the norm' and to regard ongoing changes, including those caused by human activity, as freak events disturbing what would otherwise be 'steady state' equilibrium. There is little doubt that human activity is affecting the Earth's atmosphere as a system but this can be viewed simply as an additional, if undesirable, short-term contributory factor to those natural processes which are occurring independently of human involvement.

In this paper I have reviewed and summarised some of the processes at work in mountain glaciers.

Glacial History

Ice currently covers about 10.8% of land and 7.3% of the ocean surface. At its greatest extent during the last major glacial event, 32% of the Earth's land surface was ice covered. The valley glaciers and small mountain ice caps of the northern hemisphere (excluding Greenland) contain only 4% of the world's ice.

Advance and retreat of ice sheets and mountain glaciers have occurred in irregular cycles, since onset of the latest widespread global cooling, about 17 million years ago. During the last 3 million years there have been at least 17 major continental ice glacial cycles. Each cycle comprised cold and temperate intervals, leading to the inter-glacial event during which we live.

Numerous advances and retreats of continental ice sheets occurred within the last 900,000 years, culminating with the Late Devensian cycle (25,000 to 6,000 years ago). During this period, northern Europe, including most of the British Isles, was covered to depths of 1000 metres by an ice cap which reached its maximum extent about 18,000 years ago. This event and the retreat of the ice sheets from Britain and North America some 6,000 years ago shaped the hills and mountains of northern Europe and large parts of North America. Hominids, including *Homo Sapiens Neanderthalensis* (150,000 to 30,000years ago) and *Homo Sapiens Sapiens*, which evolved in its present form about 100,000 years ago, lived through some of these climatic changes. Human cultural records, in the form of cave paintings dating from 35,000 years ago, survived the last major glacial advance.

Composition and behaviour of Glaciers

Glaciers are made of snow, ice and rock debris. In some cases liquid water is also present. A glacier's existence depends on a budget for which the income is snow supply and the outgoings are loss of ice by ablation (melting, run-off and evaporation) and/or loss of ice by detachment of blocks from the snout or margin (falling séracs or 'calving' of floating icebergs).

Snow falling on to the glacier, together with avalanche debris, undergoes a transition through an intermediate hard snow stage (firn or névé) to water ice. During this transformation, snow re-crystallises into a mosaic of interlocking water crystals which resemble marble in microscopic texture.

A glacier, as a system, is in equilibrium with its environment when the supply of snow is matched by loss of ice by ablation etc. In temperate climates, snow supply and melting vary with season. In consequence, there is a net gain of ice in winter and a net loss in summer. During winters, snow commonly accumulates over the whole glacier but in summer it disappears from significant areas to reveal bare ice (so called 'dry glacier').

For a glacier to maintain meta-stability, the net accumulation of snow must at least equal loss of ice over a period of years. Surge and retreat of glaciers occur rapidly as responses to short-term climatic fluctuations. The *Rivista* of the CAI (Vol.123, May-June 2004) contains a summary of research into the behaviour, over the last 75 years, of 115 valley glacier 'units' of the approximately 800 in the Italian Alps. The results indicate widespread retreat between 1925 and 1960. There was then a significant advance between 1960 and 1980 in 90% of the glaciers studied. This was followed by further retreat between 1990 and 2003. Taken with the geological record, these results serve only to show that retreat and advance in valley glaciers is unpredictable and can occur on cycles both of long and short timescale. Glacial change on the scale of a human lifetime is insignificant in terms of Earth history.

Glacier Types, Systems and Mechanisms

In addition to precipitation, the existence and movement of glaciers depends on thermal energy from the atmosphere and geothermal heat from within the Earth. There are two basic types of glacier; so-called 'cold' and 'warm' glaciers.

Cold glaciers, typified by the major polar ice caps, are terrestrial ice bodies whose surface interface with air is almost always below freezing point ($0°C$). To qualify as 'cold', a glacier must have a surface temperature low enough to prevent melting at the ice base by the earth's internal heat. Pressure

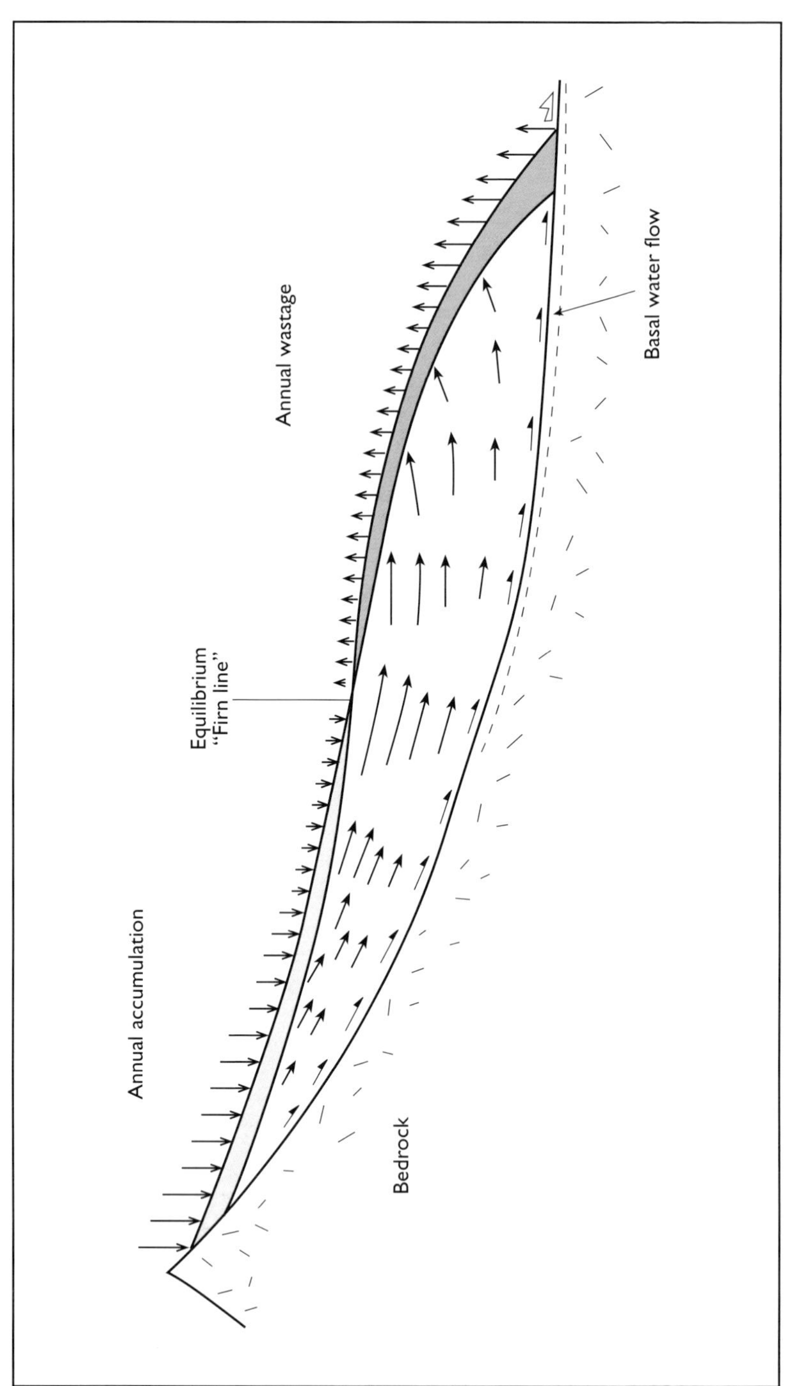

Annual accumulation
Annual wastage
Equilibrium "Firn line"
Bedrock
Basal water flow

exerted by the 'head' of ice, lowers the freezing point and so the bottom of a 'cold' ice sheet or glacier is normally −1°C or colder. With air temperatures below freezing, the whole system remains below freezing temperature and the rock below the ice is maintained in a permafrost condition. Liquid water cannot, except in very special circumstances, exist in a cold glacier.

In contrast, 'warm' glaciers generally contain melt water. This is the typical state of mountain glaciers in a temperate climate, many of which have air above 0°C in contact with the ice surface for long periods. Liquid water can exist within a warm glacier as well as at its surface. Furthermore, geothermal heat can be conducted from rock into the ice. This allows liquid water to exist and flow at the interface with the underlying rock, a phenomenon that has some profound effects on the dynamics of mountain glaciers in temperate climates such as that of the Alps. The effects of geothermal heat flow are significant. Some impression of the energy supplied from the earth is given by conditions in Alpine tunnels. For example, despite an efficient forced ventilation system, temperatures in the centre of the Mont Blanc tunnel, approximately 3000m below surface in granite, a notably 'hot' rock, are 18-20°C, when air temperatures at the portals may be −10°. Without ventilation, the rocks in the centre of the tunnel would reach temperatures not far short of the boiling point of water.

A valley glacier, as a system, can be represented by a longitudinal profile model (Fig 1). Above the equilibrium point – also known as the Firn Line – permanent snow, including névé, normally covers ice (Photo 83). This is the area of net accumulation. Below the Firn Line is the zone of net wastage. For a glacier in equilibrium, the volumes of water represented by the accumulation and wastage wedges will, in three dimensions, be the same.

A glacier cannot become larger in the accumulation area and smaller in the wastage wedge. There must be a transfer of material past the equilibrium line. This occurs by the action of gravity and is achieved by several mechanisms. Fig.1 also shows vectors representing the direction and relative velocity of ice movement within the glacier. The downward direction of vectors in the accumulation area leads to the assimilation into the ice of objects on the surface, eg crashed aeroplanes, the bodies of First World War Italian and Austrian soldiers etc. After burial periods of years or decades, flowage in the direction of the vectors leads to exhumation in the wastage wedge (Fig 1).

Fig 1. Longitudinal vertical section model of a valley glacier, showing equilibrium point ('Firn Line'), accumulation and wastage wedges. Open-tipped arrows show the relative amounts of water added to and removed from the system in different parts of the glacier. Solid head arrows represent movement vectors in the glacier; vector orientation indicates direction of movement and length of arrow represents speed. The form of the vector pattern allows the glacier to maintain its shape as material is transferred from the accumulation to the ablation wedges.

83. The 'Firn Line' forming the boundary between the snow-covered accumulation zone and 'dry glacier' ablation/wastage wedge of a valley glacier (summer). (*John McM Moore*)

The continued existence of a glacier depends on many factors, the most important of which are snow supply and annual ambient temperatures. Ice conservation depends more on low melt rates than high levels of snow precipitation. Antarctica has relatively low precipitation but very low melt rates. In contrast, in Scotland, relatively high precipitation but high melting rates mean north-facing corries do not quite meet the boundary condition for perennial conservation of snow and thus ice formation.

Glacier flow rates vary enormously. Glaciers in humid areas are generally, more active than those in cold dry climates. The 12-17km per year reported for the Jakobshvn Isbrae in Greenland is exceptional. More usual is a flow rate of 200-300m per annum but 1-2km per year is not uncommon in steeply inclined glaciers and icefalls. Each glacier has its own identity in terms of flow rate, surge or retreat. These are dependent on setting, local climatic conditions, morphology of the glacier bed and form of the valley. Inclination and evenness of the valley floor appear to be the most important factors influencing glacier flow rate.

84. (*right*) Viscoplastic deformation in dry glacier ice below the firn line, demonstrated by folding of dust and silt lenses in the ice matrix. Mer de Glace, Chamonix (summer). (*John McM Moore*)

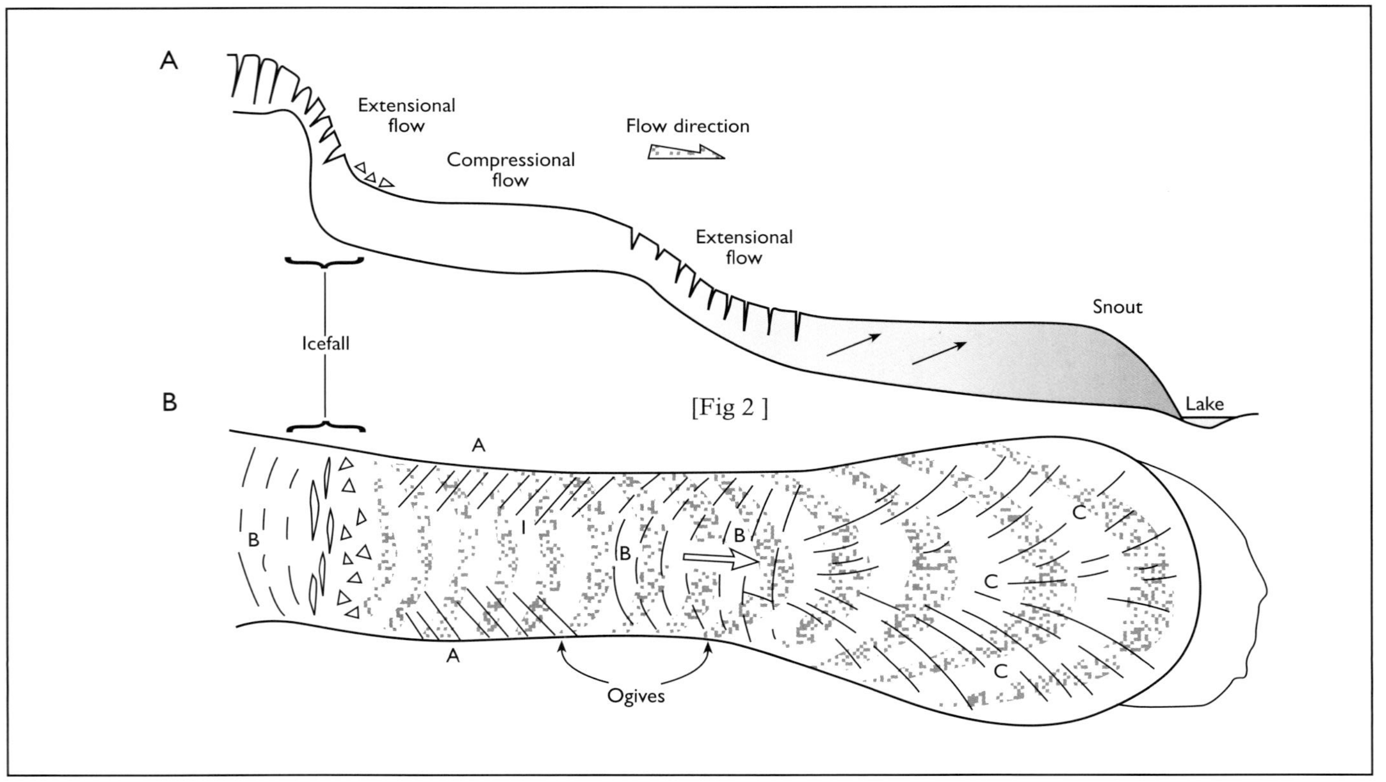

A
Extensional flow
Flow direction
Compressional flow
Extensional flow
Snout
Icefall
Lake
[Fig 2]
B
A
B
B
B
A
Ogives
C
C
C

Ice Movement

Ice is a mosaic of interlocking water crystals. Mechanically, it deforms in analogous ways to many other crystalline solids, notably geological materials, albeit over much shorter time scales. Maintenance of a glacier as a dynamic system depends on both the mechanical and thermal properties of crystalline ice.

Shape change within a body of glacier ice is induced by complex quasi-plastic or visco-plastic processes, causing progressive re-crystallisation within the mosaic of ice crystals. There is almost no deformation when ice is subjected to low shear stress for short time periods but under greater stress, applied for longer periods, the crystal aggregates respond at first rather like a fluid and then as a plastic substance. Layers and films of dark silt or dust trapped in the ice record internal deformation as streaks and folds (Photo 84) similar in appearance to those observed in metamorphic rocks.

Bulk movement in a warm glacier is achieved by combinations of internal creep, re-crystallisation and widespread but localised, brittle fracture, together with mass slippage of ice across rock, lubricated by liquid water. Basal slip is a major factor in warm glacier movement. It has been uniquely documented in a hydro-electric facility under the Argentière glacier, above the Chamonix valley, where there is access to the base of the ice by a rock tunnel. A 'bicycle wheel' type distance-measuring device has been rigged against the ice sole. This monitors rates of ice movement over the shaft mouth. Seasonal variations in flow rate can be clearly seen in time-lapse films of the tachometer monitor wheel. Indirect evidence of basal slip is given by polished 'boiler plate' slabs and striae scored by rock fragments, on exhumed bedrock. Glaciers therefore 'flow' by a combination of sliding on bed rock, lubricated by pressure melt, percolating surface meltwater and by internal visco-plastic deformation whose rate varies with load.

Flow velocities in a valley glacier vary in a complex three-dimensional pattern. Ice nearer to the surface moves faster than that at the base. Friction with the banks causes the central parts of ice streams to flow faster than the edges. Seen in plan, a line of markers placed transversely across the surface will 'deform' to an arcuate shape over time as the central region moves

Fig 2 (*left*) Generalized models of a valley glacier.
A   Longitudinal Section: note areas of extensional and compressional flow and transverse crevasses.
B   Plan. Note ogives below ice fall and generalized crevasse types:
    A   Marginal. The marginal crevasses marked 1 are older – like 1 they originally pointed upstream, but were subsequently rotated and re-oriented by the differential movement rates between the central ice stream and its peripheral zones.
    B   Transverse. The curvature of transverse crevasses is changed by the same process as that which modifies the marginal crevasses.
    C   Splaying.

downstream faster than the flanks. Similarly, a vertical borehole to the base will deform with time, to a roughly parabolic shape in longitudinal, vertical cross section.

Ice Falls and Crevasses

Where a glacier passes over a step in the rock floor, the rate of deformation may be too fast for a visco-plastic response, and the ice then behaves as a brittle material and fractures to form the crevasse fissures and séracs of an icefall. Where the channel gradient decreases, the ice thickens and compressional shear failure can occur, creating thrust and wrench 'faults' analogous to those in rocks. The crevasse-bounded tottering ridges and pinnacles which comprise an icefall are imperceptibly 'nudged' in the direction of flow, creating that fearsome and completely unpredictable danger sérac collapse/ice avalanche which, over the years, has killed a number of eminent mountaineers. Below the icefall, sérac debris is re-incorporated into the ice continuum and viscoplastic flow resumes.

Several geometrical systems of crevasse fractures are common (Fig 2). The simplest is a set of fissures on the crest of a convex bulge, where the ice is in extension over a substrate step or bump. Although initially approximately transverse to the direction of flow, as they are transported downstream, these crevasses change shape because of the differential rates of flow between the centre and margins of the ice stream. Stresses caused by frictional drag of the rock walls and floor near glacier edges create complex belts of marginal crevasses near the banks. These too become distorted by differential rates of movement across the glacier and in some places several crevasse generations cut across each other, transforming the marginal zones of the glacier into a 'crazy paving' of crevasse-bounded blocks. There are good examples of this on the Mer de Glace below Montenvers station (Photo 86). A third type of crevasse forms in the centre of the flow whenever the valley widens and ice can spread laterally. These are splaying crevasse systems and are particularly noticeable in the fan-shaped snouts of glaciers which spread as they discharge on to an outwash plain.

As is typical with brittle fracture, creation of a crevasse is a sudden event. It occurs by instantaneous nucleation and rapid propagation of a crack. A quiet night on a glacier can be disturbed disconcertingly by the sudden 'explosive discharge' of crevasse creation and propagation. There are dramatic reports from those who have experienced the appearance of a fissure in a tent floor.

Study of a dry glacier, particularly from viewpoints above, can help the mountaineer to understand the patterns of crevasses which may lie beneath the snow above the firn line. A summer glacier walk on the Mer de Glace can make skiing the Vallée Blanche in spring a matter for greater circumspection than is awarded to it by most piste skiers on an exciting day out from the Midi téléférique. Louis Lachenal was killed in a crevasse accident while skiing the area above the Glacier du Géant icefall.

86. Marginal crevasses in the 'dry' section of the Mer de Glace, Chamonix (summer). Note the Glacier du Géant icefall in the background. (*John McM Moore*)

87. Ogives and lateral and medial moraine debris trains on the Mer de Glace (summer), viewed from above the Géant icefall, looking towards Montenvers. (*John McM Moore*)

88. Icefall and snout of the Haut Glacier de Tsa de Tsan, near the Rif Aosta (summer 1973). Note discharge of water from the base of the ice. (*John McM Moore*)

89. Glacier des Bossons and Glacier du Taconnaz flowing from Plan Glacier and Les Grands Mulets towards the Chamonix valley. Note the firn line. The periodic surges of the Glacier des Bossons towards the village may be due in part to the steepness of its channel. (*John McM Moore*)

Surface Features

Rock is an important part of most valley glaciers. It accumulates as material is plucked or ground from the glacier walls, or as debris falling on to the ice surface. Debris plays an important role in the wastage wedge. Clastic fragments and fine ground dust accumulate as moving belts of debris along the edges of the ice. Adjacent to the sides of the dry glacier, they form ridges known as lateral moraines, whose crests are stable but slopes are at the angle of rest – a fact soon appreciated by the frustrated alpinist trying to climb off the ice. Where glaciers converge to a single stream, lateral moraines merge to form a ridge-like train of debris, known as a medial moraine, riding upon the ice, parallel to the flow direction.

When a glacier is stable for a reasonable length of time, debris accumulates around the snout as a terminal moraine. If preserved by abandonment as ice retreat occurs, terminal and other moraines remain as distinctive relics and indicators of the ephemeral presence of the glaciers.

Where a glacier emerges from an icefall, a curious phenomenon of arcuate dark debris bands, called ogives, can be observed on the surface in summer (Photo 87). Ogives are seasonal features with a complex three-dimensional geometry representing the alternating relics of summer seasons' debris, and cleaner 'winter' ice. Their curved form is another indication of differential flow rate between the axial line and flanks of an ice stream. Being annual features, ogives can be used to calculate rate of ice flow. Based on ogive count, the transit time taken by ice in the Mer de Glace from the Géant icefall to the snout is approximately 50 years.

Warm air, particularly as wind, in daytime and not infrequently during summer nights, causes widespread melting acting on the surface of temperate climate glaciers. The melt water flows on the surface and forms torrents whose polished runnels are potentially so dangerous to cross. The water disappears into crevasses and meltwater pipe systems in the body of the ice, and thence eventually to the base where it lubricates and speeds basal slip. Evidence of the volumes of water moving through and under warm glaciers can be seen in snout discharge torrents (Photo 88) and lakes like the Lac du Miage. This lake was the scene of a tragedy several years ago when the sudden 'calving' of sérac blocks into the lake created a tsunami surge which killed several tourists on the opposite bank.

Direct interaction of solar radiation with glacier surfaces also produces some interesting features. Clean snow approximates to the physical concept of a 'black body radiator' – that is to say that it absorbs and then re-emits almost all the solar energy which falls upon it. Consequently, on a sunny windless day, clean snow is less vulnerable to melting than in cloudy, warm and windy conditions. When snow or ice is covered by a film of rock dust or layers of debris the physical response is different. Rock dust absorbs solar radiation and does not re-emit the energy. This results in clusters of tubular pits 0.5-4cm deep floored by one or two millimetres of dark silt. The pits continue to deepen until shadow and water depth limit further melting creating the 'pockmarked' appearance so typical of many glaciers with a silt, dust or gravel veneer. In contrast, thicker blankets of debris insulate the underlying ice, creating the ice-cored hummocks and ridges which can make walking so unpleasant. Erratic blocks protect the underlying ice from melt by insulation and shade and become 'rock tables' perched on an ice column. The height of some 'perched' blocks illustrates the high rates of ice loss by ablation from the unprotected surfaces of dry glaciers in temperate climates.

Postscript

Although there is debate about what is happening to the major cold-glacier ice caps, there is no doubt that the majority of mountain glaciers have been in net retreat since the end of the 'Little Ice Age' of the 18th -19th century. At various times in recorded history, however, mountain glaciers have surged dramatically. There are several instances of the inhabitants of the Chamonix valley being threatened by rapid advance of the Argentière, Bossons and other glaciers (Photo 89).

One such event led to a notable entrepreneurial initiative by the Bishop of Annecy, whose visit in 1690 to pray for the salvation of the villagers from the advancing ice was followed by a reported retreat of 250 metres and a large invoice for services rendered. The overall picture over the last 150 years has been one of widespread retreat. Perhaps the time has come to retain the current Bishop's services for the opposite purpose.

BIBLIOGRAPHY

F Fleming, *Dragons: The Conquest of the Alps*. Granta Books, London, 2000.
M Hambrey & Alean Jürg, *Glaciers*. Cambridge University Press, 2004.

MIRELLA TENDERINI

Watching the Cavalieri della Montagna

When the *AJ* editor suggested that I might like to set down my recollections of the famous mountaineers I have met and the changes I have witnessed in alpinism during 40 years of close association with Italian climbing, I wondered at first whether this would be of interest to British readers. But it is true that I have lived a large part of my life on the mountains and have always been in touch with people who had a part in mountaineering history. So I liked the idea and shall try not to be too tedious.

I was born to a Milanese family and grew up as a real city animal. I have always loved big, busy cities and think that if I could not live in splendid alpine isolation, as we do, the only other place where I'd want to live would be in a garret, even a tiny one, in the very centre of a big, big city.

The magnet that drew me, and settled my destiny to live all my adult life on the hills, was the Grigna, a mountain above Lake Como, laced by beautiful crests and pinnacles. I could see it from my home in Milan and it was the ground for my first scrambles up rocks and screes. At that time I was a teenager and did not realise that I moved in the heart of the mountaineering world and that many people I used to cross on trails up or down the mountain were, or were to become, famous climbers. But so it was.

The Grigna is the most accessible mountain from the lowlands of Lombardy, at the very centre of northern Italy, and was therefore a nursery for passionate would-be mountaineers from the whole region. Aldo Bonacossa, Vitale Bramani and several other climbers who lived in Milan spent many Sundays on the vertical spires of that small mountain before venturing on to higher and more challenging peaks in the Alps.

In the 1920s and '30s there was an extraordinary development of the climbing activity in the area around the Grigna, especially in Lecco, a small town in the throes of rapid industrial growth. Those years witnessed the birth of mass mountaineering, a working-class revolution which spread everywhere after the Second World War. Before that time, climbing was almost exclusively the preserve of wealthy people from the cities, accompanied by local guides.

The development of industry left more free time to the workers than traditional peasant economy. Several worker clubs with recreational and sporting aims were created, and many labourers also practised sports individually. That was easy in a place like Lecco, with a lake for swimming and mountains to climb practically on the doorstep. No wonder, therefore, that Lecco produced so many strong climbers, who were called, after the war, the *Ragni*, or Spiders.

The best known was Riccardo Cassin. His ascents of the north face of the Cima Ovest di Lavaredo (1935), north-east face of Piz Badile (1937) and the Walker Spur of the Grandes Jorasses (1938) earned him a fame that obscured the names of several other Lecco aces who were his equal in climbing skill. However, Cassin also possessed natural qualities of boldness and endurance and was a born leader. It was this combination of qualities, in addition to technical skill, that accounts for his impressive record of achievement in a climbing career that lasted into old age. Without these multiple gifts he would never have succeeded in his ascent of the south ridge of McKinley in 1961.

The Grigna, however, was not the sole property of the Lombards. In the early Thirties, the most famous Dolomites climber of those times, Emilio Comici, came to Lecco with Mary Varale, a fine climber and a pioneer of women mountaineering in Italy. Comici taught Cassin and his friends a few techniques that he had developed on the vertical walls of the Dolomites. Thanks to those advanced rope tricks and to his familiarity with the granite and ice of Masino and Bergel – the logical next step after the Grigna – Cassin acquired a confidence that made him unmatched.

At the time I started climbing, Cassin was to be seen frequently in the Grigna area, and so were several climbers of his generation worthy of mention, like his mates Gino Esposito and Vittorio Panzeri, and the Milanese Nino Oppio, author of some very hard 'artificial' routes. Aid climbing had developed in the Dolomites and was particularly popular in those years. All the routes which could be climbed free with the means then available had already been done, and the only way to win awesome overhangs or smooth vertical rock was to use pitons, ladders and complicated rope procedures. Cassin and other climbers working in the Lecco iron industry made their own pitons and karabiners.

The first important aid climb in the western Alps was the east face of Grand Capucin by Walter Bonatti. He too had taken his first steps on the Grigna and climbed there often. For his fine ascents he was chosen to join the national expedition to K2 in 1954. He was the youngest and strongest member but, sadly, in the course of the expedition, certain actions high on the mountain led to unjust accusations that caused him a lifetime's bitterness.

The following year, in a gesture of revenge, Bonatti soloed the first ascent to the south-west pillar of the Petit Dru (the Bonatti Pillar), one of the boldest ascents in the history of mountaineering. His deeds gained him great popularity and he was particularly loved because of his unassuming attitude and natural amiability. At Piani Resinelli, a tiny village on the slopes of the Grigna, he often joined friends in a refuge, staying up till late at night, and then disappearing to bivouac in some secret place before starting a hard route at sunrise.

At that time Bonatti often climbed with Carlo Mauri from Lecco. Together they accomplished some fine ascents in the Mont Blanc area and in 1958 made the first ascent of Gasherbrum IV on an expedition led by Riccardo Cassin. They reached the summit by the hardest route above 7000 metres then climbed, and never repeated to this day. Later the same year, Bonatti and Mauri went to Patagonia to attempt Cerro Torre. Cesare Maestri, a strong Dolomite climber with a stunning record of first solo ascents, was there at the same time with a Trento team and with the same aim. Both expeditions failed.

Maestri went back to the Torre in 1959 with the Austrian Toni Egger, an exceptionally skilled ice climber, who was killed by an avalanche on the way down. Maestri claimed they had reached the top and nobody doubted his word until Mauri advanced suspicions, igniting a controversy that is still far from settled. Egger had spent some time in the Grigna area, climbing with friends from Lecco, astonishing them with a skill they regarded as absolutely ahead of the times. In 1970 Maestri made a winter ascent of the south-west ridge of Cerro Torre with the aid of a cumbersome compressor.

He ran out of food 350m short of the summit and went back once again in the summer to finish the job.

It was on a tower of the Grigna that I first saw two women climb together. At that time this was something really unusual. I remember a little crowd gathering at the foot of Nibbio, heads peering up, while the pair ascended a Cassin route! The two girls were Silvia Metzeltin and Maria Antonia (Tona) Sironi. A few years later, Tona married Kurt Diemberger, while Silvia married Gino Buscaini, forming a most admirable life-long climbing partnership.

There were a lot of strong climbers at Piani Resinelli at that time. Gigi Alippi and Annibale Zucchi, who were later to climb McKinley with Cassin, accomplished some fine first ascents and first winter ascents with Romano Merendi and Luciano Tenderini, who were the first Milanese to become mountain guides.

I married Luciano, and we settled in a refuge hut in Switzerland. The city-born couple had made their dream of a life in the mountains come true. We spent 13 years wardening huts in different places in the Alps, from Tessin to the Simplon area. It was a hard life, with long periods of isolation during winter, exhausting work during the summer, much strain, no comforts, little money, and completely apart from the rest of the world. But it was wonderful.

During those years I only had news about the outside world from the visitors to the hut. I learnt that the mountaineering scene was changing, slowly but substantially. The era of aid ascents was fading and even the rush to first winter ascents was slowing down. One after another, the highest mountains in the world were being climbed. In the Mont Blanc area, British and American mountaineers – utter foreigners! – had accomplished incredible ascents.

Bonatti had bid farewell to dedicated climbing with a spectacular first ascent of the north face of the Matterhorn, solo and in winter. Now he had been hired as a reporter by the weekly magazine *Epoca* and travelled all over the world, filing his *photo-reportages* from the remotest and wildest places. Bonatti had been the first mountaineer to gain fame outside the restricted world of mountain lovers. With his articles from the Yukon to the African jungle, he became a national star. He is still the most popular climber in Italy, known by everybody, even by people who do not care a bit for mountains and mountaineers.

Cassin had led a successful expedition to Jirishanca and an ambitious attempt on the south face of Lhotse. Mauri had gone back to Patagonia with younger climbers from Lecco for another failed attempt on Cerro Torre. Finally, in 1974, the *Ragni* were successful on the Torre's west face under the leadership of Casimiro Ferrari. In the meantime new stars were rising in the Italian mountaineering firmament: Alessandro Gogna, Renato Casarotto, Reinhold Messner.

91. Carefree young wardens at the Pairolo hut: Luciano and Mirella Tenderini. (*Tenderini collection*)

When we decided to leave the hut-wardening life, we settled at Piani Resinelli, a convenient place for Luciano to work as a guide with his clients and courses, and a beautiful place for me who did not mind commuting every day to Milan where I went to work in publishing. It was very exciting to be back in town and yet to be able to sup and sleep each night at 1100 metres on the mountainside high above Lecco.

Eventually I started to write for mountain magazines – a way for me to stay in close touch with a world to which I felt I belonged. Paradoxically, Luciano and I had more opportunity to climb together than we ever had when we lived on the heights. We even visited distant mountains. As I also travelled a lot for my main work, I got to know climbers from all over the world and to appreciate better the further evolution and specialisations within mountaineering.

One of the most unexpected things for me was the discovery of rock climbing for its own sake, without necessarily reaching a more or less pointed summit. Hundreds of climbers of my generation – let alone the older ones – had walked for year after year below the stunning granite faces of Val di Mello to reach the peaks in Val Masino, without ever thinking of establishing routes on them. The practice of crag climbing spread very quickly all over Italy, in fact all over continental Europe. Here it was something of a novelty, though it had been the norm in Britain for decades. Soon in its wake came the use of bolts and the introduction of competition climbing.

Certainly Cassin and Bonatti had a newer, less trampled, world at their disposal than contemporary climbers who, lacking higher or more prestigious summits, have turned to records: to do something more difficult, to do it faster, the fourteen 8000ers, the seven summits, and so on. These are all admirable achievements in their way, but they lack the inspiring drive of the search for 'that untravelled world, whose margin fades / for ever and for ever ...'

However, new hard and beautiful routes established by fair means on the peaks of the Himalaya, of Patagonia and of other regions of the world show that the margins for adventure are still there, fading on, for ever and for ever. The quest is not over. I know a couple of fine mountaineers who have climbed dozens of unknown and unnamed peaks in a remote part of the world. They have never publicised or announced their ascents, and that has been going on for several years. They have just built a cairn on each summit. When in the future other climbers reach one of those summits, they can either report that they reached the top and found a cairn, or just kick away the cairn and claim the first ascent for themselves. But there is another solution: they can leave the cairn where it is, and say nothing. The gods will smile on them.

Issues

T H Somervell *Gorge through Himalayas to East of Nanda Kot*
1926. Watercolour
Lakeland Arts Trust

ROBERT MARSHALL

Re-writing the History of K2 ~
a story *all'italiana*

For the past half century there has been a simmering controversy about what happened during the first ascent of K2. In the past two decades a combination of unlikely and quite fortuitous events has allowed the writer (a mere onlooker from the other side of the world) to become involved in untangling the web of deceit that has blighted the life of one of the climbers – Walter Bonatti.

Bonatti was one of the greatest mountaineers of the last century. When only 19 he climbed the north-east face of the Badile, and two years later made his remarkable first ascent of the east face of the Grand Capucin. In 1953, at the age of only 23, he was chosen to take part in the forthcoming Italian expedition to K2. He was the baby of the party.

The expedition, led by Professor Ardito Desio, was a huge project involving 11 climbers and more than 500 porters. The summit was duly reached on 31 July by Achille Compagnoni and Lino Lacedelli. But the price of that success has been 50 years of unresolved argument. The whole affair has become a black joke, or perhaps more accurately a story *all'italiana* – a dark and nasty story, full of tragedy, betrayal and villainy as well as bravery, selflessness and dedication.

In the early 1950s few believed it possible that Everest or K2 could be climbed without the use of supplementary oxygen, and the oxygen used by the summit pair was carried up to camp 9 by Bonatti and Mahdi, a Hunza high-altitude porter. But they did not reach camp 9, and were compelled to bivouac in the open on a steep ice slope. As a result, Mahdi suffered severe frostbite and lost most of his fingers and toes; astonishingly, Bonatti escaped uninjured.

In his autobiography *Le Mie Montagne* in 1961, and more recently in *The Mountains of my Life* (Random House, 2001), Bonatti recounts how the climbing group at camp 8 on 29 July discussed their pre-summit tactics. Bonatti volunteered to go down almost to camp 7 with Pino Gallotti to retrieve the two pack-saddles of oxygen and get them up to camp 8 – then carry them up to camp 9, which Compagnoni and Lacedelli were to set up on the 'shoulder' at a much lower altitude than had been originally planned back in Italy.

Next morning Compagnoni and Lacedelli climbed up to establish camp 9, while Bonatti and Gallotti descended 200 metres, then started back up again with the oxygen, helped now by Erich Abram and the Hunza porter Mahdi, who had come up from camp 7. Gallotti barely managed to reach camp 8 and, just above that level, Abram too had to give up. It was left to Bonatti and Mahdi to carry the oxygen up to camp 9. But when they reached the relatively flat shoulder late in the afternoon there was no sign of the tent. Up and up they went into the gathering dusk until finally, by 9.30pm, it was pitch dark. Bonatti shouted repeatedly and more and more desperately for help. No answer. Finally a light appeared from among the rocks on the other side of the very steep couloir to their left, only a little higher than the point they had reached. It was Lacedelli, who shouted, 'Do you want us to stay out all night to freeze for you? Leave the oxygen there and go down!' 'We can't!' yelled Bonatti. 'I'd be all right, but Mahdi's off his head and couldn't make it.' Silence. The light went out.

In desperation, Walter dug out a shelf where he and Mahdi could sit. They had no protection whatever, but somehow they survived, despite a storm that blew up during the night and buried them in snow three times. Next morning, Mahdi staggered off down the slope as soon as it was light, and Bonatti followed him later after the sun had restored his batteries a little, leaving the bivouac site at exactly 6.30am. He could still see the oxygen bottles on the slope above him at 7am as he crossed the shoulder, and the summit pair still had not appeared.

Desio's official book in 1955 told a very different story. Camp 9 was to be placed 'as high as possible'. Compagnoni and Lacedelli therefore set up camp 9 on the rocky spur beyond the couloir, and Bonatti simply failed to reach it. Because of this, the bivouac site was 'much lower than camp 9', which made communication difficult, and there was a 'misunderstanding', so that Compagnoni and Lacedelli thought Bonatti and Mahdi had gone down. The summit pair left camp 9 at '4 to 4.30am', crossed the couloir, descended to the oxygen bottles, and started up for the top, on oxygen, at about 6.30am. Their oxygen packs ran out simultaneously at 4pm at 8400m, 200m below the summit. The account describes how they felt an 'agonizing feeling of complete suffocation', tore off the oxygen masks, but then climbed on (without discarding the pack-saddles of now empty oxygen bottles) for another two hours. They reached the top just before 6pm, as confirmed by Bonatti, Gallotti and Abram, who could see them on the eastern summit slope from camp 8.

Back in Italy, Compagnoni and Lacedelli were fêted as national heroes who had restored Italian pride after the humiliating end to the war, in particular because they had reached the summit without supplementary oxygen. The time-table of their heroic climb was told and retold to generations of Italian schoolchildren – and indeed still is, 50 years later.

Amazingly, Bonatti's role in the ascent was not even mentioned in the official movie of 1955. He also was ostracised by the mountaineering establishment for no apparent reason and fell into deep depression. In desperation, to 'prove he was not finished', he climbed the south-west face of the Petit Dru solo, via the now famous 'Bonatti Pillar'. Over the following decade he threw himself into climbing extreme routes, often solo, and so became the best known climber in Italy. But he had no idea why he remained *persona non grata* in certain Italian mountaineering circles.

Then in 1964, on the 10th K2 anniversary, Compagnoni told a reporter that Bonatti had tried to race Lacedelli and himself to the summit, had used some of the oxygen to avoid frostbite, and then deserted Mahdi. The whole concoction was published in the *Gazzetta del Popolo* in successive weeks, labelling Bonatti a liar, thief, cheat and coward.

Bonatti started libel proceedings against the newspaper. He felt totally disillusioned, and while the case was pending, in 1965, he gave up climbing after an extraordinary farewell solo ascent of the Matterhorn north face *direttissima* in midwinter. He subsequently became even more famous in Italy as a roving photo-journalist for the magazine *Epoca*.

The libel case in 1966 completely exonerated Bonatti, because Compagnoni and Lacedelli had the oxygen masks at camp 9; Bonatti and Mahdi had no oxygen masks and therefore could not have used any of the oxygen even had they wished. But the court case changed nothing. In 1984, on the 30th anniversary, Compagnoni and Lacedelli were still telling the same story about leaving camp 9 at 4am.

Infuriated, Bonatti wrote *Processo sul K2 (Trial on K2)* – a detailed discussion of the whole affair. He insisted they could not have started for the summit before 8.30am, so the ten-hour oxygen supply *must* have lasted to the summit at 6pm: it was impossible for them to have climbed 300m, using oxygen, in eight hours and then take no more than another two hours for the final 200m, carrying the empty bottles. He also protested against the incorrect site of his bivouac indicated in all the official maps. Bonatti's book contained a full transcript of the 1966 libel case, including an extraordinary deposition made by Mahdi in Pakistan, in which the Hunza porter spontaneously and independently accused Bonatti of trying to race Compagnoni and Lacedelli to the summit. Mahdi also made a large number of other statements that seemed to the Turin tribunal so absurd and contrary to the most elementary common sense that his evidence was judged unacceptable and discarded.

This was when I became involved. I came across *Trial on K2* quite by accident and it dawned on me as soon as I read it that Bonatti had not really understood what had happened on K2. Although Mahdi's evidence had been discarded by the tribunal and by Bonatti himself as nonsensical, I thought it made perfect sense from Mahdi's point of view, and was indeed the key to understanding the whole unsavoury affair.

So I wrote a commentary about the climb and later, somewhat diffidently, sent it to Bonatti. In it, I theorised that Compagnoni envied young Bonatti and was afraid of being upstaged by this parvenu. He purposely held out the bait of a summit attempt to Bonatti without the slightest intention of allowing this to happen. He deliberately put camp 9 completely out of Bonatti's reach and stayed in his tent until well after dark to make this quite certain. Compagnoni presumably *did* think Bonatti and Mahdi had gone down after dumping the oxygen, but was totally indifferent to their fate. Compagnoni and Lacedelli left camp 9 just after 7am, crossed the couloir, retrieved the pack-saddles of oxygen, and started off for the summit at about 8.30am. The oxygen lasted all the way to the top.

Because they did not reach Camp 9 that evening and were on the other side of the couloir on the direct route to the top, Mahdi concluded that Bonatti had been leading him on an unauthorised summit attempt. Back at base camp with gangrenous fingers and toes, he was questioned by the liaison officer, Ata Ullah, and told him Bonatti had tried to race Compagnoni and Lacedelli to the summit. Ata Ullah must have then confronted Desio, who then questioned Compagnoni about Mahdi's accusations.

Compagnoni had a brilliant idea that he believed would increase his own fame, exonerate himself from any possible blame, and utterly destroy Bonatti at the same time. He adjusted the altitude of the bivouac and said he and Lacedelli had left Camp 9 soon after 4am, picked up the oxygen, then started for the summit at about 6am: the oxygen had run out on the way up because Bonatti had used some during the bivouac. He also said Bonatti had deserted Mahdi, thus neatly absolving himself of blame for Mahdi's frostbite. Ten years later, Compagnini told the reporter this same story.

But no one was interested in what I had surmised except, of course, Bonatti himself. Another decade passed; then, just before the fortieth anniversary, while leafing idly through *The Mountain World* for 1955, I came upon Desio's original article about the ascent of K2, illustrated by two summit photographs. I was flabbergasted, because the pictures show Compagnoni standing on the summit still wearing his oxygen mask, while Lacedelli has a circle of rime around his mouth just the shape of a mask. Here at last was objective proof that Bonatti had been telling the truth. So I sent them off to Italy.

When these pictures appeared in the Italian magazine *Alp* there was a furore. The press had a field day. But there was no comment from the Italian Alpine Club (CAI). In an effort to ensure that at least the English-speaking world would know the truth, I embarked on preparing a definitive edition of Bonatti's mountaineering books. *The Mountains of my Life* was published in 2001 and consists of an annotated translation of Bonatti's most significant climbs, together with an exhaustive discussion of the K2 affair. In 2003 Bonatti's most recent book *K2 - the Truth* was published in Italy. However, there was still no response from the CAI, obviously hoping desperately that this unhappy business would fade away if ignored. But in 2004, K2's golden jubilee year, came several new dramatic developments.

First, in February 2004 Roberto Mantovani, the editor of *Rivista delle Montagne (Mountain Review)*, wrote an open letter to the CAI, co-signed by 24 other eminent Italians. They demanded that the club *must* set up an inquiry into the first ascent of K2 so that an official revised version of the climb could be published in time for the 50th anniversary celebrations in

August. The CAI duly appointed three eminent senior authorities, the *tre saggi* (*three wise men*) – professors Fosco Maraini, Alberto Monticone and Luigi Zanzi – to examine the matter.

Their 39-page report was published in April 2004. They decided that the true version of the events of the summit eve was precisely as set out in Walter Bonatti's book *Le Mie Montagne*, and that the version given in Desio's book *La Conquista del K2* was completely misleading. They concluded there had been 'two victories' on K2 in 1954 – the first by Compagnoni and Lacedelli in reaching the summit, the second by Walter Bonatti in performing prodigies by carrying up the oxygen necessary for the summit climb, then surviving an unprecedented bivouac at 8100m. But the report made no mention whatever of Compagnoni's accusations on the 10th anniversary, which had led to the libel case of 1966. As for the contentious issue of the oxygen, they concluded that Compagnoni's story of the supply running out 200m below the summit at 4pm was completely unbelievable. However, they generously conceded that perhaps he had merely become confused about events because of the effects of altitude. Concerning the true site where the bottles became empty, the report wavered back and forth, finally stating that it was 'possible' that the oxygen might have run out 'just below the summit', though certainly not at 8400m. Reading their report, it is difficult to avoid the suspicion that the *tre saggi* had been specifically briefed by the CAI to stick to the events of the summit eve and summit day and avoid any reference at all to Bonatti's court case.

Nevertheless, the report concluded with a very strong recommendation that the CAI should publish immediately a new official history of the Italians on K2 to set the record straight. But there was *still* no reaction from the CAI: for my part I would urge the Alpine Club to use its influence and press the CAI to accept this advice, and publish a revised history.

Second, Lino Lacedelli has now at last published a book, *K2 - il Prezzo di Conquista (the Cost of Victory),* written by a journalist, Giovanni Cenacchi, and based on some long interviews with Lacedelli. In a quite stunning about-face, Lacedelli completely repudiates Compagnoni and totally (or almost totally) confirms Bonatti's version of events. It is difficult not to feel a little sorry for Lacedelli, who emerges as a simple man, embroiled in matters largely beyond his control, who for the most part simply kept his head down and tried to stay out of the firing line. It is obvious that he was terrified of Desio; indeed, he says as much quite specifically and thought he would be 'destroyed' if he as much as opened his mouth. Nevertheless, it is impossible to condone the fact that he has said nothing for 50 years when he could have cleared Bonatti's name at any time with the greatest of ease, and has only chosen to speak out now that Desio is dead. (He died in 2003 at the age of 104.) Lacedelli says that Desio was incompetent and authoritarian, hated by all the climbers except Compagnoni, and that even on the approach march the team was on the verge of 'mutiny'.

Lacedelli notes that back in Italy there were no fewer than four court cases as a result of the expedition; Compagnoni sued the CAI for compensation for his frostbitten fingers as a result of taking photographs on the summit; the CAI sued Desio in an attempt to recover several million lire missing from the expedition coffers; Desio sued the expedition photographer, Mario Fantin, over some missing film (which had in fact been taken quite legitimately by one of his own scientists); and of course Bonatti sued the *Gazzetta del Popolo*.

Lacedelli is absolutely scathing about Compagnoni, insisting he should never have been appointed head climber. He was a complete sycophant who toadied to Desio at all times. He describes giving Compagnoni his own left glove on the summit when one of Compagnoni's blew away and his fingers were going white, but never receiving the slightest thanks; his fury when Compagnoni told a reporter soon after their return to Italy that he had 'pulled the totally exhausted Lacedelli up to the summit'. He confesses that the story of the climb in the official account was based solely on Compagnoni's diary and that he, Lacedelli, had signed it even though he knew it was inaccurate; he wished only to avoid controversy.

Concerning the summit eve and summit day, Lacedelli confirms that Bonatti's version of events is correct in almost every respect. He agrees that camp 9 was supposed to be placed 'as low as possible' – that is, on the shoulder at 7950m – to enable Bonatti to reach it with the oxygen. He says Compagnoni insisted on putting it higher, against his (Lacedelli's) wishes, and that Compagnoni then also insisted on crossing the couloir to place camp 9 in what Lacedelli describes as a 'most dangerous and stupid position'. He agrees with Bonatti that the bivouac was just across the couloir from camp 9 and almost at the same altitude and states that Compagnoni told him quite explicitly at camp 9 that he did *not* want Bonatti there and that 'nobody but the two of them were going to attempt the summit next day'. Lacedelli believes that Compagnoni was afraid Bonatti would be fitter than he was, and might replace him in the summit attempt next morning. He says that Compagnoni wouldn't leave the camp 9 tent to speak to Bonatti that night and sent him out instead.

Lacedelli denies they left camp 9 next morning at '4 to 4.30am' and ventures that their departure was perhaps at about 6am, though he admits this is only an estimate because he did not look at his watch all day. To support this statement, Lacedelli's book contains a photograph taken by Compagnoni, which shows Lacedelli sitting outside the camp 9 tent putting on his crampons in broad daylight – so it was certainly taken well after dawn and definitively contradicts Compagnoni's statement about the time they left.

Lacedelli agrees they took an hour and a half to reach the oxygen bottles at the bivouac site, and insists they left for the summit at 'about 7.30am', though this too is merely 'an estimate' because again he did not look at his watch. According to Lacedelli the oxygen *did* run out on the way up, though certainly not at 8400m as Compagnoni has always insisted. He himself puts the site of exhaustion of the oxygen at about 60m below the summit 'just before we reached the top at ten to six', the only time he did look at his watch – and this time is of course verified by Bonatti, Gallotti and Abram, who could see the eastern summit slope from camp 8.

Lacedelli refers repeatedly to my commentary throughout his book, and agrees that all its conclusions are completely correct – except about the oxygen. He speculates that perhaps the oxygen supply may have been exhausted early because they had been 'breathing too hard on the way up'. Concerning the summit photographs in *The Mountain World*, he insists that once they had reached the summit Compagnoni replaced the mask on his face for five minutes merely to 'protect his lungs from the cold'. (But surely this alleged hasty replacement of the mask would imply that the straps of Compagnoni's face mask should be visible outside his cap in the summit photograph? Why would he first take off his fur cap, settle the straps comfortably around his ears, then replace the cap over the straps?)

He agrees there was a plot hatched after the event between Desio and Compagnoni to discredit Bonatti, and that Bonatti was indeed made a 'sacrificial goat'. Lacedelli states, in conclusion, that Bonatti was a completely honourable man and under no circumstances would have contemplated using the summit oxygen even had he been able to do so – but in any event he also confirms that Bonatti and Mahdi had no masks.

Lacedelli's co-author Cenacchi insists that the story of the oxygen lasting to the summit must be accepted and asks: 'Why would he lie about such a relatively minor matter of a few minutes?' The answer to this question seems all too obvious: Lacedelli wishes to preserve at least some scraps of his own integrity and heroic reputation.

Compagnoni responded vigorously to these revelations. In a full-page interview by Aldo Cazzullo published in *Corriere della Sera (The Evening Courier)* on 9 August 2004 he flatly denied all the allegations in Lacedelli's book. He heaped scorn on his former climbing partner — and on everyone else. He asks '...Have the tre saggi ever even *seen* K2?' [*Maraini photographed it in 1958 – Ed*] Concerning the events of the summit eve Compagnoni says '...Bonatti didn't make any effort to be punctual. Our appointment (at camp 9) was for 3.30pm, and at that time he was still in the tent, or perhaps he had only just left camp 8.' He insists that '...we started at six in the morning – seven at the latest.' The only point on which he and Lacedelli still agree is that '...it isn't true that we arrived on the summit breathing oxygen. The bottles were empty.'

Third, late last year Bonatti sent me a copy of a letter he had just received from Erich Abram, the engineer who was in charge of the oxygen bottles on K2. Heaven knows why Abram has remained silent for the past 50 years, but he has now volunteered some staggering news about the oxygen bottles. He first makes clear that the rate of supply was completely invariable because the control tap was a simple on-off affair, unlike modern bottles with which the rate of flow can be varied. Heavier breathing would merely increase the proportion of outside air drawn in. The fact that the two pack-saddles became exhausted simultaneously (according to both summit climbers) speaks volumes for the Germanic precision with which they functioned and indicates that they were indeed full.

But the real bombshell is Abram's news that there were two different types of bottle on K2. Most were made in Italy, were destined for use at the lower camps, and were indeed scheduled to last for 10 hours – but those intended for the higher camps were German Dräger bottles filled at a higher pressure, which supplied oxygen for 12 hours! So, even if one were to accept Lacedelli's story that they left the bivouac site at 7.30am, there would still be one and a half hours of oxygen supply remaining when they reached the top.

There has now been one more unhappy development in this saga. Just before Christmas 2004, Walter Bonatti was invited by the President of Italy to attend the Quirinale Palace to be awarded the Grand Cross of the Knights of Italy, the highest Italian civilian honour. He was surprised and delighted. However, on arriving at the palace he found himself face to face with Compagnoni who was to be presented with the same honour. (Lacedelli, after the publication of his scurrilous book, was not invited.) Bonatti was outraged, but held his peace out of respect for the office of the President. Next day, however, he sent the medal back to the palace with an icy note to explain why he was rejecting it.

Honours of this sort are awarded on the recommendation of others, not as a personal Presidential initiative. One can only conclude that the gesture was a CAI initiative in response to the report of the *tre saggi* and its conclusion that the club should recognise 'two victories' on K2. Presumably the committee members thought Bonatti would be satisfied at last and cease his embarrassing efforts to discredit the official history of the ascent. If so, they were sadly mistaken. Bonatti has said many times that, in the end, '...the official record is the *only* thing that counts'.

The Editor would like to acknowledge the part of Terry Gifford in securing this article for the AJ, as Terry gave Bob Marshall a platform to air this controversy at the International Festival of Mountaineering Literature at Bretton Hall in April 2005.

SKIP NOVAK

Breaking the Ice

The Israeli-Palestinian Friendship Mountain

There have been many initiatives to promote understanding between the Israelis and the Palestinians, orchestras and soccer matches among them, but the idea of climbing a virgin summit in the Antarctic must be among the most bizarre. 'Breaking the Ice' was conceived as a flagship for a recently created foundation in Germany called Extreme Peace Missions. The idea was to make a spectacular media success of 'an extreme peace mission' in order to raise capital to fund adventure sports projects between young Israelis and Palestinians. The intended message was that Palestinians and Israelis could work for a common goal on an individual basis, politics aside, although the political differences would not be ignored by design. A high-risk project indeed, especially after it secured the endorsements of Kofi Annan, Shimon Peres, Yassar Arafat, the Dalai Lama, Mikhail Gorbachev, the German Parliament, the European Parliament et al.

The architect of the concept was Heskel 'Hezi' Nathaniel, an Israeli businessman living in Berlin. His friend and mountain hero Doron Erel, Israel's answer to Chris Bonington, Robin Knox Johnston and Ranulph Fiennes all rolled into one, was chosen as team leader. Climbing Everest and the 'seven summits' may not raise eyebrows anymore in extreme sports circles, let alone among the general public, but Doron's film making, lecturing and writing about his adventures in remote areas provides a much needed distraction from the daily dose of death and violence in Israel and the occupied territories. His exploits as a young commando in an elite unit are less well publicized.

The initial idea was to take a joint team to a peak somewhere in the Himalaya or elsewhere in the high mountains of Asia. However, Hezi and Doron realized that wherever they went the host country would put a political spin on the project. The solution lay in choosing a neutral territory and nowhere better fits that description than Antarctica. That's where I came in. Among our shared adventures as friends, Doron and I had sailed and climbed together in 1994 in the Antarctic, using my expedition sailing vessel, *Pelagic*, a veteran of 15-years of logistical support operations, based in Puerto Williams on the Beagle Channel.

In December 2000 we spent some time with Doron in Israel while my wife, a news coordinator with the European Broadcasting Union, was working on the millennium story from Bethlehem. I remarked what a quiet period it was in the conflict. Doron was visibly nervous and constantly looking over his shoulder while giving us a tour of old Jerusalem. 'It won't last. I'm very pessimistic,' he said. But like many people on both sides of the conflict, despite their pessimism, when an opportunity arises they do what they can. Doron, whose responsibility it was to select the team of four Israelis and four Palestinians, almost bit off more than he could chew.

After eight months of planning, including a press conference in Berlin in July 2002 to whet the media appetite, we set sail from Puerto Williams in Chile near Cape Horn on 1 January. My new vessel *Pelagic Australis* carried the eight team members plus boat crew, cameraman, editor and satellite technician. My old boat was seconded in to ferry the 'extras' in this entourage of mountain cameraman/Chamonix mountain guide, journalist, doctor and a camp manager. Between the two boats there were 21 people. Unlike so many 'expeditions' that have felt hijacked by the media and their purpose lost in the telling, in our case it was understood by all from the beginning that the telling was in fact the only purpose.

In order to enhance this, the team was not a youth squad but people with a history – history of the tragic kind, which is not hard to find in the Middle East. In the Palestinian contingent we had Sulemain Al-Khatib (32). In the 1987 Intifada, at the age of 14 he knifed someone in the street and lost his youth in an Israeli jail where he spent the next 10 years as a political prisoner. He is now head of Al Fatah in his village of Hismeh in the West Bank. Nasser Gous (38) is number two in Al Fatah in Jerusalem. He spent three years in jail for throwing a Molotov cocktail in the same Intifada. Ziad Darwish, at 52, was our elder Palestinian spokesman, a journalist and fixer for foreign news teams. Among other things he was close to Arafat and it was he who managed to secure Arafat's approval of the project (without which the Palestinian team probably would not have showed up at all) and Arafat's signature on the joint venture flag that was to be flown at the summit. None of these three looked like adventure types, but Olfat Haider was the exception. Lean and mean at 33 years old, Olfat is a distractingly attractive Israeli Arab who teaches sport in Haifa and is admittedly non political. She was the only Israeli Arab to represent Israel in a national volleyball team.

'You would not believe how hard it was to find the people on the Palestinian side,' Doron explained to me as the swell in the Drake Passage kicked in and before he along with most of the others got deathly seasick. 'First of all, it sometimes takes week to get permission to meet some of the people who are candidates. Then it may take weeks for them to get a pass to enter Israel to have another meeting.' Maybe it should have been obvious, but it quickly became evident that Palestinian mountain climbers, sailors or adventurers are almost non-existent. A doctor was originally on the team but after pressure from 'associates', which included death threats to himself and his family, he finally threw in the towel when someone in his family hid his passport two days before a training week for the group in Chamonix in early November.

3. *Pelagic Australis* was chosen as a base in Antarctica from which a joint Israeli-Palestinian team would attempt a virgin summit as a symbol of co-operation. She carried the eight team members plus boat crew, cameraman, editor and satellite technician. (*Skip Novak*)

4. The old expedition sailing vessel *Pelagic*, a veteran of 15-years' support operations, ferried the 'extras': mountain cameraman/Chamonix mountain guide, journalist, doctor and camp manager. (*Skip Novak*)

95. The Israeli-Palestinian team on board *Pelagic Australis*. (*Skip Novak*)

The Israeli team was not at all problematic. In addition to Doron and Hezi were Avihou Shoshoni (44) and Yarden Fanta (27). Avihou, an articulate civil litigation lawyer from Tel Aviv, had been in the same commando unit as Doron, bonding their friendship. He has acted for the state of Israel in many disputes during the last two Intifadas and it is therefore no surprise he is right wing. Yarden migrated from Ethiopia at the age of 13 with Operation Moses in 1989 and lost five family members on the year-long walk and through the rigours of the refugee camp in the Sudan. She is now working through her PhD, studying the minds of illiterate people with a view to developing technological solutions.

The Drake crossing was relatively mild, but bumpy enough to put a fear into the team of the return journey three weeks later. Our first landfall in Antarctica, at Deception Island, gave the team the chance of a run ashore. This was an enlightening experience, as the walk across a small mountain to the Chinstrap penguin colony on the opposite coast finished in a full-blown Antarctic snowstorm. It was clear that some in the group had struggled on a trek no more than a refreshing day out for a tourist hiker in the Alps. Back on board they all took stock of the situation. The original plan touted in the media was for the team, after having battled the Drake Passage and the pack ice of the Antarctic Peninsula, to spend three-to-four days trekking to the chosen mountain, climb it and return – an ambitious outing given the nature of the place. There would be no rescue here except self-rescue.

As we threaded our way between the diamond-studded icebergs of the Gerlache Straits, the main inner passage in the central section of the Peninsula, Hezi was constantly on the phone to Germany, Doron to Israel and Ziad to Ramalla, massaging their media contacts. There were financial black clouds on the pristine Antarctic horizon, as the cash sponsorship that was to have paid not only for this project, but also towards the foundation for the young people, had not materialized. With the media plan well in hand, including daily news feeds via satellite, everyone involved expected the money if not to fall out of the sky like rain, at least to flow easily from a tap. It was not to be. 'Too risky', 'too political', 'What if the team breaks down?' were typical responses. Reprisals from extremists in the 'peace process rejection front' were not beyond possibility. Even Lan Chile, when approached about sponsoring air tickets, refused because of a perceived likelihood of passengers cancelling when they discovered that Israelis and Palestinians were on the same plane. 'Everyone talks about solving the conflict, but we got almost no support except equipment and clothing. It was a shocking revelation. So Hezi and I wound up paying for it all,' admitted Doron.

En route the team had been working surprisingly well together. They cooked together, helped sail the boat and cleaned house together. Avihou even helped Nasser fix the head (the toilet) when it jammed. They joked about their different cultures, language and habits, but when asked by the film team to 'engage' in a serious discussion about the political background, the fangs inevitably came out. Avihou and Nasser would lock horns for hours on the subject of Jerusalem accusing each other of fundamental ignorance on the religious history of the Temple Mount and the Dome of the Rock. Although this demonstrated that a dialogue could take place without killing each other, and maybe the Antarctic had a pacifying effect, it was clear that lines were drawn in the sand. And that in turn demonstrated the whole problem in the Middle East where any compromise is a clear signal of weakness and eventual defeat.

Last year's sea ice was still fast to the shore in some places in Crystal Sound, near the Antarctic Circle. It was my intention to get us in to land at Prospect Point, a good place to disembark with an easy glacier to ascend and several unnamed peaks at its head. After a day of tricky navigation skirting the sea ice and pushing our way through the brash ice, we off-loaded 16 people and 400kg of equipment and the pilgrimage to the mountain began. Threading our way through the crevasses and seracs, pulling sleds and carrying heavy packs was slow work. But the team, now with the climbing rope between them for 'encouragement', somehow gelled and moved together like an amateur army.

Camp 1 was on the middle of the glacier and Camp 2 below the base of our mountain. Doron was now more relaxed as he and the team had overcome so many obstacles to get this far. So many things could have gone wrong: the politics, the lack of money, the sea voyage and its possible

96. The Israeli-Palestinian Friendship Mountain, 882m, climbed in January 2003 as a symbol of co-operation. (*Skip Novak*)

97. The support team. (*Skip Novak*)

vagaries, and the ability of the team itself to cope with such an ambitious undertaking. But now we had reached a stage where only the weather could throw a serious spanner in the works.

Until now, Allah and God had blessed us with perfect conditions for the preparation and the trek up the glacier. Optimism for mountaineering soars on a windless sunny day and in the Antarctic it is no exception. The air is crystal clear and all things are pure. But 14 January, the day of the climb, dawned snowy and the sky was closed. Getting breakfast and getting a move on was a solemn affair. The harder route on the face above the camp was voted down by the Chamonix guide Denis Ducroz and we opted for a safer traverse of the summit ridge above a col further up the glacier. It was a procession in a white out – all tied together and the symbolism could have not been stronger.

Four hours later, after a few technical manœuvres, the team of eight, with the media on their heals, topped out at 882 metres above sea level. Hezi made a speech to camera and named the mountain 'The Israeli-Palestinian Friendship Mountain' which had been jointly agreed. Hugs and kisses were offered and received all around and then Ziad, Nasser and Sulemain went down on their knees and prayed to Allah. The expedition's peace flag was broken out, but Arafat's signature at the bottom was enough for Avihou to refuse to stand together with the team for the group photos. This was an unpleasant surprise and a bit of a dark moment on the summit, but it underpinned the reality back home.

The goals of the project had been achieved in relative calm, so much so that the television news pickup was weak. They were expecting a disaster or two and none came. Good news is no news especially in the Antarctic, but life and the bad news goes on as usual in Israel, in the occupied territories and on your TV screen.

Summary In January 2003 a team of four Israelis and four Palestinians climbed a virgin summit in Antarctica as a symbol of co-operation. They named the peak 'The Israeli-Palestinian Friendship Mountain'. For more information on the expedition go to www.breaking-the-ice.de

BEN AYERS

Five Sheets to the Wind

A Foreigner's Place in the Himalaya

We don't start drinking *chang* until noon. The ancient stone and mud house is warm and cluttered with raisin-faced old women and chanting monks. Smoke from the open fireplace sifts up through the blackened rafters and out of gaps in the eaves. The dusty glass in front of me is filled with an alarming frequency by the clutch of women with an endless pitcher of the warmed millet brew. There is a chair in the corner of the crowded room that appears to be constructed of salvaged airplane parts. Outside, the late spring clouds gather and gossip against the Himalaya.

It is time to bring the monsoon rains to Chaurikharka. The fields of this remote Nepali hamlet are already choking with ankle-high potato plants desperate for rain. At an altitude of 3500 metres, potatoes and wheat are the only major crops that can survive the unpredictable mountain weather. It is our job on this auspicious day to praise and placate the deities that will exchange the merciless spring hailstorms for nourishing summer rains.

I have called Chaurikharka my home for the past four years, after founding a local NGO called Porters' Progress. We advocate for safe working conditions and basic human rights for the migrant workers who carry loads for trekking and climbing expeditions in the Everest region. I first came to the Khumbu valley with a handful of dreams and a gut filled with fury. I was determined to end the gross exploitation and abuses that trekking and expedition porters face while working for foreign clients on the trails that wind up to base camp. Every season since I started coming to Nepal, I have seen porters die from preventable altitude sickness while foreign trekkers get whisked to safety on rescue helicopters at the slightest provocation. I have also seen thousands of porters shoulder loads of 60kg or more, and set off for altitudes exceeding 5000m wearing little more than sandals and thin cotton trousers.

Few people in Chaurikharka work as porters anymore. Due to family connections and a genetic inclination for strength at altitude, most ethnic Sherpas have access to higher paying jobs fixing ropes and ferrying loads high above base camp. Some of those who choose not to climb run luxurious teahouses for trekkers or work as well paid guides and expedition leaders. A staggering number of men from Chaurikharka have traded in the wood smoke and snow-clad summits of home for the sidewalks and canned beer of any western country that will grant them passage. As I sit contemplating the tsampa flour balanced in blessing on the edge of my glass of *chang*, (said to symbolise a mountain, and the milky liquid underneath a glacial pond), at least a dozen men from Chaurikharka are hard at work somewhere high on Everest setting camps and fixing ropes for paying western climbers.

This year is no different to previous years at this time. Trekking and climbing are in high season, and there aren't enough men remaining in the village properly to carry out the Chhirim Lapsang ceremony. It came as no surprise when the village elders commissioned me to carry one of the sacred flags in this year's procession. Two years ago I carried one of the sacred books. Being given no real choice in the matter, I joined the festival with true Sherpa zeal and watched the afternoon dissolve under an avalanche of *chang*.

Chaurikharka is a 20-minute walk from the bustling airstrip in Lukla, starting point for the Everest Base Camp trekking route. Despite its proximity to the tens of thousands of intrepid trekkers that pass along the trail each year, Chaurikharka village has somehow managed to avoid the creeping westernisation that follows adventure-based tourism like a lost dog. The residents here are mostly ethnic Sherpas who for decades have reaped the economic benefits of the world's infatuation with Everest while still managing to preserve their traditional culture and community. As with all human ideals, however, this too is beginning to slip.

Today's Chhirim Lapsang festival is a cornerstone of the Sherpa community and their Tibetan Buddhist tradition. The entire town comes out to worship and appease the local deities – many of them incarnated as the toothy Himalayan peaks that encircle the village. The festival itself is something between midnight mass and a keg party.

For us lay people, the true fuel of dharma – *chang* – is kept in old blue plastic expedition drums. Great care is taken to keep the local brew pure and clean, as any spoilage or failure to ferment is seen as a bad omen. During the ceremony, *chang* is consumed with the great devotion and hyper-generosity of Sherpa culture. Once a glass is poured it must be refilled by the host at least twice. One's standing as a guest is directly linked to how much one drinks between refills. Things get hazy quickly.

While the slow ballet of consumption is going on in the open room of the house, a chorus of monks in the small adjacent shrine blesses the religious icons and sacred texts that have been removed from the local monastery for the occasion. Only when this is completed can we begin to parade the icons and books along the narrow footpaths that circumnavigate the town, stopping to perform ceremonies at all four cardinal points and blessing the village residents along the way.

Borne on thick clouds, the afternoon crawls up the valley. By the time we begin the procession there is dense blanket overhead. The novice monks set out first, blowing a set of seven-foot-long brass horns, followed by older monks with shorter horns, and then still more monks with drums and cymbals. We sound like an opera of geese as we venture into the grey Himalayan afternoon.

I am leading the group of flag bearers. We each carry one of five primary colours lashed to a bamboo pole that constantly snags the low-hanging trees and thorn bushes. Blue, white, red, green, yellow: each flag represents the five elements of sky, snow, fire, vegetation, and earth. They also stand for the five sacred syllables, *om mane pad me hum*, meaning '*blessed be Lord Buddha, the jewel of the lotus.*' The flags dance and flap like Tibetan dragons in the chill wind, each twist releasing karma, prayers, and our devotions into the mountain ether in which all gods reside. The gods, in turn, keep the rain and hail tucked safely within the darkening clouds as our makeshift jamboree swerves and clatters across the potato fields. The cold spring breeze sweeps steady now, like a prayer across the flags to which, thanks to the *chang*, we cling for support.

The premise of our expedition seems simple enough – to walk once around the village. However, every house we come to refuses to let us pass without a glass of *chang* and the requisite refills. The blessing of the Eastern and Southern corners pass without event. We stop at each and place our offerings of rice, wheat, coins, and small idols made from wheat flour onto small boulders. At each corner, the head monk plants a handkerchief-sized white flag illustrated with mantras into the ground, says a few prayers, and our parade ambles on. Eventually, we encounter a high stone wall across our path. Helping the elderly members of our expedition over is an orgy of shoulders and mis-steps. The *chang*, it seems, has temporarily robbed these Sherpas of their famed climbing ability. Once this obstacle is overcome, we celebrate our achievement with more *chang* poured out of a container that once held motor oil. As we pass the Western corner and head north, our team begins to fracture.

Two years ago, as we reached the Northern corner during the same ceremony, I was in a similar state of disrepair. The sky was heavy with clouds and freezing winds, and the head monk wrapped his shawl around himself as he read the final mantras. The gods, it seemed, were somehow watching us – at the very instant that the final white flag was planted into the ground, a wall of hail thundered across the valley and overtook us. It was one of the most violent storms I have ever encountered. The hail covered the ground with three inches of icy marbles and left welts on our shoulders, arms, and necks as we fled. It was like hell trapped in a snow-globe.

Later that evening, as the entire town nursed their wounds with more *chang*, I sought forgiveness from the monks. I was convinced that having a *bideshi* – a foreigner, a non-Buddhist – carry a sacred object had upset the gods and severely damaged the crops. Yet as I bowed my head in humility and prostrated myself before the monks, the room erupted in laughter at my foolish assumption. Everyone knew that the hail had been summoned up by an elderly local man appointed to carry the most important object in the village – a sacred book written in golden ink. Halfway through the procession, for reasons not altogether mysterious, he had lost his way and

decided to recover his bearings over a few glasses of *chang* at home. He was found there, asleep, long after the ceremony had finished and the hail had ceased.

This year, the ceremony ends without event. We plant the final white flag and return to the old house to join arms and dance through the night. The dance is another foreign language to me – all shuffling and stomping without any apparent regard to metre or pattern – and as I stagger through the motions, the clouds clear outside and Chaurikharka falls asleep under a sheet of stars and moonlight across the high summits. A few days later, the fields are soaked with deep and steady rains. The potato plants grow greener and the sky seems a touch more blue.

Our world simultaneously shrinks and expands like a storm cloud, throwing people and cultures together with dangerous and beautiful abandon. Culture and life, like weather, can never be static. They are unpredictable and fluid like shadows in a sunrise. This fact would be well carried as a mantra for all those who travel to, and seek to help, cultures separate from their own. By approaching impoverished communities with humility and with our hats in our hands, we give ourselves the opportunity to discover gratitude, and the strength and capability that exists alongside the very hunger and desperation that we wish to change.

A great many development projects tragically underestimate the populations they intend to assist. This fact is aggravated by the linguistic, cultural, and logistic barriers that loom, sometimes on a Himalayan scale, between those who provide help and those who receive it. One area of interest to the climbing communities, worthy of examination, is the recent enthusiasm for constructing porter shelters along the trekking routes in Nepal. At first glance, the idea is a sound means of providing life-saving shelter and warmth to porters who are routinely denied such by unscrupulous trekking companies. Shelters can also, if managed correctly, help reduce deforestation caused by porters seeking cover and warmth in local caves. Many of the shelters that have been constructed to date, however, have been built with little regard for long-term management and local investment

98. *Left*

Porter Ganesh Nepali on the trail from Namche to Machermo. The blue trunk will become a locker for medicines at a porter shelter being built at Machermo by Community Action Nepal in conjunction with the International Porter Protection Group. (Medical supplies are prone to pillaging by rats unless stored in tin.) While Ben Ayers is critical of porter shelters as maintaining segregation between porters and trekkers or climbers, Ganesh took a more pragmatic approach and welcomed the idea of any kind of roof over his head at Machermo. For years, porters arriving at this trekker hamlet in the Khumbu have had to make do with curling up for the night in the lee of a large boulder, a miserable prospect at 4500m in sub-zero temperatures. Some have not survived.

(*Stephen Goodwin*)

in the project. Moreover, shelters are typically located on inexpensive land and set apart from the lodges that house trekkers and guides. The result is a form of segregation that, in effect, both justifies and encourages the denial of shelter for porters by local lodge owners and the provision of tents on camping treks. This, in turn, could distance porters from access to life-saving medicine and rescue should a porter contract altitude sickness in the night, and enforces a potentially fatal distance between sick porters and their oft-compassionate clients. In essence, porter shelters may actually aggravate the very problems that they intend to solve.

There are numerous examples of projects such as these that have unforeseen consequences. True and durable solutions can be as elusive and mysterious as the yeti. Solutions to the crisis of shelter that porters face at altitude must continue to be pursued, but greater attention should be given to their social ramifications. One option may be to favour subsidised construction of dormitory rooms for porters as additions to already established lodges. Constructing these buildings will be less expensive than separate shelters and allow for management of firewood and natural resources; the implementation of a nominal charge system to be paid by trekking groups per porter will ensure their sustainability.

Navigating other cultures is not an easy task. Sometimes we bring rainbows, and other times we bring hail. The key is time, patience, asking the right questions and, most importantly, listening to the answers. Our survival and success as a species depends upon our diversity as a whole and upon our capability and compassion as individuals. Be this the strength and endurance of porters; be this the tranquillity and wisdom of a monk; be this something as simple as some tall westerner with a belly full of *chang* and a sky-blue flag rattling madly in the spring wind.

To learn more about the plight of Nepali mountain porters, and how you can contribute to their welfare, please visit the website of Porters' Progress at www.portersprogress.org

Art & Literature

T H Somervell *Tinki Dzong*
1922. Watercolour
Lakeland Arts Trust

DAVID SEDDON

'Something the Artist Wishes to Say'

T H Somervell 1890-1975

Theodore Howard Somervell has a record of achievement extending beyond his mountaineering exploits that has hitherto been only partly appreciated. First and foremost, he was a family man and a man of profound Christian belief who devoted his professional life to the health of the people of southern India. In 1922 and 1924 he climbed high on Everest without supplementary oxygen. He was President of the Fell and Rock Climbing Club (1954-56) and President of the Alpine Club (1962-65). He was a musician and an author, and as recent exhibitions and picture cards testify, he was also an accomplished artist. Yet even those aware of Somervell's output think of him as a painter of only Himalayan scenes. This study seeks to cast more light on the man and his artistic *œuvre*.

Surgeon

After Rugby, Somervell went to Caius College, Cambridge, graduating with a double first in Natural Sciences in 1912. He completed his studies at University College Hospital. Although he considered enlisting in 1914, he was advised to qualify first. The Army List records that he was commissioned as a Captain in the Territorial Army in November 1915. He was within a few miles of the front line as the battle of the Somme began on July 1916 (but managed to fit in some climbing near Marseilles when on leave later that year[1]) and was also very near the front at the time of the final German offensive in March 1918. On one occasion he operated almost continuously for 70 hours and this immense experience in wartime surgery would serve him well throughout his professional life. He completed his training in Liverpool and Leeds and was awarded Fellowship of the Royal College of Surgeons in 1920.

After the 1922 Everest expedition, with £60 in his pocket, Somervell travelled through India and eventually arrived at the town of Neyyoor in Travancore. He had arranged to meet Dr S H Pugh, a surgeon at Neyyoor Hospital whom he had met in England, and while there took on some of Pugh's workload. Somervell's life was to change forthwith. Hitherto his ambition had been to secure an appointment as a consultant surgeon, and on his return to Britain he was offered such an appointment at University College Hospital, London. Yet he turned his back on everything this could offer to accept a post as Medical Missionary at Neyyoor for the London Missionary Society and sailed for India on 3 October 1923.[2] A few young doctors today might spend some months or a year in such a post before returning to practise in the United Kingdom. To devote one's entire professional life in such a way is a remarkable demonstration of Somervell's humanity.

His life and work at Neyyoor and elsewhere in southern India is described in three books, *After Everest* (London, 1936), *India Calling* (London 1947) and *Knife and Life in India* (London 1941). Suffice to say, he was not just a general surgeon. He was orthopaedic surgeon, anaesthetist, obstetrician and physician as well, managing epidemics of cholera and malaria. He purchased X-ray equipment that was the only such equipment available to many millions of people in southern India and became particularly skilled in the surgical management of duodenal ulcer, writing a book and several papers on the subject. He even had an operation for duodenal ulcer named after him, though it is no longer performed. He also wrote papers on subjects as diverse as trench foot, the surgical management of tuberculosis and cancer of the mouth and jaw. During the 1924 expedition he attempted to measure oxygen and carbon dioxide from the lungs of the climbers at various altitudes.

In July 1935, Somervell took leave for one year and returned to Britain. During that year he completed *After Everest* and climbed in the Tatras with his brother and Bentley Beetham.[3] He exhibited at the Lake Artists Society and at the Alpine Club in 1936.

From 1948 to1953 he was Professor of Surgery at the Christian Medical College at Vellore, southern India, some of the staff from Neyyoor moving with him. At Vellore he founded a climbing club for the medical students, who usually climbed barefoot.[4] Somervell retired to the Lake District but returned to India for two short periods of service in 1955-56 and 1961.

Mountaineer

Somervell's record in the Alps and on Everest is well documented. After his first summer season in 1913 he returned to the Alps in 1920 and with various companions, including Bentley Beetham and JHB Bell, climbed the Aiguilles des Grands Charmoz, Aiguille du Midi and Dent Blanche and traversed the Matterhorn and Zinalrothorn before moving on to the Dauphiné.[5, 6] Despite this not unreasonable tally of peaks, his application to join the 1921 Everest expedition was turned down.

He had been a member of the Fell and Rock since 1915 and in February 1921 was elected to the Alpine Club. Amongst his supporters was Noel Odell. In June 1920 he became the first person to traverse the Cuillin of Skye from Sligachan to Glen Brittle solo. The Alpine routes of his 1921 season included the Aiguille du Géant, the Grépon and traverses of the Weissmies and Portjengrat, Mont Blanc, Dom-Täschhorn and others. He was working at University College Hospital in London when he heard that he had been invited to join the 1922 Everest expedition. He would have to travel to Darjeeling at his own expense but, once there, all further costs would be met by the expedition committee. He was 'transported with joy' at this news and responded that as his salary was £150 a year he would be quite happy to comply with this requirement and might even be able to support himself further by selling paintings of the expedition.

In *After Everest* he gives his own account of the avalanche on 7 June that killed seven porters and ended the expedition's third attempt on the summit. With Mallory and Norton, he had already taken part in the first summit attempt and on 21 May reached almost 27,000ft without supplementary oxygen. Mallory had already written an account of the accident for Bruce's *The Assault on Everest:1922* (London 1923) but Somervell, writing more than 10 years later, makes a number of important observations. He records that the initial walk of half a mile from Camp III to the foot of the slopes leading to the North Col took two hours through '...snow of a most unpleasant texture...' but higher up the '...snow trod firmer... we were gaining height more rapidly than we thought the condition of the snow would allow...' This firmer snow was almost certainly windslab. After light wind it may feel like powder snow, but after strong winds the original snow crystals have been so fragmented and packed down so densely that the edge of a boot may barely grip. Mallory described '...unremitting snowfall ...' and '...fine glistening particles driven by the wind through our (tent) walls...' on the nights of 3 and 4 June.

Once on the initial slopes below the North Col, Mallory, Somervell and Crawford excavated trenches to see if they could trigger an avalanche. They could not and feeling secure they began with one porter to climb up towards the North Col. The angle of the slope began to ease and with the firm surface underfoot their spirits rose. Somervell was leading and had reached about 600ft beneath the North Col when '...with a subdued report ominous in the softness of its violence, a crack suddenly appeared about 20 feet above me. The snow on which I was standing began to move, slowly at first, and then faster.' Somervell and his rope were lucky. They were able to extricate themselves. The 13 porters below were less fortunate. The avalanche swept them over an ice cliff and seven were killed.

The weight of the first rope of four men had not been enough to trigger the avalanche but once the whole party was on the slope the combined weight of 17 men and equipment was. Ruttledge was later to write that the avalanche had occurred because the snow slopes beneath the North Col had been softened by the warm winds of the monsoon.[7] This was not a wet snow avalanche. Somervell had seen the fracture line of a slab avalanche.

Somervell and Crawford left the expedition a few days before its departure from Rongbuk to explore the valleys and mountains to the north of Kangchenjunga. Despite the arrival of the monsoon they were able to climb five peaks of more than 18,000ft before crossing the Lhonak La and returning to Kalimpong.[8] Once at Darjeeling Somervell set off on his journey to Neyyoor.

In 1923, with his brother, Beetham, Frank Smythe and others, he climbed the Weisshorn by the Schalligrat, the Ober Gabelhorn, Jungfrau, Wetterhorn and Schreckhorn, and traversed the Bietschhorn. Somervell's party also traversed the Eiger from Scheidegg carrying the provisional oxygen equipment destined for use on Everest the following year. He submitted a report critical of the weight and awkwardness of the apparatus to the Mount Everest Committee.[9] The account of his Alpine season was written while on his way to India.[10]

Somervell was selected again for Everest in 1924 and considered to be one of the ablest climbers in the party. Nevertheless, the slopes leading up to the North Col must have been full of foreboding for porters and climbers alike, and if anything the weather was worse than in 1922. On 23 May, and with Camp IV on the North Col only just established, Hazard returned to camp III with the disturbing news that four porters were marooned at camp IV.[11] As Norton selected his most able climbers, Mallory and Somervell,[12] for the rescue, he must have appreciated that if an accident befell them, the expedition would be as good as over. The following morning the pair retrieved the four frightened, frostbitten men, with no little demonstration of cool and courageous mountaineering skill by Somervell.

Seven days later, on 1 June, Somervell and Norton with Odell, Irvine and six porters in support moved up to camp IV. Norton and Somervell occupied camp V on 2 June and the following day, and with three porters, established camp VI. On 4 June, Norton and Somervell, without supplementary oxygen, reached a height of more than 28,000ft with Norton going a little higher than his companion.[13] Many years later, Younghusband conjectured that but for the exertions of the rescue, Norton and Somervell might have climbed higher.[14] However, these achievements were overshadowed by the loss of Mallory and Irvine, last seen by Odell on 8 June.

Although not involved in any major Himalayan expeditions after 1924, Somervell continued to explore and climb with his family, with friends, and sometimes on his own. In 1926, with Hugh Ruttledge and Roger Wilson, he explored the north-eastern side of Nanda Devi. Somervell contributed some notes to Ruttledge's account of this expedition, commenting on the huge north-east face of Nanda Devi and the north face of Nanda Kot.[15] In 1928 he was in Sikkim for an unsuccessful attempt on Pandim, following which, with his companion ill, he climbed and sketched alone on a number of peaks south of Kangchenjunga. In 1933, while his wife was in England, he travelled over the Tragbal and Burzil passes wanting to '...enjoy Nanga Parbat, not to climb it – to paint it, not to struggle with it...' From the Rupal Nallah he climbed a number of lower peaks.[16] In 1943 he returned to Darjeeling with his family and took a party onto the Singalila ridge '... sketching at every opportunity ...'. His last visit to the Himalaya was to Kulu and Lahul in 1944 though it seems possible that he travelled to Nepal and Pakistan at some later date as he was to paint both Dhaulagiri and Rakaposhi.[17]

Artist

Somervell was encouraged to sketch by his father, William Henry Somervell
(1860-1934), a competent watercolourist and a collector of modern art. A
studio photograph exists of Howard, aged six or seven, with paint tray in
hand. As a boy he was soon painting local scenes in Kendal and as an
undergraduate exhibited at the Cambridge Drawing Society (*Albemarle Street,
watercolour*) in 1910.[18] In 1911 Somervell and fellow students also organised
a 'spoof' art show of the *avant garde* artists then in vogue.

Somervell painted many hundreds if not thousands of paintings. His
family describe him as a compulsive sketcher and painter. He would just sit
down and in 20 minutes or so complete a simple sketch or watercolour. Of
some 540 titles that I have been able to identify, 201 are of the Himalaya or
Tibet. Of these, 125 date or relate to the 1922 or 1924 expeditions although
there are certainly another 30 or so, exhibited at the Redfern Gallery in
1926, that I have been unable to trace. He seems to have been more active
in 1922 than in 1924, with upwards of 80 paintings from late March to late
July 1922, perhaps his most prolific period.

Of the rest, there are 54 paintings of India, 86 of the Alps and other
mountain ranges, 86 of the Lake District, 23 of Scotland and Wales, and
others from all over the world. These figures can only be a guide to his total
output. In retirement, he continued to paint and was, like his father, invited to join the Lake Artists Society (LAS). He exhibited a total of 136
paintings at the annual exhibitions of the Society from 1920 onwards,

101. T H Somervell *Nanga Parbat from Gulmarg* 1951. Watercolour. (*Lakeland Arts Tr*

102. T H Somervell *Nanda Devi* 1959. Oil on canvas. (*Lakeland Arts Trust*)

at first intermittently but following his return from India, he exhibited almost every year until his death.[19] He painted specific scenes for friends and gave many of his paintings away. In 1934 he painted *The Grepon, Chamonix* (private collection) in memory of a climber who had died on Mont Blanc. He exhibited his work on at least 30 occasions and held six exhibitions as sole artist.

Many of Somervell's watercolours are painted on what may be no more than brown or off-white wrapping paper. The paper has a ribbed appearance and some of that used in 1922 was watermarked 'Michallet, France'. He usually painted with the ribbing set horizontally, though in some paintings it appears vertically. He used this paper as early as 1913 and was still using it in the 1970s. I am not aware of any other artist who used a paper such as this. He often used bodycolour; that is watercolour mixed with gouache, in preference to watercolour alone and often used pastel either alone or with watercolour. Watercolour was his favoured medium in Tibet, the Himalaya and India.

He painted during the First World War and, although not a member, exhibited at the New English Art Club in 1917 (*Ypres 1917, Stone Quarry, Pas de Calais*) and again in 1921 (*Dent Blanche*).[20] Another painting dating from his war service, *The Somme Valley*, was exhibited in 1921 at the LAS. There are, however, no Somervell paintings held in the Imperial War Museum. Also exhibited at the LAS in 1921 was *The Matterhorn from Rothorn*. He was to paint at least another nine views of the Matterhorn, the last, an oil, dated 1969.

Somervell exhibited nine paintings of the 1922 expedition at the Alpine Club in December that year in an exhibition mainly devoted to ET Compton who had died in 1921. These were exhibited again in January 1923 when the Mount Everest Committee mounted a major exhibition of 204 photographs, including 12 by Somervell, and 57 of his paintings. The most expensive of these was *Mount Everest's Western Shoulder* at £50 10s but most were priced at 12 guineas or less. Surprisingly, only five are of Everest itself. Twelve of the paintings relate to Somervell's foray into Sikkim following the expedition, including *Fluted Peak, Sikkim*; *Jonsong Peak* and *Siniolchum*. Half the proceeds of sales of his pictures went to the Mount Everest Foundation. In 1929 his father exhibited five of Somervell's pictures at the AC in an exhibition of mountain paintings by a variety of artists. These included *Pancha Chule*; *Northern Peaks of Pancha Chule* and *Mountains near Neyyoor Travancore* (1929, private collection). He was sole exhibitor at the AC in 1936 (101 paintings), 1954 (103 paintings) and 1974 (94 paintings). The 1936 exhibition included 37 paintings of southern India.

The Alpine Club is fortunate in possessing 30 paintings by Somervell. Of these, 23 date from the Everest expeditions, the majority from 1922. Of the others, there is an oil, *Jannu,* dated 1943 and two watercolours of Nanda Devi: *Nanda Devi from Marloti looking west* dated 1933 and *Nanda Devi from Kwal Ganga-Ka Pahar* dated 1926. The latter was probably exhibited and for sale at the AC in 1929. It was then exhibited again at the Club in 1936 and at some later date given to the Club by Somervell. The view is from about 18,000 feet on the mountain Kwal Gang-Ka Pahar about 10 miles to the north of Nanda Devi and shows the north ridges of Nanda Devi and Nanda Devi East plunging downwards.

The Abbot Hall Gallery in Kendal has 13 very fine Somervell watercolours and one oil. All the watercolours are unframed and I presume have never been exhibited. The watercolours include one of his earliest mountain pictures, *Mountain*, dated 1913, a view of the Peuterey ridge of Mont Blanc. Five of the watercolours date from 1922 or 1924. *Rain over Tibetan Foothills* and *Everest Base Camp* are both dated 1922 but the latter is in fact a camp scene with figures at Kampa Dzong. There are two views of Tinki Dzong: *Tinki,* dated 1922 with a reflection of the Dzong in an adjacent lake and a chorten in the foreground and another, also *Tinki*, dated both 1922 and 1924. There is a photograph of Tinki Dzong in Howard-Bury's *Mount Everest, The Reconnaissance 1921* (London 1922) from almost exactly the same place as the first of these paintings. Of later works there are *Gorge through Himalayas to East of Nanda Kot* (1926) and *Everest, Lhotse and Makalu from Sandak* (1943), a view from the Singalila ridge with the Kanshung face of Everest glimpsed beyond Makalu. The oil is *Nanda Devi,* one of Somervell's largest works, and was used to illustrate the cover of the LAS annual exhibition catalogue in 1990, the centenary of his birth. It was exhibited at the LAS in 1959 and was for some time in the possession of his brother's family. The mountain is viewed from the east with the summit seen beyond the slopes of Nanda Devi East.

The Royal Geographical Society holds a large watercolour, *Gaurisankar from the North West* (1924), although this may in fact be a painting of Menlungtse.[21] Another, *Nanda Devi and Nanda Kot*, is dated 1923 and bears the signature of Somervell's father. WH Somervell visited India as treasurer of the London Missionary Society. Younghusband suggests in the foreword to *After Everest* that there are paintings of Everest itself by Somervell in the RGS but this does not seem to be the case.

When the 1922 Everest expedition arrived at their base camp, Somervell assisted with the organisation of stores for transport to higher camps whilst others prospected the route. He thought Everest stately rather than fantastic and was struck by the cubist appearance of the northern aspect of the mountain. In the first eight days of May he painted six oils and 10 watercolours of Everest. Amongst these would have been *Mount Everest's Western Shoulder* (AC 1922 and 1923*)* and *The Western Shoulder of Everest* (AC 1923). I suspect that also amongst these are *Everest from Base Camp,* probably oil, included in *The Fight for Everest:1924* referred to below. In the possession of the AC are *Ice Pinnacles, East Rongbuk Glacier, Everest*, pastel, 1922 as well as a pastel, *Everest from Rongbuk,* and an oil of the same name, 21x35cm. Somervell painted another, larger oil, *Everest from Rongbuk*, 50 x 57.5cm, possibly from the same piece of canvas, now in private ownership.

Everest from the North (oil, 30x40cm, undated, private collection) shows a view of the mountain from well above the Rongbuk glacier, high upon the slopes to the west above base camp, and may date from May 1922. I have been unable to trace the remaining eight pictures that were painted in those eight days.

Unclimbed: North Side of Everest (oil, AC 1954) was probably painted at a later date. From Camp I he painted *Pumori from Camp I* (AC 1922 and 1923). Later in the expedition and prior to his own summit attempt, he climbed to the Rapiu La from camp III. This gave him views onto the Kangshung glacier and the south-east face of Everest. The view probably inspired *South East Face of Everest* (oil, AC 1954) and *East Face of Everest from Point 6833m*, oil, even though the latter is dated 1924. He also took photographs from the Rapiu La of Makalu and Chomo Lomo as well as the east face of Everest.

Two years later, Somervell recorded sketching Chomolhari at least twice on 9 April 1924 although his brushes froze. There had been five paintings of Chomolhari in 1922. On a solitary excursion away from the main body of the expedition on 28 April, he painted *Gyachung Kang from Gyachung La*. He certainly painted base camp scenes again such as *Everest* (watercolour, private collection), however I suspect he spent less time at base in 1924 than in 1922, as there would have been no need to prospect the route. With bad weather and the rescue delaying summit attempts, he may not have had the time to seek out new views to sketch. However *From Camp VI* (oil, AC 1954) must have been inspired in 1924 as there was no such high camp in 1922.

Although General Bruce did not use any of Somervell's paintings to illustrate *The Assault on Everest:1922*, Norton selected eight out of a shortlist of 12 for inclusion in *The Fight for Everest:1924*. One, *Everest from Base Camp*, is dated 1922; three: *Kinchenjau from Kampa Dzong*, *From Lingga looking west – evening during monsoon* and *A typical camp in the plains of Tibet*, are dated 1924. The remaining four: *Sunset on the snows of Cho Rapsang*, *Chomolhari from the West*, *Kampa Dzong* (unfinished) and *Gyachung Kang from Gyachung La* are undated, although the last certainly dates from 1924. All are watercolours except perhaps the first named. *The Fight for Everest:1924* was published in June 1925 and although well received there was some comment that Somervell's paintings had not been adequately acknowledged. Arthur Hinks, secretary of the Mount Everest Committee, had been some-what lukewarm about Somervell's paintings and at one stage suggested to Norton that he might like to include some of his own sketches.

The eight *Fight* paintings were exhibited with 42 others at the Redfern Gallery at 27 Old Bond St in April 1926. There are press cuttings relating to this exhibition in the National Art Library but no catalogue seems to have survived. The paintings, mostly watercolours and pastels, included two views of Everest itself as well as *Gaurisankar, Rongshar Chu, Forest above Sedongchen, The View from Lingga at 5.30am, A Valley in Sikkim* and *Climbers Camp at 26,000 feet*. Only the last was not completed on the spot.

The exhibition was arranged by his father and opened by William Rothenstein who also wrote an introduction to Somervell's work in the catalogue. His brother Leslie purchased the now finished *Kampa Dzong*, undated, and an aunt, Rachel Dora Howard, purchased *A Valley in Sikkim*, a simple pencil and watercolour sketch on off-white paper, dated 1922. *Kampa Dzong* shows a scene from the hillside just behind the fortress looking south across the plains of Tibet. The hills of north Sikkim are in the distance. There is a photograph in Tilman's *Mount Everest 1938* taken from a comparable position. Comparison with the unfinished *Kampa Dzong* in *The Fight for Everest:1924* shows that the sky and distant hills have been heightened in blue and some foreground detail has been completed. *A Valley in Sikkim* shows dense monsoon clouds and was probably painted in July 1922 when Somervell returned through Sikkim after the end of the Everest expedition.

Somervell had painted three views of Kampa Dzong during the 1922 expedition, *Kampa Dzong* (two paintings) and *Kampa Dzong, The Gateway of the Fort*, all exhibited at the AC in 1923. There were to be further paintings of Kampa Dzong, an oil exhibited at the Alpine Club in 1954 and two exhibited also at the Club, possibly in 1974. There are several watercolours of Shekar Dzong, including *The Holy of Holies, Shekar Monastery* (AC 1923) and *Shekar Dzong* held by the AC, dated 1922, a view of the interior of the monastery. There is another *Shekar Dzong* (1924, private collection) that shows the fortress from the valley floor. Somervell selected *Everest from Base Camp: looking south towards the Rongbuk Glacie*r, oil, dated 1924, to illustrate *After Everest*. There is a photograph in the *Westmorland Gazette* of a very spry Noel Odell inspecting this picture when Somervell's paintings of the Himalaya were exhibited at the Abbot Hall in April 1979.[22]

I have traced four watercolours of Kangchenjunga. *Kangchenjunga from below Darjeeling* (1925) is of particular interest in that it bears the inscription 'EFN from THS.1925'. Edward Norton remained a close friend of Somervell after the Everest expeditions and Somervell may have given this painting to Norton to mark the publication of *The Fight for Everest:1924*. Another watercolour, *Southern Aspect of Kangchenjunga* (1928), depicts the valley to the south of the Guicha La from the slopes opposite Pandim and was exhibited at the AC in 1929. *Kangchenjunga from Tiger Hill* is dated 1947 and another, *Sunrise over Kangchenjunga from Darjeeling*, is undated. All are in private collections and the last was the AC's Christmas card in 2004. Two more watercolours, *Domed Peak, Kangchenjunga* and *Forked Peak, Kangchenjunga*, as well as *Pandim, Sikkim* and *Kabru, Sikkim* were exhibited at the Club in 1936.

There are at least three oils of Kangchenjunga: *Kangchenjunga from Darjeeling* (1932, AC col) and *Kangchenjunga* (1939) and *Kangchenjunga at Dawn* (undated) both in private collections. The last may have been exhibited at the LAS in 1960. Finally there are paintings including *Kangchenjunga from Darjeeling*, *Kangchenjunga from Gangtok* and *Pandim from Gangtok* that were exhibited at the AC in 1923 and *Kangchenjunga from Jongri* (AC 1936) and *Kangchenjunga* (AC 1954) that I have been unable to trace.

I know of seven watercolours of Nanga Parbat, five of which were exhibited at the Club in 1936, including *Camp near Nanga Parbat, East of Nanga Parbat, Nanga Parbat from Das Khurm* and *Nanga Parbat in Cloud.* The other is probably *Nanga Parbat*, dated 1933 and in a private collection. There is a further watercolour, *Nanga Parbat*, also privately held, which Somervell describes on the reverse as one of a pair. It shows the top of the Rupal face as seen from above the Rupal Nallah. Abbot Hall holds a very splendid watercolour, *Nanga Parbat from Gulmarg, early morning* (1951), which shows the massif seen from the south. At least two oils, *Nanga Parbat from the South* (AC 1954) and *Nanga Parbat and its satellites* (AC 1954), exist, although I have been unable to trace them or *Nanga Parbat* (LAS 1967).

Of other Himalayan paintings not already referred to are oils: *A Shoulder of Everest* (AC 1936), *Everest and the Rongbuk Stream* (AC 1936), *Everest from Base Camp* (AC 1936), *Mount Everest from Rongbuk* (AC 1936) and *Nanda Devi* (AC 1954). I have traced an oil, *Nanda Devi*, probably the last mentioned, to private ownership. It is similar but smaller than the large oil, *Nanda Devi*, at the Abbot Hall. Watercolours include *Nanda Devi from North East* (AC 1936), *A Mountain near Nanda Devi* (AC 1936), *Pancha Chule, Nepal Border* (AC 1936), *Everest from Sandakphu* (AC 1954), *Everest from Phalut* (AC 1954), *Nanda Kot, Himalayas* (LAS 1956), *Himalayas from Gulmarg* (LAS 1960), *Dhaulagiri* (LAS 1964) and *Jannu, early morning* (LAS 1965). There are also paintings in existence of *Kabru* and *Lingtren*, dated 1924, and *Gaurisankar, Makalu and Lhotse*, dated 1928, in private collections. The latter is very probably a view from the Singalila ridge. There are possibly a further four paintings of Gaurisankar dating from 1924.

Somervell continued to paint scenes from Tibet and the Himalaya well into his retirement. There is, for instance, an oil, *Chomolhari*, dated 1922 and 1972 (private collection). One presumes that the original dated from 1922 and continued to provide inspiration half a century later. Sadly, of some two hundred scenes of Tibet and the Himalaya that Somervell is known to have painted, I have been able to trace less than half. Similarly, I have been able to trace very few of his paintings of southern India.

Almost every Lake District fell and hillside is represented amongst paintings that I have been able to trace. Scenes of Great Gable, Wetherlam, the Langdale Pikes and Helvellyn seem to have been amongst his favourites. Paintings of Scotland include watercolours *Liathach, Rannoch Moor and Schiehallion*, and *Storm leaving Slioch* all held privately.

Five paintings were exhibited by the LAS posthumously in 1975. These included appropriately paintings from India (*In Sind Valley Kashmir*), the Lake District (*Dale Head from Robinson*), Switzerland (*Dawn over the Dom*) and Scotland (*Loch Eriboll*, watercolour, private collection).

In 1979, Somervell's widow, Margaret, opened an exhibition of selected Himalayan paintings at the Abbot Hall. In 1981 the Fell and Rock held an

103.   T H Somervell *Marmolada, Dolomites* circa 1954. Oil on hessian.
(*Private collection*)

exhibition to mark its 75th anniversary when three Somervells were exhibited by his wife, *Jannu* (oil), *Garhwal* (watercolour) and *Great Gable*.

Somervell had sketched with William Rothenstein (1872-1945), an official war artist during WWI, and remarked on his attention to detail in drawing even the humblest of objects. In his autobiography Rothenstein records meeting Somervell in March 1918 but makes no other comment about him.[23] Somervell later wrote that the aspiring mountain artist must first draw his mountain, simplifying detail, 'cubifying' as he put it. Another source of influence on Somervell was Nicholas Roerich (1874-1947) who, in 1946, was described by Somervell as '...the greatest mountain painter alive...'. Roerich was a Russian who travelled through India and North America in the 1920s before settling in Kulu. Somervell stayed at his house for a few days in 1944. Roerich's paintings demonstrate a similarity in style with those of Somervell. The cubist influence on both artists is clear although Roerich saw and developed mysticism in his work while Somervell did not.[24] Other influences would have included his father, other Lake artists such as the Heaton Coopers and also Edward Norton who himself painted and sketched with skill on both the 1922 and 1924 Everest expeditions.[25]

Somervell wrote of the colour and atmosphere of Tibet in *Assault on Everest: 1922* and his pictures capture the distances, space and remoteness of Tibet and the Himalaya.[26] Yet in *After Everest* he wrote 'People at home will say my sketches are hard, lacking poetry or mystery but that is just where they are true records of this extraordinary clarity.' He was not the first European to paint the Himalayan peaks. An exhibition of paintings of Tibet, Kashmir and India by William Simpson was held at the Pall Mall Gallery in 1869 and Edward Lear had painted three oils and several watercolours of Kangchenjunga following a visit to Darjeeling in 1874.

Somervell wrote in a note to his 1936 exhibition that a picture must 'communicate something the artist wishes to say' as well as being 'in some measure descriptive of its subject'. Although Somervell sold some paintings, he gave many away and should not in any way be regarded as a commercial artist. This allowed his style to develop much more freely than it might otherwise have done. Probably no other artist applied Cubism to the high mountains in such a consistent and authoritative way as Somervell. This is particularly true of his later works and he deserves more recognition as an artist in his own right. Most would regard his paintings of the great Himalayan peaks and Tibet as unique and they are an important part of the heritage of the Alpine Club as well as the history of mountain art.

REFERENCES

1 T H Somervell, 'A New Climbing Zone – in France', *FRCC Journal* 4, 1916, 4 38-9.
2 London Missionary Society Register of Missionaries 1796-1923 Council for World Missions, London.
3 T H Somervell, 'Climbing in the Tatra Mountains', *AJ* 48, 1936, 15-25.
4 T H Somervell, 'Climbing in Southern India', *FRCC Journal* 18, 1958, 132-7.
5 Election papers of T H Somervell, AC archive.
6 T H Somervell, 'Five Weeks of Good Weather', *AJ* 34, 1921-22, 280-292.
7 H Ruttledge, *Everest 1933*, London 1934, 15.
8 T H Somervell, 'Climbing North of Kangchenjunga', *FRCC Journal* 6, 1923, 222-226.
9 RGS archive.
10 T H Somervell, 'Rock Peaks and Snow Peaks 1923', *AJ* 35, 1923, 200-209.
11 A Salkeld, 'The Scapegoat', *AJ* 101, 1996, 224-226.
12 E F Norton, 'The Mount Everest Expedition of 1924', *Geographical Journal* 64, 1924, 224-226.
13 T H Somervell, 'The Mount Everest Dispatche', *Geographical Journal* 64, 1924, 156
14 F Younghusband, *Everest: The Challenge*, London, 1936, 27
15 H Ruttledge, 'Wanderings in the Kumaun Himalaya 1925-26', *AJ* 39, 1927, 71-79, and T H Somervell, 'Round About Nanda Devi in 1926', *FRCC Journal* 7, 1927, 342-352.

16   T H Somervell, 'A Pilgrimage to Nanga Parbat', *FRCC Journal* 10, 1934, 89-100

17   T H Somervell, 'A Holiday in Kulu', *FRCC Journal* 14, 1946, 195-199 and 'Some Minor Expeditions in the Himalaya', *HJ* 13, 1946, 28-40.

18   *The Caean* 1910, 189.

19   Catalogues of the annual exhibitions of the Lake Artists Society, Armitt Museum and Library, Ambleside.

20   Dictionary of Exhibitors at the New English Art Club, Hilmaston Manor Press 2002.

21   M P Ward, *Everest: A Thousand Years of Exploration*, The Ernest Press, 2003, 104.

22   'Height of Achievement' *Westmorland Gazette*, 27 April 1979.

23   W Rothenstein, *Men and Memories*, London 1931, 336 & 338.

24   J Decter, *Nicholas Roerich: The Life and Art of a Russian Master*, London 1989.

25   M P Ward, 'The Everest Sketches of Lt Col EF Norton', *AJ* 98, 1993, 82.

26   T H Somervell, 'Colour in Tibet' in *The Assault on Mount Everest*, CG Bruce, London 1923, 309-312.

In addition, I have drawn on Somervell's three books: *After Everest* (London, 1936), *India Calling* (London 1947) and *Knife and Life in India* (London 1941).

A C K N O W L E D G E M E N T S

I am very grateful to members of the Somervell family for their support in writing this article. I thank members of the Alpine Club, the Fell and Rock Climbing Club and the Association of British Members of the Swiss Alpine Club who have let me have details of the Somervell paintings in their possession. I acknowledge the assistance of Yvonne Sibbald of the Alpine Club Library, London and Hannah Neale, Curator of the Abbott Hall Gallery in Kendal.

Three Early Influences

In April 2004 Royal Robbins took up an invitation from Terry Gifford to speak at the International Festival of Mountain Literature, Bretton Hall, about his favourite American climbing authors. Restricting himself to those writing prior to 1960, he assembled an impressive pack that included Charles Houston, Bob Bates, Allen Steck and Brad Washburn. His top three, however, were as follows, in reverse order.

James Ramsey Ullman is not known for a string of first ascents, nor for the difficulty of the climbs he made. He was, primarily, not a climber but a writer. He earned his bread with *words*. He wrote fiction and non-fiction about other subjects as well as climbing, but, in my opinion, his one book that stands out, like Everest above the lesser peaks of his other works, is his story of mountaineering titled *High Conquest*.

While discussing this book with Nick Clinch, I was surprised and delighted to hear him describe it as 'the Bible of our generation'. I had never talked to anyone else who had read it. It hadn't been recommended to me. I came across it by chance in the Los Angeles Public Library when, as a 15-year old, I was casually looking for mountaineering titles. It changed my life. This book, published in 1943, in the middle of the Second World War, attempts, in Ullman's words, 'to offer a word of suggestion and encouragement to the reader who would follow the Mountain Way himself'. The 'Mountain Way'! What an idea. I was ready for that way and *High Conquest* was just the kick in the pants to get me off and running. After reading this book I was convinced that the 'Mountain Way' was the way for me. Ullman paints a picture of mountaineering as a glorious enterprise, a calling worthy of one's best endeavours. It was something I could believe in, partly because it didn't claim to be socially useful. Through climbing one could grow toward one's potential. Climbing would help one get there.

The book is superbly well written, pulling one into the narrative and holding one there. The captions on the illustrations suggest the romance of mountaineering as Ullman saw it: 'The Last Citadel' (the Mustagh Tower), 'That Awful Mountain' (The Matterhorn), 'White Death' (an avalanche), and (my favourite) 'Hard Rock – Thin Air – A Rope' (a climber in extremis). It's a persuasive history by a gifted, professional writer. At the end of the book Ullman sums up his message:

For it is the ultimate wisdom of the mountains that a man is never more a man than when he is striving for what is beyond his grasp and that there is no conquest worth the winning save that over his own weakness and ignorance and fear.

    'Have we vanquished an enemy?' asked Mallory. And there was only one answer:

    'None but ourselves.'

    It is not the summit that matters, but the fight for the summit; not the victory, but the game itself.'

'The game itself.' I was a sucker for heroic prose like that. More than any other American climbing writer, James Ramsey Ullman captured in words the magnetic pull of mountains on those with mountaineers' blood in their veins.

That brings me to my penultimate climbing writer, **Clarence King**, whose lone book about climbing, *Mountaineering in the Sierra Nevada*, made such exciting reading and so strongly influenced me as a young climber. Clarence King was a geologist who travelled and worked under some of the great names in California geology such as Whitney and Brewer. King roamed the Sierra about the same time as John Muir, that is, the 1860s, though there is no record of their ever having met. King was an extraordinarily gifted writer, approaching in skill the likes of Mark Twain and Brete Harte, who, like King, also wrote about life in the Sierra foothills.

Although the title suggests the book is all about mountaineering, and although climbing forms the core and centrepiece, *Mountaineering* is at least as much devoted to travel, geology, and character sketches as to thrilling ascents. Nevertheless, the key chapters in the book are 'The Ascent of Mt. Tyndall' and 'The Descent of Mt. Tyndall'.

King asks his chief, Brewer, for permission to attempt, with his friend, Richard Cotter, to reach what they believe to be the highest point in California:

> It was a trying moment for Brewer...he felt a certain fatherly responsibility over our youth, a natural desire that we should not deposit our triturated remains in some undiscoverable hole among the feldspathic granites.

Brewer, overcome by a desire for scientific knowledge, decides to risk the lives of his lieutenants and grants permission. There follows a fascinating description of a cross-country journey to reach the mountain, crossing gorges, climbing over difficult terrain, bivouacking on the chilly heights:

A sudden chill enveloped us. Stars in a moment crowded through the dark heaven, flashing with a frosty splendour. The snow congealed, the brooks ceased to flow, and, under the powerful sudden leverage of frost, immense blocks were dislodged all along the mountain summits and came thundering down the slopes, booming upon the ice, dashing wildly upon rocks.

The next day finds them encountering more hair-raising adventures, including lassoing spikes and climbing the rope hand over hand. Two days of adventures brought them to the base of their mountain, which they climbed, with great difficulty, the third day, naming it Mt Tyndall, and realising, as they could see higher peaks to the south, that they were not on top of California's highest point. King describes vistas of cold, dark, inhuman hardness, summed up in his words: 'Looking from this summit with all desire to see everything, the one overmastering feeling is desolation, desolation!' How different this point of view is from that of John Muir, who, in such a place, would see light and beauty, and hear God's voice.

On the descent they need to climb up at one point. Cotter goes first over difficult terrain and calls King to come ahead and 'don't be afraid to bear your weight'. King climbs up but distains using the rope, insisting upon getting up on his own power. When he reaches his friend he finds Cotter on a sloping shelf with no anchor. If King had pulled on the rope or fallen they both would have perished. The climbing was so 'on the edge' that Cotter avoided saying so for fear that King might stiffen up and climb less freely. Of this act, King writes: 'In all my experience of mountaineering I have never known an act of such real, profound courage as this of Cotter's.'

This 'edge of one's seat' description of climbing Mt Tyndall, and the noble sentiments expressed, strongly affected me as a young climber and I held Clarence King in the highest regard until I climbed Mt Williamson and could look across at Mt Tyndall and see it was much less fearsome than King's writings had led me to believe. I came to the reluctant conclusion that he must have exaggerated. And so it is that we must ascribe to King the fault of hyperbole, and deduct a few points from his stature as an American mountaineering author.

Still, as a writer, *qua* writer, King is superb, particularly when it comes to capturing the comic aspects of man or beast. Travelling through the Sierra forest, King comments upon the mule he is riding:

My Buckskin was incorrigibly bad. To begin with, his anatomy was desultory and incoherent, the maximum of physical effort bringing about a slow, shambling gait quite unendurable. He was further cursed with a brain wanting the elements of logic, as evinced by such *non sequiturs* as shying insanely at wisps of hay, and stampeding beyond control when I tried to tie him to a load of grain. My sole amusement with Buckskin grew out of a psychological peculiarity of his, namely, the unusual slowness with which waves of sensation were propelled inward toward the brain from remote parts of his periphery. A dig of the spurs administered in the flank passed unnoticed for a period of time varying from twelve to thirteen seconds, till the protoplasm of the brain received the percussive wave, then, with a suddenness which I never wholly got over, he would dash into a trot, nearly tripping himself up with his own astonishment.

In a chapter titled 'The Newtys of Pike', King describes a family who have left Pike, a town somewhere in the Midwest, to seek a better living in California. He meets them in the Sierra foothills:

> The mother…rocked jerkily to and fro, removing at intervals a clay pipe from her mouth in order to pucker her thin lips to one side, and spit with precision upon a certain spot in the fire, which she seemed resolved to prevent from attaining beyond a certain faint glow. I saw too that (the daughter) …was watching with subtle solicitude that fated spot in the fire…which slowly went into blackness before the well-directed fire of her mother's saliva.

King displays a strong appreciation of the good things of life, especially after coming through a Sierra storm:

> In anticipation of our return the party had gotten up a capital supper, to which we first administered justice, then punishment, and finally annihilation. Brief starvation and a healthy combat for life with the elements lent a marvellous zest to the appetite.

And now we come to my numero uno, the last man standing, so to speak, among my early American mountaineering authors. It is hard to know where to begin with **John Muir**, so vast is his output. There is so much that could be said about 'John o' the mountains', and so much that has been said, that I need to confine my remarks to, not Muir the climber, as such, but Muir through a *climbing perspective.* I suppose a logical starting point is to acknowledge that he is known not primarily as a climber but rather as a conservationist, or even a *prophet* of conservation. We might more accurately say, a prophet of *preservation.* For, in his heart of hearts, Muir wanted not merely to keep resources from being wasted; he wanted to preserve them in their natural state. And this, frankly, has been Muir's great contribution to America's climbing mores – the idea of leaving the mountains, including the rock upon which we climb, as much as possible in their natural condition. Thus Americans, particularly in the western states, early came to see fixed pitons as not desirable, as interfering with the natural experience of finding the rock as the first ascensionists did. We were just following in Muir's footsteps.

Muir's 'mountaineering' often took the form of ranging over the mountains, rather than climbing specific peaks, and was usually in the service of science – glaciology, geology, mapping the wilderness. Muir certainly had the true climber's instinct to climb for its own sake, and once, viewing a panorama of Sierra peaks, effused: 'Hope I may climb them all.' Still, he rarely did a climb without using it to further his scientific investigations, once spending a life-risking night in a storm on Mount Shasta because scientific measurements caused him to linger longer than prudence counselled.

Nature was very much a religious experience for Muir. He had little sympathy with and patience for the Christian religion as it was practiced in his day, and observed, upon reaching the top of Cathedral Peak, that it was the first time he had been to church in California. Still, he often invoked God and the words of Christ in his writings, even while finding fault with the idea of man 'having dominion' over the rest of the creatures of God. He saw this religious 'splitting up' of man and nature as, well, unnatural. Muir always saw things as part of a whole. He was a great synthesizer.

Muir led a grandly adventurous life. In fact, his was a life of adventure. There was recently published in America a book titled *22 Adventures of John Muir*. Of the 22 adventures, only five or six could properly be called 'climbing stories'. Of these, three stand out: his ascent of Mount Ritter, the night out on Shasta, and a rescue of a friend on an Alaskan peak. Most climbers consider the description of his solo first ascent of Mount Ritter to be his most memorable climbing writing, especially the section where he describes a close call spread-eagled in the middle of a steep face high on the mountain. The writing sings with the ring of truth. Anyone who has done a little climbing says, 'Yes, I recognise that moment. I've been there!'

Muir describes his first ascent, alone, of Cathedral Peak with off-hand nonchalance. Leaving the north side of Tuolumne Meadows at daybreak, he attained the summit by noon 'after loitering along the way' to study trees, flowers, rocks, chipmunks and squirrels. He gives us a detailed description of the peak, but no comment about climbing it. His reticence about any climbing difficulty is remarkable. Even today a rope is recommended for this ascent. He did it ropeless in hiking boots, probably with hobnails, hardly the best footwear for gripping the hard granite of this 'temple of marvellous architecture'.

But Muir's greatest legacy to climbers was the intensity and eloquence with which he captured not just the climbing experience in particular but the mountain experience in general. He showed us, in word and deed, how to view the mountains, how to climb them, and how to care for them. He was like an Old Testament prophet. Receiving the word directly from God through the trees and rocks, the waterfalls and animals, he had little patience with those who didn't share his religion. Like many modern environmentalists, he, at times at least, viewed humans as blights upon the landscape, referring to them as 'the moiling, squirming, fog-breathing public', 'Babylonish mobs', and 'rough vertical animals…who occur in and on these mountains like sticks of condensed filth'. Muir saw the wholeness of things, especially of nature, and was in arms against anything that threatened to split that wholeness asunder.

Muir made an early ascent of Half Dome, 'a month or two after' the Scotsman George Anderson had gained the summit by drilling holes, leaving a fixed line. Muir climbed the Dome on November 10, 1875, right after a snowstorm. The snow on top apparently kept Muir, who was a keen observer of glacial phenomena, from noting the lack of glacier polish on top of the Dome. He was under the impression that ice rivers had overridden Half Dome, as they had many of the other Yosemite domes. Muir was mostly right in his original interpretations of how glaciers formed Yosemite. Except for snow that day he might have realized and corrected this minor error.

Well, this is what it has come to, after so many throes and convulsions – my pick of Muir as the top American climbing writer. John Muir was a mountaineer – wide-ranging, peripatetic, climber of many summits, of different types of mountains; gifted and eloquent chronicler of his ascents, no exaggerator, telling it like it was; a writer and prophet, who by his pen and voice and actions spoke to us climbers about how to think about the mountains and how to treat them; and, finally, an author whose output far exceeds that of any other American mountaineer. For all these reasons we have no choice but to accept John Muir as the number one American climbing writer.

There is one final thing we haven't mentioned – his quotability. His sayings alone are enough to give him first place. His most famous and most often repeated quote is one with which many are familiar:

> Go to the mountains and get their glad tidings. Nature's peace will flow into you as sunshine flows into trees. The winds will blow their freshness into you, and the storms their energy; while cares drop off you as autumn leaves.

Here are some others:

'All the world was before me and every day was a holiday.'

'But where do you want to go?' asked the man. 'To any place that is wild,' I replied.

'Canyons 2,000 to 5,000 feet deep, in which once flowed majestic glaciers, and in which now flow and sing the bright, rejoicing rivers.'

Speaking of climbing to get a better view:

'One must labour for beauty as for bread, here as elsewhere.'

'A climb of about 1,400 feet from the valley has to be made. There is no trail, but to anyone fond of climbing this will make the ascent all the more delightful.'
'My first view of the High Sierra, first view looking down into Yosemite, the death song of Yosemite Creek, and its flight over the vast cliff, each one of these is of itself enough for a great life-long landscape fortune — a most memorable of days.'

'Who wouldn't be a mountaineer! Up here all the world's prizes seem nothing.'

'I wish I could live, like these junipers, on sunshine and snow, and stand beside them on the shore of Lake Tenaya for a thousand years. How much I should see, and how delightful it would be!'

Speaking of clouds building in the late afternoon sun:

'I watched the growth of these red-lands of the sky as eagerly as if new mountain ranges were being built.'

'I came at length to the brow of that massive cliff that stands between Indian Canyon and Yosemite Falls [Muir is referring here to Yosemite Point], and here the far-famed valley came suddenly into view… the noble walls – sculptured into endless variety of domes and gables, spires and battlements – all atremble with the thunder tones of the falling water. The level bottom seemed to be dressed like a garden – sunny meadows here and there, and groves of pine and oak; the river of Mercy sweeping in majesty through the midst of them and flashing back the sunbeams.'

But, in the end, in the final analysis, Muir's words can be summed up in the one injunction with which we started these quotes, and I will leave you with that:

'Go to the mountains and get their glad tidings!'

CHRIS SMITH

Wordsworth and the Mountains

Over the last two hundred years, Samuel Taylor Coleridge has had rather a good mountaineering press. Coleridge, you will recall, was the great conversationalist, the experimenter, the risk-taker, and above all the man who descended Broad Stand alone, in what probably ranks as the first recorded act of mountaineering adventure in Britain. His great friend William Wordsworth, by contrast, has come down to us through the ages as being much more staid, worthy rather than wild, and someone who strolled through the daffodils along the shores of Ullswater instead of conquering the crags. This is a thoroughly unfair and inaccurate portrayal of Wordsworth, fuelled I suspect by the fact that he lived to a ripe old age, became increasingly conservative as the years advanced, and with a few rare exceptions allowed the poetic fire to die out at the same time. But the *young* Wordsworth: ah, there is a poet and poetry to be conjured with. And his work in those early years is shot through with the lure, the magic, the soul of the mountains. It is time to rediscover Wordsworth as a mountaineer, and as a poet of the hills and crags.

Wordsworth was someone, of course, who thought nothing of walking twenty miles to post a letter. He composed *Tintern Abbey* – one of the great, iconic poems of English literature – in his head as he was walking from the Wye Valley to Bristol. He roamed the hills from his earliest years as a schoolboy at Hawkshead. He deliberately chose to settle in a simple cottage in what was then one of the most remote parts of the country. Walking was second nature to him. And I could lead you through his poetry, poem by poem, line by line, and recapture for you the power of mountain landscape that probably had more impact on his writing than on that of any other major poet.

Take his early poem *Michael*, for instance. It is a poem about a Grasmere shepherd, and when the storm calls all other travellers to shelter, it summons him up into the mountains: '… he had been alone / Amid the heart of many thousand mists, / That came to him, and left him, on the heights.' Or take *Tintern Abbey* itself, where he describes his youthful enthusiasm for nature, '… when like a roe / I bounded o'er the mountains, by the sides / Of the deep rivers, and the lonely streams, / Wherever nature led …'; and then goes on to reflect how maturity has brought a deeper love for nature, tinged with a more perceptive recognition of the human condition. Or read the passage in the first book of *The Prelude*, where he describes skating by starlight on Lake Windermere, and the way he feels the crags wheeling round him as he retires from the throng into a silent bay, 'To cut across the image of a star / That gleamed upon the ice …'

Later in *The Prelude* Wordsworth describes his walk through the Alps, starting from Calais and walking through France, past Mont Blanc, and over the mountains into Italy – and the sense of exhilaration when he suddenly discovers that he has crossed the watershed of the Alps. But above all, perhaps, read the passage in the final book of *The Prelude* where he describes the ascent of Snowdon in a cloud inversion, climbing steadily through the cloud and mist and then suddenly emerging into sunlight:

> ... and on the shore
> I found myself of a huge sea of mist,
> Which, meek and silent, rested at my feet.
> A hundred hills their dusky backs upheaved
> All over this still ocean; and beyond,
> Far, far beyond, the vapours shot themselves,
> In headlands, tongues, and promontory shapes,
> Into the sea, the real sea ...

This surely is mountain poetry at its best. This is a poet who has lived amongst, climbed, roamed, and loved the hills and who writes about them with a sensitivity that few have ever matched.

But Wordsworth is more than this: together with Coleridge, he brought about nothing less than a revolution in English literature. It is hard for us to conceive now, but just over two hundred years ago when the first edition of the *Lyrical Ballads* appeared – a joint project by the two poets – it heralded a complete change in the course of English poetry and thought. And Wordsworth went on to build on that during the whole of the next decade.

For a start, Wordsworth's poetry is written in a simple, straightforward style, using the rhythms of ordinary speech, but in a remarkably powerful way. He describes the act of writing poetry as being 'a man speaking to men'; and not only does he talk about the lives and experiences of ordinary people, often vagrants and outcasts, but he does so in a way that is completely different from the carefully crafted, overtly 'poetic' writing of much of the eighteenth century.

And of course in his greatest poem, *The Prelude*, he writes something that no one had ever done before: an epic poem about himself, his own life and experiences, and the thoughts and feelings they bring. This is a new poetry, focused on the interior life, reflective, exploring the boundaries and relationships between mind, soul and experience, that would have been undreamed of in earlier times.

So Wordsworth is a pioneer in what he writes about, and how he writes it. But the revolution goes far deeper. Along with his fellow Romantic poets, he believes profoundly in the transformational power of the imagination. For him, it is the special task of the poet to see the world afresh, to see beyond the surface of things into the deeper reality, to take the most ordinary of people or things and find in them the revelation of something powerful and special. Looking out over the huge sea of mist from the upper slopes of Snowdon, for example, he sees a great chasm in the clouds, through which he hears an immense roaring of waters, and senses a glimpse of infinity, where nature has lodged 'The soul, the imagination of the whole'. Reaching out to touch a sense of the infinite which is implicit in the material world around us is at its heart what much of Wordsworth's poetry is about; and not only Wordsworth, but Coleridge, Keats, Shelley, Byron, Blake and others too. It is the great Romantic legacy for our contemporary world.

Wordsworth is also distinctive in that much of his poetry is an exploration of the interrelationship and interdependence of the individual human soul and the world around it – especially the world around as expressed in the mountain landscapes and wild country to which he is passionately devoted. Many of his early poems, from the *Lyrical Ballads* onwards, describe a succession of solitary people, strange looming figures who come towards us in an empty landscape: the Old Cumberland Beggar, the Leech-gatherer, the old Soldier, Lucy Gray. The Leech-gatherer is perhaps the strangest of them all. When he comes across this very old, still man sitting beside a wild moorland pool, he describes him in the most inanimate of terms: 'As a huge stone is sometimes seen to lie / Couched on the bald top of an eminence ...' or, later, 'like a sea-beast crawled forth, that on a shelf / Of rock or sand reposeth ...'. The Leech-gatherer's essence is existence, rather than activity; he hardly speaks or moves throughout the whole poem, and towards the end it is as if he merges back into the landscape whence he first appeared. The exploration this prompts in Wordsworth's own mind, however, about the nature of existence, and about the relational power of mind or action, is profound. The poem may end with a jovial attempt to laugh off the encounter, but it has had a deep impact.

As Wordsworth takes us through his own life story in *The Prelude*, the same exploration – applied to himself, his friends, and his thoughts – keeps appearing and re-appearing. If I have a favourite passage from this greatest of English poems it is the one in Book V (which also appears as a separate poem in the second edition of the *Lyrical Ballads*) where he describes a young friend on the shores of Windermere:

> There was a Boy: ye knew him well, ye cliffs
> And islands of Winander! – many a time
> At evening, when the stars had just begun
> To move along the edges of the hills,
> Rising or setting, would he stand alone
> Beneath the trees or by the glimmering lake,
> And there, with fingers interwoven, both hands
> Pressed closely palm to palm, and to his mouth
> Uplifted, he, as through an instrument,
> Blew mimic hootings to the silent owls,

> That they might answer him; and they would shout
> Across the watery vale, and shout again,
> Responsive to his call, with quivering peals,
> And long halloos and screams, and echoes loud,
> Redoubled and redoubled, concourse wild
> Of mirth and jocund din; and when it chanced
> That pauses of deep silence mocked his skill,
> Then sometimes, in that silence while he hung
> Listening, a gentle shock of mild surprise
> Has carried far into his heart the voice
> Of mountain torrents; or the visible scene
> Would enter unawares into his mind,
> With all its solemn imagery, its rocks,
> Its woods, and that uncertain heaven, received
> Into the bosom of the steady lake.

I have quoted the whole passage, not just because it is a fine and beautiful piece of writing, rolling from peaceful mountain setting to breathless noise and back to silence, but because in the process it encapsulates perfectly the interrelationship of human mind and surrounding world which lies at the heart of Wordsworth's work. Note for example that line-ending which produces such a pregnant pause, where he 'hung' … 'Listening' – a pro-active and re-active moment at one and the same time. And note also the way in which the sound of torrents is carried far into his heart, and the visible scene enters into his mind. The human mind and soul themselves act, and are also acted upon. Their identity and experience are shaped by what they are intrinsically, but also by the experiences they receive whilst in the midst of nature's finest scenery.

How often have I remembered that line about carrying far into the heart the voice of mountain torrents, as I've been descending from some high mountain in the late afternoon, and have stopped on a rock beside the path to reflect on the day and what it has brought. And the sound of the streams fills the air, comforting, reassuring, reflective, a little elegiac perhaps. These are some of the most exquisite and moving moments of our time in the hills. And they do speak to the heart.

As we struggle in our modern world to understand better our relationship as human beings with the natural world around us – as we try to make sense of the way we use and abuse the elemental environment – we can do worse than return to the wisdom and understanding that Wordsworth brings to his greatest poetry. He puts his love of mountain country directly into his work, yes. Few have done it as well as he has. But he also explores what that means for us, and how the experience of mountains and landscape deepens what we are as human beings.

Coleridge will always have Broad Stand to his credit. But Wordsworth has the whole world of the mountains to his; and his poetry at its best helps us to see the world with new eyes and new feelings. He, too, is a true mountaineer. Perhaps the last word is best left with another great, more recent, Cumbrian poet, Norman Nicholson. In a poem addressed ostensibly to the River Duddon, he writes profoundly about Wordsworth's poetry:

> A hundred years of floods and rain and wind
> Have washed your rocks clear of his words again,
> Many of them half-forgotten, brimming the Irish Sea,
> But that which Wordsworth knew, even the old man
> When poetry had failed like desire, was something
> I have yet to learn, and you, Duddon,
> Have learned and re-learned to forget and forget again.
> Not the radical, the poet and heretic,
> To whom the water-forces shouted and the fells
> Were like a blackboard for the scrawls of God,
> But the old man, inarticulate and humble,
> Knew that eternity flows in a mountain beck ...

From 'To the River Duddon', in *Five Rivers* (1944)

That really is what Wordsworth's poetry is all about. For those of us who love the mountains, it's something we instinctively know, but always need to learn – and re-learn.

Note: Quotations from *The Prelude* are from the 1805 version, as edited by Ernest de Sèlincourt.

History

T H Somervell *Kampa Dzong*
1925. Pencil and bodycolour
Exhibited at the Redfern Gallery 1926
Private collection

HEINRICH HARRER
'Friends for a Lifetime'

A personal tribute to Anderl Heckmair
who died in February 2005, aged 98

*'First we were opponents, on the wall we became partners
and afterwards friends for a lifetime.'*

These were the words Anderl Heckmair used when he gave interviews or spoke to audiences. The course of the climb up the north face of the Eiger during the July days of 1938 is known to the readers of the *Alpine Journal*, therefore I shall concentrate on anecdotes of Anderl Heckmair to whom this tribute is dedicated. Even if you have not the faintest idea beforehand of the person's character, when you climb together for days under extremely difficult conditions, nothing can be hidden. Every weakness and all merits of the necessary comradeship will be revealed.

Though Anderl and his partner Wiggerl Vörg were much better equipped than myself and Fritz Kasparek, the Bavarians shared with us Austrians a conviction of the necessity for speed whenever possible. This was especially so while climbing the Spider, when suddenly a storm broke upon us with lightning and thunder, and communication became impossible. Heckmair and Vörg, who were already on the upper part of the open ice field, feared for our lives. They gave Kasparek, who had been hurt on his left hand by a stone, the rope and safeguarded both of us to the uppermost brim of the Spider.

Here we found a ledge as broad as a boot on which to bivouac. It was already the third night on the face for Kasparek and myself and the second for our friends. Wiggerl melted snow for hot coffee and the pot went shuttling back and forth, hanging from a snap link on the 3m-traverse line we had fixed between us.

Anderl had to keep his 12-pointer crampons on so as to get some kind of a stand in the ice. With his head resting on the broad back of Wiggerl he fell asleep. And no wonder, for the ramp had turned out to be more difficult than it looked. It took us several hours to overcome just two overhangs. It was typical of Anderl that after falling twice from an ice bulge to the belaying Wiggerl he simply got furious. The rebuff could not stop him, he immediately balanced himself up the ice-covered overhang and tackled the obstacle again.

The night was an ordeal in wet clothes. Fritz and I pulled the Zdarsky-sack over us. Through the little window in the tent-sack I could see that the weather was bad. There was an occasional small snow slide, which made a gentle swishing sound. But I wasn't worried about the weather. I was possessed of a great feeling of peace. Though the bivouac was the smallest endurable in terms of room, in spite of that it was the best. The reason was the rest, the peace, the joy and the great satisfaction that next day we would reach the summit. Of course I thought also of my ropemates and felt assured that they too were happy. Anderl slept the sleep of the just.

At dawn the rocks were white and it was still snowing. We lightened our rucksacks by throwing down the precipice that part of the equipment which had become superfluous. Among it was a whole loaf of bread. It was the point of no return. Anderl was leading and it became his day. All four of us were fit and confident but Anderl was the best. Thinking back, our euphoria might have been due to the fact that we were capable of producing the pain-killing endorphin. But this kind of morphine, as well as the word itself, was unknown to us. All we felt was a happy confidence.

We were all on one rope and knew that there was no other way but to go on. Again, as on all parts of the wall, the so-called Exit Crack turned out to be difficult. After one rope length I waited an endless time for the call to follow. I was on a small knob while 30m above stood Vörg, safeguarding Heckmair as he grappled with icy rock and snow-slides in the mists and driving snow. We couldn't see either of them.

Still no order came from Vörg to come up. We could here voices and short, muffled cries. What could have gone wrong up there? Then we could only hear a murmur of voices. At the same time a snow-slide came down on us. That was nothing unusual and we were quite used to it by now; but this wasn't white snow. It was stained red with blood. Definitely blood, because the next thing to come down was an empty bandage cover, followed by a small empty medicine bottle.

'Hallo!' we yelled. 'What's happened?'

No reply. We waited for what seemed an age, racked with doubt and anxiety. Then, according to schedule, another avalanche came down with savage force. Not till it had passed did we obtain relief in the shape of an invitation to move on up. Vörg was hauling on the rope so hard that it took my breath away. But I understood what this manhandling meant. No longer was there time to climb pitches neatly according to the rules. Time was now the watchword, if we were to escape from the face. And evidently something had happened up there to cause great delay.

When I reached Vörg's stance, a great weight fell from me. They were not seriously hurt. Vörg had a blood-soaked bandage on one hand, but Heckmair was already a whole rope higher up, on a tiny, exposed, rickety stance. Later on, he reported in his dry but lively way how Vörg came by his injury:

'The point of the ice-piton on to which I was clinging for dear life only went a little way in and so did the pick of my ice axe. Suddenly the piton came out, and at the same moment my axe gave way. If I could only have straddled, I could have kept my balance. But with my legs crossed, there wasn't a hope.

'I shouted, "Look out, Wiggerl!" Then I came off.

'Wiggerl was looking out all right. He took in as much rope as he could, but I bore straight down on him – not through thin air, for the gully was inclined, but in a lightning-swift slide. Just as I fell, I turned face outwards so as not to go head over heals.

'Wiggerl let the rope drop and caught me with his hands, and one of the points of my crampons went through his palm. I did turn head over heels, but in a split second I grabbed the rope-piton, which gave me such a jerk that I came up feet first again. I dug all 12 points of my irons into the ice – and found myself standing.'

As Heckmair bandaged Vörg's hand he urged his partner, who was deathly pale, to 'pull himself together, because it was now or never'. Anderl recalled:

'Just then a little phial of "heart drops" came to hand in the first-aid bag. That devoted woman Dr Belart of Grindelwald had made me take it along in case of emergency, remarking: "If Toni Kurz had only had them along, he might even have survived his ordeal."

'We were only supposed to use them in the direst need, though.

'On the bottle it said … "ten drops". I simply poured half of it into Wiggerl's mouth and drank the rest, as I happened to be thirsty.'

(Quotations from: Andreas Heckmair, *Die drei letzten Probleme der Alpen*, Bruckmann Verlag, München, 1949.)

We climbed on with Anderl in the lead. Minutes passed into hours. Up we went, yard-by-yard, rope-by-rope. Eventually we gained a lodging on the wind-battered ridge and plodded our way over it to the summit of the Eiger. It was 3.30pm on 24 July 1938. We were the first to climb the north face of the Eiger from its base to its top.

Joy, relief, tumultuous triumph? Not a bit of it. Our release had come too suddenly, our minds and nerves were too dulled, our bodies too utterly weary to permit of any violent emotion. Fritz and I had been on the face for 85 hours, Heckmair and Vörg for 61 hours.

We had not had a hair's-breadth escape from disaster; on the contrary, our bond of friendship had throughout given us a firm sense of mutual reliance. And hard as the climb had been, we had never doubted its successful outcome.

The storm was raging so fiercely on the summit that we had to bend double. We just shook hands without a word and started down at once. But it wasn't easy. The descent was full of spite and malice. We kept on slipping and recovering ourselves. We suddenly felt tired, terribly tired. I had been given the job of finding and leading the way down because I already knew the route; I didn't always find the correct route immediately; then, my companions hauled me over the coals.

We could see how Anderl was collapsing, not in a physical but in a spiritual sense. Uncomplainingly, mechanically, he moved forward; but by now he had given up the leadership. The fantastic nervous tension under which we had lived for days and nights on that mighty face just had to induce a reaction. During those endless hours of danger he had excelled himself; now he could afford to be an ordinary man again, with all an ordinary man's weakness, susceptible and exposed to all the caprices of normal life.

For instance, take the matter of Anderl's trousers. The elastic band of his overall had broken. Anderl kept on pulling his trousers up and they kept on falling down again. This man, who had reacted with the speed of lightning when he fell in the icy gully and so saved us all from disaster, the man who had so often withstood the pressure of the deadly avalanches, who had climbed ice-bulges in a blizzard and, with unexampled endurance, fought a way to freedom for himself and his three team-mates – this same man was almost driven to desperation by a broken elastic.

So Anderl had given up the lead. He had every right to expect to be led down on the descent just as surely and safely as he had led up that appalling face; and he had every right to swear now when, racked by the exhaustion of a body exerted to the uttermost, he was asked to climb up a few hundred feet again because, in the mirk and the blown snow, I had led the wrong way down.

Suddenly there was a young boy in front of us, staring at us as if we were ghosts. His face expressed embarrassment, incredulous astonishment. Then he summoned up his courage to ask:

'Have you come off the Face?'

'Yes,' we admitted, 'off the Face!'

Then he turned downhill and ran away screeching in a high treble: 'They're coming! Here they are! They are coming!'

We had made an excursion to another world and come back, but we had brought the joy of life back with us. And now that earth was welcoming us home..........

Nearly 70 years have passed since then. At the end I think with sadness of Wiggerl Vörg, that strong, calm, magnificent climber, who fell in the war. Fritz Kasparek, a true child of the sunshine, fell to his death in 1954 when the summit cornice of Salcantay in Peru gave way.

As for Anderl Heckmair, who saved our lives, I would need a special chapter to sum up his merits.

Twenty years after climbing the *Nordwand* Anderl received the Gold Medal at the International Mountain Film Festival in Trento. Yet despite all successes and honours Anderl remained modest, likeable and reliable – a typical classical mountaineer. He satisfied his love for mountains on all continents, from the Karakoram to Africa's 'Mountains of the Moon'.

He had built up his life organically; however even the fame of a top climber diminishes. Anderl was wise to realise it and with the help of his wife Trudl he gradually changed from the pursuit of physical extremes to more cerebral interests – walking through the mountains with young people, teaching safety and explaining minerals and flowers.

He remained outspoken when asked his opinion and he also remained forever fond of those Swiss cigarillos with the good sounding name 'Toscanelli'. When I took him a packet of these strong Virginian 'Stumpen' for his birthday, there, at the same time, was his personal physician from Oberstdorf. He gave Anderl several bottles of Schnapps saying: 'This strong alcohol will neutralise the strong tobacco.' Quick-witted Anderl remarked to me: 'You see, he is a really good doctor.' Anderl and Trudl came regularly to celebrate my birthdays, but with Anderl being six years older than me, they did not arrive for my 90th in 2002.

Then there came his funeral when a great crowd assembled around the grave of honour and among the mourners fittingly stood the mountain guides of Grindelwald with their flag, from the resort beneath the scene of Anderl's greatest climb. I remembered his words again:

> *'First we were opponents, on the wall we became partners*
> *and afterwards we were friends for a lifetime.'*

RICHARD DAVY

The Oldest Guide in the World

By the time he died on 14 June 2004, at the age of 103, Ulrich Inderbinen's fame had spread far beyond his home town of Zermatt, largely because of his astonishing ability to continue climbing and skiing into old age. He remained an active guide until he was 95, by which time he was almost certainly the oldest guide in the world. He was nearly 90 when in 1990 he climbed the Matterhorn for the last time during the celebrations of the 125th anniversary of the first ascent in 1865. According to John Hunt, who reported on the event in *AJ96*, he reached the top only four hours after leaving the Hörnli Hut. 'Not surprisingly,' wrote Hunt, 'he was the centre of many admirers and much media attention that evening.'

Already well-known among climbers and ski tourers in Zermatt, his renown spread when his biography was published in 1996. It became a best-seller in Switzerland and Germany and was translated into English, French and Japanese (*Ulrich Inderbinen* by Heidi Lanz and Liliane De Meester; in English *Ulrich Inderbinen: As old as the century*, 1997). That brought him celebrity status. Journalists and photographers sought him out for interviews and tourists queued for his autograph. In 1996 he was received by the Pope in Rome.

One of the best-loved of many stories about Ulrich is told by the guide Hermann Biner. A client engaged Ulrich to guide him up the Dufourspitze but was then horrified to see on the official list that his guide was 87. Unwisely he complained to a hut warden. Next day he returned exhausted, having been first on the summit and first back, and was rash enough to grumble that Ulrich had gone too fast. 'My dear sir,' replied Ulrich, 'if you want to climb more slowly you must engage an older guide next time.'

But it was not only his age that endeared him to so many people. He was a man of quiet charm and transparent integrity, preserving the honesty and dignity of his early village life amid the pace and glitter of modern Zermatt. At his funeral he was described as having 'wisdom of the heart'. He was also known for his patience, modesty, a nice line in dry humour and impeccable manners (as we noticed when, at the age of 95, he startled us by leaping up to help my wife with her anorak).

Fame did not noticeably change him or his way of life. He continued to live in the house he had built in 1933-5, chopping his own wood for heating and cooking and never owning a car, bicycle or even a telephone (people knew where to find him when he was needed). He remained a devout Catholic all his life, attending mass without fail, carrying a rosary at all times and crossing himself with holy water before going to bed or leaving home.

105. Matterhorn guide Ulrich Inderbinen, at age 97, with 'his' mountain. (*Richard Davy*)

As a climber he undertook no new or spectacular ascents but he built up a reputation as a thoroughly steady, reliable and considerate guide, always patient with his clients and helpful to younger guides. Until the 1980s he kept up with modern techniques and equipment but thereafter, being by then in his 80s, he did not embrace new developments in sport climbing. Nor did he use some of the new climbing gear that came in around that time. He was essentially a traditional climber who was more interested in the mountains than in advanced techniques for climbing them. Like most Zermatt guides he was particularly competent in rope handling for fast progress on mixed terrain, especially on the Matterhorn, which he climbed about 370 times, but he preferred less crowded peaks such as the Zinalrothorn and the Gabelhorn.

For the last 50 years of his career he had so many regular clients and recommendations by word of mouth that he no longer needed references in his guide's book but early entries are lavish with praise. One of his most faithful clients was Sergei de Vesselitsky Merriman (1882-1957), an AC member who had been London correspondent of a Russian newspaper, *Novoe Vremya*, until the Russian revolution (obituary *AJ61*). After two expeditions with Ulrich in 1928 taking in the Rimpfischhorn and, a few days later, the Obergabelhorn via the Wellenkuppe, returning by the Arbengrat, he wrote that Ulrich 'combines great energy and keenness with prudence and painstaking attention to details'.

After a month of climbing with Ulrich in 1950 a member of the AC whose signature I could not decipher wrote that 'on all occasions his guiding has been sure, reliable and such as to inspire confidence. A quality in him which is very satisfactory is that he is ready to go on in the face of poor conditions both of weather and mountain.'

In 1940 a supervisor on a course he attended wrote: 'his outstanding technical competence, inexhaustible strength and quiet manner make him an excellent mountain guide'. In 1933 an American climber wrote simply that 'our guide was the best', to which Ulrich's dry comment was, 'Perhaps he knew no other guides'.

His only climbing accident in 70 years of guiding was in August 1958 when a client fell while descending the Italian ridge of the Matterhorn. Ulrich held him on the rope but dislocated his own shoulder in the process. Fortunately two colleagues were on hand to wrench the joint back into place and bind his arm.

He also qualified as a ski guide for high tours, but his first expedition, in January 1931, was not auspicious. Engaged by a young Swedish visitor to climb the Breithorn, he lacked climbing skins and simply wound thin rope around the skis, which must have made the 10-hour climb particularly exhausting. All went well until the descent, when he broke a leg as his skis, which lacked metal edges, lost their grip on the glacier. He struggled on in acute pain to Schwarzsee, where he removed his skis and sat on them to slide slowly downhill to Zum See. There he left his skis in his father's sheep shed and hobbled down to Zermatt supporting himself on two ski sticks. The client's rather surprising written comment was 'in spite of that, a good run home'.

However, he went on to be a first-class ski guide, particularly on the Haute Route from Chamonix to Zermatt. He became known for his uncanny sense of direction in bad weather, a skill he must have refined during his military service in the Second World War, when he often had to patrol the high frontier areas above Zermatt on skis alone at night, forbidden to use a torch. Hermann Biner tells of an occasion when some guides and their clients were sitting out a blizzard in the Britannia hut. Late in the day the door suddenly opened and in came Ulrich with a client. To the astonishment of the assembled guides he had made his way from the Monte Rosa hut through the foul weather without a compass, a piece of equipment he regarded as superfluous for an experienced guide on home ground.

He continued to ski until the age of 94. On one of his last outings I watched him set off confidently down the red run from the top station of the Trockener Steg cable car above Zermatt, not fast but very steady and in full control. He told me later he had been practising for the international guides' ski race, an event he always won, as he liked to boast, adding reluctantly, after a suitable pause for effect, that he was the only entrant in his age group.

The story of Ulrich's life is also the story of Zermatt's evolution from a small, isolated village with only 741 inhabitants to one of the world's top winter and summer resorts. He was born on 3 December 1900 in an exceptionally cold winter. Infant and maternal mortality were high in those days, especially in winter. There was no doctor in the village in winter and the 22-mile path to the valley was often blocked, so even a minor illness could be a death sentence. None of the children of his father's first wife reached adulthood, and she herself died young. Ulrich's mother then lost two children herself. The cog railway from Visp, which had opened in 1891, did not start winter services until 1929.

Ulrich's parents were farmers who lived only just above subsistence level. Resisting the pull of the growing tourist industry, they moved in the summer between Zmutt and Blatten, small settlements on the high pastures above Zermatt, with nine children, four cows and several hens, returning to Zermatt in the winter, when the children had to attend school.

There was no school in summer because children were expected to work. Ulrich started at the age of four, tending cows and collecting firewood. He remained a farmer until the age of 20, when he decided to improve his prospects by training as a guide. Before being admitted to the course, however, he had to show that he had climbed a mountain, which he had never in fact done, so he got together with his sister, a friend and the friend's sister, none of whom had any serious climbing experience, and set off up the Matterhorn. The girls wore long skirts and carried flickering lanterns, which often blew out as they groped their way up from the Hörnli hut in the pre-dawn darkness, following the scratches left on the rock by the nailed boots of previous climbers. Astonishingly they all returned safely from this foolhardy trip.

But even after qualifying as a guide it was difficult to find work, especially as he had no connections in the hotel trade, so life remained hard. His first climb as a guide – the Matterhorn – did not come until July 1925, and he spent many long hours waiting for clients or climbing about 1500m to the top station of the Gornergrat railway to meet the first train of the morning (he could not afford a ticket). He also took a variety of other jobs out of season, such as construction work and clearing snow from the Gornergrat railway, as well as helping on his parents' farm.

He learnt rudimentary English from his English aunt who lived in Zermatt. She was married to his uncle Moritz Inderbinen, a guide who had spent time in the household of Dr Montagu Butler, headmaster of Harrow and subsequently Master of Trinity College, Cambridge. (An obituary of Moritz appeared in *AJ* November 1926.)

In 1928, while bringing in the harvest, he met Anna Aufdenblatten, three years his senior, and married her five years later after several postponements caused by poverty and deaths in both families. As was the custom in those days, the brief wedding was at 6am so that everyone, including the couple, could get back to work immediately afterwards. Honeymoons, or even holidays, were unheard of. They had a son, German-Ulrich, and a daughter, Maria, who cared for him after the death of his wife in 1984.

Not until after the Second World War did Ulrich start to earn a comfortable living. Yet he looked back on his early hardships with affection, regretting that tourism had destroyed much of the neighbourly solidarity of Zermatt: 'In the old days life was hard but good. Everyone had little and helped everyone else. People were more content than they are today.' But he gave every impression of enjoying life until almost the end and was tolerant of modern ways. He approached death with serenity. Asked by a young journalist if he was afraid of dying, he replied humorously that he was not worried because when he looked at the local paper he scarcely ever saw a death notice for anyone of his age.

C A RUSSELL

One Hundred Years Ago

(with extracts from the *Alpine Journal*)

A terrible blizzard has been raging for the last 24 hours over the whole of Switzerland. An icy north wind has been whirling tremendous falls of snow before it. The mountains are already covered with two feet of snow, and all the passes are blocked.

Several Alpine villages are isolated, and it is feared that many lives have been lost. The telegraphic and telephonic services have been interrupted.

The bitter wind and exceptionally low temperatures experienced in many parts of the Alps in January 1905 persisted for several weeks and only the most determined parties were able to take advantage of occasional breaks in the weather. On 6 February Julius Kugy with Anton Oitzinger and Giuseppe Pesamosca completed the first winter ascent of the Jôf del Montasio, or Montasch, the second highest summit in the Julian Alps. Kugy later recalled[1] the moment when he completed the ascent from the southern side of the peak.

> As if freed from this earth, I stood over the vast abrupt, in the luminous heaven, on this small white island of my hard-won summit, and enjoyed an hour of such pure happiness as will never return, listening to the music of the heavenly hosts, and dreaming the loveliest mountain dream of all my life.

On 10 February in the Bernina Alps E L Strutt,[2] accompanied by Martin Schocher and Anton Rauch, arrived at the Boval hut which

> ... proved to be in a better state than usual; the door, on arrival, was actually found closed, not more than a foot of snow lay on the floor, which had of course drifted in through the interstices of the roof, and day-light could only be discerned through half a dozen holes in the walls. As usual the party did not suffer from heat, or a surfeit of blankets during the night.

On the following day Strutt and the guides made the first winter ascent of Piz Argient, reaching the summit in a piercing north-east wind.

In the western Alps a notable contribution to the development of ski mountaineering was made by Dr Michel Payot who organised an expedition to complete the Tour of Mont Blanc on ski. Payot, who had taken part in the first attempt[3] to complete the high-level route – the Haute Route – from Chamonix to Zermatt, was accompanied on this occasion by H E Beaujard, Joseph Couttet, Emile Fontaine and the guides Jean and Joseph[4] Ravanel. Leaving Chamonix on 21 January the party crossed the Col du Bonhomme and the Col de la Seigne to Courmayeur, continued over the Petit Col Ferret to Praz de Fort and Martigny and returned to Chamonix on 27 January by way of Champéry and the Col de Coux.

Later in the year another successful expedition on ski was undertaken by Fritz Otto with Josef Kuster and Martin Schocher. On 28 December, after reaching the Fuorcla Crast' Agüzza, Otto and his guides completed the first ski ascent[5] of Piz Bernina.

The severe winter was followed by unsettled weather which continued for much of the climbing season. Although conditions on the high peaks were, in the main, unfavourable many parties were in the field and as in previous years a number of new routes was recorded. In the Mont Blanc range several notable expeditions were undertaken in the Chamonix Aiguilles where on 9 July Albert Brun and Count Robert O'Gorman with Joseph Ravanel and Edouard Charlet made the first ascent of the Aiguille des Pèlerins. Another successful climb was completed by V J E Ryan who on 14 July with Franz and Josef Lochmatter opened the first route on the north face of the Aiguille des Grands Charmoz, following a line in the upper section of the face from a point on the north-west ridge. On 15 July H E Beaujard, accompanied by Joseph Simond, reached the north point and the slightly lower south point of the unclimbed Aiguille des Deux Aigles – named after the two eagles which flew near the party during the ascent. A few days later, on 20 July, Emile Fontaine with Jean Ravanel and Léon Tournier completed the first ascent of the Dent du Caïman, reaching the peak by way of the north-north-east ridge of the neighbouring Dent du Crocodile and making the first descent and ascent of that ridge during the expedition.

Later in the season, on 15 August, Fontaine and the same guides completed another fine expedition: the first complete traverse of Les Droites from the Col des Droites to the Col de l'Aiguille Verte. Elsewhere in the range two strong guideless parties were climbing on the Italian side of Mont Blanc: on 21 July Karl Blodig and E T Compton made the first complete descent of the east face of the Aiguille Blanche de Peuterey; and five days later E H F Bradby, J H Wicks and Claude Wilson made the first recorded ascent of Mont Rouge de Peuterey, at the lower end of the Peuterey ridge.

In the Arolla district on 20 July A Stuart Jenkins with Jean Bournissen and Jean Gaudin made the first ascent of the steep north-north-east ridge of Mont Blanc de Cheilon. Further along the chain on 28 August V J E Ryan, accompanied on this occasion by Gabriel and Josef Lochmatter, joined forces with Geoffrey Winthrop Young and his guide Josef Knubel to open a new route on the south-east face of the Weisshorn, completing the climb less than two metres from the summit.

In the Bernese Alps on 31 July Heinrich Buttmann with R Müller and P Rieppel made the first ascent of the north-east ridge of the Mittelhorn in the Wetterhorn group. In the following month, on 18 August, the guideless party of R P Hope and W T Kirkpatrick descended the Nesthorn by moonlight after reaching the summit by way of the unclimbed north-north-west ridge.

> The mountain was in very bad condition, all but the very steepest rocks being covered with 18 inches of new snow, which had to be scraped away to find the holds, and this made the time abnormally long.

Despite the unfavourable weather several new routes were completed in other districts. In the Graian Alps in July Helene Kuntze and a companion with the guide Pierre Dayné scaled the west-north-west ridge of the Roccia Viva. In the Austrian Alps on 23 August Viktor Pillwax, accompanied by Johann Unterweger and Andreas Hutter made the first ascent of the dangerous west face of the Grossglockner, his second notable route[6] on the peak. In the Dolomites two outstanding expeditions were completed: the first ascent of the long north ridge of the Crozzon di Brenta by Adolf Schulze and Fritz Schneider on 20 July; and, on 11 August, the ascent by Georg Leuchs, solo, of the unclimbed south-west face of Cimone della Pala.

Elsewhere in the Alps further progress in connection with a major engineering project was announced on 24 February.

> The piercing of the Simplon Tunnel was completed at twenty minutes past seven this morning. ...
>
> The final connection was made by the explosion of charges placed in holes driven into the roof of the south gallery, which left a gaping hole on a level with the floor of the north gallery. The water in the latter, the pressure of which had been diminished by pumping from the northern side, flowed rapidly away down the southern side, without doing any damage. An hour later, the water had subsided to its normal level. The direction and length of the works show no apparent deviation from the plans. The heat in the galleries is suffocating.

Later in the year ceremonies were held to mark the official opening of the road on the Italian side of the Great St Bernard Pass.

> The first automobile reached the Hospice from Aosta on July 1. There was then snow on the last part of the ascent. It is reckoned that an automobile will ordinarily take about 1½ hr. from Aosta to the Hospice as against the 7 hrs. required by the diligence.

106. Camp on Nanda Devi Saddle, 8 June 1905. (*T G Longstaff*)

On 10 May T G Longstaff, accompanied by Alexis and Henri Brocherel of Courmayeur, arrived at Almora in northern India to commence his first expedition to the Himalaya. During the following months Longstaff and the guides, supported at intervals by small teams of local men, travelled widely and climbed to a considerable height on several occasions. Starting in the Garhwal region the party established a camp in the Goriganga valley to investigate the eastern approaches to Nanda Devi (7816m). On 8 June, after ascending the Lawan glacier and finding the tracks of a snow leopard, Longstaff and his companions reached the saddle – later known as Longstaff's Col – at 5910m on the rim of the Nanda Devi basin where they built a platform for a small tent. After passing a very cold night they climbed for some distance up the south ridge of Nanda Devi East (7434m) before descending to the Lawan valley. Longstaff then attempted to reach the summit of the neighbouring Nanda Kot (6861m) and on 11 June had reached a height of some 6450m on the north-east ridge before dangerous snow conditions forced the party to retreat.

After reaching Askot at the end of June Longstaff accompanied C A Sherring, the Deputy Commissioner of the Almora district, on a journey into Tibet during which he investigated the northern approaches to Api (7132m) and Nampa (6755m) in the north-west corner of Nepal. In Tibet Longstaff and the guides made a determined attempt to ascend Gurla Mandhata (7728m) from the west, reaching a height of some 7270m on 25 July after surviving a serious fall in an avalanche below the west ridge.

Before the guides left in October the party spent several days examining the southern and western approaches to Trisul (7120m). After this remarkable journey Longstaff, who had also investigated the Pachhu, Shalang and Poting glaciers, made a number of corrections to the existent map and provided a detailed description of his route. Inspired at an early age by an account[7] of climbing in the Himalaya he now made his own important contribution to the exploration of the region.

In a paper read before the Alpine Club in the following year Longstaff explained that he had hoped to visit Sikkim after the monsoon, one of his aims in that region being to reconnoitre the Yalung glacier with a view to identifying a possible route on the south-west face of Kangchenjunga (8586m). 'This part of my programme I gave up as soon as I heard that another mountaineering expedition was on its way there to try this very route.'

The expedition in question was undertaken by an international party which left Darjeeling on 8 August. Dr Jules Jacot-Guillarmod, Charles Reymond and Alexis Pache, an army officer, all from Switzerland placed themselves under the leadership of Aleister Crowley and the party was completed by A C Rigo de Righi, the Italian manager of an hotel in Darjeeling. On 1 September, after the party had spent several days forcing a route up the Yalung glacier, Pache and Reymond reached a height of some 6500m before returning to the seventh and highest camp which had been established at 6200m. At this point Pache, who had endured three unpleasant nights after his bedding had been mislaid, indicated that he was content to have climbed to such a height and that he wished to descend to a lower camp. Late in the day Guillarmod, de Righi, Pache and three porters formed a single rope and began the descent. As they were traversing a steep slope one of the porters slipped, starting an avalanche in which Pache and the three porters lost their lives.[8] Following this disaster and the loss of another porter who had fallen to his death the expedition was abandoned and the survivors returned to Darjeeling.

Although the expedition ended in tragedy it had not been entirely unsuccessful. By climbing for some distance up the slopes above the Yalung glacier and returning with a number of photographs the party made a useful contribution to the exploration of the approaches to the south-west face of Kangchenjunga.

In October D W Freshfield, accompanied by A L Mumm and the guide Moritz Inderbinen, travelled to Uganda with the aim of exploring the peaks

107. Members of the AACB including Albert Hitz, the first President (*seated, right*), at the Restaurant Sonne in Bern, May 1906. (*Akademischer Alpenclub Bern*)

in the Ruwenzori range. After engaging local porters and a young Englishman named Moggridge to act as interpreter Freshfield and his companions arrived at Fort Portal on 21 October and approached the peaks in very bad weather by way of the Mubuku valley. On 2 November Mumm and Inderbinen reached a height of some 4300m on the Moore glacier[9] at the head of the valley but on the following day, to Freshfield's disappointment, a further deterioration in the weather forced the party to retreat.

In South Africa members of the Mountain Club explored the Hex River Mountains where several new routes were established. On 31 December a notable climb was completed by G F Travers-Jackson and Hugo Lambrechts who made the first ascent of Buffel's Dome (1448m), an imposing peak connected with the main range by a narrow ridge. After crossing this sensational knife-edge during the descent Travers-Jackson considered that 'the bottoms of the gorges on both sides of this ridge are not far off 2,000 feet below.'

In South America the German geologist Fritz Reichert explored a large area of the Puna de Atacama, the elevated plateau containing some of the highest peaks in the Andes. In May Reichert climbed alone for some 1700m from a high bivouac to complete the first recorded ascent of Cerro Socompa (6051m), a volcanic peak on the border between Chile and Argentina.

In Britain experienced parties were active in all the principal regions. In Wales during May G D and A P Abraham opened two notable routes: *Monolith Crack* 'involving an excursion into the depths of the mountain' on the Gribin Facet; and, with Andrew Thomson, *Hawk's Nest Buttress* on the main cliff of Glyder Fach. The Abraham brothers also investigated Clogwyn Du'r Arddu where in September they established *East Wall Climb* on the West Buttress. Another visitor to this famous cliff was P S Thompson who in July led a party up *Deep Chimney* on the Far West Buttress. In September J M Archer Thomson and Oscar Eckenstein returned to Lliwedd, completing *Horned Crag Route* on the East Buttress. In the Lake District on 17 August G F and A J Woodhouse continued their exploration of Dow Crag, making the first ascent of *Woodhouse's Route* on 'B' Buttress. On the Isle of Skye on 21 April Harold Raeburn and Erik Ullén accompanied by W C Slingsby and G A Solly established the line now known as *Raeburn's Route* up the slabs of An Caisteal.

A welcome event during the year was the formation of the Akademischer Alpenclub Bern on 27 October following a meeting on 18 October at the Café Merz in Bern. The first President of the Club was Albert Hitz and the names of the original members were recorded in the first issue of the Club's annual publication – *the Jahresbericht*. Many famous mountaineers have belonged to the ranks of the AACB.

Another event of note was the publication of the first volume of *Kaukasus*, the account by the Hungarian explorer Maurice de Déchy of his seven expeditions to the range. This comprehensive work in three volumes, illustrated with photographs by the author, was reviewed in the *Alpine Journal* where it was noted that as de Déchy had 'visited every important mountain group from the Tsagerker Pass in the W. to Basardjusi in the E., his book might not inaptly be entitled *The Caucasus from End to End*.' [10] Other books published during the year included *The Central Tian-Shan Mountains, 1902-1903*, a record by Gottfried Merzbacher of the exploration and scientific observation completed during his expedition to that range.

On 20 October the death occurred of C E Mathews, an original member and a former President of the Alpine Club and the first President of the Climbers' Club. In a notice which appeared in the *Alpine Journal* it was recalled that Mathews had made twelve ascents of Mont Blanc 'which exercised over him a singular fascination' before the publication of his book *The Annals of Mont Blanc*.[11]

In conclusion it is interesting to note the following extracts from the announcement made by Freshfield during his address to the British Association at Durban in September 1905.

Lord Curzon,[12] acting on his own initiative, had expressed his desire that some further endeavours should be made to explore, and, if possible, to climb, either Kangchenjunga or Mount Everest, and with this end in view had proposed to Mr. Freshfield to act as an intermediary in organising such an attempt and obtaining the sympathy and material support of the Alpine Club, the Geographical Society, and any other scientific bodies likely to be interested. On his own part he promised to recommend to the Indian Government to contribute substantially to the cost of the expedition, and to do his best to get permission from the Nepalese authorities for its sojourn in their territory.

The matter was accordingly brought before the Council of the Royal Geographical Society and our Committee. The Council instructed their President to make further inquiry of the Viceroy as to the exact scope of the proposed expedition before deciding on any action. The Alpine Club Committee promptly requested our President to express their most cordial appreciation of the Viceroy's suggestion, and their willingness to co-operate as far as was in their power. ...

Meantime the resignation of Lord Curzon has delayed any further steps in the matter. To his personal initiative the proposal was doubtless due. It is not every Viceroy of India who is an enthusiastic geographer, and we know as yet nothing of what his successor's views may be. We have good grounds, however, for hope. Lord Minto[13] has long been a member of the Alpine Club. There is, moreover, a growing interest among the Survey officers in India in mountain work, and we trust that after due deliberation a joint and competent party of surveyors and mountaineers may be organised to explore the environs of the highest mountain of the world, and to climb as far as possible towards its summit.

REFERENCES

1   Dr Julius Kugy, *Alpine Pilgrimage*. London, John Murray, 1934.
2   Colonel Strutt, the second-in-command of the 1922 Mount Everest Expedition, was President of the Alpine Club from 1935 to 1937 and Editor of the *Alpine Journal* from 1927 to 1937.
3   See *AJ108*, 216, 2003.
4   The famous guide Ravanel, *le Rouge*.
5   A ski ascent is defined by Sir Arnold Lunn as 'an expedition on which ski were used until the foot of the final rock or ice ridges.'
6   Pillwax, accompanied by the guides Sebastian Hutter and Peter Unterberger, had made the first ascent of the south face on 29 June 1891.
7   By W W Graham who had spent several months in the Himalaya in 1883.
8   The bodies of the victims were recovered three days later. Pache's grave, on the site of the party's fifth camp at a height of some 5500m, was marked by a large cairn, a wooden cross and a granite plaque engraved with his name and the date of the accident.
9   Named after the naturalist J E S Moore who reached a height of some 4540m on the main, summit ridge of Mount Baker (4843m) in March 1900.
10   *The Alps from End to End* by Sir Martin Conway had been published in 1895.
11   Charles Edward Mathews, *The Annals of Mont Blanc*. London, T Fisher Unwin, 1898.
12   Viceroy of India 1899-1905. Foreign Secretary 1919-1924.
13   Governor-General of Canada 1898-1904. Viceroy of India 1905-1910.

Valedictory Address

ALAN BLACKSHAW

(Read before the Alpine Club on 7 December 2004)

When our then President, CE Mathews, first put forward the idea of a Presidential Valedictory Address, back in 1880 (*AJ* 10, 251, 1881), it was on the basis that the outgoing President should not just '*slink away*' but should say something of moment to the Club.

He referred in particular to the President being acquainted with what he called '*the traditions of Alpine government*'. Nowadays such issues are perhaps more the concern of the British Mountaineering Council (BMC) or, as regards overseas ones, the International Mountaineering and Climbing Federation (UIAA). I have been involved with both of these bodies from time to time over the years, as well as with the Alpine Club, and will venture some personal comments on some of the issues of which I have had direct experience, and which may still be of some interest for the present. Mathews was evidently himself attracted to international collaboration, attending two Congresses of alpine clubs in 1878 and 1879 (*AJ* 9, 154, 333, 1879).

My starting point is that good administration is important for mountaineering; and that it is worth the various mountaineering bodies – especially the Club, the BMC and UIAA – trying to help people to climb or travel in the mountains, more or better or more safely.

The Club has a special role of leadership and influence, given its very long tradition of mountaineering and its commitment to mountaineering freedoms and ethics. It also has the ability to comment on and defend these freedoms and ethics, notably through the independent viewpoint of the *Alpine Journal.*

The fact that the Club is so firmly within the world of mountaineering for its own sake – with practically no links with commerce or officialdom – is perhaps its greatest strength. I speak, as regards the latter, as someone with both a commitment to the public service and a recognition of its limitations in dealing with, for example, customary freedoms or mountain traditions.

Early days

A number of valedictory addresses have been autobiographical, so it may not be out of place for me to say something also of my own relationship with the hills. I first experienced them when I was evacuated to South Wales during the Second World War, living for some time on a Welsh-speaking hill-farm in the shadow of the Carmarthen Van. In 1947, I cycled from my home in Liverpool to Land's End and back, for my fourteenth birthday; and the following year cycled to Glencoe and Lochaber. It was there that I met a young climber, John West, who encouraged me to walk over the Mamores; and who subsequently sold me his nailed climbing boots and hemp rope when he became engaged to be married.

Thereafter, I entered the friendly world of the impecunious young climber described by Dennis Gray in his book *Rope Boy* (1970). Most travel was by hitchhiking; and we either camped or stayed in a range of barns, notably at Ogwen (Williams), Wall End in Langdale, Altnafeadh (Cameron) and Glen Brittle (Macrae), or sometimes at Idwal Cottage or other Youth Hostels.

Climbing partnerships also depended on something like hitchhiking – meeting up with whoever might be available and willing to team-up at the time. When joining a party of three, it would usually be necessary for me, as the incomer, to offer to lead the second rope, an effective but inadvisable way of developing climbing skills.

I was fortunate to become a member of the Wayfarers' Club in about 1950 and benefited from more regular climbing partnerships, notably with George Bintley and John Walton. By then we had started doing climbs like the Great Slab and the East Buttress routes on Clogwyn D'ur Arddu, which were little frequented at that time.

In 1951 I was offered, through school, a spare place on a Workers' Educational Association party going to Annecy, which gave me the chance to get to Chamonix. There I met Geoffrey Sutton, and we climbed the Aiguille de l'M, surviving a scary lightning storm that night, camped on the Nantillons Glacier.

After starting at Oxford in 1951, I mainly climbed with the Oxford University Mountaineering Club (OUMC), mostly with Hamish Nicol, but initially at least very much in the shadow of the previous Oxford generation, including Tom Bourdillon, Derek Bull, Anthony Rawlinson and Michael Westmacott. David Cox was constantly supportive, as Senior Member in residence.

The following summer, 1952, however, I found myself unexpectedly alone in Chamonix again, and met up with an FRCC member, Desmond Stevens, at the Chalet Bioley. Together we were to traverse the Aiguilles du Diable, but unfortunately without the guidebook which we had left behind at the Col de la Fourche hut. The atmosphere of the time is conveyed by his subsequent article:

> My companion of 19 summers was inexperienced but full of confidence. Blackamoor' [*sic*] 'led the first Diable as a matter of course. ... I would have enjoyed leading the second pinnacle, but my friend was half-way up before I could make my wishes known. ... We now stood on the summit of the Chaubert and an amusing discussion took place, to decide who should rappel last. Blackamoor appeared to regard my

160ft of nylon string as a joke and eloquently presented his case. In short that I should have sufficient faith in my own rope to descend last. This was *unanswerable*.[1] It can only be good to see yourself as others see you.

By way of night climbing at Oxford, I helped Hamish one Eights Week to put a neon sign on top of Trinity Tower, flashing on and off '*Bloody Trinity*', apparently as retribution by Balliol for some Trinity aggression earlier in the week.

In the OUMC I particularly enjoyed the lectures and Dinners, which gave us the opportunity to meet well-known figures of the time, like Sir John Hunt, Douglas Milner, Eric Shipton, Ken Tarbuck and, very memorably, Geoffrey Winthrop-Young.

My best season was in 1955, on the Stage des Etrangers at the Ecole Nationale in Chamonix, when Bob Downes and I did the south face of the Aiguille du Geant and the north face of the Aiguille de Triolet; and Eric Langmuir and I did the Republique Arête of the Grands Charmoz. All three of us, and Geoff Sutton, also did the south face of the Pointe Gugliermina and the north face of the Piz Badile.

By that time I had started National Service and shortly afterwards became an instructor in the then Cliff Assault Wing of 42 Royal Marine Commando, commanded by Mike Banks.

In the summer of 1956, I, like a number of others, was greatly shaken by the tragic accident to Tom Bourdillon and Dick Viney on the Jagihorn (*AJ* 61, 357, 1956). It was a terrible shock and we had to think very deeply about mountaineering, the ethical issues involved, and the question of obligations to families and civil society.

I came to realise that the very hard forms of mountaineering no longer held quite the same appeal for me. But I continued to enjoy the hills in various ways, notably through: expeditions with Sir John Hunt to the Caucasus (1958) and Greenland (1960); writing my Penguin *Mountaineering* (1965); climbing and mountain warfare instruction in the Royal Marines Reserve (until 1974); ski-touring or ski-mountaineering, including a traverse of the Alps from Kaprun to Gap in 1972, and of Scandinavia end to end over the period 1973-77 (*AJ* 83, 91, 1978); and completing the Scottish Munros (1978).

George Band discussed the problem of how to balance work with mountaineering in his Valedictory Address, which he said he might appropriately have called '*I Chose to Work*' (*AJ* 95, 1-10, 1990). In my own case, I had joined the Civil Service in 1956, and fitted in these mountain activities with a number of jobs, mainly in the Ministry of Power in London where I was Private Secretary to various ministers for about five years altogether, but with secondments to the Diplomatic Service (UK Delegation to OECD, Paris, 1964-66) and to the City (Charterhouse Bank, 1972-73). In 1974 I was very pleased to move to Scotland to set up the HQ of the

Offshore Supplies Office in Glasgow for the burgeoning North Sea oil and gas programme. I will mention later some of the difficulties which were to arise, following this period, when I was to attempt to switch to more of a mountain way of life, at the end of the 1970s.

Some mountain issues to 1980

I had joined the AC in 1954, on attaining the age of 21, which was the minimum at that time; and received a nice welcoming letter from Basil Goodfellow, the Club's Hon Secretary.

We were in parallel setting up the Alpine Climbing Group (ACG), modelled on the Groupe de Haute Montagne, and I became Editor of its *Bulletin*, which disseminated information about current alpine activity, a role now mainly fulfilled by the modern climbing magazine.

I was also involved in 1955 with the working party set up by Sir Edwin Herbert (later Lord Tangley), our then President, to examine ways of improving recruitment to the AC; and repeated this in 1967-68 when Sir Charles Evans led another group on the future of the Club (*AJ* 75, 285, 1970). These recognised that the Club needed to be more accessible and should give better value for money through improved services, really the same issue we face now.

Dick Viney, who, as I mentioned a moment ago, was the victim of a tragic accident in 1956, was an immensely energetic and effective Hon Secretary of the Climbers' Club at the time, and had won the MC in the Parachute Regiment during the Rhine crossing. As I was his Assistant Secretary, it fell to me to succeed him (1956-61). There was a lot to do in such an active Club, with five huts; a major guidebook programme; meets and Dinners; and a need to relate to the other 'Senior Clubs' and the BMC. We bought freeholds of the huts in order to secure them for the longer term; but also faced the difficult issue of reducing the unduly powerful position of some of the hut custodians in relation to the active climbers or elected members of the Committee. I enjoyed working with the several successive Presidents – HRC Carr, David Cox and AB Hargreaves.

My first connection with the UIAA was in about 1961, when I attended a meeting in Switzerland at the request of the BMC, and met Egmond d'Arcis, *The Times* correspondent in Geneva, who had been involved in the foundation of the UIAA in 1932.

I was pleased to be asked to edit the *Alpine Journal* 1968 -70; and changed it, after much consultation, into a single volume, with black and white illustrations integrated with the text. It is very good that Stephen Goodwin, in producing the present AJ, has taken this to such a splendid further stage, with coloured photos throughout the text.

One of the main issues in the 1970s was the reform of the BMC, of which I had become President in 1973. Based in Knightsbridge, it could not attract enough active climbers locally for its range of Committees, so we moved it to Manchester where, happily, it proved possible to gain considerable support. We also set-up a Future Policy Group to determine its strategic objectives and main functions.[2] The main priority was to keep the BMC in close touch with the 'grass roots' of climbing and ensure that, by constantly rejuvenating itself, it did not become monolithic or a bureaucracy. One of the ideas of the time was that the AC should have a strong role on the international side of the BMC,[3] and I will return to this later.

I was also much involved with the Mount Everest Foundation (MEF) over the period 1968-74, as one of the Trustees nominated by the AC. This was in the Club's capacity as one of the two co-equal Constituent Societies of the MEF, the other being the Royal Geographical Society (RGS).

The MEF had by then run down its resources with generous grants and there was a suggestion that it should be wound up, its main tasks having been completed. The AC, through a working group led by Anthony Rawlinson, however, successfully argued that the MEF was still needed in the longer-term in the interests of small expeditions. This in turn led to a need to secure the MEF's financial future; and David Cox and I were appointed, for the Club, to the MEF's Administration Sub-Committee which recommended that the MEF should move on to a much cheaper voluntary basis, more like say the Climbers' Club, thus economising on the cost of the Secretary and of the room in the RGS. As President of the BMC at the same time I was also able to facilitate the setting-up of a parallel system of BMC grants (funded by the Sports Council) to help offset the shortage of MEF funds; these grants have recently been running at over £40,000 annually, and must have a made a useful contribution to the current excellence of British exploratory mountaineering overseas.

In consequence of the MEF giving up its room at the RGS, the MEF Trustees asked the RGS in 1973 to take over the administration and storage both of the Everest photos and of the documentary archives, broadly as the RGS had done in the period 1921-55, before the MEF was set-up. This was on the basis that the RGS would receive payments in the form of photo-royalties and rent.

This issue has recently come to the fore, with the current claim by the RGS that the MEF had not only transferred the administration and storage of the Everest photos to them in April 1973, but had also '*assigned*' the ownership and copyright.[4] In consequence the RGS appear to be treating the surplus income from the Everest photos, after recovering their costs, as RGS '*commercial funds*' available for RGS purposes generally; and not as MEF funds for mountain exploration and research, as was the original intention both of the AC and of the RGS in gifting the photos to the MEF in 1955-56.

Partly because of my residual obligations as a former Trustee at the relevant time, and partly because of the significance of this loss of funds for mountain exploration, I have thought it necessary to research the MEF and AC archives over the past year to check on the available historical evidence relevant to the RGS's claim. My Report [5] confirms that the MEF

Trustees collectively never even discussed the question of transferring the ownership and copyright of these photos to the RGS in April 1973, the date stated by the RGS; nor at any other time during my time as a Trustee 1968-74; nor indeed thereafter until they queried the position with the RGS in 1990-91. But it was mentioned retrospectively in correspondence between Staff of the RGS and MEF after I had left in 1974 and in the 1975 AGM papers. Such an issue, had it been considered by the Trustees in 1973, would have raised questions on, for example, the MEF's powers of disposal; on the need for income from MEF assets to be used only for the MEF objects; on the conditions to be attached to such a disposal of assets and the related income; and on the potential for conflict of interest for the RGS-nominated Trustees in participating in any such decision.

The Club's Committee has recently requested the views of the MEF and the RGS as to what they now consider to be the correct position, in the light of this historical research.

More of a mountain way of life

By the end of the 1970s, the problem of how to combine work with mountaineering posed me the difficult choice of whether or not to leave the Civil Service. This had become a serious issue firstly because I had had to return from Scotland to London to head the Coal Division there. This meant that I had to leave my post as Director General of the Offshore Supplies Office, which I enjoyed both because of the interest of the work and because of its location in Scotland. But, secondly, I also needed time to revise my Penguin *Mountaineering*, which was out of print, and for other mountain writing.

By a freak of fate, my resignation from the Department in August 1979, unknown to myself, was to coincide with a Parliamentary investigation of what was at that time alleged to be mis-spending on North Sea oil grants; and a number of newspapers incorrectly concluded that I had left the Civil Service because of this.

Although I was exonerated by the Government in Parliament[6] and was subsequently to receive Government compensation,[7] the *Daily Telegraph* and the *Daily Mail* would not withdraw or apologise. It was not until two years later, in 1981, that I was to secure libel damages and costs in personal actions against them in the High Court; and it was to be not until two years after that, in 1983, that the issue was to be finally disposed of, when an appeal by the *Telegraph* was to be dismissed in the Court of Appeal.[8]

This long trauma effectively destroyed my hopes of pursuing mountain writing as a second career, firstly because it was extremely distracting, and secondly because subsequently I had to spend most of my time working as a management consultant, for financial reasons. But I often reflected that this catastrophe was far preferable to those much worse ones caused by mountain accidents, from which my family and I have so far, mercifully, been free.

By leaving the Civil Service, I have at least been able to live nearer the mountains, either in Scotland or in Le Tour, Argentiere.

Mountain training

The review of future policy for the BMC in the 1970s[2] had left to one side the difficult issue of mountain training, on which a serious dispute was emerging between the BMC and the mountain training boards. The dispute centred on what was the correct role for the BMC with, on the one hand, its prime interest in maintaining the freedoms and traditions of mountaineering as a sport, and on the other, its responsibilities towards the Mountain Training Boards, with their emphasis on mountain training often as a form of outdoor education.

This complicated issue had been addressed instead in a separate report to the BMC by Lord Hunt,[9] and eventually there had been a formal Arbitration by Emlyn Jones (with George Band and David Cox), on the initiative of Peter Lloyd as President of the AC (*AJ* 85, 12,1980). One of the recommendations of this Arbitration was that the BMC should set up a Standing Advisory Committee on Mountain Training to provide a mechanism by which such disputes might be avoided in the future; and the BMC asked me to chair this.

One of the first issues we were asked to address was the nature of the BMC's relationship with Plas y Brenin, the Sports Council's national centre for mountain activities. We advised that this should be seen not just as a mountain training centre, important though that role was, but more as a centre of gravity for British mountaineering, with a much wider role in support of the BMC. In 1985, I was asked by the Sports Council to be the Chair of the Plas y Brenin Committee, and continued to promote this co-operation between the BMC and the Centre until the late 1990s.

A second main issue was the future organisation of mountain training in Britain, and in particular how to produce a UK perspective while maintaining the independence of the mountain training boards in the home countries. We recommended the setting up of a UK Mountain Training Board to replace the then Joint Co-ordinating Committee, with a remit to consult regularly on those issues requiring a UK perspective.[10]

At that time there was also the question of how to relate British mountain training with overseas schemes, such as the emerging European Mountain Leader qualification. In my then capacity of President of the Mountaineering Commission of the UIAA (1989-98) (supported by Roger Payne (BMC) as Secretary), I encouraged it to set up a working group to advise on the possible introduction of International Model Standards for mountain training. Once these standards had been brought into operation,[11] the BMC applied for the British mountain leader and mountain instructor awards to be accepted as meeting them. In consequence, these British awards are, quite rightly, recognised internationally as being in line with international standards.

The success of the UIAA model training standards is due in no small measure to the support which the scheme has received from Britain, especially from Iain Peter (BMC) as Secretary of the initial Working Party (1992-94), and from John Cousins (UKMTB) as Secretary and now Chairman of the Sub-Committee which runs the scheme, since 1998.

Freedoms of mountain access

Probably the most important single mountain issue with which I have been involved since the 1980s has however been the recent legislation to secure statutory rights of public access in Scotland.[12]

It brings to an end the campaign started by our former President, James Bryce OM, one-time Professor of Civil Law at Oxford, with his Access to Mountains Bills from 1885 onwards. His speech of 4 March 1892 in the House of Commons[13] was perhaps the best-ever exposition of the need for free, responsible, public access to mountains, in its correct historical and customary context. Before him a previous AC President, Sir Leslie Stephen, had also taken a stand on access with the adventurous excursions of his Sunday Tramps society.

James Bryce stood for a civil liberty of harmless and responsible public access to mountains, reflecting earlier public customs and freedoms which were being eroded in practice at that time by some landowners and their lawyers. My understanding of the existing freedoms of Scottish access is closely in line with his perception, namely that there is a long-standing general freedom in Scotland to take harmless responsible access to land not in cultivation without any need to seek consent, and without trespass, generally recognised by landholder and public alike as an accepted normal convention of society.

However, when I became a Board Member of the Government agency, Scottish Natural Heritage (SNH), in 1991, with a responsibility on the Board for access issues, I came to realise that the current official view treated public access not as a civil liberty but as a privilege tolerated by land-managers who could, in the SNH view, bring it to an end at any time.

This was so different from the long-standing traditional position in Scotland as I knew it, that I undertook historical research from 1994 onwards, supported by Scottish Environment LINK and the Ramblers' Association Scotland (especially David Morris), to explore how such a very different official view, so strongly favouring the land-owner or land manager, could have become established. This research (14) confirmed that James Bryce's more liberal approach was indeed broadly in line with long-standing Ministerial, Law Officer and other official views going well back into the 19th century. These were to be very usefully summarised in 1942 by the then Secretary of State, Tom Johnston, who advised Ernest Bevin officially that '*in Scotland anyone is at liberty to walk over land outside the curtilage provided he does not breach the poaching law or harm fences etc*' and that '*there is no law of trespass in Scotland*'.[15] It became clear that, quite remarkably, these earlier more liberal official views had been replaced within the official system by the present more repressive ones in the late 1960s through the efforts, not of lawyers, but of a small group of planners, administrators and land-managers, notably the Master of Arbuthnott (later Lord Arbuthnott), Land Agent to the Nature Conservancy.[16]

When the Land Reform (Scotland) Bill was passing through the Scottish Parliament in 2002, I was asked to give evidence to the Justice 2 Committee, mainly in a personal capacity; and took the opportunity to enlarge on the earlier freedoms of public access as described by James Bryce and Tom Johnston, linking them with one of the fundamental principles of British civil liberties, namely that, as a general rule, what is not expressly prohibited is permitted.[17]

Although all of my historical research on the earlier more liberal official views had been made available to SNH since 1994 as it had progressed, I became the subject of public attacks in the Justice 2 Committee by their representatives,[18] who, along with the Law Society of Scotland (LSS), were still arguing for the new, more repressive, land-management approach developed within the official system since the late 1960s, claiming, incorrectly in my view, that this had always been the position.

At the invitation of the Convenor of the Justice 2 Committee, Pauline McNeill MSP,[19] I made a further submission to her Committee, aiming to show how these new views appeared to be out of line with the Tom Johnston letter and other earlier historical evidence and, where this was indeed so, were perhaps unlikely to be soundly based.[20] The Justice 2 Committee effectively accepted this with their conclusion that:

> *The SNH and Law Society position is not the position understood by the majority of people taking access in Scotland and reflected in many of the written submissions on the Bill. Alan Blackshaw's extensive historical researches have also demonstrated that understanding of the legal position as interpreted in government statements (and statements by key organisations such as the SLF) has changed over time. For example, Government statements since the 1960s which refer to a Scottish law of trespass are compared to the statement by the Secretary of State for Scotland (Tom Johnston) in 1942 that "there is no law of trespass in Scotland" and that there is a presumption of freedom to roam so long as no offence is committed and crops and fences are not damaged.*[21]

The Convenor also subsequently advised the Scottish Parliament that she had '*rejected*' the legal opinion of SNH on trespass, on the grounds that '*there is a widely-held view that there has been a right of access in Scotland and that there is no evidence that there is a prohibition*'.[22]

SNH have however continued to attack me openly on their website until earlier this year, but without mentioning these Parliamentary conclusions.[23] This raises a number of issues about the propriety of an executive agency using public resources to attack an independent Parliamentary witness, especially when, as in my case, his evidence has been broadly upheld by the Parliamentary Committee concerned.

Suffice it to say that James Bryce might well have been pleased with the access provisions of the Land Reform (Scotland) Act 2003 as they finally emerged. They may even have exceeded his expectations by applying not just to mountains, but to virtually all land, water and air in Scotland.

I hope that this Scottish Act, and the related Scottish Access Code, may serve as an example of what might be aimed for elsewhere, including even in the rest of Britain, given that there are customary freedoms of harmless access in many areas there, for example in the north of England and in Wales, and also on many sea-cliffs, not dissimilar to the Scottish ones.

Further progress otherwise may need to look more to a Fundamental Human Right of the Enjoyment of Nature about which I wrote briefly in 2002.[24]

The life of the Alpine Club

I have very much enjoyed the opportunity of being so closely involved with the Club over the past three years, which would not ordinarily have been the case, living as I do in the North of Scotland. The regular lectures, the mountain art exhibitions, the meets, and the two annual dinners which we have held in the Lake District (on the initiative of Doug Scott), have all been well attended; and the *Journal* and the new *Bulletin* a great success.

A highpoint was in May 2003, on the occasion of the 50th Anniversary of the first ascent of Everest, when there were major celebrations organised by the MEF (chaired by Charles Clarke) with the administrative support of the RGS, and also an excellent party at the Club. It was a busy month for me, as the Centenary of the Ski Club of Great Britain (SCGB), of which I was also President at the time, was only a few days apart.

It will not come as a surprise that we have had a small Future Policy Group to look at the future direction of the Club. One of the Group's main conclusions was that the Club continues to have a very important role for networking among active exploratory mountaineers; in the provision of the information needed for active mountaineering worldwide; and in arranging for meets overseas. Another is that the Club should consciously seek to develop partnerships primarily with the BMC and the UIAA, but also, for example, with the RGS, the Himalayan Club, the Kendal Film Festival and the Festival of Mountain Literature. The Group also recommended to the Committee that those responsible for the Club's heritage assets, especially of books and pictures, should review them so that any not required in fulfilment of our important heritage role (eg second or third copies of books) might be considered for sale, in order to help provide funds for a separate climbing or development fund, whether charitable or not. It also drew attention to the need to prepare for the Club's 150th Anniversary in 2007; and recommended that there should be a new publication on the Club's history, which, I am pleased to say, George Band is undertaking.

We have, finally, also introduced a category of Associate of the Club. This is different from any of the forms of Membership and is intended for those unable to qualify for membership but who support the objects of the Club and may be able to help in achieving them.

Throughout my time as President of the AC, there has been a very heavy burden of administration on the Club's officers, Committee and key individuals both voluntary and staff, especially in relation to the Clubhouse and the many Club activities here, and also the Library Council. It must be evident that we owe a considerable debt to all of them, and I would like to thank every one of them on the Club's behalf.

Relations with the BMC

I mentioned earlier this evening that one of the ideas in the reorganisation of the BMC back in the 1970s was that the Club might have a stronger role on the international side of the BMC.[3] And I am pleased that the BMC and the Club are now looking at this issue together.

Peter Lloyd, in his Valedictory Address (*AJ 85*, 3-15, 1980) drew attention to the need for regular discussions between the Club and the BMC. The BMC is growing rapidly, particularly by attracting more and more individual members. I do not see this as being in anyway detrimental to the AC, which itself needs more members; indeed it must be welcomed. A closer association between us may help to make the Club better known and more readily accessible.

I hope that if, at some point in the future, the BMC decides to move to larger premises and offers the Club the possibility of sharing them, then the Committee of the day will consider the issue on its merits, bearing in mind the success of the American Alpine Club's move to larger premises in Golden. We considered the possibility of combining premises with the RGS some 15 years ago, so it is not really a particularly new idea.

We have also floated with the BMC the idea of a British Mountain Heritage electronic network which might record on a common or inter-linked database the contents of the Club's and other British mountain libraries, and perhaps also the locations of archives, paintings, photos, and artefacts of heritage value. Within that, I hope that there might be an enhanced role, and perhaps improved public financing, for the Club's library and other archives.

It is essential also that there should be some recognised focal point in Britain for the documentary and photographic archives of key individuals, which might otherwise be lost to posterity.

The UIAA

The main area of international collaboration with the BMC will be in relation to the UIAA, on which the BMC represents the UK, but which the AC has recently rejoined. I say 're-joined' because the Club was involved when the UIAA was being set up in 1932-34, though we dropped out thereafter.

The UIAA brings together some 98 member Federations or other mountain organisations in 68 countries and the Club's membership should offer us the opportunity of extending our links among them. As it happens, I have recently been elected President, in succession to our member Ian McNaught-Davis, who has served in that capacity since the untimely death of Pietro Segantini almost 10 years ago. There are also of course quite a number of our members who have been nominated by the BMC to serve the UIAA in other ways, of whom I should mention Lindsay Griffin in the UIAA Expeditions Commission; Robert Pettigrew, the President of the Access and Conservation Commission; Anthony Rich, the Legal Advisor to the UIAA; and Martin Wragg in the UIAA Legal Experts Group. Many more have served previously. Roger Payne is employed by the UIAA as Sport and Development Director.

The UIAA is recognised by the International Olympic Committee as the international sporting federation responsible for mountaineering; and this in turn may be helpful to member federations in gaining recognition, and government funding, in their own countries. The UIAA has developed over the last 15 years an important responsibility on competitions in climbing, ski-mountaineering and ice-climbing, seeking to reconcile this with its continuing traditional responsibilities, which remain the main interest of its 2.5m members. My personal view is that mountaineering, including exploratory mountaineering in the Club's tradition, is very much in line with the modern Olympic ethic of *'stronger, faster, higher'*, so the gap may not be quite as great as might appear.

The UIAA is also a member of the United Nations' Global Mountain Partnership which has developed from the UN's work on mountain issues, following the Rio agreements of 1992. The UIAA made a commitment to this Global Mountain Partnership in 2002,[25] on the basis that everyone should be able to enjoy the natural environment, including mountains and cliffs, with freedom of responsible access. It saw itself as having a particular role on clarifying and enhancing the economic benefit of mountain tourism to local communities; in developing codes of good practice for responsible mountain tourism; in helping with the training of, and the setting of standards for fair employment of, local guides and porters in those parts of the Greater Ranges where this might be helpful; and perhaps of identifying material in the archives of the older alpine clubs, showing the extent of changes over time, for example in the state of the glaciers. There are a number of substantive initiatives within the Partnership, including one on

Policy and Law, and others on the Hindu Kush-Karakoram-Himalaya, the Andes and Europe, requiring some mountaineering input.

The UIAA has, to its credit, also been active, usually in support of the World Conservation Union (IUCN), in quietly promoting the idea of Cross-Frontier (or Peace) Parks, most notably in the case of the Siachen Glacier, to which our Honorary Member Harish Kapadia has made a special contribution.

It is potentially to the benefit of our all-important access freedoms, wherever we go, that the UIAA should actively demonstrate that, on such environmental, economic and social issues, mountaineers are part of the solution and not part of the problem; and I hope that the Club and its members, individually, may make a contribution to this.

That concludes my Valedictory Address,[26] and it only remains for me to wish my successor, Stephen Venables, and the Club, all success in the future; and to thank the Club most sincerely for the honour of being its President.

Mountaineering needs a strong and active Alpine Club and I am confident that that is what the Club will continue to be.

REFERENCES

1   *Fell and Rock Climbing Club Journal,* 54, 1954.
2   *Future Policy,* BMC, November 1976. See '*The first fifty years of the British Mountaineering Council*', BMC, 51-54,1997.
3   *ibid,* page 3.
4   Letter and enclosure dated 15 November 2003. See the Report at Note 5 below, Annex C1.
5   '*Research on the ownership and copyright of the Everest photos*', Alan Blackshaw, 4 October 2004 (2 vols).
6   *Official Report,* Commons, 28 October 1979.
7   *Third Report of the Public Accounts Committee 1978-79, Annex.*
8   *Blackshaw v Lord and the Daily Telegraph,* Court of Appeal, *All England Law Reports,* February 1983.
9   *The Hunt Report on Mountain Training,* BMC, 1976. See '*The first fifty years of the British Mountaineering Council*', 59-65, 1997.
10   *Future of mountain training in the UK,* Standing Advisory Committee on Mountain Training, BMC, 1991.
11   *UIAA Model Training Standards*
12   The Land Reform (Scotland) Act 2003.
13   *Official Report,* Commons, 4 March 1892.
14   Summarised in '*Implied Permission and the Traditions of Customary Access*', Alan Blackshaw (LINK Access Research Project), *Edinburgh Law Review,* Vol 3, September 1999, pages 368-80.
15   *ibid,* pages 370-71; and National Archives of Scotland (NAS), file AF45/244.

16 *ibid*, page 373; and NAS file DD12/86/1, enclosure 3, February 1965.

17 Letter to Justice 2 Committee of 21 December 2001; and oral evidence of 14 January and 6 February 2002. See *Stage One Report on the Land Reform (Scotland) Bill*, Justice 2 Committee of the Scottish Parliament, published on about 10 March 2002, Vol 2, pages 65-67, 77-83 and 249-254, respectively.

18 Letter from SNH Board Member to Justice 2 Committee, in a personal capacity, 24 December 2001; and SNH oral evidence of 6 February 2002. See *Stage One Report*, Vol 2, pages 103-11 and 232, col 1007, respectively.

19 6 February 2002. See *Stage One Report*, Vol 2, page 249, col 1042.

20 *'Conflicts between the views of the Law Society of Scotland and the historical evidence of the LINK Access Research Project'*, Alan Blackshaw, 12 February 2002.

21 *Stage One Report*, Vol 1, para 19

22 *Official Report*, Scottish Parliament, 20 March 2002, col 10399.

23 An SNH letter to the Justice 2 Committee, dated 5 March 2002, was left on the SNH website, as the sole item on the passage of the Land Reform (Scotland) Bill, without any mention of the Justice 2 Committee's subsequent criticisms of the SNH position (as in Notes 21 and 22 above), until February 2004. See also the references to SNH in *'Comments on some of the criticisms of the Link Access Research Project published by the Scottish Rights of Way and Access Society'*, Alan Blackshaw, 20 February 2003.

24 *'Human rights and mountain freedoms: Is Nature a missing link?'* Alan Blackshaw, Proceedings of UIAA Conference, Trento, 3 May 2002, p101. See also *AJ* 107, 139, 2002.

25 *UIAA Summit Charter 2002*.

26 For the author's historical research on the ownership of the Black Cuillin, see *AJ* 109, 402, 2004.

Alps 2004

The following report only provides a snapshot of significant ascents during the 2004 winter and the following summer/autumn. Thanks are due to Antonella Cicogna, Sebastien Constant, Andrej Grmovsek, John Harlin, Geoff Hornby, *Klettern*, Vlado Linek, François Marsigny, Tony Penning, Hilary Sharp and *Vertical*.

ECRINS RANGE

Pic du Casset In 4½ hours on 9 February 2004 Sebastien Constant and Cécilie Thomas climbed a new route *Si tu t'Emmêles, Je m'en Mêle* (890m: D/D+: IV M4 c60°) up the mixed N face immediately left of the ultra-classic Davin Couloir (c600n: AD+).

Ailefroide On 4 June Sebastien Constant and Mathieu Meynadier climbed a new ephemeral ice route on the E face of **Ailefroide Orientale** (3847m). *Au-Dessus du Vide les Fantoches s'agîtent,* which starts up the 1904 route left of the main rock face before branching right to a hidden vertical ice wall, took 7 hours and was 480m V/5 and M6.

On the N face of Pointe Fourastier (3907m) Arnaud Guillaume and Hubert Pirat climbed a fine new rock/mixed route between the classic Y-Couloir/Fourastier Route and the Pilier des Séracs: *Premier Pas* (800m: TD).

Pointe de Bonne Pierre Julien Désécures and Arnaud Guillaume put up *Passy-Bonne Pierre Direct,* largely to the left of the classic Girod-Sandoz. Completed in 13 hours over 8-9 September, the ED1 route has 15 main pitches up to 6b+ and is traditionally protected.

MONT BLANC MASSIF

Mont Blanc A new Superdirect Route on the **Innominata Ridge**, *From Dawn to Decadence* (TD: 5.10+ and A0, though the crux was climbed free at 5.11 on an attempt in 2003) was completed on 19 September by Julie-Ann Clyma, John Harlin and Roger Payne (*see 'From Dawn to Decadence', p153*).

Mont Maudit To the right of the great Central Couloir on the E face above Combe Maudit, Marco and Massimo Farina, and Ezio Marlier climbed a new route named *The Brothers* (550m: III/4+). The route was completed on 15 December and appears to be based on the line erroneously marked as the 1888 *Anderson Route* (which actually lies further to the right) in *Neige, Glace et Mixte*.

Mont Blanc du Tacul Pierre Darbellay and Patrick Gabarrou chose 6 June to climb the ice/mixed route, *D Day,* to the left of the 1996 Andy Parkin/Harry Taylor route, *Non Stop*. Two months earlier, on 14 April, the late Massimo Farina and Ezio Marlier climbed what they felt to be a new line up the right side of the Gervasutti Pillar, finishing up a runnel/corner system left of the Tour Carrée. *Matador* is ED2 IV/4 M6+.

Mont Rouge de Peuterey On 4 August Tony Penning with Robin Wilmhurst-Smith and Dave Hope with Nic Mullin completed a new route *Forgive and Forget* (seven pitches, some of them quite bold, at E4 5c, F6c) up the left side of the NE face.

Tour Ronde Philippe Batoux and Patrick Gabarrou added another line to the NW face, when on 29 June they climbed *Supermattia* up mixed ground and a conspicuous red pillar (6a+) right of the 1977 *Cordier Route*; they then followed the ridge past the exit to the Rébuffat Couloir to the summit.

Gros Rognon The central of the Batoux/Robert trilogy, *Pas d'Agonie II,* which was formerly III/5+ and A2, has been climbed free by Andy Parkin at WI 7R (direct up the poorly formed stalactite on the third pitch).

Grandes Jorassses On 30 September Benoit Jacquemot and François Marsigny made probably the fourth and by far the fastest ascent of the legendary *Bonatti-Vaucher Route* on **Pointe Whymper**. They reached the summit in just 14 hours finding sections of M5+ and F5c and some thinly-iced runnels of 85-90°. The far left side of the face was visited on 23 August by Maciej Sokolowski and Michal Wiodarczak from Poland, who climbed the relatively short rock ridge left of *Coulée Douce. Ma-Ika* follows the right side of a black pyramid in the upper section and gave difficulties of UIAA V and 80°. During the summer a number of parties repeated the ultra-classic *Cassin Route* on the *Walker Spur*, finding that the large rockfall of 2003 had not intrinsically damaged the line. However, parts are now quite dusty and gravel-covered. This slows progress and many climbers were forced to bivouac.

L'Evêque Above the Italian Val Ferret, Nic Mullin, Tony Penning and Robin Wilmhurst-Smith made a difficult and dangerous approach to climb a new route on the SE face of the Evêque. On 7 August the three climbed a rightward-slanting line up a pale-coloured ramp to give 630m (11 pitches) of E2 5b. It seems almost certain that this area has never been visited before.

Rognon du Plan Clean aid or free? Take your choice on *American Beauty* (8a or 6b and A1), a new route on the 200m W face just left of *Toru Nakano* by François Pallandre and a team of aspirant guides on a 'training outing'.

Dent du Requin On 3 September Gilbert and Nicolas Pareau, the former guardian of the Requin Hut, climbed a new 325m line on the Central Pillar, weaving around the *Renaudie Direct* at 6b, 6a obl.

Aiguille du Fou In an amazing linked ascent, Slovenians Andrej Grmovsek and Marko Lukic climbed both *Les Ailes du Desir* (Colas/Grenier, 1988: 7c) and the *American Route* (Frost/Harlin/Hemming/Fulton, 1963: 7c) all free in one day at the end of July.

Grands Charmoz – Breche de la Republique Over 13-14 February Mathieu Cortial, Sebastien Franc, Jean-François Reffet and the perennial Benoît Robert climbed an ephemeral line up the NE (Envers) face of the 3222m Brèche de la République: *Banan'ice Republic* (500m: M6 a little A1 and F5c to finish).

Petit Dru   One of the highlights of the 2004 winter was another repeat of the 2001 *Lafaille Route* (originally graded A5, F5+ and M7) on the W face of the Dru, this time with the addition of a four-pitch *Direct Finish* to the Shoulder. Guillaume Avrisani, Philippe Batoux and Christophe Dumarest spent eight days of perfect weather in mid-February completing the original line exactly but down-rating the crux pitches to A3 and A3+.

Le Minaret   Starting just 20m right of the classic SE spur, Pascal Ducroz, Paul Dudas and Nicolas Potard have opened *Rasta Metal* (250m: 6c maximum). Completed on 31 August. The new route joins the SE spur at the Second Tower and gives probably the best-equipped rappel descent from the Minaret.

VALAIS

Sadly, perhaps the most notable and well-publicised event in the Valais during 2004 was the death of the one of the most famous icons of French alpinism, **Patrick Bérhault**, who fell while traversing from the Täschhorn to the Dom on 28 April. The 47-year-old mountaineer was moving unroped with Philippe Magnon during an attempt to complete a continuous ascent of all 82 tops over 4000m in the Alps. The pair had just completed their 64th, having started in the Ecrins on 2 March.

Matterhorn   The late Massimo Farina and local guide Hervé Barmasse made the first winter and possibly second overall ascent of *Padrepio prega per Tutti* on the S face of 4190m **Picco Muzio** (Gabarrou/Ravaschietto, 2002: 1200m: ED3 on sound rock at 7a, 6c obl).

URNER ALPS

On the isolated east face of **Titlis** (3243m) Markus Dortfleitner and Stefan Glowacz created another very hard, multi-pitch Alpine sport route when on 4 July they redpointed the bolt-protected *Last Exit Titlis* (500m: 13 pitches: 8b: no pitch less than 6c). It was repeated on 18 September by Ines Papert and Ueli Steck who found it superb and on sound rock, but they down-rated the difficulties to 8a+.

BERNESE OBERLAND

Scheideggwetterhorn (3361m)   Starting just to the right of the classic *Niedermann Route* on the N face, Denis Burdet, Julien and Nicolas Zambetti have created the 1100m and 34-pitch *Baston la Baffe. T*o date the crux pitches, 7b+, 7b+ and 7c, have yet to be climbed without rest points. This is now one of the most difficult big Alpine climbs on Swiss limestone.

Eiger   There have now been a couple of repeats of *La Vida es Silbar* (first redpointed in 2003 by Stefan Siegrist and Ueli Steck: 28 pitches: 7c), notably the fourth ascent from 21-year-old Florian Behnke.

Bietschhorn   The ubiquitous Batoux-Gabarrou partnership have climbed the steep golden pillar left of the classic *Tissières-Rham Route* on the S face to create *Wildnis (*4c to 6a+ on superb rock).

BREGAGLIA

Badile The most impressive performance of the winter was the first solo and second overall winter ascent of the legendary direttissima *Ringo Starr* (Fazzini/Fazzini/Gianola, 1985: 700m: ED1; VI/VI+) on the austere NW face by local activist Rossano Libera. He climbed it on-sight in five days and, due to a route-finding error, created a new seven-pitch variation finish to the right of the final characteristic dièdre. He was then trapped in a storm for three days in the summit bivouac shelter before safely descending to Italy.

    Cascata Wall The big aid climb of the year came from Gabor Berecz and Thomas Tivadar who created *Acqua Senza Grappa* up the wall of the waterfall left of *Sasso Remenno*. The route is nine pitches long and has the most delicate aid climbing over roofs that the highly experienced big wallers had encountered. Berecz led the crux and the route was graded V 5.11a New Wave A4+ c/d.

DOLOMITES
Tre Cime di Lavaredo

Cima Ovest Over 15-16 February 2004 Rolando Larcher made the first winter and first solo ascent of *Akut* (Kurt Astner/Urban Ties, 2000: FFA Astner/Ties, 2001: 450m: 8a, 7b obl). Larcher had already made the fourth ascent of this route in 2003, estimating the obligatory difficulties to be no more than 7a. Climbing with their respective wives, Andrej Grmovsek and Marko Lukic made the third and fourth free ascents of the *Couzy Route* (Desmaison/Mazeaud, 1959: 500m: 17 pitches: originally A4 and 5+: FFA Bubu Bole, 1999 at 8b) reporting, like the second ascensionists, that grades proposed by Bubu were a little 'soft', being one or two notches too high.

    Cima Grande In September Dusan Beranek and Riso Nyeki made the third free ascent of the *Camilloto Pellesier Route* (Mauro/Minuzzo, 1967: 550m: V and A2e with 340 bolts. FFA Mauro Bole/Kurt Astner, 2003: 8b). In common with the second ascensionists Andrej Grmovsek and Marko Lukic, the Slovaks found the crux to be no more than 8a+, as did the Czechs Dusan Janak and S Hovanec, who made the fourth ascent and thought it 8a/8a+.

Tofana Group

Tofana de Rozes On the big south wall of the 3225m Tofana, on the pillar left of the start of the ultra-classic 1901 *Dimai/Eötvös/Eötvös/Siopaes/Verzi Route*, Diego Stefani and Ferruccio Svaluto opened the 500m *50th Anniversary of the CSNAS,* which they redpointed on 22 July at 7b. Another good performance on the Tofana was achieved by the young Austrian, Florian Behnke, in his on-sight ascent of *Good Bye* (7c).

08. Marko Lukic on the very bold Specchi di Sara (Maurizio Giordani/
    Rosanna Manfrini, 1988: 500m: FFA by Roland Mittersteiner in 1989 at F7c),
    S face of the Marmolada di Ombretta. This route is a must for the talented adventure
    climber and athough it features bolt protection, some of it is well-spaced:
    Giordani took a 30m fall during the first ascent. (*Andrej Grmovsek*)

Civetta Group

Torre Trieste A direct route on the famous SW face was put up in July by
Christophe Hainz and Roger Schäli. *Donna Fugata* is 750m (but 900m of
climbing), 26 pitches long, 7a obl and A2, and climbs though the friable
yellow overhanging rock on the lower central section of the wall between
the 1959 *Piussi/Redaelli Direttissima* and the classic 1934 *Carlesso/Sandri*.

Two months later a second direct route further left was created by Mauro Bubu Bole and has been dedicated to the late *Patrick Bérhault.* The 20-pitch route is largely protected by hand-drilled 8mm bolts and has a crux pitch that sports a full 50m of strenuous, fingery wall-climbing at 8a.

Marmolada Group

Marmolada The big event of the summer on the Marmolada was Pietro Dal Prà's first free ascent of the *Via della Cattedrale* (Maffei/Leoni/Frizzera, 1983 and 1985: 850m: A4 and VI+) on the S face of the **Roccia.** With Michelle Guerrini and Lorenzo Nadali, Dal Prà strung together the two A4 pitches through the roofs at half height to give a 40m pitch (with no possibility of a no-hands rest) at 8a+. Of the 19 pitches on this 850m route, two are 7c and apart from the crux the rest lie between 6b and 7b. Protection and belays use either pegs or natural gear.

Sella Group

Piz Ciavazes Mauro Bubu Bole has been continuing a project to systematically free climb hard Dolomite aid with an ascent of the *1961 Italian Route* (250m: A3 and VI) at 8a. The route was repeated in the same style during early September by Germans, Florian and Martin Riegler.

   Passo Gardena – Mur del Pisciadu Toni Lamprecht and Michi Wärthis climbed *Blumen am Arsch der Hòlle* (400m of climbing: eight pitches: VII+, VII obl: some bolts) on the steep rock on the magnificent Torre Brunico, the famous pillar jutting from the wall that is home to the 1920s classic *Via Normale* (V+).

Pala Group

Three new guides published in the last couple of years have transformed the Pala from a backwater of outdated information into the most well-covered region in the Dolomites. One was put out of date two weeks after publication, when on 14 August Geoff Hornby and Moreno Tomaselli (the great grandson of Tita Piaz) added a direct finish, *Non Smettere di Sognare* (110m: VII-), to the 1978 route, *Sogni Tenui* (700m: V+) on the south face of the south summit (Punta Frassené) of the **Spiz d'Agner**.

   Campanili dei Lastei The well-known Maurizio 'Manolo' Zanolla, with Riccardo Scarian, redpointed his own 2003 route, *Cani Morti* on the NW face of the Campanile Basso. The five-pitch route, which is sparsely bolted, is now 8b/8b+, 8a obl, with the first three pitches at 8a or above.

Brenta Group

Cima Tosa In August the great Italian alpinist Ermanno Salvaterra put up a new route, solo, on the big central pillar of the west face. *Carpe Diem* (VI+) follows an elegant slanting crack system that cuts through the yellow overhangs on the upper part of the pillar.

PAUL KNOTT

Russia & Central Asia 2004

This report owes much to the reports submitted by climbers from Russia and the CIS to information websites including mountain.ru (Moscow), alpin.nm.ru (Buryatia), vvv.ru, mountains.dgu.ru (Dagestan), basecamp.kg (Kyrgyzstan), stolby.ru (Krasnoyarsk), and alpclub.ur.ru (Sverdlovsk). Thanks are due also to Ingrid Crossland for help with correspondence in Kyrgyzstan.

The level of reported activity by climbers from Russia and the CIS continued to be high, and included exploration of new routes in both established and little-known ranges. Some of the hardest new routes were climbed in areas that have yet to be visited by non-Russian climbers. Protracted ascents of difficult faces remained popular, particularly in the context of climbing championships, but international styles of climbing are also in evidence. The grades given in these reports generally use the Russian scale for overall difficulty (eg 6A). Where roman numerals are used, these refer to the free-climbed technical rock standard unless stated otherwise.

The Caucasus

Climbing in this range continues to be inhibited, although not prevented, by the widespread violence and instability in the region. Horrific incidents have occurred even in the formerly calm republic of Kabardino-Balkaria in which the Central Caucasus is situated. However, the Bezengi mountaineering camp continues to operate as normal.

In the western part of the range in June a Krasnodar team led by Roman Gubanov climbed a new route at 5B (VI, A1, F6b max, 1500m) taking a buttress on the SE face of **Dombai Western (4036m)**. They took 5 days over the route, which lies to the R of the 2000 *Zagimayak Route* (6B), commenting on the availability of unclimbed granite even in this well-established climbing area. In February 2005 an Irkutsk team including Pavel Kolesov climbed a new 6th class route on the N face of **Dombay-Ul'gen (4038m)**. In the Central Caucasus in July there was a climbing visit to the southern side of **Koshtan-Tau (5150m)**. This side of the mountain (the third highest summit in Europe) has been little visited during the last 20 years. In the Adylsu valley in February 2005, climbers from the Moscow Demchenko club made an ascent of **Bashkara (4241m)**.

Further east, the project to climb the Caucasus 5000m peaks in winter continued with the ascent in January 2005 of **Kazbek (5033m)** via the Genaldonskoye valley in North Ossetia and the *Pastukhov Route*.

Most of the Caucasus new route activity was on the big rock faces of **Erydag (3925m)** and the surrounding massif in Dagestan. Over 15 days from 1-19 July, Makhachkala-based climbers Shanavaz Shanavazov, Vitaliy Afanasjev, Oleg Bibin and Konstantin Dorro climbed a 665m new route through the overhangs on the R bastion of the NW face. They graded the route 6B VI A3. Much the same team returned to the face in January 2005, again climbing through the overhangs on the right side of the face at 6B. They climbed the 23 pitches from 21 January to 14 February in cold conditions with little sun on the face. The ascent won the Russian winter championship. In February 2005 a Sverdlovsk team including Sergey Kofanov and Alexander Shabunin made the first winter ascent of the 2002 6B *Efimov route*, climbing from 11-23 February in 29 pitches. On 4 March 2004 the Sverdlovsk team of V V Popvich and A G Stolbov reached the top of the 6A 1981 *Shchedrin route* on the L part of the NW face. They had spent 13 days on the route, which is 1200m in length with 6b-6c and A2 climbing.

In the same massif a 265m new route was climbed on **Sel'dy (3664m)** from the Chekhychai valley. Sel'dy is the highest point of the plateau SW of Erydag, across the Azerbaijan border. The Dagestan State University team of Evgeniy Pashuk, Gadzhimurad Nurbagandov and Tagir Mazanov climbed the central W face from 3-4 July at 5B VI A2.

Russia and Ukraine

In the **Crimea** a new rap-bolted route was climbed on **Shaan-Kaya (871m)**. The 220m 7a to 8a+ *Atlant-M* was climbed in September by Serik Kazbekov and Igor Solovey, partly on sight. The route interesects and climbs to the R of the *Grishchenko* and *Samurai* routes. In March 2005 Ukrainian climbers made winter training ascents of *Centre* on Foros Kant, *Cave* on Zamok, *Centre* on Morcheka, *Dana* on Chelebi and *Arsenal* on Shaan-Kaya, all at 6A. Conditions were frosty, with iced-up cracks and snow on the routes.

In the Sablinskiy Range of the **Prepolar Urals** a Sverdlovsk team led by S A Kofanov climbed a new route on **Sablya (1497m)**, taking the L bastion on the NE face. They climbed the 17-pitch route from 3-7 May, achieving third place in the first ascent class of the Russian climbing championships. Graded 6A VI A3-A4, the route was considered by one of the team members to be harder than the *Semiletkin route* on Svobodnaya Korea.

The Pamir Alai

Russian and CIS climbers have been returning to this range in significant numbers, reflecting a perception that the security problems have lessened. Climbers from Odessa returned to the Karavshin area in August, finding their journey several times longer and more expensive than on their previous trip in 1998. From this group the team of Vladimir Mogila and Aleksandr Lavrinenko, Viorel Cheban and Vadim Nikolayev climbed a new 6B route on the NW face of **Asan (4230m)**, claiming it as the hardest route on the mountain. The route lies between the 1986 *Moroz route* and the 1986

Gorbenko Route and took 19 pitches to the summit ridge. The same team also climbed the *Timofeev Route* despite poor weather. A second team of Pugachev and Maksimenya climbed another new route on the R part of the face. The Karavshin area was also visited in August by climbers from Novosibirsk, while in the Laylak valley a Moscow Demchenko team including A Adamov climbed **Pik Bloka** by the SW ridge at 5B.

The **Fann mountains** were once again the venue for a CIS mountaineering championship. In all, over 200 people were involved. July snowfall made the routes harder than normal, with the walls of **Chapdara (5049m)**, **Bodkhona (5138m)** and others covered with ice and snow. Despite this, some of the hardest routes received ascents.

The Pamir

There was a healthy level of activity in this range driven by the return of a degree of normality to the region. During the summer season **Pik Lenin (7134m)** was attempted by over 500 people, of whom approximately a third summited. There were several deaths. The camp on the Moskvina glacier operated for a second year after many years of absence. Operated jointly by Tashkent and Dushanbe-based companies, the camp hosted 124 people, of whom 72 ascended **Korzhenevskaya (7105m)** and 21 **Kommunizma (Somoni, 7495m)**. In doing so, five attained the coveted Snow Leopard status awarded for making ascents of all 7000m peaks in the former Soviet Union. Four Tatarstan climbers made ascents of all three Pamir seven-thousanders during the season. They reached the summit of Pik Lenin on 26 July, were the first of the season to summit Korzhenevskaya on 3 August, and on 11 August were the first of the season to ascend Kommunizma.

In the **Eastern Zaalaiskiy Khrebet** a UK team led by Paul Hudson visited the western end of the range, close to the Tajikistan border, where they climbed a number of peaks up to 5513m. There was also a Russian expedition to the region of the Sarezskiy Lake in the **Muzkol range**. On 11 August the expedition made the ascent of a new summit and named it **Poytakht**.

The Tien Shan

The mountains of Kyrgyzstan continue to attract the bulk of the attention from climbers from outside Russia and Central Asia. Reflecting this, a detailed map of several of the ranges has been produced by the American Alpine Club. At the local level P I Solomatin, V N Biryukov and V P Lyakh have published a new guide book (in Russian) to the mountains of the central section of the Kyrgyz range including the Ak-Say, Adygine, Ala-Archa, Alamedin and Issyk-Ata areas.

In the Inylchek area the summer season was marred by an avalanche on the Semenovskiy glacier on 5 August which killed 11 climbers from the Czech Republic, Ukraine and Russia. This glacier is used to access the standard *West Ridge Route* on **Khan Tengri (6995m)** from the south.

The objective risk on this glacier was earlier highlighted by fatalities to guided British climbers in 1993, since when many organised groups have used the longer but objectively safer approach from the north. Despite the avalanche and the major rescue operations that followed, ascents of Khan Tengri continued from the S side. The relatively high summer snowfall also did not prevent activity on **Pobeda (7439m)**, including a number of successful ascents and an attempt to traverse its three summits by a Bratsk-Irkutsk expedition led by M L Krivosheev.

From the N Inylchek glacier a team from the Sverdlovsk region climbed a new route on the NE summit (6010m) of **Pik Maksim Gorky (6050m)**, making the main ascent from 17-24 August. The first face route on this mountain was climbed in 2001 on the NW face of the NE summit by Yu Ermachek's Sverdlovsk team. The 2004 route took the L part of the NW face, with 6A mixed climbing, an average steepness of 75° and a height gain of 1500m. Team members included Alexander Korobkov, Nikolai Smagin, Alexander Cheryavskiy and Alexander Shabunin.

In the little-explored area SW of the Inylchek glaciers, the UK pair, Ingrid Crossland and Graham Sutton, visited the **Djungart** region. This forms part of the Kokshaal-Too range SSW of Maida-Adyr and ESE of the settlement of Akshiyrak. The only previous exploration in this area had been by a non-climbing party of glaciologists. The pair accessed the area by helicopter and explored the valleys E and W of the highest **Peak 5318m**, finding the area to have complex mountain terrain with steep rock towers of a granite-type rock. Peak 5318m also appeared to require steep climbing from all aspects.

In the **Ala-Archa** area, from 17 to 21 February 2005, Tatarstan climbers A Akhmadiyev, E Rozhnov and Yu Kruglov completed a new route taking the central chimney of the N face of **Svobodnaya (Free) Korea (4778m)** R of the *Ruchkin* and *Myshlyaeva routes* and L of the *Bagayeva route*. Routes climbed in the summer season included the 1988 *Nikiforenko route* on the W face of **Semenov Tienshanskiy (4875m)** by a Tomsk team, and the 1963 *Glukhovtsev route* on the W face of the 6th tower of **Korona (4860m)** by an Altai team, both at 5B.

In September an ISM guided expedition led by Pat Littlejohn, Adrian Nelhams and Vladimir Komissarov climbed peaks in the central **Borkoldoy Range**. Because this part of the range is difficult to access, the only previous climbing visit had been by Danil Popov's 2003 team (see below) that unsuccessfully attempted the highest peak (5170m). Using all their manpower the ISM group made passable an old track accessing the river leading to the main glaciers in the heart of the range. They made several ascents from the R branch of the double-headed glacier running southwards (later named Ilbirs Glacier): the dominant peak on the R side **Pk Ilbirs (5017m)** at PD+; the rock pyramid on the E side **Zoob Barsa 4685m** at PD+; and **Trident Peak** N of Pk Ilbirs via a traverse at AD. Another group explored the glacier to the W and climbed **Pk 4857** by its W ridge.

09. North face of Peak 5318m in the Djungart area, seen from c4000m in the valley to its west. (*Crossland / Sutton Collection*)

From the E branch of Ilbirs glacier several summits were climbed including Twin Peak **(Dvoinay Vershina 5041m)** and the forepeak of Pk 5170m, Sakchi **(Sentry 4915m)**. An attempt on **Pk 5170m** via a couloir on the W flank and N ridge was aborted at c5000m as the ridge became sharp and corniced. On the 100-500m walls above the base camp two routes were climbed at E2 and HVS on good limestone.

The nearby **Western Kokshaal-Too** was visited by Scottish climbers Es Tresidder, Guy Robertson, Pete Benson, Matt Halls and Robin Thomas in September. Robin and Matt made a probable second ascent of **Kyzyl Asker (5842m)**, avoiding séracs low on the N face by approaching via a gully from the SE (1 pitch of Scottish VI) to the col between Kyzyl Asker and Panfilovski Division. From here they traversed onto the N face with skis and hence climbed to the W summit, finding the two summits indistinguishable in height. They had aborted an earlier attempt on the SE face at 5200m due to poor conditions. Members of the team also climbed four new mixed routes on the nearby walls. On the S face of **Panfilovski Division (5400m)** Es, Pete and Guy climbed *Haggis Supper* at WI 5+ 500m taking a prominent corner/gully system (due to bad weather they omitted the summit). On the S face of **Jerry Garcia** Robin and Matt climbed a 500m gully at Scottish V. On the **Great Walls of China** Es and Guy climbed the 500m *Border Control* at Scottish VII and A1. This took a 28-hour round trip. On **Ochre Walls** Es and Pete climbed *Fire and Ice*, an ice smear L of *Beefcake* with climbing at ED and Scottish mixed VII, afterwards reaching the nearby unnamed summit.

In summer 2003 Moscow climbers continued their earlier activity in the eastern part of the same range. From the Nalivkin (Aytali) glacier a 5-person party led by Danil Popov made the first ascent of **Peak 5471m** which they named **Letavet**, climbing by the SE rib at 2B. From here they traversed over several cols close to the border with China before making the first ascent of the W ridge of **Krylya Sovetov (5560m)** via Pik 5120m.

Siberia and the Russian Far East

In the **Altai** the only new route to report is a new 5B variant on the N face of **Karatash (3534m)**, climbed from 1-8 August by a Kemerova team led by A V Foygt. There was, however, an interesting attempt in February 2004 by a group of climbers from Irkutsk and Biysk including Andrey Afanasev on a serious new route on **Cherniy Belok**. This peak is situated in the Myushtu-Ayry valley in the Katun range, W of Bielukha. The route was 800m in length with vertical walls and overhangs looking like 6B climbing, but the group retreated after 150m due to rockfall and an avalanche that injured several party members.

Significant exploration and new route activity continued in the **Barguzin Range** E of Lake Baikal (highest point **Pribaikalya 2841m**). From 1-2 July a team of Buryatia and Amur climbers including I. Sherstnev climbed a new 5A route on the R part of the E face of **Argada (2340m)**. Meanwhile on nearby **Medved'** (Bear), Sergey Zurbulayeva and Aleksandr Shelkovnikov completed a new route by the NE ridge at provisional 4B. At the same time other local climbers completed a traverse over Argada, Medved', Kreyser Varyag and Obzornaya, also at 4B. From 21-26 June, a team of Buryatia and Amur climbers including I.V.Sherstnev completed a new route on **Gordelan (2512m)** taking the centre of the L bastion of the E face at 6A. This ascent achieved first place in the first ascents class of the Russian alpinism championships.

In the nearby **South-Muyskiy** range a new 5B route was climbed on the NE buttress of the highest peak **Muyskiy Gigant (3067)** from 20-22 July by A E Afanasev's team from Irkutsk. In the **Western Sayan** in July, a team from nearby Krasnoyarsk climbed a new route on **Tugodum (1740m)** taking the E face by the overhangs at 5B.

Krasnoyarsk climbers also continued their earlier exploration in the **Kodar Range** with a visit in January-February 2005. This comparatively little-explored range has beautiful sharp summits and technically interesting walls up to 800m high. The team led by Nikolay Zakharov flew for 90 minutes by helicopter from Taksimo village on the Baikal-Amur road to the Vodopadny stream on the N side of the range. After nine days' climbing up a mixed technical wall, they reached the summit of a new peak which they named in honour of the 70th anniversary of **Krasnoyarsk region**. The climbers countered temperatures down to -43°C using heated base camp tents. At the end of the trip they waited for several days without food as their helicopter was detained for non-payment of debts.

DEREK FORDHAM

Greenland 2004

These notes are less comprehensive than the author would wish because of a lack of responses from many expeditions. The response rate for traverses of the inland ice was particularly low. Those who visit this region or have information on other expeditions are strongly encouraged to make contact.

Inland Ice

The lure of the Inland Ice seemed to diminish in 2004, only 21 of the 35 sporting expedition permits issued being for traverses, all but one by what is now the trade route between Ammassalik and Kangerdlugssuaq. Five of these planned to travel west to east and 16 east to west with one group following the shorter, more southerly, original Nansen route.

The first trans-Greenland expedition to start, on 2 April, was the Estonian Greenland Expedition of Rain Lond and Marko Kalve who starting from Isortoq reached Kangerdlugssuaq on 3 May (32 days). This first Estonian expedition to tackle the Inland Ice had to endure strong winds on the east coast and lost a total of 5 days to bad weather. Snow conditions were poor on the eastern flank of the ice cap and limited progress in temperatures that bottomed at –32°C.

Gurkha Extreme (UK) was a project by ten members of the Brigade of Gurkhas to complete a series of extreme challenges. These included running six marathons in 6 days, completing the Devizes to London canoe course, and finishing with a crossing of the Inland Ice. Starting from a helicopter drop on the Hahn glacier on 16 April, thus avoiding the access problems often encountered by parties starting from sea level, the group reached the Russell glacier on 15 May (29 days). This achievement is perhaps remarkable in that five of the team had never skied until a month before the expedition began. The team carried out a number of scientific projects in the areas of human metabolism and psychological coping strategies. They also reported that conditions were unusually cold and that of nine expeditions on the Inland Ice at the same time only three successfully completed their crossings, showing that the lessons that should have been learned from the series of rescues last year have not been fully assimilated by the authorities or many expedition planners.

The Scottish Trans-Greenland Expedition consisting of Alistair Simpson and Patrick Lewtas (UK) started on 23 May also from the Hahn glacier and reached Pt 660m on the Russell glacier on 4 July (41 days). Their first major problem was a ski binding which repeatedly detached itself from the ski and was finally positioned by an arrangement of which Heath Robinson

110. Paddy Lewtas with 30-35kg pulk, near Pt 660m at the end
     of the expedition. We walked for 15 kilometres like this
     over broken fissured ice. (*Alistair Simpson*)

would have been proud. The second major problem was the supra-glacial
drainage system which establishes itself every year in early summer over
an extensive area on the steep and broken Russell glacier and which presents
a daunting finish to expeditions that choose this route. Both team members
fell through the ice into melt pools and, due to the broken and fissured ice
which was engulfing the remains of the ice road to the car test facility, as
they neared Pt 660m were forced to relay their equipment off the ice.

It is perhaps worth noting that the Russell glacier is a truly appalling
place to choose to access or exit the Inland Ice and that it is used by the
majority of crossing parties only because it leads directly to or from the
airfield at Kangerdlugssuaq. There are many other places where access

onto and off the Inland Ice is much easier, and even pleasant, but their use requires a little bit of extra effort to establish a transport link between Kangerdlugssuak and the chosen location.

On 23 June, three members of the Karlsen family led by Finn Yngve Karlsen (Norway) set off from Umivik to follow the route Nansen used when he made the first crossing of Greenland in 1888. They made a difficult 250km boat journey down the east coast from Kulusuk but were able to ski onto the Inland Ice immediately from sea level. In 6 days of excellent weather they passed most of the marginal crevassing to reach 2000m, but once they reached the central area of the Inland Ice at 2800m the weather deteriorated, the temperature dropped to –35°C and the group lost 5 days. At 2300m the weather improved and a favourable wind allowed the use of ski sails until crevassing and melt water near the west coast presented the inevitable problems and forced the abandonment of some equipment. From the Inland Ice the expedition walked 40km to Ameralik Fjord and camped at Nansen's tent place on the fjord. Unlike Nansen and Sverdrup they did not build their own boat, but instead walked a further 12 hours to an Inuit settlement where they were able to organise a boat to Godthab.

The 4-man Imperial College Trans-Greenland Expedition under the leadership of Daniel Carrivick (UK) made a late start from Isortoq on 11 August and reached the western edge of the Inland Ice on 9 September (29 days). Starting with pulk weights of 70-100kg according to each individual's perceived pulling ability, they made good early progress in favourable weather. Up to day 15 they achieved a daily average of 20-22km, after which their progress was slowed by increasing cloud and fresh snow. Progress was stopped entirely on day 18 by strengthening winds that reached 125km/h. The following day the wind dropped and allowed good progress to be made on the now wind-hardened surface, although this gain was somewhat cancelled out by one member having to ski on one ski due to a broken binding. Softer snow reached after a few days allowed the re-attached binding to function and the expedition achieved its daily distance record of 28km just before reaching the abandoned ice road. Unable to use the road as an easy exit as planned, the expedition had to ferry their equipment to the ice edge, meeting the same problems as earlier parties. By this late in the season most of the melt water was frozen and presented little problem. The expedition claim to have eaten 4500 calories per day and encountered temperatures ranging from 0°C to –20°C.

Watkins Mountains

There was considerable activity in the Watkins Mountains, mainly centred on the easily accessible (by aircraft!) area near **Gunnbjørnsfjeld**.

The first reported expedition was a 5-person group arranged by Tangent Expeditions (UK) and led by Phil Poole who flew in towards the end of April. In generally good weather they climbed Gunnbjørnsfjeld (3693m), Dome (Qaqqaq Kershaw, 3682m), Cone (Qaqqaq Johnson, 3669m),

111. Per Ove Oppedal on Istind. A first ascent on the last day of climbing for the Norwegian G4 Expedition. The view is south to south-east. (*Jan-Frode Myklebust*)

Outpost and two unnamed peaks near Gunnbjørnsfjeld. One team member suffered suspected appendicitis at 3000m near Dome, but fortunately it cleared sufficiently that he only had to be hospitalised on the return to Iceland.

On 15 May the 6-man G4 Expedition (Norway) flew in to the glacier below Gunnbjørnsfjeld and from there made ascents of Gunnbjørnsfjeld, Dome and Cone. Per Ove Oppedal and Torstein Skage carried skis to all three summits and made the first ski descents of Gunnbjørnsfjeld and Dome. They also made the second ski descent of Cone, having been beaten to the first descent by a team of their countrymen from Tromsø who were just one day ahead of them. In a long day from their base camp the team then climbed a twin-horned peak they referred to as Styggehorn (3503m) overlooking the Christian IV glacier which they believed to be the highest unclimbed mountain in Greenland. They then moved to the east to the Bergen gletscher area and set up a new base from where they made claimed first ascents of peaks named as Anita Fjeld (2466m), Ebeth (2628m), Snefjeld (2650m) and Istind (2667m) with ski descents of the first two. In the early part of the trip they experienced temperatures of –10°C to –30°C, but towards the end of May it warmed to –5°C - +5°C.

Jim Hall, Bob Kerr, Rae Pritchard and Ros Murray from The Rucksack Club (UK) were the next group to visit the area in late May. They made ascents of Gunnbjørnsfjeld and Dome as well as the claimed first ascents of two peaks of 3020m and 2908m around the head of a tributary of the Woolley glacier. They also made attempts on a 2775m peak at the head of the Woolley glacier and on Julia (3455m), the 7th highest in Greenland, both unsuccessful due to cold feet described as 'literal and metaphorical'.

East Coast
Further north on the east coast and running the risk more of wet feet than cold feet was the 7-man Greenland White Sea Expedition (UK) who sailed their own boat (skipper Ron Newton) from Portsmouth to **Kangerdlugssuaq**. They left the UK on 19 May and, despite a broken boom off Iceland, reached Kangerdlugssuaq on 2 August. Access to the inner fjord was thwarted by a combination of a heavy swell and extensive pack ice, so they adopted plan B and established a camp at sea level at the head of Mikis Fjord. From here, they made several excursions into the coastal mountains of up to 1200m. The limited window of opportunity such a sailing dependent expedition has available meant that the expedition had to sail on 10 August, reaching Iceland on 12 August where the boat was left for the winter.

Perhaps more suitable Arctic vessels were used by the 3-man Greenland East Coast Kayak Expedition led by Martin Rickard (UK) who starting on 16 July kayaked from Kulusuk northwards to **Lake Fjord** and back to Ammassalik. Lake Fjord is where Gino Watkins drowned while kayaking in 1932 and one of the expedition's objectives was to re-erect the cross left there in his memory. This was duly done and the return journey to Ammassalik was completed on 29 July where the team continued their work with the local kayak club that they had helped establish some years previously.

In the interior of **Scoresbysund** a 3-man party led by Hugh Mackay (UK) was helicoptered on 3 July to the watershed of the Korridoren glacier where they established a base camp. During a couple of weeks at this site the group made five ski-mountaineering first ascents of peaks ranging from 1513m to 2065m in perfect weather.

Also in the same area of Milne Land, from 21 July to 9 August were the 29 (!) members of the West Lancashire Scouts East Greenland Expedition (UK) under the leadership of Dick Griffiths. During their stay in the area they made ascents of over 20 peaks (19 thought to be first ascents) in addition to carrying out botanical investigations of Arctic willow.

The weather experienced was more changeable than it had been for the earlier expedition with 10 'bad' days during two of which snow fell.

Further north in the 'Arctic Riviera' Hans Laptun (Norway) and 2 companions, starting from Nathorstfjord, continued his expeditions tracing the travels and huts of his father who had been a trapper in the area before WW2. The weather was not as it should have been on the 'Riviera' and they encountered much rain, wind and mist.

The Nanok group who every year carries out a programme of restoring the old trappers' huts was active again in the region between Germania Land and Shannon. On Shannon they worked on restoring the Alabama hut erected in 1910 from the wreck of the expedition ship 'Alabama'. This is where Ejnar Mikkelsen and Iver Iversen spent an enforced 2 years alone after returning from a long sledging expedition to find their shipwrecked companions had been picked up by a passing sealer.

South Greenland

The 7-person British 2004 **Torssukatak Fjord** Expedition led by Leanne Callaghan (UK) was in the field between 26 July and 25 August. The weather was good for all but 4 days, and they climbed six new routes of considerable difficulty on The Baron and The Baronet, the main twin peaks dominating the island of Pamiagdluk. Tim Riley was injured in a rock fall 9 days into the expedition and suffered chest injuries that required his evacuation. The expedition members lowered him from the mountain and got him to base camp but it was 5 days before a passing boat saw the group's signals from the shore, their satellite telephone having been damaged on arrival at base. Tim has made a good recovery.

The Karabiner Mountain Club (UK) also mounted an expedition to **Kangerdluarssuaq Fjord** on Pamiagdluk Island where they experienced poor weather but managed to establish a number of mountain routes of up to AD+ and rock routes to E3.

West Coast

Bob Shepton, leader of The Greenland Arctic Challenge (UK), sailed his boat across the Atlantic in June/July and in poor weather made his first mountaineering stop at **Kangerdluarssugssuaq** north of Nuuk (Godthab). A long mountain day resulted in him and his companion finding a 'dirty great cairn' on Pt 1650m, their chosen summit! Sailing on to the Akuliarusinguaq peninsula, his team had as their objectives four 2000m+ peaks that Bob's earlier expeditions had opted to leave. This was for good reason it seems, since the peaks did not entirely submit to this year's onslaught either! Various groups also made a number of small sorties at different points on the peninsula. On 13 August Bob made a solo ascent of Solo Snow Dome (2065m), and in the following days the crew in various combinations made first ascents of 4 peaks on the Qeqertarssuaq peninsula.

After various crew changes the boat sailed north to Etah, and following that probably established a furthest north record for a fibreglass boat at 78°32' in Smith Sound – at the same time noting 'attractive ski-mountaineering possibilities' in NW Greenland. On the return south Polly Murray and Tash Wright made a ski traverse along the length of Herbert Island before the expedition pressed on to Upernivik where the boat and Bob were to spend the winter to await the second stage of the expedition due to take place in 2005. Bob spent his 70th birthday on the boat frozen into the ice of Upernavik harbour but, sadly, during the over-wintering, while he was re-fuelling the boat, it caught fire and was totally destroyed.

These notes started with a statement that the lure of traversing the Inland Ice had perhaps begun to diminish. It is interesting, therefore, to end with the contrast posed by an expedition whose leader Kasuo Kojima (Japan) had as his goal a traverse of the Inland Ice. Nothing surprising in that except that this expedition started in Irkutsk in Siberia in 1997 and its leader was lured by that goal for all the intervening years. Kasuo wanted to trace the route followed by the prehistoric Mongoloid people as they expanded from central Asia into the Arctic, and his original plan was to cover some 22,000 km by dog sledge in 4 years. However, many delays arose or were created to impede his progress (he was imprisoned by the Russians for 35 days). It was not until 30 June 2004 that he reached Ammassalik. His route with his dogs had taken him through Siberia, across the Bering Strait, through the Canadian Arctic islands, and then from Grise Fjord on Ellesmere Island across Smith Sound to Siorapaluk in NW Greenland. From there he travelled by dog sledge, with one re-supply, southwards down the Inland Ice to finish at Ammassalik after a total distance covered of 28,000km. Beat that!

SIMON RICHARDSON

Scottish Winter 2003-2004

Opinions differ on the 2004 winter season. For some it was a good winter with long settled spells in the West. The air was clear and the sky blue for many days through February and March, and if you wanted to front-point classic gullies on squeaky névé this was the season for you. On the other hand, lack of any significant snowfalls until late March (when it was too late), meant that there was never enough build-up for the likes of Orion Face to form on the Ben. Few of the classic Grade V climbs were in condition, and many Grade III climbers became unwitting Grade IV leaders as routes were typically at least one notch harder than their advertised grade. For the technical mixed climber it was a frustrating time too, for the infrequent snowfalls were swiftly followed by deep thaws that stripped even the highest crags.

Despite this, the 2004 winter saw some outstanding achievements. Arguably the finest example was the first winter ascent of *Marathon Corner Direct* (VIII,8) on Ben Loyal by Guy Robertson and Pete Benson. With a summit elevation of only 764m, Ben Loyal is not an obvious winter climbing venue, especially in a lean season, but when bitterly cold strong NW winds swept southwards across the country in late January, the Aberdeen based pair took the gamble and made the long journey north up to Sutherland to visit the little known 300m-high cliff on Sgor a'Chleirich, Ben Loyal's westerly top. *Marathon Corner* is an E1 summer climb that was first climbed by Les Brown and A Turnbull in 1969. The guidebook description of the cliff is particularly enticing for a winter climber, mentioning that several summer parties have been repulsed by extraordinarily steep vegetation, loose rock and a distinct lack of protection. All this made for a superb seven-pitch winter route climbed on a mixture of turf, snowed-up rock and icy smears. For many climbers, climbing a new route of this length and quality on a cliff that was previously untouched in winter is close to the ultimate, and *Marathon Corner* joins the likes of *Magic Bow Wall* and *The Godfather* as one of the most significant ascents in the Northern Highlands in recent years.

By contrast, the other major new route of the season was made three days earlier at the other end of the Highlands. Over the last couple of seasons Dave MacLeod has been pushing the winter envelope with a series of difficult ascents such as his on sight repeat of the *Demon Direct* in the Northern Corries. During the cold snap near the end of January, Dave pushed the technical limit yet further when he succeeded on his long-standing roof project on the Cobbler. *The Cathedral* (X,11) climbs up to a tight niche at the back of the cave on the front face of the Centre Peak, and then climbs across a six metre horizontal roof crack across the middle of the cave to gain turf at the lip and easy ground above. The 30m-long line is not taken by a summer route and is an ideal winter only line as it features wet, dirty rock with lots of turf.

The Cathedral is the largest continuous roof ever climbed in Scottish winter and was climbed ground up at the second attempt. Dave had tried to on sight the route in January 2003 but had failed due to lack of physical endurance. This time he was full of confidence having just returned from a very successful visit to Uschinen in Switzerland where he had climbed several of continental Europe's hardest mixed routes including the M12 test piece *Vertical Limit*. One only has to imagine a route that combines the technical difficulty of *The Cathedral* with the stature of a route like *Marathon Corner* to see that the long hoped-for quantum leap in traditional mixed climbing standards is not far away.

Big news on Ben Nevis was the first winter ascent of *Arthur* (VIII,8) by Bruce Poll and Tony Shepherd. This steep four-pitch HVS runs up the centre of the front face of Number Three Gully Buttress and was first climbed by Klaus Schwartz and Gordon Webster in 1971. They used a point of aid on the third pitch and it is possible their route has never been repeated. Lying high on the mountain *Arthur* was a likely candidate for a winter ascent, but recent mild winters have thwarted several hopefuls as the line has failed to carry much snow or hoar frost. Bruce and Tony timed their climb to perfection and nipped in to make a very smooth ascent just after New Year when the cliff was white with frost and the cracks free of ice. *Arthur* is only the third Grade VIII to be climbed on Ben Nevis and, along with *Marathon Corner*, joins a very small number of Grade VIIIs that have had on-sight first winter ascents.

The Ben also saw some new additions to the Douglas Boulder. Gareth Hughes and James Edwards climbed *Turf War* (V,6) based on the summer line *Militant Chimney* and also climbed an alternative start to *Left-Hand Chimney*. Further right Jonny Baird and Andy Turner made a winter ascent of *Jacknife* (IV,6). A new winter route on the Ben always feels extra special, and it was particularly fitting that Nevis regular Jonny Baird should at long last have a Nevis climb to his name. Iain Small and I took advantage of a heavy early April snowfall to climb *Central Rib Direct* (VI,7) on Creag Coire na Ciste. The original line climbed by Jimmy Marshall and Robin Campbell avoided the steep central section by taking a line close to *Central Gully Right-Hand*, but an improbable sequence of holds led up the outside edge of the impending right arête to give a spectacular and unique pitch.

Aonach Mor saw heavy traffic and many climbers enjoyed the easier gullies that held good ice and névé throughout much of the season. Steve Kennedy and Bob Hamilton showed that Coire an Lochain still has routes to yield with a handful of good new lines including *Pro Libertate* (V,6), a sustained mixed route on the buttress between *The Guardian* and

Stirling Bridge. A little further north, Andy Nisbet and Dave McGimpsey visited their old haunt of Stob Coire an Laoigh in the Grey Corries and added a clutch of new routes including *Socialist* (V,7) which climbs the centre of the left wall of Centrepoint buttress. Further east Kevin Neal and Iain Rudkin made a productive visit to Geal Charn above Loch Ericht near Drumochter. Their first addition was called *Map and Compass* (III,4) and implies that they were a little unsure of their location on the mountain but they capitalised on this with the fine steep ice line of *Flight of the Navigator* (VI,6) when they returned with Kirk Watson the following day.

The high crags in Glen Coe saw some action in the cold snowy snaps in late December and January. Of note was the first ascent of the short but good *Tuberculosis* (VI,6) in Stob Coire nan Lochan by Dave Hollinger and Guy Willett. This takes the impending groove right of *Crest Route* and gave excellent climbing, although well-frozen conditions are recommended to cement everything in place. *Bishops' Buttress* on the West Top of Bidean saw a couple of technical additions on the same day in late December. Donald King and Andy Nelson made a winter ascent of *The Crook* (VI,7) and Gareth Hughes and James Edwards found *Under The Weather* (VII,7) a difficult climb on the upper tier of the buttress.

James Edwards had a very good season with new routes across the Highlands. If you're serious about seeking out unclimbed lines, you have to be prepared to put in the groundwork and James made a useful reconnaissance visit to Coire nam Fhamhair on Beinn Bhan the previous summer. The intention was to scope out the wall right of *Die Riesenwand* for a possible repeat of *The Godfather*, but Edwards noticed a couple of lines left of *Genesis* on the left side of the crag. He returned at the end of December with Sam Barron and climbed *Revelations* (VI,6), a superb natural line of weakness near the left end of the cliff. Three weeks later Edwards was back with Gareth Hughes to climb *Biblical Knowledge* (VI,5), the second line he had spotted, which takes the left edge of the fault-line taken by *Genesis*.

The other major addition on Beinn Bhan was the steep buttress between *Mad Hatter's* and *March Hare's* gullies by Malcolm Bass and Simon Yearsley. This was a well-known objective and is mentioned in Cold Climbs as a new route objective, but nobody had stepped up to the challenge of a direct ascent of the wall. Bass and Yearsley were concerned about how much weaving around they would have to do to find a way through the succession of rock tiers, but they managed to find a logical direct line. Conditions were good with a thin covering of good névé, hard frozen turf and bits of ice but not enough to choke the cracks. The seven-pitch *Realisation* (VI,6) is a major addition to the mountain and deserves further repeats as it has good belays and protection.

Other notable new route activity in the North West included the first ascent of *Aquila* (VI,7) on Ben Damph by Andy Nisbet and Jonathan Preston, *Expanding Universe* (VI,5), on Sail Mhor by Guy Robertson and Es Tressider, *Avalanche Goose* (VI,7) on Slioch by Iain Small and Neil Wilson, and the excellent sounding *Underground Resistance* (V,6) on Stac Pollaidh by Erik Brunskill and Daffyd Morris. All these climbs show that even on relatively well known cliffs there are still good new routes to discover.

Further west, John Mackenzie continued to develop the Stratchconon and Ben Wyvis crags with an astonishing 11 new routes. With the increased focus on climbing new winter lines across Scotland, it is difficult to believe that Mackenzie will retain a monopoly on his home turf for much longer, but his unrivalled knowledge of the these crags gives him a head start over the competition. His finest additions were *Oh Dearie Me* (III,4) that takes thin discontinuous turf streaks on the 250m-high East Buttress of Creag Ghlas, and the superb *Temptress* (V,5) in Coire Mor on Ben Wyvis. Both routes were climbed with Alan Dennis.

The Cairngorms were particularly quiet for most of the season. Beinn a'Bhuird held snow well and saw the most activity with a handful of new routes. Chris Cartwright and I were particularly pleased with the first ascent of *Archtempter* (VII,8) in Coire na Ciche, a good winter line based on the prominent arch in the unclimbed section of crag right of *Jason's Chimney*. This one had been on the list a long time but went without a struggle on the first attempt. *Nipped in the Bud* (V,6) in Coire nan Clach was a different story and only succumbed on the fifth visit with all previous attempts being stymied by horrific weather or lack of conditions. Persistence pays in the Scottish winter game! The Nisbet-McGimpsey team joined forces with James Edwards for a good weekend in February when they made the first winter ascent of the all too obvious *Ribbon Ridge* (IV,4) on Stacan Dubha and *Dreadlock* (V,6) a new addition on the Upper Tier of Carn Etchachan. Those that thought the Northern Corries are worked out will be surprised by the addition of *Lagopus* (V,6), a direct start to *Snow Bunting* in Coire an Lochain by Ian Taylor and Neil Carnegie.

The finest winter climb in the Cairngorms however was Guy Robertson's and Jason Currie's ascent of *The Winter Needle* (VIII,8) on the Shelter Stone. The route was first climbed by Andy Nisbet and Colin MacLean in February 1985. They used a point of aid and spent two days on the route with a bivouac, but the route was so far ahead of its time that it took thirteen years before it was repeated by Alan Mullin and Steve Paget in October 1998 with a major variation in the lower section. The second ascent created a storm of controversy, because many climbers believed it was climbed too early in the season to be a valid winter climb. This was rectified by Alasdair Coull and Sam Chinnery who made a free ascent of the Nisbet-MacLean line over two days in February 2000. The next logical step was a one-day free ascent and this was achieved by Robertson and Currie on a perfect day at the end of February in a swift eleven hours to give a powerful demonstration of the continual progression of Scottish winter standards.

For many, the exploratory nature of Scottish winter climbing is the big attraction, and the season revealed a number of new venues. The fine crop of routes that Andy Nisbet, Dave McGimpsey and Dave Allan pioneered

112. Chris Cartwright on *Goldfinger* (VII, 7) on Ben Cruachan. (*Simon Richardson*)

on Creag an Lochan Ulbha on Meall Horn one superb day at the end of February sound particularly intriguing. I am surely biased, but in my view some of the finest exploratory climbing took place high up on the north side of Ben Cruachan. The superbly steep granite cliff above Coire Chat is seamed by cracks and grooves. It was first climbed by Dave Ritchie and Mark Shaw in February 2002 when they added *Noe Buttress* (IV,4) and the Grade II gully to its left. Chris Cartwright and Iain Small visited the cliff during winter 2003 and were immediately struck by the climbing potential of the unclimbed wall to the left of *Noe Gully*. They left their mark with the first ascent of *In the Knoe*, a fine VI,6 that cleaves a central line up the wall.

The cliff proved to be an ideal location for the variable weather of the 2004 season as it faces north, lies above the 1000m contour and comes into condition very quickly. Although the routes are relatively short, typically between 80 and 100m high, they are continuously sustained from the first move to the very top of the crag. Cartwright methodically set about developing the cliff adding a dozen routes along with Iain Small, Andy Hume, Roger Webb and myself. The finest additions were *Goldfinger* (VII,7), the impressive central line that takes the impending crack splitting the clean wall high on the buttress, and *Dr Noe* (VI,6), the stepped ramp line running left to right up to a point overlooking Noe Gully.

New winter crags are developed every winter in Scotland, but what is remarkable about this discovery is that the quality of the climbing is so good and that it lies on a relatively accessible mountain. One of my abiding memories of the 2004 season will be climbing the superb corner line of *Tainted Elixir* (V,6). As I pulled through bulge after bulge on good solid hooks and torques, the cloud cleared behind us to reveal a magnificent view down Loch Etive across to Glen Coe with Ben Nevis standing regally behind. It was the very essence of Scottish winter climbing, and it makes me wonder just how many other great winter crags are out there still waiting to be discovered.

TONY HOWARD

Jordan 2004 - 2005

Despite the surrounding Middle East turmoil, Jordan is busy with tourism including climbing. New route developments in Wadi Rum have continued through winter – spring 2005.

Nevertheless, the summit of **Jebel um Ishrin** – one of the most dominant in Rum, guarding the east flank of the main valley – still remains elusive. Regular Rum visitor, Gilles Rappeneau, hopes to track down the long-forgotten Bedouin way and has gathered more information from the locals. Meanwhile a copy of his small topo booklet to other superb Bedouin hunting routes – amongst Rum's best adventure climbs – will be found in the Rum Rest House. Another is with Talal Awad, an 'aspirant' Bedouin guide and regular companion of Gilles. Also see website list below. The only new climb on this massif is south of the summit and of considerably smaller scale: A Nevin and L Kamphausen climbed the bold overwidth chimney above the abseil from **Rakabat Canyon**, into **Kharazeh Canyon** at 6a (all grades in French system).

To the east of **Jebel um Ishrin**, the enjoyable and easily accessible west facing cliff of **Jebel M'Zaygeh** has had two more climbs added, up cracks 50m left of *Runner Up*, at 6a and 5c/6a, by three French climbers and Bedouin guide M'salim Sabbah (eldest son of Rum's first Mountain Guide, Sabbah Atieq). Both routes were climbed in traditional style unlike last year's new additions on this crag that were bolt protected, contravening the Rum Protected Area (National Park) regulations. I will say again, as I said in my last *AJ* report, that after the safety of the bolts, anyone moving on from here to the traditional routes of Rum is likely to find a cool head at least as much of a requirement as technical ability. Writing in the New Routes Book in 2004, Andrew Walker says 'save those scary, unprotected but beautiful lines for climbers with the ability to "run it out" and create bold, committing routes in the future'. A bolt has already appeared on pitch 3 of *Aquarius* on **Jebel Rum's** E face on a line originally climbed using traditional gear, and a heated debate is taking place about bolts placed on an exposed traverse on the committing Bedouin climb of *Mohammed Musa's Route*. Apparently an aspirant Bedouin Guide requested them to protect clients, as happened with *Sabbah's Route*, which set an unfortunate precedent. Still having a grump about bolts, another (actually a peg in a drilled hole) has appeared in the top wide chimney of *Sundown* in **Barrah Canyon**. It is to be hoped that this retrogressive trend does not spread insidiously onto other traditional lines. Climbers adding new routes should also endeavour to use traditional ethics and gear – Rum is a wilderness area, let's do our best to keep it that way.

Still in **Barrah Canyon**, Omar Auda and Mohamed Hammad, Rum's youngest 'aspirant' guides (see weblinks below) made their first new route, *Welcome to the Gazelles*, with 2 pitches of 5+ which clients seem to enjoy. Nearby, on **Jebel Barrah**, A Moore and T Pidsley broke left from *Hunter's Slabs* to climb the *East Ridge*, giving 'a worthwhile traverse of the summit'. They also added some grade 3 climbs on **Jebel Sabata**, SSW of **Jebel Khazali**. East of **Khazali**, on **Jebel Qabr Amra**, a seldom climbed massif, half a dozen new climbs were opened up by Omar Auda's elder brother, Mountain Guide Atieq Auda, all at about 5+, some with sections of A1/A2.

Rum regulars Albert Precht and Sigi Brochmeyer have been busy again on **Jebel Rum**, adding the *South Wall of the West Pillar* – 7 pitches with a 6b crux and, together with Oswald Ölz, the *West Pillar* itself – 9 pitches, 6a max, 'superb'. The trio went on to climb *Gourmet* right of the *West Pillar*, 5 max, 'perfect rock, a real pleasure', descending by four 50m abseils on good gear. They finished their trip with the 8-pitch *Mumien Express*, 6b max, on **Jebel Rum's** remote **Amen Dome**. As always, all routes were done in clean traditional style.

Heading to the far south now, near *The Hajj*, the *West Buttress* of **Jebel Suweibit** provided a 300m TD inf with a 6b crux for R Durra and R Austin and gave C and R Lewis and S Grey *The Fear of Flying*, 3. Finally, on the last day of their trip, A Walker and F Horacete added the excellent *Songline*, 'four exciting pitches' 6c, 6a, 5c, 5c/6a, up a 'perfect Barrah-style straight crack on the S Face of **Jebel um M'goor**. Good nut pro throughout.'

The weather was again a bit weird. The Khamsin (fifty day) wind blew for much of April, bringing some dusty days and a few days in mid-April with temperatures over 38°. The Visitor Centre at the entrance to the valley is now open and charges a 2JD (£1.50) admission fee to the Rum Protected Area. The Rest House and Campsite are still in use and it is possible to hire vehicles and local guides from the Rum Village, though the official system is to make arrangements at the Visitor Centre on arrival (not really possible for long stay climbers). There is still no adequate rescue equipment (though there has been another helicopter rescue aided by local Bedouin) and there are still only three local 'qualified' guides, though half a dozen others are working regularly as guides on the popular Bedouin routes. The Aqaba Authority (ASEZA) is responsible for the area but have not indicated when there will be further training of these guides or provision of equipment.

Useful websites and contacts:
Gilles Rappeneau – http://wadirum.userhome.ch
Mohamed Hammad: Mohamed-climber@yahoo.com
Rum Bedouin Mountain Guides: http://bedouinroads.com
Wilf Colonna and the Desert Guides: http://www.desertguides.com
Website on Jordan and Rum: http://www.jordanjubilee.com
Walter Neser's Rum climbs website: http://www.wadirum.net
Tony Howard: www.nomadstravel.co.uk – info on Rum, Jordan, Mid East
    and North Africa

HARISH KAPADIA

India 2004

While the world is opening its doors to mountaineers and mountain lovers, there is distressing news from the new Uttaranchal state in India. The state contains some of the most beautiful areas in the Indian Himalaya with peaks like Nanda Devi, Kamet, Shivling and several others. Unfortunately, it has imposed severe restrictions on climbing and special royalty charges for mountaineers (minimum US$ 1400). This is *in addition* to charges payable to the Indian Mountaineering Foundation. Moreover, separate permissions must be obtained from officials in the state, forest departments and local authorities. At least half the number of porters must be employed from local villages and each village is to be paid a fee as you trek through. The forest department is to be paid a special fee to camp on its land. Indian mountaineers and trekkers are not spared and for the first time they will have to pay peak fees to climb peaks in their own country. After many discussions, negotiations and protests, all of which were brushed aside, the state government has decided to impose these rules from the beginning of the 2005 season. Please check full details, rates and addresses on the website www.indmount.org.

An Indian army team climbed Kangchenjunga from Nepal to celebrate the 50th Anniversary of the first ascent of the peak.

Another major event was the exploration of the Tsangpo-Siang Bend from the south. A team of three Indians pioneered a route through the thick forest of Arunachal Pradesh to reach the Line of Control, between India and China, where the Tsangpo enters India and is called the Siang. The same river is called the Brahmaputra as it flows into the plains of Assam. The full exploration of the Tsangpo gorge was thus completed.

SIKKIM

Tingchenkang (6010m)
An expedition organised by the Himalayan Club, Kolkatta Section, led by Air Vice Marshal A K Bhattacharyya (retd), made the second ascent of this mountain on 6 November. The summit was reached via the north face (a new route) in extremely cold conditions. Subrata Chakraborty and Pasang Phuter Sherpa reached the summit. The first recorded ascent was made in 1998 by the Indo-British Territorial Army's team by the west ridge.

GARHWAL

Adi Kailash (5925m)

An international team of climbers led by Andy Perkins and Martin Welch made the first ascent of Adi (also known as Chota or Little) Kailash in the Kumaun Himalaya. The mountain is revered due to its similarity to the holy mountain of Kailash in nearby Tibet. Andy Perkins, Tim Woodward, Jason Hubert, Martin Welch, Diarmid Hearns, Jack Pearse, Amanda George (all UK) and Paul Zuchowski (US) made the first ascent of Adi Kailash by the SW ridge on 8 October in perfect weather. Out of respect to local sensitivities, the team stopped a few metres short of the summit.

Nikarchu Qilla (5750m)

From the same expedition, Welch, Woodward, Hearns, Pearse, George and Gustavo Fierro-Carrion (Ecuador) made the first ascent of this peak which is located 3km NE of the unclimbed Nikurch Rama (5995m). This team also stopped a few metres below the summit..

Arwa Spire (6193m)

A four-member German team, led by Thomas Hüber, attempted the popular peaks of Arwa Spire in Central Garhwal. They followed the west ridge and despite some poor weather, Thomas Hüber with Alexander Hüber and Peter Auzenferger reached the summit on 28 September.

Bhagirathi III (6454m)

A German/French team led by Walter Hoelzler climbed two routes on Bhagirathi III, first by the W pillar on 19 May and then by the N ridge on 20 May. Summiters on the W pillar route were Walter Hoelzler and Joerg Pflugmacher. Jerome Blanc-Gras, Christopher Blanc-Gras, Lionel Deborde and Philippe Albouy reached the summit by the north ridge.

Chaturangi I (6407m)

A four-member German team led by Joachim Gnoyke had excellent weather in September and the summit was reached on the 13th by Joachim Gnoyke, Nadine Bagnoud, Mathieu Aste and two high-altitude porters.

Chaturangi IV (6304m)

All the peaks of this group are very inviting to climb and are situated on the Gangotri glacier. Five members of an Indian expedition from Bengal, led by Ms Jayanti Chaudhuri, reached the summit on 21 September.

Chaukhamba III (6974m) and IV (6853m)

An expedition from the Nehru Institute of Mountaineering, led by Col Ashok Abbey, made the first attempt on these unclimbed peaks. A high point of 6300m on the western flank was reached on 8 July in poor weather.

Chiring We (6599m)

The first ascent of this peak was made in 1979 by a team from Mumbai under the leadership of Harish Kapadia. The 12-member team led by Martin Moran completed the second ascent on 26 September. They followed the west ridge (route of first ascent) after establishing four camps above base camp and the summit was reached by Martin Moran, Alex Moran, Jonathan Preston, Liam Warren, Paul Watson, Stuart Reid, Christopher Wheatley, Geoffrey Dawson and Christopher Harle.

Januhut (6805m)

A British/New Zealand team led by Malcom Bass attempted this unclimbed peak near Chaukhamba I in the post-monsoon season. Following the SW ridge they reached a height of 6400m on 10 November. However, heavy snowfall caught them unawares and they were forced to retreat.

Kalanka (6931m)

An expedition led by American Carlos Buhler attempted this peak in the pre-monsoon season by the north face. Unfortunately they encountered serious bad weather and snowfall which could have avalanched. All three team members – Buhler, John M Lyall and Sandy Allan – reached a high point at 6075m on 30 May.

Kamet (7756m) and Abi Gamin (7355m)

This large team from Bengal, led by Samir Sengupta, comprised 15 members, five Sherpas and four high-altitude porters. They climbed both peaks on 29 May. The route followed on Kamet was from the NE face and on Abi Gamin via the W ridge. Both mountains were climbed an hour apart on the same day from a common last camp. The Kamet summiters were Samrat Basu, Dawa Sherpa, Thukpa Sherpa and Na Dorjee Sherpa. The Abi Gamin summiters were Prodyut Bhattacharjee, Sandip Roy, Nima Sherpa, Debender Singh Rana and Shohan S Martholiya.

Kedarnath (6968m)

A Japanese five-member team, led by Yosuke Narisue, attempted the normal route on Kedarnath. Not using any high-altitude support, members ferried their own luggage and reached 4400m by the normal route, but they were too tired to continue further.

Mana Northwest (7092m)

A team of eight members from Bengal, led by Arupam Das, attempted this subsidiary peak of Mana in Central Garhwal. The peak is situated near Kamet. The team reached 6900m on 21 June via the Purvi Kamet glacier.

Meru (6660m) and Shivling (6543m)

A five-member Japanese team, led by Hiroyoshi Manome, attempted both these peaks in the post monsoon season in different pairs. In the early stages of the expedition one member had a serious fall and was hurt in the leg. All the members helped in the rescue but some equipment was lost. Later they attempted Meru, reaching 5850m on 3 September by the NE face. Another team reached 5900m on Shivling on 4 September while attempting the W face. They had to give up the further climb.

Parvati Parvat (6257m)

A 10-member team from the Indian Mountaineering Foundation, led by Lovraj Singh Dharamshaktu, approached the peak from the south via the Panpatia Bamak. On 17 September Nadre and Balwant with three high-altitude porters reached the col between Nilkanth and Parvati Parbat. From the col, in whiteout conditions, they climbed the east ridge to a high point. They placed a snow stick there and returned. On 21 September, the leader with Ashish, Deepesh, Surender and Umesh and two high-altitude porters reached the same high point in clearer weather and could see two more tops (estimated 100m higher). They were unable to reach either of them.

Saf Minal (6911m)

A two-man team of John Varco (USA) and Ian Parnell (UK) made one of the best ascents in the Indian Himalaya this season. They climbed the N ridge and NW face of this high peak situated on the northern rim of the Nanda Devi Sanctuary. The summit was reached on 6 October. Except for four days, they had excellent weather throughout. (*See Parnell's account 'Saf Minal North-west Face' on page 83*.)

Sudarshan Parvat (6507m)

This peak, rising above the Gangotri glacier, was climbed on 19 June by the popular east ridge. The summiters from this 10-member team from Bengal, led by Biswadeb Ghosh, were Dalip Sahoo, Dev Jyoti Datta and four high-altitude porters.

Thalay Sagar (6904m)

A strong Swiss-American-German climbing team of six members, led by Stephan Siegrist, climbed the NW buttress route to reach the summit on 27 September. Summiters were Thomas Senf, Dennis Burdet, Ralf Weber and the leader. They encountered excellent weather throughout the ascent.

Yogeshwar (6617m)

A six-member Indian team from Maharashtra, led by Chandrashekar Shirsat, attempted this peak from the Shyamvarna valley in May and June. Gautam Raut, Datta Chalke and Rajendra Shinde reached a high point of 6250m on June 1.

HIMACHAL PRADESH

First Ascent of Khhang Shiling (6360m)
A three-member team, Divyesh Muni, Vineeta Muni and Shripad Sapkal, sponsored by the Himalayan Club, made the first ascent of Khhang Shiling (6360m) on 19 September, assisted by Sherpa Lakhpa Bhote. They explored the Khamengar valley in Spiti, a rarely visited area in Himachal Pradesh. Khhang Shiling is a prominent mountain at the head of the Khamengar valley. Camp I at 5880m was established in a basin formed between a large rock feature and the Shigri Parvat massif. After climbing along the glacier to a bergschrund below the col between Shigri Parvat and Khhang Shiling they dumped equipment there. Next day they reached the top at 1.30pm. The party returned to Kullu via the Pin Parvati pass.

Dharamsura (6445m)
A 10-member, all-women team, sponsored by the IMF and led by Ms Deepu Sharma, climbed Dharamsura (also known as 'White Sail') on 14 August via the E ridge. The summiters were Nari Dhami, Asmita, Chandra Bisht, Bhuvneshwari Thakur and Krishna Thakur.

Indrasan (6221m)
On 30 August Basanta Singha Roy, the leader, with three high-altitude porters, reached the summit of Indrasan. This was the first ascent by an all-Indian team of this formidable peak. The E ridge was followed to the summit.

Unnamed Peaks (6240m, 6100m)
A 12-member team from Bengal led by Ujjal Ray climbed both these peaks situated in the Pakshi Lamur river basin of the Spiti valley. They approached the peaks after crossing Parang La and established their base camp near the confluence of Pare Chu and Pakshi Lamur Nala. Peak 6240m was climbed on 28 August and Peak 6100m on 29 August via the SW face.

Lahaul
CB - 9 (6108m)
A nine-member IMF sponsored expedition led by I D Sharma approached this peak on the Milang glacier after establishing three camps above base camp, but on 25 August bad weather and technical difficulties stopped the attempt at 5600m.

CB-13 (6264m)
A twelve-member team from Bengal led by Pijush Kanti Das climbed this popular peak in summer. The peak was climbed by the traditional route on 27 July by Samar Prasad, Mithun Talukdar, Biplab Mondal with Sonam Rana (high-altitude porter).

CB-14 (6078m)

A large 14-member Indian team from Bengal, led by Anal Das, climbed CB-14 (6078m) on 19 August. The summiters were Swaraj Ghosh, Ajoy Mondal, Subrata Banerjee, Sanjay Ghosh, Moloy Mukherjee and Arindam Mukherjee, with three high-altitude porters. They followed the west ridge to the summit. On their approach to the mountain the team located the wreckage of a plane which had crashed here in 1968. They reported the matter to the nearest authorities and in a large recovery effort many parts of the plane were brought back and a major mystery solved.

KR-7 (6096m)

An eight-member Polish team led by Adam Sredniawa climbed the E ridge in three different ascents. The summit was reached on the 6th, 17th and 22nd August respectively. All climbers reached the top.

Menthosa (6443m)

This high peak in Lahaul's Pangi valley was climbed by Japanese and Indian teams in the past following a route from the Urgus pass and then going up an ice wall to the summit. This large 12-member team from Bengal, led by Bikash Roy and accompanied by two Sherpas and two high-altitude porters, reached above camp II on 1st September through Urgus pass but could not establish camp III, which was to be their summit camp. They reached 5850m on the mountain.

Kinnaur

Phawararang (6349m)

This peak is situated in a little known valley of Kinnaur. The circular route round Mt Kailash passes at its foot. A nine-member team followed the north ridge and the leader Dhananjay Bhagat, with guide Manoj, reached the summit on 31 August.

Zonikanda (4250m)

This 11-member Indian team, led by Chanchal Bhaduri, had some strange experiences with bureaucracy. In spite of having permission from the IMF they were not allowed to go beyond base camp at Zonikanda (4250m). The local army and the Indo-Tibet Border Authorities refused permission to proceed on 20 September.

LADAKH – ZANSKAR

Harong (6210m)

A seven-member Japanese team, led by Masato Oki, attempted the E face of this peak near the Pangong lake, Ladakh. On 18 August Hideho Masudu, Sherpa Pem Tsering and Sherpa Sangay Pun reached the top.

Exploring the Tsangpo Gorge from the south

The romance of exploration of the Tsangpo gorge has puzzled geographers for centuries. The Tsangpo (as it is called in Tibet) originates near Lake Manasarovar at the foot of Mt Kailash. Flowing east across the Tibetan plateau, its progress is blocked by Namcha Barwa and the Gyala Peri massif and between these peaks the river takes a huge turn called the 'Great Tsangpo Bend'. From here onwards the Tsangpo descends steeply towards the south from the Tibetan plateau to the Himalayan divide leading to the McMahon Line and India.

As the river enters Indian territory at 580m, it takes an 'S' loop, the 'Tsangpo/Siang Bend'. In Arunachal Pradesh it is called by different names, like the Siang and Dihang, and is joined by various tributaries. On reaching the Assam plains it is joined by the Dibang and Lohit rivers and from that point onwards the river is called the Brahmaputra.

The exploration of this mighty river started in 1715. Although the 'Great Tsangpo Bend' in the north (the Pemako area in Tibet) had been explored, the 'S' bend at the border of India-China had never been reached owing to the inhospitable nature of the terrain. After the 1962 war with China the whole area became 'out of bounds'.

In 2004, a three-member team, Harish Kapadia, Motup Chewang and Wing Cdr V K Sashindran, travelled from the Brahmaputra river in the Assam valley along the Siang river to the Tsangpo gorge where it enters Indian territory, thus completing the exploration of the Tsangpo.

Books

Capt M S Kohli published his autobiography entitled *One More Step* covering his illustrious career in the Himalaya and in the Navy. *J B Auden A Centenary Tribute* was published by the Geological Survey of India, paying tributes to this foremost geologist in the early part of the last century. Towards the end of the year came *Adventure Travels in the Himalaya* by John Jackson, covering his lifetime of travels and climbs in the range.

Save Siachen

The war-torn Siachen glacier remains peaceful due to a lasting ceasefire. But soldiers continue to die there, as they stay for too long at altitude. Pollution is prevalent and the shrinking glacier is a warning against future disaster.

A conference, chaired by Dr Saleem Ali, a young professor from the United States, was held in Mumbai. It considered various proposals and possible methods of protecting the glacier. Political talks between India and Pakistan are moving, albeit slowly, towards a peaceful solution.

DICK ISHERWOOD

Nepal 2004

Correspondents who provided assistance with this report include Lindsay Griffin, Alexander Odintsov, Tamotsu Nakamura, Nick Bullock, Bill Ruthven, Bernard Newman, Tom Briggs, and above all Elizabeth Hawley, whose detailed reports are of great value to all who are interested in climbing in Nepal.

Probably the most notable climbing event in Nepal in 2004 was the Russian ascent of a very direct route on the north face of **Jannu (Khumbakhama, 7710m)** in the spring. This face is the 'Wall of Shadows', and the Russian line is close to that claimed by Tomo Cesen as a solo ascent in 1989 but now generally discredited. After several attempts in previous years, an eight-member team led by Alexander Odintsov fixed over 3000m of rope, mainly on very steep and sometimes loose limestone, in cold and often windy conditions. A hanging portaledge was used for the highest camp at 7400m. The climbing was graded VII, 6b, A3+, ice 4, M6 and seems to have maintained this standard until very close to the top. After seven weeks' work Alexander Ruchkin and Dmitry Pavlenko reached the summit on 26 May, followed by Sergei Borisov, Gennady Kirievskiy and Nikolai Totmyanin on the 28th. They descended by the same route and left base camp for home on 30 May. This expedition received the 2004 Piolet d'Or award.

In the post-monsoon season Tomaz Humar went to the east face of **Jannu** which Slovenian groups had tried several times before. Humar soloed to around 7000m in four days, up a steep and apparently dangerous mixed face, before abandoning the attempt owing to hazardous snow mushrooms on the south-east ridge. He took several falls during both ascent and descent, and said he had no plans to return.

A Spanish expedition attempted the east ridge of **Dome Kang (7264m)** which rises from the Jongsong La north of Kangchenjunga, reaching a height of 6650m.

On **Makalu** a British Services team led by Colin Scott attempted the south-east ridge in the spring, reaching 7500m before retreating in bad weather. They fixed a lot of rope with assistance from a three-man French team who had started in Tibet, attempted the north-east ridge of Makalu, retreated in bad conditions, lost most of their gear to thieves, and finally moved round to the Nepalese side to try the south-east ridge. Late in May the weather improved and the French continued up the ridge and descended into the eastern cwm, as previous parties have done on this ridge. Yannick Graziani reached the summit alone on 29 May. The crest of the south-east ridge still has not been followed all the way to the summit.

113.   North face of Jannu (Khumbakhama, 7710m) showing the 2004
        Russian line. (*Alexander Odintsov*)

Also in the spring, Jean Christophe Lafaille climbed a difficult line on the north-west ridge of **Makalu II (Kangchungtse, 7678m)** solo from the remote Chomo Lonzo glacier in Tibet. He joined the 1976 Japanese route, which climbed this ridge from the Nepalese side, at around 7100m. The remainder of this ridge, with only bits of ancient fixed rope for help, was technically difficult (M5/6). He was unable to continue to the main peak of Makalu as he had intended and instead went down to the Barun base camp and took a long route back into Tibet, returning to his base camp after seven days.

A four-man Italian/Kazakh team climbed the north-west face of the north summit of **Baruntse (7057m)** by a variant on the 1994 Czech route.

A Slovenian team went to **Pasang Lhamu Chuli (Nangpai Gosum I, 7351m)** just south of Cho Oyu in the post-monsoon season and climbed a new route up its south-east face to the south ridge. This involved steep rock and ice and a very narrow initial section on the south ridge.

Two members of the same party made the probable first ascent of the south-west face of **Dzasampa Tse**, a 6295m summit on the ridge immediately south of Nangpai Gosum. The pair climbed most of the 600m face unroped, the ascent taking seven hours. The route was graded TD+ (50–65° and Mixed).

Nick Bullock and Nick Carter made the first ascent of the 1600m north-west face of **Teng Kangpoche (6500m)**, alpine style, in two days in late October. They soloed much of the climb, mainly on steep ice often covered by powder. The upper part of the face was very steep rock and ice with little protection, and the last 300m took a full 12-hour day. In very cold conditions they reached the west ridge around 1 km from the summit of the mountain. They decided to leave the rest of the corniced ridge for someone else, and descended by the same route. They graded their climb ED1/Scottish IV. They observed considerable scope for further hard climbing on this face, which they compared to the north face of the Droites, but considerably higher.

On the Tibetan side of **Everest** a large Russian expedition led by Victor Koslov made a new and direct route on the north face, using 5000m of fixed rope, oxygen and some Sherpa support. Much steep loose rock was encountered. Eight people reached the summit and descended the North Ridge route with help from another Russian expedition.

The mainstream Everest scene continues unabated. In the 2004 pre-monsoon season no less than 319 people reached the summit, from the north and south sides combined. Peak traffic was on 16 May with 61 summiters. There were seven deaths, which is perhaps not a bad rate for this sort of activity. Only two parties went to Everest post monsoon, both from Tibet, and neither was successful.

Other highlights included:

- A new speed record, from the Khumbu Base Camp to the top, of 8 hours 8 minutes, was claimed by Pemba Dorje. This astonishing achievement was not surprisingly disputed by the previous record holder, but seems to have been accepted by the Nepalese Government.

- a Sherpa with an artificial leg got to the top. He was the second amputee to achieve this but he had lost more leg than the previous guy.

- an American, Gheorghe Dijmarescu, became the first non-Sherpa to reach the summit six years running, always by the standard Tibetan route.

- Apa Sherpa made his 14th ascent which is yet another record.

- a new ladder has been placed on the Second Step, bigger, better and longer than the old Chinese one, courtesy of Russell Brice.

One thinks Mallory must be turning in his icy grave.

In other largely commercial activity 52 parties went to **Cho Oyu** and 29 to **Ama Dablam** in the post-monsoon season. On Cho Oyu there is plenty of room, but on Ama Dablam things got distinctly crowded and testy. Parties accused others of doing it on the cheap, stealing food and gear, and kicking rocks down.

A Japanese Alpine Club senior party attempted the north ridge of **Tengi Ragi Tau (6943m)** north of the Tesi Lapcha, but was stopped by steep icy slabs at around 6250m on the north side of its northern outlier, Langmoche Ri.

A Japanese expedition succeeded on the French route on **Annapurna I** in the spring, while another was unsuccessful in the autumn, losing two climbers in an avalanche below the Sickle.

Elsewhere, four members of a Japanese Alpine Club student party made the first ascent of the peak of **Chhiv (6555m)** in Mustang in September. They climbed the north-east ridge and reported 60° snow and a final narrow corniced ridge. They fixed 850m of rope. Several other small peaks were also climbed in this general area.

By late 2004 the political difficulties in Nepal had clearly not inhibited climbing in Solu Khumbu, or in the recently opened smaller peaks of the Damodar and Peri Himal north of the Annapurnas, but it does appear that few if any parties tried to go to the more remote areas of western Nepal, where much of the country is under Maoist control. Tales abound of trekkers being held up for so-called 'donations'. One hopes this situation will improve, but it is difficult to be optimistic in the short term.

LINDSAY GRIFFIN

Pakistan 2004

Thanks are due to Desnivel, Doug Chabot, Kelly Cordes, Dario Crosato, Xavier Eguskitza, Chris Geisler, Jeff Hollenbaugh, Steve House, Lev Ioffe, Tomaz Jakofcic, Matic Jost, Jan Kreisinger, Nikolas Kroupis, Vlado Linek, Luca Maspes, Michael 'Much' Mayr, Tom Nakamura and the Japanese Alpine News, Anna Piunova and the Russian Extreme Project, Marko Prezelj, Jens Richter, Nazir Sabir, Vasek Satava, Silvestro Stucchi, Markus Walter and Simon Yates.

With Pakistan now in full swing after a couple of lean years following the terrorist activities of 2001, around 57 different expeditions took up permits to climb peaks above 6500m. Eleven of these had more than one goal, in some cases permits for three different peaks. Of these 57, only nine were attempting mountains other than the five 8000m peaks, Spantik and Diran. Most of the remaining 48 were commercially organised groups to well-trodden standard routes. In terms of any evolution in mountaineering, only three of the 57 produced successes of note; on K2, Gasherbrum III, K7, Nanga Parbat and Kapura. However, on peaks below 6500m, which currently do not require a peak royalty, there was much significant activity.

In 2003 and 2004 the Ministry dropped all peak fees by 50% to encourage more mountain tourism to the country. This has been extended to 2005 and there is both internal and external pressure on the government to abolish royalty fees for all peaks below 7000m (ie raising the height from 6500m). It is estimated that over 6000 climbers and trekkers visited Pakistan's mountains during 2004.

HUSHE REGION

Charakusa Valley
K7
In what was arguably the most significant ascent in Pakistan during 2004, American Steve House soloed a new route on the huge SW face of 6973m K7. House lifted his Alaskan-grown, single push tactics on big alpine faces up a notch to the higher altitudes of the Karakoram, and completed his 2400m line in a continuous 41 hours and 45 minutes from base camp on the Charakusa glacier. Showing great determination he climbed a predominantly ice and mixed line to the left of the SW ridge, having already reached 6650m on an attempt a week previously. This was the long awaited second ascent of the mountain first climbed by a full scale siege in 1984 and the difficulties of his route were rated 5.10a A2 WI 4 M6+. This ascent, which

advanced the style and ethics of modern mountaineering, gained House a well-deserved Special People's Prize at this year's Piolet d'Or.

In the meantime Doug Chabot and Bruce Miller were repeating the original 1984 *Japanese Route*, which reportedly used 450 bolt and peg placements, and took 40 days plus 6500m of fixed rope. Chabot and Miller took three days' food and one sleeping bag between them for their alpine-style ascent. Climbing some significant variants, including a WI 5+ runnel in the Fortress instead of the Japanese A3 seam, they reached the top in three days and were full of praise for the young Japanese and their sustained efforts plus the motivation needed to complete what is actually a very beautiful route (2400m: VI M6 A1 WI 5+). They reversed House's line, making a number of rappels and down-climbing huge distances on ice, reaching base camp from the top of the Fortress in one day.

K7 West
Jeff Hollenbaugh, Marko Prezelj and Steve Swenson, from the primarily American expedition above, attempted the unclimbed 6858m K7 West, following the line of the 1982 Japanese attempt. They took two days to gain the crest of the NW ridge (M6 and WI 4) and the following day continued until Prezelj, in the lead, triggered a small slab avalanche. The climbers were fine but Swenson's rucksack took a 1000m ride to the glacier. The three descended from this point, several hundred metres below the summit, having found much evidence of the 1982 attempt in the form of bolts, pegs and electron ladders.

Kapura
On 4 July, Doug Chabot, Steve House and Steve Swenson made the first recorded ascent of 6544m Kapura. Bruce Miller and Marko Prezelj followed them next day. All climbers used the same route; SW face and NW ridge. The last section of the ridge provided mixed terrain, cornices and deep snow, as well as being quite sharp in the upper section, giving difficulties of M4. The last two pitches involved near vertical névé – excellent to climb but impossible to protect. Later, Tine Cuder and Matej Mejovsek from Slovenia climbed the east face in a single-push round trip of 16 hours (1600m: ED2/3).

Naysar Brakk
On the wonderful 5200m granite pyramid of Naysar Brakk, which stands above the north bank of the Charakusa, Steve House, Marko Prezelj and Steve Swenson climbed the upper SE ridge to create *Tasty Talking* (300m: III 5.10+: 11 pitches of which 10 were in the 5.10 category and the final pitch a wonderful 5.8). Two days later Prezelj returned with Bruce Miller to climb the entire ridge from its foot: *No More Tasty Talking* (900m: IV 5.10+).

K7 Lower Rock Towers

Miller and Prezelj climbed a new route on one of the unnamed rock towers that rises to c4900m from close to the lateral moraine of the Charakusa glacier below the SW face of K7. *Difficult Life* (650m: 6c+ and A0) follows a fine and exposed arête up a slender pinnacle.

Chogolisa Glacier

A six-person Italian team climbed four routes from the Chogolisa glacier. Their first foray took them into the Buesten glacier where they climbed Pointed Peak (c5400m) via the NW face and west ridge. This involved an 800m snow couloir to a col, followed by nine rock pitches (to UIAA V+) to the summit. Maurizio Giordani, Luca Maspes and Nancy Paoletto reached the top, with Hervé Barmasse, Ezio Marlier and Giovanni Pagnoncelli stopping two pitches below. Signs of passage around the summit area confirmed that this peak had been climbed before.

Then Marlier, Maspes and Pagnoncelli climbed on the walls of a formation, dubbed the Chogolisa Cathedral, on the west side of the glacier overlooking their base camp. On the right side of the east face the three climbed eight pitches to the top of a pillar that they named the Pilastro Kekka (c4500m). The 300km route was graded VI+ and A1. Barmasse and Giordani later made the first ascent of Sheep Peak (c6000m) which lies above and to the north-east of Raven's Peak on the north side of the Buesten. Finally, Barmasse, Maspes and Pagnoncelli climbed the south face of Raven's Peak (c5300m). This is an obvious challenge from the Buesten but at the time the Italians were completely unaware of the 1987 Hardwick/Littlejohn ascent and their route was similar to the British line for much of its length. *Luna Caprese* gave 1000m and 22 pitches of climbing at 6c+.

Nangma Valley

Amin Brakk

The Russian Extreme Project, comprising climbers Sergey Kovalev, Alexander Lastochkin, Valery Rozov and Arcady Seregin with cameramen Lev Dorfman and Dmitry Lifanov, climbed a partial new route on the c1250m west face of Amin Brakk. Rozov, as is usual in these projects, made a sensational BASE jump from high on the wall. The Russians spent 22 days on the route, the first 11 fixing rope on a line between *Sol Solet* and *Czech Express* but much of the time very close to *Namkor*. However, prolonged bad weather when they were a little over half-height forced a traverse right to the *Czech Route* and a faster finish to the summit. The Russians climbed a total of 31 pitches, mainly on aid up to A3, after which Rozov, wearing his winged suit, made a jump from a point where the rock wall meets the easier-angled upper ridge c300m below the summit – a soul-searching experience as the wall is not totally vertical.

Drifika

Slovenians Gregor Blazic, Matic Jost, Zlatko Koren and Vlado Makarovic made probably the first attempt to climb the beautiful snow and ice pyramid of Drifika (6447m) from the South Drifika Cwm. They first tried the face just right of the SW ridge, eventually joining its crest at around 6200m, above which they were unable to find a way through a rock wall and retreated. Later, all but Koren made an attempt on the Central Spur of the SSE face. After one bivouac they reached the east ridge and later gained the crest of the north ridge just below the summit.

Just as the three were contemplating how to negotiate the final section, they heard the sound of a large avalanche. Looking down they saw that a Spanish team, which had been attempting the face to the right of their spur, had been hit by a large sérac fall. They were obviously in trouble so the Slovenians immediately began to descend. One climber (David Aris) died and his body was later evacuated together with the injured survivors. Although they didn't quite reach the summit, the Slovenians joined an existing line and have therefore christened their route *White River* (1200m: D+: 40-60° with one section of 90°).

Korada Peak

Blazic, Jost and Makarovic also made the probable first ascent of Pt 5944m, a summit on the long multi-topped ridge that runs east then south from Drifika around the eastern rim of the Changma glacier. They climbed the SW face, which they considered rather harder than the *Swiss Route* on Les Courtes, to create *Bostjan Arcan Memorial Route* (750m: TD+: 75° and V). A GPS reading at the last belay, 15m below the top, gave an altitude of 5955m.

Zang Brakk

Several new routes were added to the golden granite walls of Zang Brakk, the impressive 4800m rock spire rising from grassy slopes at the entrance to the valley leading to Amin Brakk's west face. Janez Skok on-sighted pitches of 7a and only used aid (A0 and one section of A1) on the last four pitches, which were common with the Korean line, which terminates just below the summit (at a bunch of prayer flags) where the last section of the Central Pillar is completely blank. Hannes Mair and Much Mayr, who were part of the same team, made a significant variation to the first half of *Ali Baba*, then followed this, climbing the whole route, on sight, all free in a day at 7b+. They named it *Ali Baba's Hadsch*.

Prior to this Mair and Mayr had tried a very thin crackline on the right side of the south face but gave up at a blank section having on-sighted some demanding pitches up to 7c. On the main section of the previously untouched SW face, Italians Enea Colnago, Anna Lazzarini and Silvestro Stucchi, with Elena Davila from Spain, put up the 18-pitch, 750m, *Hasta la Vista, David* (6b and A1), named after the young Basque climber who died on Drifika. Aid (including two pendulums) was only used on five pitches.

Denbor Brakk

During the poor weather of July, Czechs Pavel Jonak and Vasek Satava climbed a new route on the west face of c4800m Denbor Brakk. The Czechs were able to complete their route, *Bloody Mary*, on the left pillar in 14 pitches at UIAA IX– (F7b) and A2. Ropes were fixed to the top of the 10th pitch before going for the summit. Pitches eight and nine followed a brutal off-width through a big roof (VIII and A1). The climbers only had one big Camalot of that size (from below it had looked like a hand crack), so by the time they emerged from the struggle they 'looked like butchers': hence the name of the route.

Changi Towers

Spanish big wall climbers Nestor Ayerbe, Cecelia Buil and Oscar Perez spent most of August establishing *Ankhé Ashahé* (Clear Eyes: 1150m: VI 6b+ A3) on the east face of the c5800m Changi Towers, a collection of huge granite walls and spires close to the main valley SSE of Amin Brakk. In unsettled weather the team used fixed ropes and established two camps, at 4900m and at 5200m. They appear to have followed *Ludopatia* or a similar line on the upper tower for eight pitches to a point dubbed the South Top (c5700m), where they terminated their ascent. There are now five recorded routes on this complex formation.

Roungkhanchang

Three Italians, Dario Crosato, Stefano Zaleri and Marco Zebochin, made the first ascent of Roungkhanchang I (4600m), a small rocky summit on a ridge immediately north-east of Shjingu Charpa. This is the smallest and most westerly of the pillars on the formation sometimes referred to as No Name Wall. They climbed the north face, which gave 14 pitches and 540m of climbing up to 6b+ with some A1. Unfortunately *Troubles, Cough and Fever* has around 100 bolts, all placed with a power drill, a totally condemnable act on such a relatively minor wall in a wild and remote area.

Shjingu Charpa

Two teams attempted the magnificent line of the north ridge on Shjingu Charpa (aka The Great Tower, c5600m). Experienced Canadians Dave Edgar and Chris Geisler more or less followed the line tried in 2000 by a four-man American team, which climbed c700m up to 5.10 and A3 in five days before one of the team broke a leg. The Canadians made three light-weight attempts, all thwarted by bad weather. On their last they continued past their previous high point to arrive at a small ledge atop the 22nd pitch. To this point the climbing had been 5.10+ and A1 but on disappointing flaky and vegetated granite. Above, the ridge reared to vertical and overhanging rock leading for 800-900m to the summit. Judging that they had only completed the easier half of the ridge and with no chance of completing the upper section in a couple of days, the Canadians went down.

BALTORO REGION

K2

31st July 2004 marked the 50th anniversary of the first ascent of 8611m K2 by Achille Compagnoni and Lino Lacedelli from Ardito Desio's Italian expedition. To mark the occasion, 11 expeditions bought permits. One of these, a Korean 'Clean Up' expedition, met with early disaster. On or before 11 June three of these climbers, Lee Hwa-Hyong, Kim Jae-Young and Pae Kyong-Kyu, were at their Camp 1 on the mountain when an avalanche overwhelmed them. All were found dead in their sleeping bags.

K2 had not been climbed since José Garces's ascent on 22 July 2001. Reasons for this involve the threat of terrorism, weather, and most of all the collapse of the sérac forming one side of the Bottleneck at c8300m. Sérac fall sometime after 2001 made the lower section of the Bottleneck much more difficult and dangerous, stopping climbers in 2002 and 2003.

By the summer of 2004 things had settled down in this area but for a long time it still appeared as if it was going to be another non-year for K2. Then towards the end of July a fine spell of weather coincided with many climbers in position for a summit push. During the night of 25th-26th nine climbers set off from the top camp at the Shoulder and progressed slowly upward, the Bottleneck proving passable but very difficult and time-consuming.

Silvio Mondinella and Karl Unterkircher led a team of five Italians to the summit, although the work through the Bottleneck, general trail breaking through deep snow and the fixing of ropes (this year ropes appear to have been fixed through the Bottleneck and up the final slopes above, leading to K2 being almost fixed from base to summit) was shared with the Basque climber Ivan Vallejo, from the Al Filo de lo Imposible team. Fittingly, given the year, the Italians were first to summit and one of them, Michele Compagnoni, is the grandson of the first ascensionist. Last to summit, at around 5.30pm, was the second pair of four Basques, Juanito Oiarzabal and Edurne Pasaban. With her ascent (and safe descent), 30-year old Pasaban became the leading female 8000m peak collector, having now climbed seven of the 14 giants. Only the late Wanda Rutkiewicz climbed more. In addition, the Basque mountaineer is the solitary living female to have summited K2.

Pasaban regained her tent on the Shoulder at around midnight, 24 hours after leaving, but Oiarzabal never showed. He was subsequently discovered sitting in the snow only 100m above camp by more Basque climbers leaving for their summit attempt on the 27th. Many summiters and others on the mountain rallied to evacuate Oiarzabal and Pasaban, who had both sustained frostbitten feet. Pasaban eventually lost two toes but Oiarzabal's condition was much worse. Back in Spain medics were unable to save any of his toes and he is making a slow recovery. However, with his ascent, this highly experienced 48-year old Basque became only the third person to climb K2 twice and also set a record of climbing to an 8000m summit no less than 21 times.

On the 27th and benefiting enormously from the opened trail, more climbers summited, including six members of Sam Druk's China-Tibet expedition, members of which have now climbed 12 of the 14 8000m peaks. The 28th saw another batch including 65-year-old Carlos Soria, who became the oldest summiter and the only man to have climbed three 8000m peaks over the age of 60, and Mario Lacedelli, a nephew of the first ascensionist. By the time four Japanese and their two Sherpas had reached the top on 7 August, a total of 47 climbers had summited during the season but, notably, only 19 of these climbed without oxygen, a far cry from former years when climbing K2 with bottled gas was simply not the done thing.

Sadly, three more people died high on the mountain in a similar scenario to the 1986 disaster. On the 28th Davoud Khadem Asl from Iran and the experienced Sergei Sokolov from Russia were camped on the Shoulder. Unlike their teammate Alexander Gubaev, they hadn't left for the summit that morning but decided to wait another night to see if the weather would improve (it had gradually deteriorated overnight). It is thought that Gubaev, climbing without oxygen, reached the top (the first mountaineer from Kyrgyzstan to reach any 8000m summit) but he did not return. Asl and Sokolov could not be persuaded to go down and were subsequently trapped by a big storm. They didn't attempt to descend until 1st August, after which nothing more was heard from them. Some of the remaining climbers at base camp mounted a rescue but heavy snowfall forced them to abandon their attempt.

One more climber was to summit, bringing the total for the season to 48 and the overall total to 246 ascents. This was the Catalan, Jordi Corominas, achieving what was undoubtedly the finest ascent on K2 or any Pakistan 8000m peak last year, the second ascent of the elegant SSW ridge, dubbed by Reinhold Messner *The Magic Line* when he went to attempt it in 1979. He never set foot on the route, deeming it far too difficult and dangerous. In 1986 Peter Bozik and Poles, Przemyslaw Piasecki and Wojciech Wroz, completed the route to the summit. As the three started to descend the Abruzzi, Wroz slipped and was killed. Since then the route has gained a reputation as the hardest technical climb on K2 and until last year remained unrepeated.

On 16 August the highly experienced Cadiach, Corominas and de la Matta left their top camp for the summit. Corominas was going strongly but the other two decided to retreat at 8300m. Corominas continued without oxygen. Deep snow hampered progress and the final 100m proved particularly time consuming, meaning that the Catalan did not reach the summit until midnight. He descended the Abruzzi, finally stopping to rest in Camp 3 after 30 hours of continuous effort. The other two descended to their own Camp 3, spent the night and continued on down the next day, spending another night at Camp 2 before reaching the Negrotto Col on the 18th. Neither of the two climbers had experienced any altitude problems but at Camp 1, de la Matta suddenly complained of abdominal pain, later thought to have been the onset of appendicitis. Deterioration appears to have been relatively fast and the following morning he died.

He received a second Spanish Piolet d'Or posthumously, when the whole *Magic Line* team was awarded the prize for 2004.

Gasherbrum III

Almost as significant as the repetition of K2's *Magic Line*, was the second ascent of Gasherbrum III (7953m), the 15th highest mountain in the World. A top-class Basque trio of Jon Beloki, Alberto Iñurrategi and José Carlos Tamayo followed the *Original Polish Route*, which first climbs the SW ridge of Gasherbrum II as far as Camp 4 (c7300m), then traverses across its west flank to the base of the triangular SE face of III. In the final couloir Tamayo turned back, leaving the others to continue to the summit. Climbing the upper section the remaining pair found snow ramps at 50-55° and an old rusty peg, the only visible relic from the 1975 ascent. On that occasion the summit was reached by the foremost British female mountaineer of that period, Alison Chadwick (only one higher peak, Kangchenjunga, received its first ascent from British climbers), her Polish husband Janusz Onyskiewicz, Wanda Rutkiewicz, arguably the foremost female high-altitude climber of all time, and Krzysztof Zdizitowiecki.

Trango Group
Great Trango

Of all the rock climbs completed in the Karakoram during 2004 the finest was the first ascent of the huge SW ridge of Great Trango (6286m) by Americans Kelly Cordes and Josh Wharton. The first ascent of this 2250m ridge, one of the longest rock climbs in the world, in a committing lightweight style, features elsewhere in this journal: *Azeem Ridge* (5.11 R/X A2 M6). (S*ee artical 'Just Climbing', page 103.*)

Trango Tower

Many parties, exhibiting a wide variety of style, ethics and, seemingly, behaviour, attempted 6251m Trango Tower. The most successful were Slovenians, Tomaz Jakofcic, Klemen Mali and Miha Vali, who made the first alpine-style ascent of *Eternal Flame* on the South Pillar (Albert/Güillich/ Steigler/Sykora, 1989: 1000m and c31 pitches: 7b+ and A2: climbed almost free in 2003 at 7c+ and A0 – a 15m bolt ladder on pitch 10 – by Denis Burdet). The route was climbed at 6c+ and A2. This was the fifth ascent to the summit. Most other parties previously claiming the ascent have generally been stymied by lack of time on the final day, forcing them to stop at either the junction with the 1976 *Original British Route* (and top of the rock section) approximately 80m below the summit, or the summit ridge (as did other parties in 2004). This Slovenian ascent was also the first true alpine-style ascent of the tower.

Trango Monk

Previously thought to be unclimbed, the small c5900m spire immediately north of Trango Tower gained its first ascent from Jakofcic, Mali and Vali via the east face and a route they christened *Chota Badla* (450m: 6b, A2 and 70°). The name means 'small revenge', because they had originally come to Pakistan to attempt the huge SW ridge of Great Trango and found that it had just been climbed by Kelly Cordes and Josh Wharton.

Shipton Spire

On the ever-popular Shipton Spire (5885m) Slovaks Miro Mrava and Brano Turnek made the first ascent of *Knocking on Heaven's Door* up the middle of the SE face between *Women and Chalk*, and *Akelarre*. However, they did not complete the route to the summit. After an injury due to rockfall the pair had to terminate their line after climbing the right-slanting ramp/dièdre high on the face to join *Akelarre*. To this point they had climbed 17 pitches of 60m up to VIII and A4.

At the same time, fellow Slovaks, Jozef Kopold, Dino Kuran and Jozo Santus made the second ascent of the *Khanadan Buttress* (Brian McMahon and Josh Wharton, 2002: 1300m: 30 pitches: 5.11 and C1). Their two-day ascent was made in alpine style and due to the amount of snow, the route was considered quite dangerous. During the descent the climbers were very lucky to survive a huge rockfall.

The third team of Slovaks, Igor Koller, Gabo Cmarik and Vlado Linek attempted a new line on the right side of the SE face, eventually reaching a point three metres from easy ground and c70m below the junction with *Ship of Fools*, where the right-slanting ramp meets the NE ridge. To that point they had climbed 17 pitches up to 7a and A3 but hope to return this year to finish it off.

PANMAH GROUP

Latok I

In early July well-known Argentinean brothers, Damien and Willie Benegas, attempted the oft-tried 'Walker Spur of the Karakoram', the north ridge of Latok I (7151m). Conditions were poor. They fixed a few ropes up the toe of the lower rock buttress and then went for it in alpine style. Two bivouacs later they realised the route was a no-go that year and descended. They plan to return this summer.

Latok V

Motomu Omiya with two other companions made his fourth attempt on this unclimbed 6190m summit which stands at the end of the SE ridge of Latok III. Omiya, who made the first ascent of Latok IV in 1980, attempted V in 1999, 2000 and 2003 via the south face, reaching high on the mountain on each occasion and in 2003 getting to within 70m of the summit. Last year he again reached 6100m but failed to reach the highest point. However, there is some confusion in the naming of these peaks: the 1999 attempt was definitely on the south face of a peak previously climbed just a few days earlier by the Huber brothers, who refer to it as Latok IV (c6450m).

HISPAR REGION

Kanjut Sar

Russians, Ivan Dusharin, Lev Ioffe, Yura Soyfer and Anton Terekhov were lucky to escape disaster during their attempt on the SW face of 7760m Kanjut Sar in the Hispar Muztagh. They had established an advanced base at c4990m, close to the foot of the face yet at a point they felt was safe from avalanche.

As they were all sleeping in advanced base one night, a huge sérac fell from left of their route and although it did not reach camp, the blast picked up the tent and its occupants and hurled them down the glacier for about 100m. As one climber started to struggle out, the tent began to roll. The four climbers fortunately came to rest just 20m short of a very large crevasse. Surprisingly, only one of the team was really injured. Later, as they were limping towards base camp, they realised this first collapse had simply been a prelude to the real thing: suddenly a much bigger fall occurred and covered the entire valley with ice chips and powder.

Hispar Sar

In September Andy Parkin and Simon Yates made a spirited attempt on the attractive unclimbed Hispar Sar (6400m), only being forced to retreat c300m below the summit after climbing all the major difficulties. (*See article 'Naught but Noodles on Hispar Sar', page 96.*) The peak still awaits a first ascent.

RAKAPOSHI RANGE

Spantik

A small Japanese expedition climbed 7028m Spantik from the north-west, repeating the descent route used by Mick Fowler and Victor Saunders after their historic ascent of the Golden Pillar in 1987. The line follows a prominent snow and ice spur well right of the Pillar to reach the plateau and upper SW ridge at c6500m. Ms Kei Taniguchi and Kazuo Tobita established Camp 1 on the NW Spur at 5500m then Camp 2 on the plateau. Next day they ploughed their way up deep snow and through poor weather to the summit, relocating their camp later the same day by GPS.

Phuparash

Hideki Nakayama's attempt to make the first ascent of 6824m Phuparash in the Rakaposhi Range ended at only 4300m. The Japanese soloist was injured by a sérac fall and lost most of his climbing equipment.

NORTHERN BATURA

Sakar Sar

Kunihiko Sato made a solo ascent of 6272m Sakar Sar via the SE ridge. This remote peak, which lies on the Afghan border in the northern Batura Muztagh, gained its first and, until last year, only ascent from Miyazawa Akira's four-member Japanese expedition, which climbed the SE flank, finishing up a snow ridge. It appears that Sato's route was more or less the same.

WESTERN HIMALAYA

Nanga Parbat

Four expeditions attempted 8125m Nanga Parbat but only two primarily-German teams were successful. On 30 June, their summit day on the Standard Kinshofer Route up the Diamir Face, Günter Jung, Jörg Stingl and the brothers Christian and Markus Walter from Saxony did not reach the top until 9pm. Jung was 64 years of age, making him the oldest person to climb Nanga Parbat. The team then set off down into the night.

But a little before 1am on 1 July, Jung fell and was unable to stop himself. His body was not found.

Americans, Doug Chabot and Steve Swenson, became the first to traverse the West South-west or Mazeno Ridge as far as its junction with the 1976 *Schell Route*. Unfortunately they were forced to descend from this point due to exhaustion and a chest infection to Swenson.

Two weeks of almost fine weather, followed by high winds, had made underfoot conditions on the ridge excellent. Where previous parties had been troubled by knee-deep snow, the American pair found névé. They climbed relatively straightforward snow and ice up the long South Ridge of the First Mazeno Peak (Pt 6800m), bivouacking for a first night at c6200m. By the end of their second day on the climb (third out from Base Camp) they were cutting a tent site at 6900m beyond the Third Peak.

Next day they climbed mixed ground to the top of the fourth peak at 7,060m, then skirted the fifth peak, 7090m, via its icy flanks. The sixth, actually designated Mazeno Peak, was the highest at 7120m and proved a simple snow dome, as was the next at 7100m. A third bivouac was sited before the last peak (7070m). The next morning, with Chabot in the lead, it took more than 12 hours to reach the Mazeno Col and *Schell Route*, with the intervening ground proving to be the crux of the route, (technical pitches of M4 and AI 3 in a very airy situation).

Believing the hard part of the *Schell Route* to be fixed, they left much of their remaining food, fuel and the only climbing rope, expecting to come back up and finish the route to the summit. However, the descent, through poor visibility and huge amounts of rockfall, proved quite harrowing and the pair understandably had no desire to go back up for another crack at the summit. The Mazeno is the longest arête on any 8000m peak;

a staggering 13km from the Mazeno Pass at 5377m to where it joins the *Schell Route*, then another two kilometres up this to the summit. The Mazeno Peaks traverse was a magnificent achievement, carried out in exemplary style, but the first complete ascent to the summit of Nanga Parbat remains an unclaimed prize.

Two more members, Steve House and Bruce Miller, attempted a new route on the c4500m South East or Rupal Face, arguably the highest single sweep of steep rock and ice in the world. The pair climbed difficult snow, ice and mixed ground between the *Messner Route* and South East Pillar, making four bivouacs, the highest at 7200m. To this point they had overcome difficulties of M5, 90° and 5.7. The following day at c7550m and just below the point where the *Messner Route* makes its exit from the Merkl Gully, Miller became concerned that House was succumbing to AMS and made the decision that both climbers should descend immediately. The two regained their last bivouac and the following day rappelled and down-climbed to the *Messner Route*.

HINDU RAJ

Buni Zom Range

Greeks Nikolas Kroupis and George Zadalidis climbed in the rarely visited Buni Zom Range of the Western Hindu Raj north east of Chitral. This in itself is interesting, as the mountains north of Chitral, close to the Afghan border, were considered very much a no-go area for foreigners after the terrorist strikes of 2001. However, the Greeks climbed there without problem in 2002, when they reached 6050m on Gordoghan Zom (aka Gordoghan Zom I: 6240m and the fifth highest peak in the range). Returning last year they made another attempt on Gordoghan Zom I after first failing to find a safe access to their original goal and the highest peak of the range, Buni Zom. The pair progressed up the west ridge (40-50°) and Kroupis reached what he believed from below to be the summit, only to find that the main peak was some 300m distant along a very narrow ridge. The peak on which he was standing was not marked on the Japanese 1:150,000 map, so it was christened Gordoghan Zom III (GPS height of 6158m). Later, the Greek climbers found this peak had possibly been climbed three times before during attempts on Gordoghan Zom I. Kroupis was unwilling to continue alone, so climbed down to Zadalidis and the two descended.

China & Tibet

This is the first time for some years that dedicated Area Notes have appeared for China and Tibet and they therefore cover developments over the last two to three years.

Qonglai Shan

There has been a resurgence in interest in the Qonglai and Daxue Shan in Szechuan Province, which are relatively easy of access from Chengdu. There seem to be fewer permit problems than for Tibet, and the area provides opportunities for climbing of all kinds at the highest levels.

In the Singuniang area, Mick Fowler and Paul Ramsden's epic ascent of the ice couloir on the N face of **Singuniang (6250m)** in 2002 was followed by a second British expedition in the spring of 2004, comprised of Tom Chamberlain, Dave Evans, Dave Hollinger and Andy Sharpe. Poor conditions did not allow an ascent of the peak but ascents were made of **Camel East** and **Camel West**, both c5510m. Tim Boelter, Jon Otto (US) Chen Junchi, Chenzi Gang, Kang Hua and Ma Yihua (China) made a successful ascent of **Singuniang** in November 2004 by the original *1981 route* on the SE ridge.

The nearby Shuang Qiao Gou valley was visited in August 2002 by Naoki Ohuchi (Japan) and an attempt made on the W face of **Niuxim Shan (4942m)**. Anne and John Arran (UK) made the first ascent of this peak in summer 2004 via the N face and W ridge as well as putting up a new route on **Mi Mi Shan (5018m)**. In the autumn of the previous year Andrej and Tanja Grmovsek (Slovenia) made impressive ascents of the S face of **Tan Shan (4943m)** and the W face of **Putala Shan (5428m)**.

Daxue Shan

Minya Konka (7556m), received an ascent in the Autumn of 2002 by a French expedition organised by the Groupe Militaire de Haute Montagne. Antoine de Choudens made a fine solo ascent of the last 500m of the original *1932 route* on the NW ridge. The expedition also made ascents of **Gomba (5605m)**, **Nochma (5575m)** and **Eva Shan (5705m)**. In the spring of 2003 Andy Cave, Mick Fowler, Neil McAdie, and Simon Nadin (UK) made two attempts on the NW face of the unclimbed **Grosvenor (6376m)** but failed due to poor weather. In the autumn Roger Payne (UK) and Julie-Ann Clyma (NZ) succeeded in making the first ascent of Grosvenor over a period of eight days by the NW face and the SW ridge, descending via the E ridge and S face.

An attempt in April 2004 on the unclimbed **Edgar (6618m)** by another UK team was less successful: Angela Benham, Chris Drinkwater, Titch Kavanagh and Andrew Phillips were unable to find a safe approach to the upper part of the mountain. **Longemain (6294m)** and **Daddomain (6380m)** are snow peaks lying on the main ridge between Grosvenor and Minya Konka. They were climbed for the first time in October 2004 by Jo Kippax and Sean Waters (NZ). **Haizi (5820m),** which lies in the northern part of the Central Daxue Shan, was attempted by Geoff Cohen, Dick Isherwood, Martin Scott and Bill Thurston (UK) in April 2004 via the NE ridge and North Peak (5700m) but the team ran out of time on the summit day.

Eastern Tibet

The little known but spectacular Kangri Karpo range has received considerable attention in recent years, particularly from Y. Matsumoto and the JAC Fukuoka section who conducted explorations in 2001, 2002 and 2003, concentrating on the Mizui valley. John Nankervis' New Zealand expedition in 2001 explored the peaks surrounding the upper Lhagu Glacier. The highest peak, **Ruoni (6882m)** was unsuccessfully attempted in October 2003 by Kazumasa Hirai's nine-strong Kobe University team.

The Jarjinjabo Range was explored for the first time by Tamotsu Nakamura in 2000 and has been the target of two expeditions. In July 2001 Naoki Ohuchi, Eiji Daigo, Yuriko Kowaka and Taizo Yoshida (Japan) made the first ascent of **Jammo Spire (5382m)** and were followed in August 2002 by Pete Athans, Robert MacKinlay, Hilarre Nelson, Jared Ogden, Kasha Rigby, and Mark Synnott (USA) who also ascended the Spire, together with the large peak to its immediate NE, and also **Jarjinjabo's Son**. Neither team climbed the Spire's final monolithic block.

In the massif just north of Batang, a Japanese team made the first ascent of **Dangchezhengla (5833m)** in June 2002, the summit being reached by Kiyoaki Miyagawa and Junta Murayama.

South Eastern Tibet

The western (Tibetan) side of the Meili Xue Shan was visited in 2003 by John Nankervis' New Zealand expedition, which climbed **Bungxung Laka (5877m)**.

On the border between Tibet and Yunnan, close to the Zhongdian - Dechen highway, Damien Gildea and Paul Macleman (Australia) attempted **Baimang Shan (5429m)** but turned back after a massive avalanche scoured their proposed route on the E face. This underlines the dangers of this and the nearby Meili Xue Shan massif, where 17 Japanese climbers were killed on Kawa Karpo (Kawagebo) by a massive avalanche in January 1991.

Nyenchentangla East

The complex of high peaks lying between Atsa, Nye and the Pasum Lake have been explored through a number of expeditions in recent years by

Tamotsu Nakamura (Japan), and John Town (UK), which revealed a wealth of spectacular unclimbed 6000m peaks. Easiest of access is the Namla Karpo group to the east of Basong (Pasum) Lake, where John Nankervis' New Zealand team made the first attempt on **Jieqinnalagabu (6316m)** in 2000 via the western edge of the South Face, followed by a US pair in 2002 who attempted the NW spur. This formidable peak was successfully climbed for the first time in September 2004 by Gabriel Voide (Switzerland) in a solo ascent of the NW spur. The only other peak so far climbed in the Namla Karpo group is **Peak 6250m**, opposite Jieqinnalagabu, by John Nankervis' expedition. The naming of peaks in this area has suffered by translation from Tibetan into Chinese and then on into English using Pin Yin transliteration. There is probably a case for returning to the more standard and comprehensible direct transliteration of Tibetan used elsewhere.

Entering from the north, via the Nye Valley, Adam Thomas, Bryan Godfrey, Phil Amos (UK) and Graham Rowbotham (Canada) suffered grievous access problems before choosing and attempting **Chokporisum (6359m)**, reaching c.6000m. The team also circumnavigated the area north of the Nye Valley.

Well to the NW of the above region lies **Sepu Kangri (6956m)**. Although it has already been well reported in the Journal, it would be wrong in any summary not to record the final resolution of a long series of attempts by Chris Bonington and others in the first ascent by Mark Newcomb's US team in October 2002.

Nyenchentangla West

In September 2002, John Anderson, Russell Luker and Bob Stewart (UK) attempted **Samdain Kangsan (6590m)**, which lies in a prominent position at the northern end of the western Nyenchentangla. They reached a height of 6400m on the SE ridge before being turned back by unstable snow conditions. This peak may have been climbed by a Chinese expedition in 2001 via the NE ridge.

As well as applying to the range as a whole, the name Nyanchen Tangla is also given to its highest peaks, which lie NW of the town of Yanpachen. **Nyenchentangla South East**, also known as **Nyenchentangla III (7046m)**, is the remaining unclimbed peak of Nyenchentangla and was climbed in Spring 2002 by Erich and Stefan Gatt (Austria). They diverted from the route of their commercial expedition, which made an ascent of **Nyenchentangla Central (7117m),** to climb the South East Peak via its SW ridge and then descend via the NW ridge.

In September 2000 Christian Haas, Erich Gatt and Hansjoerg Pfaundler (Austria) visited the Lan Puk valley which is situated not far to the south of the Nyanchen Tangla peaks, above Yanpachen. They made the first ascents of **Sir Duk (6653m)**, via the S face; **Yarlung Ri (6256m)**, via the SE ridge; and **Chorten Garpo (6415m)**, climbed first by the SSE flank and W ridge and then repeated solo via the S ridge. This area can be reached from Lhasa in half a day and contains numerous unclimbed 6000m peaks.

John Town, Derek Buckle, and Martin and Alasdair Scott (UK) visited in September 2003 to attempt **Beu-tse (6270m)**, which is situated in a small glaciated group facing the Nyanchen Tangla across the Yanpachen Valley. They succeeded in making the first ascent via the NW face and N ridge.

Himalaya

In the Lunana Himal, on central Tibet's border with Bhutan, Nam Yong Ho, Li Fua Fun, Li Ji Ryue, Chuen Oir and Kim Ze Yong (Korea) made the first ascent of **Kangphu Gang (a.k.a Shimo Kangri) (7204m)** in September 2002 via the southern face of the SW ridge and the final section of the ridge itself.

Further west, in the spring of 2004, Roger Payne (UK) and Julie-Ann Clyma (NZ) succeeded in their attempt on **Chomolhari (7326m)**. After first attempting the NW ridge, they turned their attentions in the last few days to the S ridge and SE flank, reaching the summit on 7 May.

In the Everest Region, in May 2002, Mike Bearzi and Bruce Miller (USA) made the first successful ascent from the north of **Ngozumpa Kang II (7743m)** but sadly Bearzi was killed on the descent. In the same area two successful ascents of **Hungchi (7036m)** were made from the Nepalese side in Spring 2003, but in the autumn Masakatsu Nakamura's Nagano expedition were turned back at 6800m on their attempt from the north.

A number of recent expeditions have vied for the prize of the first winter ascent of **Shisha Pangma (8027m)**. In November 2003 Victor Saunders and Andy Parkin were driven back from 6500m on the *Corredor Girona* on the SW face. In January 2004, Piotr Morawski, Jan Szulc, Darek Zaluski (Poland) and Simone Moro (Italy) reached 7700m after climbing the SW face by the above route. Next to come, the following season, was Jean-Christophe Lafaille (France), who reached the summit via a variant on the original *British route* on 11 December 2004, which technically falls within the Chinese winter season. Opinion, however, seems to be that proper winter conditions are not established until January, when Moro returned with Morawski, Szulc, Zaluski and Jacek Jawien. The team followed a new line on the SW face, reaching the summit on 14 January.

Kaqur Kangri (6859), in the Ronglai Kangri area, which lies north of the Kanjiroba Himal, was climbed for the first time in September 2004 via the E ridge and East Peak by a Japanese expedition led by Toyoji Wada.

West Tibet

In September 2004, an expedition consisting of John Town, Derek Buckle, Martin Scott (UK) and Toto Grönlund (Finland) made the first exploration of the isolated Nganglong Kangri group in W Tibet (81°00'E 32°49'N), making the first ascent of the highest peak **Nganglong Kangri I** , known to locals as **Kang Ngolok (6710m)** by the SE face, and **Nganglong Kangri I**

East (6595m) by the SE ridge. The group lies about 40 km N of the Northern Highway and the town of Gegye.

In 2003 Janne Corax and Nadine Saulnier (Sweden) made the first unsupported crossing of the Chan Tang from north to south in modern times. This extraordinary effort took a total of 46 days covering over 1000 km of virtually uninhabited country.

Chinese Pamirs

In 2003 a six-strong Russian expedition, led by Andrei Lebedev made an impressive crossing of the southern section of the Chinese Pamirs, passing the Kongur massif, crossing a number of high passes between Shindi and Gez. En route they climbed **Peak 5430m** and **Nikolaev (5975m).** Also in 2003, Pete Lardy, Chad McFadden and Tom McMillan (USA) made a new route *Golden Eye* on the W Slope of **Muztagh Ata (7546m)**, descending on ski and snowboard.

In 2004 three Russian teams successfully completed routes on the northern side of **Kongur (7719m)**. Valeri Shamalo's St Petersburg group reached the summit on 9 August via the N face. On the 18th and 19th, V Kagan, V Kulbachenko, V Legkih, A Medvedev, A Petrov and V Odohovsky from Yuri Hokhlov's large Moscow expedition were successful via a new route on the north ridge. V Arkhipov, A Mikhalitsin and S Filatov, from the Krasnoyarsk team led by Nikolai Zakharov, summited on 23 August by the same route.

Tien Shan

In July 2004 a Russian team consisting of Anatoli Dzhuli, David Lehtman, Vladimir Leonenko, Yuri Strubtsov, Alexei Kirienko and Ilya Mikhalev visited the Chinese side of the Central Tien Shan with the aim of completing a new route on **Army Topographer's Peak (6873m)** which lies close to Peak Pobeda/Tomur. Instead, they completed an epic 13 day traverse of the previously unclimbed **Kashkar Peak (6435m)** including 5 days sitting out bad weather.

Sources: Mountain Info/Climb Magazine, American Alpine Journal, internet and personal communication.

MARK WATSON

New Zealand 2004 - 2005

This report covers developments in the Southern Alps from autumn (May) 2004 to late summer 2005. The grades quoted are 'Mt Cook' alpine grades and Australasian (Ewbank) rock grades.

The Darran Mountains – Fiordland

The Darran Mountains are New Zealand's greatest multi-pitch alpine rock venue, with technical diorite slabs and faces. Because of the high precipitation and difficult access, new routing here requires time, commitment and patience.

Some sustained periods of fine weather and a group of motivated climbers saw a surge of activity in summer 2004/5. Craig Jefferies and Martin Wightman made the most notable ascent of the season by exploring the Llawrenny Peaks, situated in a seldom-visited tract of wilderness north of the Milford Track and south-west of Mitre Peak. The pair made the first ascent of the E ridge of the **North Llawrenny Peak (1925m)**. The route offered around 300m of quality rock climbing on a sharp ridge, with near vertical sections where the ridge merges with the N face.

Immediately north of the Llawrenny Peaks sits Sinbad Gully, where Kester Brown and Sebastian Lowensteijn attempted to free the *Original Line* on the upper cirque. This 10-pitch route was first climbed a year earlier by Craig Jefferies and Paul Rogers at 23 (5.11c) A2+. It had been considered a viable free route – that is until Kester and Sebastian were shut down on the seventh pitch having already freed pitches up to grade 27 (5.12d).

Another route to have its free pitches eliminated, this time entirely, was *Ram Paddock Road* (23 A4) on the Little North Face of **Mt Sabre (2167m)**. Derek Thatcher and Jonathon Clearwater gave the route an overall grade of 24 (5.11d) and added a grade 25 (5.12) pitch called *Rock Candy* near the start of *Ball and Chain*. On the S face of **Tairoa** Jonathon Clearwater and Thomas Evans climbed eight new pitches to create *Liquid Toasted Sandwich* (21).

Mount Aspiring Region

In terms of new route activity it was a relatively quiet year for the Aspiring region. However, the fact that new route potential still exists was clearly illustrated when on the same day in January 2005 two parties climbed new terrain on the S face of **Mt Aspiring (3033m)**.

Howie McGhie and Chris Fox, believing they were on an entirely new line due to a mistake in the Aspiring Region guidebook, climbed the *Whiston-Hyslop* line (5+) for two thirds of its length and then took on new

114. Mt Aspiring, south face. Dave Alderson in the overhanging rock
band of *24 Hour Party People*. (*James Edwards*)

ground directly to the upper Coxcomb Ridge. They named their alternative
finish *Perspiring*.

Forcing a direct line through the overhanging schist band at the base of
the face the UK team of James Edwards, Kevin Neal and Oliver Metherell
climbed up the centre of the S face to join McGhie and Fox's finish, shortly
after they had climbed it themselves. *24 Hour Party People* is given 5+ and is
possibly the hardest route on the face. Edwards had tried the route in the
spring with another ex-pat Brit, Dave Alderson, but the pair had failed due
to a two-day wade through deep snow and difficult conditions on the route.

The crux overhanging rock band featured 'very dubious rock and thin blobs of plastic ice' and gave several pitches of Scottish VII.

Queenstown Region

The Remarkable Range continues to be an ice playground in winter with several new lines being established this year. Most notable is *Helicampers* (M-something) by Mark Sedon and Lionel Clay at well-known ice crag Wye Creek. Mark aided and bolted the severely overhanging line and Lionel bagged the first free ascent, first shot. The route climbs a schist cave wall and links to a thin free-hanging icicle. This is the first true mixed line in New Zealand employing pre-placed bolts for protection and is no doubt a reflection of overseas trends, whilst being a staunch reminder as to how far New Zealand is behind the rest of the world in the development of mixed climbing.

Barron Saddle – Mt Brewster Region

This is a large and complex alpine region south of Aoraki Mt Cook. Judging by the number of new routes to come out of the area in the last two years it is a treasure trove of new opportunities. In the 2004 NZAJ Ross Cullen (guidebook author and one of the area's leading first ascensionists) reported 20-plus new climbs in twelve months.

In May 2004 Paul Hersey and Mat Woods climbed the 500m rock route *Tenderfoot*, grade 3, crux 13 (5.6), on **Mt Glen Lyon (2050m)** at the toe of the Neumann Range. The wall features some nice climbing with sections of good rock broken by ledges. Later in the year *Late Bloomer* was added on the same face by Mat Woods and Dave Morgan at 4–, 17 (5.9). In the Dobson valley Kynan Bazley and Yew-jin Tan made the first ascent of the east face of **Mt Glencairn (2499m)** via *Hidden Treasures*, grade 15 (5.8), overall 3-. The route started from Sutherland Stream. Ross Cullen and Bill McLeod once again teamed up for some new route exploration and after fishing around in the S branch of the South Temple valley the duo discovered and named the Salmon Slabs. This salmon-hued stretch of greywacke now has four multi-pitch routes up to grade 17.

The most notable first ascent of winter was a new line on the SE face of **Mt Ward (2645m)**, North Elcho valley, climbed in late August by Kynan Bazely and Paul Hersey. Their route *Great Dane* is a 12-pitch ice climb with an overall grade of 5-. Prior to this ascent the face had not seen a pair of ice tools for 23 years! A handful of new ice routes were also climbed at Bush Stream.

Summer 2005 saw the Cullen-McLeod team active again on the Grasshopper Wall, **Peak 2070m**, with the first ascent of nine-pitch *Knees Up*, grade 16 (5.8/5.9) In the N branch of the Huxley River James Edwards and Oliver Metherell made the first recorded ascent of **Peak 2072m**. Their 500m route is called *Matinee*.

Aoraki Mount Cook and Westland

There were a number of outstanding climbs at Aoraki Mt Cook during 2004-5, with Allan Uren and Craig Jefferies' ascent of the NE face of **Torres Peak (3160m)** being the most significant. *Godzone* (14 pitches, grade 6+) tackles consistently technical terrain as it negotiates a more or less plumb line up the face. The 500m route was climbed in early July with two bivouacs and is a definite contender for the badge of 'hardest route in the country'.

A few days later Glenn Pennycook and Tshering Pande Bhote tackled **Mt Haidinger**'s E face headwall via a prominent ice lead high above the Tasman Glacier. In a committing effort the pair climbed the route from Pioneer Hut by crossing the S ridge of Haidinger and abseiling and traversing steep slopes to access the direttissima. *White Steel* tackles 200m of ice from 65-90° and is graded 5+.

Continuing with his penchant for soloing Southern Alps classics Guy McKinnon upped the ante with winter solos of the remote and difficult to access Hidden and Balfour Faces of **Mt Tasman (3497m)**, both grade 6. The Balfour has been soloed in winter before, but not often and the Hidden Face (climbed via the *Direct*) was a first winter ascent. In January Guy attempted a solo of the N ridge of **Aoraki Mt Cook (3754m)**. Tackling the crux, the Beare Step, still shod in his big boots Guy slipped but his near-fatal plunge was cut short after five metres by a small ledge that he was lucky enough to strike and remain on. The landing broke his left fibula and he remained on the ledge for 13 hours before being rescued by the Aoraki Mt Cook SAR team.

Australian climber Gren Hinton also made some very impressive winter solos. On the S face of **Mt Hicks (3198m)** he made an ascent of the *Yankee Kiwi Couloir* (6+) and a mixed free and rope solo of *Logans Run* (6+). Other winter highlights included a first winter ascent of *The Balcony Line* (4+) on the S face of **Mt Mallory (2756m)** by Tsering Pande Bhote, Johnny Davidson and Glenn Pennycook. Pennycook also made the first winter ascent of *Albino Merino* (4) on the SW headwall of **Mt Haidinger**. Pete Camell and Nick Monteith climbed a three pitch variation to the *Valentine Gully* on the Marcel Face of **Mt Haast** and a new route on the S face of **Mt Barnicoat (2800m)**. Glenn Pennycook and Andrew Young also made the first winter ascent of the *Gray-Williamson Couloir* on the SW face of **Conway Peak (2899m)**. The readily accessible Murchison Face of **Mt Aylmer (2699m)** was climbed in September by Paul Knott and Adrian Camm. *Archbishop of Canterbury* is a sustained 400m of ice with occasional rock steps, and was given an overall grade of 4/5.

Summer 2005 saw the usual burst of activity, though few significant ascents were made. Early in the season Tim Billington and Paul Stephanus climbed a new line on the E face of **Mt Nazomi (2925m)**. In January Mike Madden made a solo ascent of the *Direct* (4+) on the E face of **Mt Sefton (3151m)**. Vaughn Thomas and Thomas Evans made a quick ascent of the *Central Buttress* on the N face of Mt Hicks – 12 hours hut to hut.

ADE MILLER

North America 2004

The Area Notes for North America would not have been possible without the help of Kelly Cordes and the American Alpine Journal (AAJ), who provided the original background material upon which these notes are based. These notes cover the highlights and major ascents. For a complete report of all activity in North America, the reader is referred to the current editions of the AAJ and Canadian Alpine Journal.

ALASKA

Unseasonably warm temperatures in the Denali Park hampered many climbing attempts with little climbing taking place outside of the popular established routes. Steve Lyall and Zach Shlosar climbed a new line, the *Tranquillor Couloir* (7000', AK 4), on the left side of Denali's Father and Sons Wall. Carl Tobin and Vince Anderson established two lines, *Durty Sanchez* (ED2/3) and *Filthy Jorge* (1200m), on **East Kahiltna Peak**. The same pair, along with Jonny Blitz, climbed *Homage to Pat* (WI5 5.7 mixed), a variation of the Callis-Kennedy (1993) also on East Kahiltna Peak.

Several parties were active in the Ruth Gorge area with significant results. Sam Chinnery and Andy Sharpe (UK) climbed *Snowpatrol* (1600m, VI WI5+) right of the *Roberts-Rowell* (1974) on the S face of **Mt. Dickey**. A few days later the second ascent party confirmed the quality and committing nature of the line. Over four days Ben Gilmore and Kevin Mahoney put up *Arctic Rage* (4500', VI WI6+ R A2) on the vast E face of the **Moose's Tooth**. The route shares the start of *The Dance of the Li-Woo Masters* (Bridwell-Stump, 1981) before moving left to take a line on the left hand flank of the Tooth. The pair completed the climb over four days on their second attempt.

Ivan Ramirez and Gilly James climbed a new line, *The Unforgiven* (350m, M5 WI6) on the W buttress of the **Bear's Tooth**. The line ends at the base of the summit sérac. On the S side of the **Moose's Tooth** Scott Adamson and James Stover established *Levitation and Hail Marys* (V M7 A0) which follows a system of ice runnels, chimneys and cracks directly to the east summit. They also repeated *The Unforgiven*.

Joe Puryear, along with several different partners, also managed a spectacular 14 routes on 13 peaks during the course of his visit including; *Cobra Pillar* (Donini-Tackle, 1991) on **Mount Barrill** and ascents of the **Hut Tower** and **Eye Tooth**. On The Stump, a subpeak of the Wisdom Tooth, Puryear and Chris McNamara established *Goldfinger* (12 pitches to 5.11). The line takes a dihedral previously attempted by Mugs Stump on the left side of the face before moving right for a direct finish.

In a two week trip to the Alaska Range Sean Isaac and Shawn Huisman climbed two new routes. The first, *Canadian Bacon* (3000', ED1 M5 WI4) on the E face of **Royal Tower** immediately left of *Spam and Legs*. They completed the route in a 17-hour round trip. The second climbed the gully left of *Ring of Fire* on **Thunder Mountain**. *Maxim* (ED1 M4 WI5) was also completed in a single round trip, this time in 14 hours.

Mike 'Twid' Turner and Stuart McAleese (UK) were again active in the **Kichatna Spires**, this time on **Mount Nevermore**. Their new line, *The Perfect Storm* (1000m, E4 A1), climbs the pillar on the far right of the E face of Nevermore. After fixing the first 200m they climbed the remaining ground capsule style over nine days. On **Tatina Spire** Mark Reeves and Steve Sinfield (UK) climbed *Groundhog Day* (14 pitches, E3 A0/A1) right of *Alaskan Rose* (Stratford-Thaw, 1996).

Elsewhere in Alaska exploration of the numerous other ranges continued. Notably the *South Pillar* of the **Devil's Thumb** received its first free ascent when Carl Diedrich and Paul Adam Haraf climbed the line with some minor deviations from the route used by the first ascensionists (Bebie-Pilling, 1991). Andre Ike and Jon Walsh also visited the Devil's Thumb massif and completed ascents of The Thumb and all its satellites including two lines on the East and West Witches' Tits: very impressive given the area's reputation for poor weather.

CANADA

Just over the border on **Mount Kennedy** in the Elias Mountains Rich Cross and Jon Bracey (UK) completed the first ascent of Mount Kennedy's NW face, finishing the line *Pair of Jacks* (Tackle-Roberts, 1996). Where Tackle and Roberts were forced traverse and descend the N spur Cross and Bracey continued through the second rock band and then up the upper ice field to the summit. The pair took three days to climb the face and descend, reporting difficulties up to Scottish 7.

In Canada's Northern Territories the **Vampire Spires** attracted several parties. On Vampire Spire itself Doug La Forge, John Sedelmeyer and Andrew McLean climbed *Nosferatu* (V 5.9 A2) while Pat Goodman and Hank Jones returned to climb *The Coffin* (V 5.11 C1) and *The Dark Side* (IV 5.11).

The publication of Don Serl's excellent *Waddington Guide* spurred a renewal of activity around **Mount Waddington** with numerous climbers of all abilities visiting the range. Many of the classic harder lines saw one or more repeat ascents, including *Skywalk* (Flavelle-Lane, 1982) on **Mount Combatant** and Waddington's *Wiessner-House* (1942) and *Risse Route* (1987). *The Waddington Traverse* (4000m of ascent in 10km, ED+ 5.9 60°) also saw its first repeat by Mark Bunker and Colin Haley. Several new lines were also established. Most significantly John Furneaux and Matt Maddaloni put up *The Smoke Show* (to 5.13, one fall) on the south face of **The Incisor**. The pair spent some time camped on a ledge 500' above the Tiedemann Glacier while they worked out the free climbing on the first 1000' of the route.

In the Bugaboos Nick Martino, Renan Ozturk and Cedar Wright successfully freed the *Italian Pillar* (V 5.11+) and the *South West Pillar* (V 5.12- R/X) on The Minaret on **South Howser**. Both routes were climbed free in 14 and 16 hours respectively with no falls. On the E face of **Lost Feather Pinnacle** Duncan Burke and Chris Weidner established *Back at Bob's* (7 pitches, IV 5.11 A2).

In the **Canadian Rockies** visiting climber Frank Jourdan from Germany made the second ascent (solo) of the *Cheesemond-Dick* (1200m, V 5.9 A2, 1982) on **Mt Assiniboine**. He also soloed the *Greenwood-Jones* (1400m, V 5.8 A1, 1969) on the N face of **Mt Temple** and *The Supercouloir* (1200m, IV 5.8, Lowe-Jones, 1973) on **Mt Deltaform**. Before returning to his native Germany Jourdan visited The Waddington range and soloed several lines there also. **Mt Alberta**'s *Japanese Route* (1925) received its first winter ascent by Raphael Slawinski, Scott Semple and Eamonn Walsh.

Slawinski and Valeri Babanov also established a new ice route on the N face of **Mt Amery**, *Aurora* (600m WI6), while Paul McSorley and Jon Walsh put up *Rivers of Babylon* (400m, WI 5+ M6+) on **Mt Wilson**, between *Mixed Master* and *Ice Nine*.

CONTINENTAL UNITED STATES

In **Yosemite** numerous parties continued to free existing lines and add new ones. Tommy Caldwell, with Beth Rodden and Adam Stack, successfully freed *Dihedral Wall* over a period of four days. The route features several 5.13 pitches with difficulties to 5.14a and is probably the most continuously technical free route today. The *Leaning Tower* was also the scene of several important ascents. In October 2003 (previously unreported) Rob Miller made the second 'free' ascent of the route.[1] Several other parties followed also repeating the route free, including Tommy Caldwell's flash ascent. Numerous other existing lines also received repeat free ascents including; *Golden Gate* (5.13b) by Steve Schneider and Justin Sjong, and a flash ascent of *Free Rider* (5.12c/d) on El Cap by Mark and Mike Anderson. Steph Davis also made the first female free ascent of the same route. Speed climbing in the Valley was also prolific this year with Ammon McNeely completing 11 speed climbs on El Capitan and breaking nine records.

In the **High Sierras** the same high standards of free climbing were in evidence. Brandon Thau and Dave Nettle made the first free ascent of *Eagle*

---

[1] The first pitch of Leaning Tower is an overhanging bolt ladder. References to free ascents of this route refer to all climbing above the first pitch.

Dihedral (IV 5.11–, Rowell-Coe, 1971) on **East Fuller Butte**. While on **The Incredible Hulk** Peter Croft, Dave Nettle, and Greg Epperson put up *Airstream* (V 5.13), currently the most difficult free climb in the Sierras. Later in the year Peter Croft and Andrew Stevens along with Hans Steingartner returned to The Incredible Hulk to establish *Blowhard* (IV 5.12+). Croft and Dave Nettle also added *The Venturi Effect* (V 5.12+). The Palisade Traverse also saw its second continuous ascent when Scott McCook and Adam Penney traversed from Southfork Pass to the summit of Mt. Agassiz, a distance of eight miles above 13,000'.

In the **Utah** desert Greg Child and several partners put up many new routes in the Castle Valley area, including *Excommunication* (IV 5.13) on The Priest. Joe Slansky was also active in the **Moab** area establishing new routes up to 400' in length.

In Colorado's **Black Canyon** an interesting development was the much publicised "dry tool free ascent" of *Hallucinogen Wall* (VI 5.10 A3+) by Ryan Nelson and Jared Ogden on North Chasm View Wall. The pair succeeded in freeing all but pitch 13 of the route by conventional means at 5.13– R, impressive in its own right. On pitch 13 however they employed dry tooling techniques normally reserved for winter ascents. This has sparked some debate in the U.S. climbing community; not least as to its impact should such a technique become widespread.

While the continuing trend in the U.S. is towards high-end free climbing, some notable winter mountaineering also took place. In the **Cascades** an exceptional 2004/5 winter allowed several long-standing projects to be completed. Most notably the complete *North Ridge* of **Mount Stuart** was climbed by Colin Haley and Mark Bunker. This was one of the few remaining 'Fifty Classics' to be still awaiting a winter ascent, while in the **Tetons** *The Grand Traverse* also received its first winter ascent (winter of 2003/4). Renny Jackson, Hans Johnstone, Stephen Koch and Mark Newcomb, climbing as two pairs, completed the traverse in four and three days respectively. Steven Koch and Mark Newcomb also established The *Alex Lowe Memorial Route* on the N face of Grand Teton.

ANTONIO Gó MEZ BOHó RQUEZ

Cordillera Blanca 2004

Translated by Erik Monasterio

The report is ordered alphabetically by mountain.

Alpamayo (5947m) – correction of route information
(from book *Cordillera Blanca, Escaladas, Parte Norte* ISBN 84-607-7937-8).
Most mountaineering publications and climbers refer to the popular central
couloir on the SW face as the 1975 *Ferrari Route* and consider the *French
Couloir* a separate route. In fact both the *Ferrari Route* and the *French Couloir*
take a line two couloirs right of the central couloir. This route is longer and
more difficult than the central couloir and experienced major changes in
1995 following an avalanche on the lower aspects. Its first ascent has wrongly
been attributed to the N American climbers, W A Barker and S Connolly,
who climbed it in June 1980. The route is also mistakenly known as the
French Direct because it was climbed in May 1977 by N Jaeger and the
following day by his climbing partners R Ghilini and B Prud'Homme. There
are others who mistakenly believe it is named in memory of French climbers
S Beriol and B Lay, who died on the route in July 1980 from a summit
cornice avalanche. On the same day, the N American climbers P Millar
and J O'Neill were on the lower sections of the same route and were
unaffected by the avalanche. The first recorded ascent of the *Central Couloir*
is attributed to R Renaud, his client Susana (France), J Gálvez and A G
Bohórquez (Spain) in 1983.

Cerro Parón (La Esfinge, 5325m)
On 29 July Diego Fernández and Maribel Elías climbed the original 1985
Bohórquez-García Route on the E face. They bivouacked three pitches from
the summit. Elías is the first Peruvian female to climb 'La Esfinge' (the
Sphinx).
    From 24 to 31 July, Spanish climbers Ángel Olmos, Antonio L Liria and
José M Cancho climbed a new route on the E face (*Killa Quillay,* 700m, VI,
A2, 6b+ UIAA). The route took 17 pitches and lies between *Cruz del Sur*
(Bole-Karo, 2000) and the original *Bohórquez-García* 1985 line. The route
was repeated several weeks later by Basque climber Aritz Labiano and
Belgian Michael le Comte. This route had a variation on the upper face
and veered toward the Polanco-Olivera-Madrid de la Cal, (*Volverás a mí,*
1987) route, and later rejoined *Killa Quillay.*

115. SW face of Alpamayo (5947m) showing *Central Couloir* (left) and *Ferrari Route /
French Couloir (right). (*Ignacio Ruíz /file Antonio Gómez-Bohórquez*)

Chacraraju, West (6112m)

On 8 July, Slovenian climbers Majan Kovak, Pavle Kozjek and Basque
climber Aritza Monasterio climbed the N face to join the E ridge in 18
hours. The route lies between the original 1956 *French Route* and the 1986
Hapala-Husicka Route. The route is 800m long and has a technical grade of
6a, A1, AI6, 90°/55°-70°.

Chacraraju, East (6001m)

Following an attempt to climb the SE ridge (with Al Powell), Nick Bullock
teamed with Adam M Kovacs to climb a new variant on the top section of
the *Jaeger Route* on the S face. On 29 July they set off from the foot of the
face at 3.40 am and solo climbed 275m (IV with short Scottish V ice) to
within 150m of the summit. They then left the *Jaeger Route* and roped up
for the three final mixed pitches (VI, VI and V– Scottish) to the right of the
1984 Hispanic-Peruvian *García-Escolar-Silverio Route*. They did not follow
the ridge to the summit and rappelled straight down the route, reaching
camp 20 hours after setting off.

Caraz II (6020m)

From 21 to 22 July Damien Astoul, Mathieu Detrie, Gaspard Petiot and Basile Petiot climbed *Couloir Superduper* on the E face. They managed to climb beyond the high point reached by Kendrick, Coull and Morton in 1997 and added a more direct finish by climbing a rock section direct to the summit. They bivouacked at c5800m. They describe poor quality on the rock section and estimate their route to be 700m ED, 90°-95°, 6a, A2.

On 25 July Australian climbers Anthony Morgan and Matthew Scholes climbed a new route on the E face (720m, TD+, V+, W3, A2) to reach the summit via the NE ridge. The route went between the *Mlinar-Jost* 2001 and the *Huber-Koch* 1955 routes.

Hualcán pt 5350m

On 10 July Anthony Barton and Dave Sykes climbed pt 5350m on the NE ridge of Hualcán (6125m). From the 'Quebrada Huichganga' they reached the E ridge (AD+) then climbed 5 pitches of Scottish IV to reach the summit. They abseiled down the S face.

Huandoy-Sur (6160m)

On 27 June 2003, Mexican climbers Jorge Colín, Emiliano Villanueva and Emiliano Fernández attempted the S face. They gave up after a one week effort, describing poor conditions on the glacier, rockfall and severe cold. Two climbers, thought to be N Americans, climbed the N face via a route to the right of the *Sole-Sphor* line. They left the Pisco base camp on 26 July at 00.30 and reached the summit at 11.30.

Yanawaca (Peña Negra c4900m)

From 1 to 7 June, Mexican climbers Carlos Bazua, Emiliano Villanueva and Luis Carlos García Ayala climbed 735m of the N face (VI, 5.10, A2) before retreating. They planned to finish the route in 2005.

'Ulloc Grande'

On 29 August N Americans Wayne Crill and Kevin Gallagher climbed nine pitches (c350m, A3, 5.12) on the northern aspect of the Ishinca valley. They named the route *Ulloc Grande*. They intended to continue the route in 2005 and left a fixed line on the sixth pitch.

Bolivia 2004

During the 2004 climbing season there were significantly fewer visitors to Bolivia than in previous years. Political instability may have contributed to this, as in September 2003 many visitors were isolated in the town of Sorata, Northern Cordillera Real. Local Aymara protestors, angry at the government's plan to privatise and export Bolivia's rich gas reserves, blocked the access roads from the highland town of Achacachi to Sorata (140km NW of La Paz). Visitors were stranded for up to two weeks and finally when the Bolivian Army forcibly opened the road there were armed clashes with the protestors and buses were shot at and stoned. During the first few months of 2004 there were widespread road blocks and protests, and many embassies advised foreigners against visiting the country. The situation improved following a nationwide referendum on 18 July which gave the government popular support.

Climbing Conditions

2004 was a very dry year with the Bolivian Andes experiencing little precipitation during the monsoon months. As a consequence the big mixed ice/rock walls were quite bare, exposed to rockfall and often threatened by unstable seracs. The weather however, was predictably very stable.

Fatalities

As far as the writer is aware there was only one fatality, an Argentinean solo climber who unfortunately slipped and fell several hundred metres on the country's highest peak, Sajama (6549m). A party of Australians somehow managed to get lost, and were rescued on the country's most popular and straightforward mountain, **Huayna Potosi (6088m)**.

Wiphala Expedition

The Bolivian-New Zealand guide and psychiatrist, Erik Monasterio and New Zealand climber, Mike Brown climbed a number of new routes in the Northern Cordillera Real.

Northern Cordillera Real – Western Aspect
Pt 5573m - Pico Wiphala

Monasterio and Brown acclimatised by climbing a new route on this subsidiary peak on the western aspect of the Illampu-Ancohuma Massif, south of the Laguna glacier base camp used for the normal route on Ancohuma. DAV Map Pt 5573m has had one previous ascent, via the

long SW ridge, *Rebeldia de los Condores* (Enz/Rauch, reported in Mountain Info July 1999). The pair left their 4700m camp at 6am on 23 July, travelling light without bivouac equipment and with only two litres of water. They reached the start of the route two hours later, at a point approximately 400m NE of *Rebeldia de los Condores.* They ascended directly up the W face, starting on the left (N) wall of an obvious gully and continuing in the gully or to its left. The climbing was exposed and threatened by rockfall. After 14 pitches the summit was still not within sight and the pair were forced to sit out the night in temperatures down to –20°C. The next day they completed the route in a further four pitches and summitted on the glacier W of the Ancohuma mountain. Descent to the Laguna glacier camp was far from trivial as they had not carried ice-climbing equipment. They graded the route TD, F6a and christened the hitherto unnamed peak Pico Wiphala. The Wiphala is the multi-coloured, original Inca flag that symbolises the wisdom of the wind and is carried by locals in their protests and search for justice and equality.

Northern Cordillera Real – Eastern Aspect
Gorra de Hielo (5760m)
On 1 August, climbing from a high camp at c5400m on the eastern aspect of the Illampu-Pico del Norte Massif, Monasterio and Brown attempted the SE ridge of **Pico del Norte (6070m)**. The newly exposed rock on the ridge was composed of broken unstable granite boulders and was extremely dangerous. Mounting fear and a nostalgic attachment to life prevailed and the attempt was abandoned after four pitches. The pair rappelled off the E face before crossing a basin of thigh deep snow (2 hours) and on the same day climbed a new route on the S face of **Gorra de Hielo (5760m)**. The 300m route followed an old avalanche gully and provided superb ice conditions. It was graded D+, AI4. Argentinean climbers G Minotti, M Falconer and L Bromessard who repeated the route a week later confirmed the grade.

Aguja Yacuma (6072m)
From the same high camp at c5400m, on 3 August Monasterio and Brown climbed a new route on Aguja Yacuma. The route ascended the unclimbed E face of the rock towers and required three pitches of technical climbing (F6b, 6a and 5+). The approach to the base of the rock tower took seven hours and crossed the E glacier at the foot of **Illampu (6372m)**. Aguja

116. *Left*
The rocky buttress of Pico Wiphala (5573m) in front of Ancohuma (6430m). The Brown-Monasterio route takes the centre of the face. The only other route on Pico Wiphala is the Enz-Rauch route which approaches the right skyline ridge from behind. (*Erik Monasterio*)

Yacuma lies directly south of the Illampu massif and is clearly visible south of the Sanchez/Mesili pass. There are many possibilities for new routes on these towers, which offer short but excellent quality granite rock.

Pico Emma Maria (5531m)

The impressive rock peaks of PK 24 aka Punta Badile (see Mountain Info July 1999) and Pico Emma Maria lie ENE of Pico del Norte and Gorra del Hielo.

There is still some dispute as to the altitude and position of Pico Emma Maria. In Jill Neate's book, *Mountaineering In The Andes* (2nd Edition 1994) it is wrongly described as point 5715m (this is most likely Pico Esperanza) and on the DAV Map it is given an altitude of 5531m. This obvious rock tower, clearly visible from the village of Coco, had its first recorded ascent via the SW ridge in August 1953 by the legendary climbers Hans Ertl and A Hundhammer. In 1983 A Mesili and C Hutson added a second route, the *East Buttress*, a mixed route graded French TD. There have been, to the author's knowledge, no other recorded ascents. On 6 August (Bolivia's Day of Independence) Monasterio and Brown approached the peak, climbing directly up from the Cocoyo-Jahuira river (DAV Map) to establish a camp at 5000m at the foot of the E face. Their attempt nearly came to a premature end as locals set fire to the grass fields directly beneath the peak. The valley became engulfed in thick, acrid smoke and the pair stumbled blindly through the choking fumes to find their camp eventually. On 7 August the smoke cleared and they struggled on with severe throat and eye irritations. The route ascended the SE face and the climbing was varied and sustained, over solid and compact granite with roofs, dihedrals and delicate corner systems, often choked with ice. The weather deteriorated through the day and the pair faced whiteout and stormy conditions by the time they reached the summit at 5pm. Struggling with frozen ropes they rappelled into the night and finally reached camp at 11pm. The route was 500m long and required 11 sustained (60m) pitches to F6c A0.

Cordillera Real – Southern Aspect
Illimani, Kolla Kollu Pyramid (6075m)

In September 2004 resident French/ Bolivian mountain guide Alain Mesili, together with Argentinean mountain guide Gustavo Lisi, Bolivian climber Jesus Catacora and French climber Denis Levaillant made the first repeat of the Mesili/ Sanchez 1972 *Kolla Koyu* route on Illimani. They climbed the S face of the Kolla Kollu Pyramid (6075m). Mesili describes dramatic changes to the 1972 route, and estimates the overall technical grade as French TD, AI4. Due to the dangerous conditions encountered on the route, the team descended via the SW face.

Cordillera Apolobamba

Between 9 and 23 July Alain Mesili and Brazilian climbing guide Waldemar Niclevicz repeated a number of routes and climbed a possible new route in the Apolobamba mountain chain.

Cololo 5915m

From the Kotani Lake (4760m and six hours from the Apolobamba town of Pelechuco), they approached Cololo by crossing south-east along the glaciers of the Khala Phusi Peak (5465m) and climbed a possible new route on the NE face. There is a 250m 60° couloir separating the NE face from the NE ridge of Cololo. Mesili and Niclevicz climbed the NE face, following a line along the vertical seracs (French D+). They encountered névé, soft snow and ice up to 70°.

Chaupi Orco Norte 6044m

On 18 and 19 July Mesili and Niclevicz repeated the central line on the E face of the northern peak of Chaupi Orco. They encountered dangerous conditions with a thin layer of frozen névé over deep wind-blown snow. The *East Face* route is to the right of the 1995 *Central Couloir* route climbed by the JDAV-Expedition Bolivien. The grade of the route was French AD, AI2. Mesili also reports that the 1957 E ridge, *Normal Route* (W Karl, H Richter and H Wimmer) is almost unreachable and very dangerous as the northern aspect is threatened by unstable seracs and rotten ice.

Katantica Central 5610m

Mesili and Niclevicz repeated the Karl Gross and Dieter Hein 1968 route on Katantica Central (Katantica III) and the Yossi Brain, Dean Wiggin and Eamonn Flood 1997 West Ridge route.

Mount Everest Foundation
Expedition Reports

SUMMARISED BY BILL RUTHVEN

Now into its fifty-second year, The Mount Everest Foundation is the original – and still the most important – charity in the UK devoted to the support of 'exploration of the mountain regions of the earth'. Founded after the first successful ascent of Everest in 1953 and initially financed from the surplus funds and subsequent royalties of the 1953 expedition, it is a continuing initiative between the Alpine Club and the Royal Geographical Society (with the Institute of British Geographers).

In order that it may continue to support expeditions long into the future, the MEF only distributes the interest from its investments as grants, which are thus dependent on the state of the stock market. Nevertheless, it has now dispensed almost £800,000 in grants to some 1400 expeditions – mostly made up of ambitious young climbers.

All that the MEF asks in return for its support is a comprehensive report. Once received, copies are lodged in the Alpine Club Library, the Royal Geographical Society, the British Mountaineering Council and the Alan Rouse Memorial Collection in Sheffield Central Library.

The following notes summarise reports from the expeditions supported in 2004, and are divided into geographical areas.

AMERICA – NORTH AND CENTRAL

'Dusk till Dawn' Alaska 04 Stuart McAleese with Dai Lampard and Mike 'Twid' Turner. April-May 2004
Middle Triple Peak (2693m) in the remote Kichatna Spires area (aka Cathedral Spires) has only been climbed a few times, and this team hoped to make the first ascent of its SE pillar as the start of a traverse from the Shadows glacier to the Sunshine glacier. However, after moving kit to their intended start point, they soon realised that with a continuous rain of car-sized boulders, the glacier snout which gave the only access to the east face was far too dangerous to move through. They therefore directed their attention to the east wall of nearby Mount Nevermore (2469m), on which they successfully climbed a new 1000m route, *Perfect Storm* (VI, M6 E4 A1) in 10 days, six of which were spent continuously on the wall. They described the weather during this period as 'very Scottish', although the sun did shine on their summit day. MEF Ref 04/10

British Mount Dickey Guy Willett with Owen Samuel. April-May 2004
This team planned a new 'laser-line' 1600m route on the E face of Mount
Dickey (2909m) in the Ruth Gorge of Central Alaska to the right of *Blood
from a Stone*, as well as 'scoping' other new route potential in the area.
Unfortunately, before even setting foot on the mountain, the leader injured
his back, and had to return home, so was unable to take any further part in
activities. Fortunately, an American team of Freddie Wilkinson and Ben
Gilmore took pity on Samuel, and with them he repeated *Snowpatrol,*
climbed by Sam Chinnery and Andy Sharpe a couple of weeks earlier.
MEF Ref 04/25 [See 04/30 below]

British Bradley 2004 Sam Chinnery with Andy Sharpe. March-April 2004
The south face of Mt Bradley (2775m) is very steep granite rising from the
Ruth glacier. So far, the only winter route on it is *The Gift* put up by Mark
Twight in March 1998 – acknowledged as one of the hardest technical routes
in Alaska. This duo originally intended to climb a mixed couloir on the
face, but on arriving on the glacier they experienced several days of snow,
so decided to attempt their fall-back objective instead. This was an amazing
1600m line on the SE buttress of Mt Dickey (2909m) which, after one
unsuccessful attempt followed by a very scary spindrift-pummelled abseil
descent, they succeeded in climbing in three days (two bivvies) of very
sustained hard ice climbing up to 90°. They called the route *Snowpatrol*
and graded it VI, WI5+. MEF Ref 04/30

British Mount Kennedy NW Face 2004 Rich Cross with Jon Bracey.
May 2004
Mt Kennedy (4234m) is a beautiful mountain in the Yukon, with Himalayan
sized walls and ridges. Although Jack Tackle and Jack Roberts attempted
its 1800m north-west face in 1995, they had to abort due to a dropped
crampon. This team was luckier – in fact slick organisation and
unexpectedly good weather saw them achieve their objective within a week
of leaving the UK. Starting on the same line (*A Pair of Jacks,* graded Alaskan
6, M6 & A15+), their route finished straight up on new ground (up to hard
Scottish grade VII) through the upper rock band. Descent was made onto
the lower Cathedral glacier at 1900m on the south side of the mountain,
from where they were picked up and flown back to Kluane. MEF Ref 04/
34 (*See article 'The Arctic Discipline Wall', page 39.*)

'Free Knowledge' Ian Parnell with John Varco from USA. May-June 2004
This team had two objectives in mind when they headed for Alaska: to
make the first free ascent of *The Knowledge* on the N buttress of Mt Hunter
(4437m), and then to climb a new route on the SE face of Mt Foraker
(5300m). Unfortunately, they experienced unusually warm and wet weather
for the time of year, and returned home having achieved virtually no
climbing during their visit. MEF Ref 04/44

AMERICA – SOUTH AND ANTARCTICA

'Four Go Free' Fitzroy E Face Mike 'Twid' Turner with Steve Mayer, Stuart McAleese and Louise Thomas. November 2003-January 2004. Despite previous experience of Patagonian weather, this team of stalwarts returned hoping to make the first ascent of a 1300m free climb on the massive east face of Cerro Fitzroy (3405m), which they thought was well protected from the storms. A snow-hole base camp was soon established (amongst several others) at the Col Superior and a potential line identified on the left of the face. However, during the next four weeks they only had eight hours of 'good' weather: continuous snow and rising temperatures led to frequent avalanches, (and burial of equipment) and although they spent 20 days in their snow hole poised to go, they never actually set foot on the route. An attempt on the *Franca Argentine* route was also unsuccessful due to deep snow. MEF Ref 04/02

Return to Cerro Torre (Maestri-Egger) Feb 2004 Leo Houlding with Kevin Thaw plus Cedar Wright from USA. February-March 2004
Whether Maestri and Egger *did* climb Cerro Torre (3102m) in 1959 is a question that continues to haunt climbers, and this was yet another team hoping to find the answer. However, with warmer than usual weather, on both occasions that they went to the bottom of the north face, they were greeted with falling ice and other unpleasantness, so they concentrated their efforts elsewhere. They were successful in making the first ascent of Cerro Pereyara at E2, M2 and a new route on the west face of De La Ese at E1-E3, which they named *The Thaws not Houlding Wright*. MEF Ref 04/06

Chacraraju East Nick Bullock initially with Al Powell, then with Adam Kovacs from Sweden. June -July 2004
The original plan of this expedition was to make the first ascent of the E face of Chacraraju East (6001m) in the Cordillera Blanca. However, on arriving in Peru, they learned that the route had already been climbed in 2000 by two Slovenian climbers, who had then both been killed in Nepal before reporting their success. The SE ridge was apparently still unclimbed, but when two very scary days on loose rock and wobbly overhanging ice had only got them two-thirds of the way up, retreat was deemed preferable to death. Powell then returned to the UK so Bullock decided on a solo attempt of the *Jaeger route* (ED1) on the S face of the mountain. At Pisco base camp he met Kovacs who had exactly the same aim, so they agreed to 'simu-solo' side by side, thus making the best use of the very limited gear that they both carried: 40m of 5mm cord, 50m of 7mm cord plus a limited collection of pegs, wires, krabs and tat. They made good progress, and in a 20-hour single push, they climbed the route, adding a 3-pitch direct finish to the ridge (VI/7) which they called *Running on Empty*. MEF Ref 04/09

Blanca 2004 Tony Barton with Nick Carter, Mike Pescod and Owen Samuel. June-Jul 2004

The Cordillera Blanca of Peru is one of the most popular areas of the Andes chain, but still offers scope for keen explorers. This team set out with several objectives in mind in the Quebradas Santa Cruz, but experienced bad weather for much of their time in the area ('worst in 18 years' according to a regular visitor), which hampered progress and caused avalanches, one of which temporarily buried two team members. They felt that Nevada Millisraju (5500m) was unattractive so was not attempted, while fresh snow but a lack of ice stopped them on Taulliraju (5830m). However, they did succeed in making the first ascent of the north face of Nevada Parón (5600m), with a 400m 10-pitch TD+ route that they have called *Bartonellosis*.
MEF Ref 04/16

British Aguilera 2004 David Hillebrandt with Chris Smith. October-November 2004

British explorers are nothing if not determined: ever since reading of an isolated peak on the Wilcox Peninsula of Chilean Patagonia spotted by Tilman in 1957, Hillebrandt has been hoping to make its first ascent. In the past he has not even managed to reach the mountain – Cerro Aguilera (2438m) – but this time, after taking 14 days to penetrate the swamp and temperate jungle he and his companion found themselves in a beautiful Hidden Valley. They compared their feelings to those of the first people to penetrate the Nanda Devi Sanctuary. Above this they set foot on the glacier snout and donned crampons for the first time. Unfortunately the approach had taken far more time and energy than anticipated, and they were forced to abandon the climb at a height of 1291m. As a consolation, during the approach they managed to bag another minor peak which gave them a good view of their objective, and inevitably a return visit is in the pipeline.
MEF Ref 04/17

University College London Quimsa Cruz, Bolivia 2004 Sarah Griffin with Jingwen Chen, Matthew Frear, Tim Moss, Ted Saunders and John Tomlinson. June-July 2004

Although the southern part of the Cordillera Quimsa Cruz has become popular with climbers in recent years, information about their ascents is confused: several 'first ascents' may have been claimed for the same peaks, but under different names. This team was keen to clarify the true position, as well as climbing new and existing routes themselves. Although the snow and ice were in excellent condition, they were disappointed to find that the metamorphic rock was very loose, making some of the climbing frightening. Nevertheless, they climbed a number of routes on peaks from 5380m to 5740m, of which they think that six or seven were first ascents. Collating previous data is proving to be a far bigger task than anticipated, and so the team is appealing for assistance from earlier visitors, results being detailed on the website: www.quimsacruz.info   MEF Ref 04/27

NZ Ancohuma/Ilampu NE Cordillera Real   Erik Monasterio with Mike Brown. July-August 2004
These NZ climbers planned to climb new routes on Ilampu (6384m) and Ancohuma (6427m), but due to 2004 being an extremely dry year in Bolivia, all the big 'mixed' walls were bare and exposed to rockfall, making them prohibitively hazardous. They therefore turned their attention to other more accessible peaks, and succeeded in climbing new routes on Pt 5573m (which they named Pico Wiphala, after the original multi-coloured Inca flag symbolising the 'wisdom of the wind'), Gorra de Hielo (5760m), Aguja Yacuma (6072m) and Pico Emma Maria (5531m). Climbing grades were up to American Alpine VI and French TD. MEF Ref 04/29

Anglo-Scottish Vilcanota   Dave Wilkinson with Geoff Cohen, Steve Kennedy and Des Rubens. July-August 2004
Although this team experienced 'the best weather ever seen in big mountains' during the time they were in the area, their activities were largely dictated by an unseasonably heavy fall of snow that had occurred during June – even down to the streets of Cusco. As a result, they had to abandon their original objectives – first ascents of several peaks from the sunless SSW – due to the dangerous conditions. However, they did manage to achieve first ascents of Nevado Ichu Anante (c5720m) by its south flank/east ridge (AD), Ninaparaco (c5930m), Jatunhuma North East (c5930m) by its north face (TD) and the 'Scottish' West Spur of its west summit (c5760m) (Scottish IV/V), although deep snow prevented them from actually reaching the summit. MEF Ref 04/32 (*See article 'Unfinished Business in the Andes', page 47.*)

Scottish Cordillera Huayhuash 2004   Iain Rudkin with Alasdair Buchanan, Gareth Hughes, Andrew McIntyre, Kevin Neal and Neil Stewart. August-September 2004
Although all members of this team had reasonable Alpine experience, only one had previous experience of the Greater Ranges. Plans to climb new ice faces – in particular the W face of Nevado Rondoy (5879m) – had to be changed when it was discovered that the area had been virtually stripped of snow. However, they were successful in climbing the E ridge of Urus Este (5420m) plus the NW side of Ishinca (5530m) (both PD–) and reaching 5900m on the NW ridge of Tocllaraju before retreating due to altitude sickness of one of the team. They then moved to the Cordillera Blanca region where conditions were more favourable. Here they made near successful attempts on the SE face of Artesonaraju (6025m) and a complete ascent of the W face of Paron Sur (c5600m)(AD+), this probably being a first ascent. MEF Ref 04/37

British 2004 Artesonaraju Neal Crampton with Clare Fennell. July-August 2004
This couple hoped to make the first ascent of the NW face of Artesonaraju (6025m) in the Cordillera Blanca of Peru and descend by the 'normal' SW face route, which they planned to equip in advance. However, abnormal weather conditions earlier in the year had left south faces covered in unconsolidated snow and north faces bare rock, so they had to seek other routes. Several were attempted, but their only success was a repeat of the 1000m Simpson TD route on the N spur of Ranrapalca (6162m), which they climbed as far as the summit plateau, descending by the NE slopes. MEF Ref 04/41

Fin del Mundo 2004 Colin Wells with Christine Goulding. August 2004
The mountains of Argentine Tierra del Fuego, although relatively well travelled and easily accessible, have not received much attention from climbers until recently, although a small community of climbers is now established in Ushuaia. This team planned to make up for that by visiting the hinterland to explore and climb new winter and mixed routes, including the unclimbed south face of Monte Vinciguerra (1450m), which the leader had 'scoped' in 2003. However the late reduction in team size from four to two made this logistically impractical, so attention was directed at Cerro Bonete (1118m) instead, which had previously only been climbed by its non-technical SW ridge. On this they achieved the first ascent of the 300m NE ridge (AD), which they plan to call *The British Route*. They also made an almost complete ascent of a couloir *(Negra's Gully)* on the unclimbed technical SE face at Scottish IV, being stopped 10 metres below the NE ridge by loose rock and a lack of ice – the result of an unusually warm winter. They also reconnoitred several future objectives. MEF Ref 04/46

Sima Pumacocha 2004 (caving) Peter MacNab with Greg Brock, Tom Chapman, Chris Densham, Martin Holroyd, Les Oldham, Phil Rowsell and Peter Whitaker from UK; also Henry Burns, Mark Hassle, Ian Mackenzie and Taco Van Lu from Canada and Nick Hawkes + two from Peru. September 2004
Although not previously supported by the MEF, this international venture was a continuation of exploration of Sima Pumacocha in the Yauyos District of Central Peru. With a surveyed depth of 638m this cave already held the record for South America but was (and still is) thought to have a potential of up to 1000m. At 4375m above sea level, it also has the *highest* major cave entrance in the world. There are actually three known entrances, and this trip successfully connected SP1 and SP2 , adding 500m to the length of the system, but only 7m to the depth. Various other caves in the area were also explored, but none with anything like the potential of Sima Pumacoch. No doubt these optimistic explorers will be returning. MEF Ref 04/55
For further info see expedition website: http://members.shaw.ca/pumacocha

GREENLAND

Greenland Arctic Challenge 2004/2005 Rev Bob Shepton with Emily Brooks, Keith Geddes, Phil Ham, Nigel Harrison and Polly Murray, plus Jeremy Howarth and Tash Wright in support. June-October 2004 Continuing his exploration of the coastal mountains of Greenland from the sea, this leader sailed his 10-metre sloop from Scotland, and initially anchored in the 24km long Kangerduarssugssuaq Fjord. From here they climbed three peaks, two of them probably first ascents. They then moved north to the Akuliarusinguaq peninsula at the northern end of Uummaanaq Fjord in the hope of climbing four 2000m+ peaks 'left unclimbed' from a previous trip. They actually reached a total of 12 summits in the area, at least 10 of which are thought to be first ascents. Sailing even further north, they reached 78° 32' N, possibly the furthest ever reached by a conventional boat – beyond Etah, which had once been the most northerly Innuit settlement. From here they crossed to Ellesmere Island and then to Herbert Island, where the first E-W ski traverse was achieved – 30km in exacting snow conditions at an average height of 850m. They then returned to Upernavik, where the leader planned to winter on his boat in preparation for next year's phase of the exploration. MEF Ref 04/19A

Karabiner MC 60th Anniversary Pamiagdluk Island Dave Bone with Rob Allen, Steve Cheslett, Ian Heginbotham, Duncan Lee, Alois Metelko, Anna Neubert, Julie O'Regan, Scott Sadler and Jennifer Varley from UK plus Helena Bestova and Karel Prochazka from the Czech Republic. (July-August 2004)
This was a typical 'club' expedition, whose numbers were limited by the capacity of the 10m boat hired to reach an inlet on the western side of Kangerdluarssuaq Fjord on Pamiagdluk Island, where they established their base camp. Weather conditions throughout were unsettled with few wholly fine days, but the team established a total of 26 mountaineering routes up to AD+ and rock routes up to E3. However they say that 'there's plenty more to do' and no doubt some of the team will be going back. MEF Ref 04/20 *For further information see website*: www.karabiner.org

Rucksack Club Watkins Mountains, 2004 Jim Hall with Bob Kerr, Ros Murray and Rae Pritchard. May-June 2004
This was a smaller than usual 'club' expedition visiting the Watkins Mountains of East Greenland. Using the services of Tangent Expeditions to access the area, their aim was to climb the country's highest peak, Gunnbjørnsfjeld (3693m) and make first ascents – mainly on ski – of other nearby peaks. However, on arrival, they were disappointed to find that a Royal Navy team had just climbed most of their identified objectives. Nevertheless, they were successful in making the first ascents of three peaks between 2750m and 3020m as well as repeating routes on Gunnbjørnsfjeld

and Qaqqaq Kershaw (aka Dome, 3682m), the two highest peaks in Greenland: they also explored a previously un-travelled glacier. MEF Ref 04/23

British Torssukatak Fjord Leanne Callaghan with Glenda Huxter, Tim Neill, Matt Perrier, Tim Riley and Louisa Wilkinson from UK and Judith Spancken from Germany. July-August 2004
Pamiagdluk Island has become a very popular destination for rock climbers in recent years. This team set out to make the first ascent of 'The Baron' (Pt 1340m) by several free routes. Seven new routes were climbed, with grades ranging from E2 5c to E4 6a, whilst two other lines were attempted but abandoned after 10 pitches due to loose rock. In addition, the team made second ascents of two routes recently climbed by another expedition. A large falling rock resulted in chest injuries to Riley, who had to be evacuated from the summit ridge by a series of lowers and abseils, and back to civilisation by a passing boat. Subsidiary plans to attempt the unclimbed Pt 1303m on the western shore of the Fjord had to be shelved as the team could not afford the extra £1000 necessary to hire a suitable boat. Inspection through binoculars revealed that it was steep, sheer and uninviting.
The female members of this expedition were awarded the Alison Chadwick Memorial Grant for 2004. MEF Ref 04/24

Greenland White Sea Peter Watson with Tim Broad, Rob Jones, Stene Lodge, Ron Newton, Luke Priest and Stewart Wright. May-August 2004
Following the example of Knox-Johnston and Bonington in 1991, some members of this team sailed a 10m steel cutter 'Elizabeth Victory' from Portsmouth to the E coast of Greenland, picking up the others in Northern Iceland for the final leg. Their plan was to land and explore some of the coastal mountain areas, but they had been warned that the area might not be sufficiently clear of sea ice to make landfall. While this was the case with Kangerdlugssuaq Fjord, they managed to enter nearby Mikis Fjord. Once on shore climbing opportunities were limited by bad weather and poor rock. Starting from sea level, they did manage to climb Red Peak (870m) – a long glacier ascent followed by a scramble over shattered rock to a broad summit – although an attempt on Mikis Peak (1289m) was aborted at 1100m. MEF Ref 04/42

HIMALAYA - INDIA

Miyar 2004 Graham Little with Brian Davison, Kevin Kelly and Jim Lowther. April-May 2004
This must surely be the first time that local politics has come to the *aid* of an expedition! To reach the Miyar glacier in Western Lahul this team had to cross the Rohtang La, but on arrival the pass was blocked by the heaviest

snow in 25 years. However the pass had to be opened in order that ballot papers for the Indian election could get through to a number of remote settlements. If a specific peak had been its declared objective, the team would have incurred the bureaucracy of a permit, LO etc, so they simply declared their aims as 'exploration and rock-climbing'. Concentrating on the Jangpar glacier, not previously visited by mountaineers, Little and Lowther climbed a minor top, Christina Peak (5420m) from which they were able to survey the surrounding mountain complex with its vast rock walls. They also climbed Lammergeier Spire on excellent rock at Alpine D. Meanwhile Davison and Kelly attempted a big mixed route at Scottish V but had to abort at 5800m due to a dropped rucksack. However, they then put up two long rock routes (UIAA V) on the slabs flanking the Miyar Nala. MEF Ref 04/18 (*See article 'Miyar Nala 2004', page 134.*)

International Kalanka North Face Sandy Allan with John Lyall from UK and Carlos Buhler from USA. May-June 2004
Several previous attempts to climb the north face of Kalanka (6931m) in the Garhwal Himalaya had failed, but with the previous experience of Buhler, this team was hopeful of success. Unfortunately they were delayed by seven days due to bureaucracy and heavy snow. The snow continued after they had established their base camp, which was promptly destroyed by a sérac fall. At this stage Buhler left the expedition, but the two Brits continued heading up, and found a site for Camp 2 at 6180m. Then the snow hit them again, with both powder and slab avalanches making further progress impossible. MEF Ref 04/21

Janhkuth 2004 Malcolm Bass with Andrew Brown and Paul Figg from UK plus Marty Beare and Pat Deavoll from NZ. September-October 2004
Janhkuth (aka Januhut) (6805m) in the Garhwal Himal is one of the few peaks of this height that had only received one previous (unsuccessful) attempt – probably due to its remoteness (near the head of the Gangotri glacier, some 20km beyond Shivling) and technicality. Bad weather with no prolonged settled periods added to the access (and egress) problem of the present team. Climbing as separate 'national' parties, each attempted obvious lines of weakness on the West face. Both routes were judged to be *difficile,* but would have been hard to descend in storm conditions. With the early arrival of winter snowfalls, the UK trio reached 5750m and the NZ pair turned back at 6400m. MEF Ref 04/35

Anglo-American Changabang 2004 Ian Parnell and John Varco (USA). September-October 2004
The original aim of this team was to climb a new route on Kalanka and then a new extremely committing route on the S face of Changabang (6864m). However, on hearing of a number of other expeditions to the area, they changed their objective to Saf Minal (6911m). On this they were

successful in making the first ascent of its N ridge and NW face in a 10-day round trip – possibly the second overall ascent of the peak. MEF Ref 04/45 (*See article 'Saf Minal North-west Face' page 84.*)

HIMALAYA - NEPAL

Teng Kangpoche North Face Nick Bullock with Nick Carter. October-November 2004
'Officially' unclimbed, Teng Kangpoche (6500m) had already been subject to an attempt by this leader in 2003, when he climbed a solo line, *Love and Hate* on the NE face to the point where it joined the east ridge, some 200m below the summit. [See 03/31 in AJ Vol 109]. With a new companion, he now planned to repeat this route, and then attempt a new one up the NW face. Due to the snow conditions, the NE face proved harder in 2004, and after triggering two avalanches and experiencing 'the most intense 12 hours of his life', they curtailed their attempt at 5400m. Fortunately, the snow on the NW face was more forgiving, and although suffering from extreme cold, they reached a crest on the W ridge at 6210m, some 1km short of the summit. It was obvious that special techniques would be required from here, so they retreated down their ascent line. They called their 1600m route *Edge of Darkness,* and graded it TD+/ED1, Scottish IV. MEF Ref 04/ 22 (*See article 'Shadows on Teng Kangpoche ', page 91.*)

'Eigerwand of the Khumbu' Rich Cross with Paul Ramsden. October-November 2004
Although appearing to be a very steep 1000m face (very similar to that of the Eigerwand) on a stand-alone 6070m summit, strictly speaking this team's objective forms the gable end to the long NE ridge of Kangtega. It was therefore necessary for them to obtain a permit for Kangtega itself. Unfortunately, whilst staying in lodges during their approach to the mountain, both team members contracted chest infections which sapped their energy. They were also very concerned regarding the condition of the snow, so although they succeeded in bivouacking at 4300m they were unable to make a serious attempt on the route. MEF Ref 04/26A

CHINA AND TIBET

British Qionglai 2004 Tom Chamberlain with David Evans, Dave Hollinger and Andy Sharpe. April-May 2004
Mick Fowler's success on Siguniang (6250m) in 2002 (MEF Ref: 02/32) has alerted other British mountaineers to the scope offered by the Qionglai Range of Sichuan Province, and this team hoped to climb a new route on the N spur or the W ridge of Siguniang itself. However, bad weather

intervened, and their attempt on the former was terminated when they met compact slabs overlaid with wet loose snow at 5200m. In view of its length and the continuing bad weather, the W ridge was not attempted, but two other peaks were tried. On Pt 5672, dangerous avalanche conditions stopped them at 5500m, and on Pt 5700 they reached 5400m before meeting similar conditions. However, they did succeed in climbing both Camel Peaks (c5510m) – snowy mountains with easy mixed ground. MEF Ref 04/05

Huanjiang Ged Campion with Dave Appleing, Bruce Bensley, Stewart Muir, Ernie Shield and Dave Williams, plus a number of Chinese scientists/ cavers. February-March 2004
The original intention of this caving expedition to Guangxi Province (SW China), was to explore caves in Huanjiang, but unfortunately this area did not live up to expectations. They therefore moved – first to Tian's County where they found a number of caves, including a doline with a 100m entrance pitch, and then to Fengshang where the caves proved to be even larger: one shaft dropped nearly 200m. These caves were also rich in wild life, including centipedes, catfish, a rat and a 2.4m snake. Apart from the snake (which disappeared, and is thought to have been eaten by the Chinese team members) specimens were brought back to the UK for identification. So impressive was the potential of these areas, that plans are already being made for a return visit. MEF Ref 04/08

New Zealand Unclimbed China Sean Waters with Jo Kippax. September-November 2004
When this NZ pair arrived in Chengdu en route for the Nyenchentangla East region of Tibet, they found that all permits for Tibet had just been rescinded by the CTMA due to illegal climbing by several teams (none supported by the MEF). Fortunately, permits for the Daxue Shan range of Sichuan were on offer instead, so they were able to select new objectives rather than return home empty-handed. From Chengdu a two-day drive and a four-day walk took them to the Moxi Gu valley, from which they were successful in making two first ascents, Longemain (6294m) and Daddomain (6380m) both by their west ridges. MEF Ref 04/11A
For further information see website: www.summitfootprints.com

Gongga East 2004 Angela Benham with Chris Drinkwater, Titch Kavanagh and Andrew Phillips. March-May 2004
Although rarely visited by westerners in the past, the mountains of Sichuan are now becoming quite popular with British climbers. This team planned to explore glaciers in the Daxue Shan mountains (the most easterly range of the Himalayan chain) and make the first ascent of the highest peak, Gongga East (6618m) also known as Mount Edgar: this was probably first sighted in 1981 by Henry Day's 'Jade Venture' expedition (MEF Ref 80/ 16). However, shortly before leaving the UK they learned that – although

never officially reported – a Korean team had climbed the peak in 2000. Nevertheless, they decided to keep it as their primary aim, but they would attempt to make its first ascent from the north. Bad weather, plus porters unwilling to carry above 3400m resulting in a lower than intended base camp, blighted their hopes. Although several attempts were made, the weather and rotten snow, ice and rock conditions forced them to abandon the climb at 5400m. They were advised that the weather in September is more conducive to success. MEF Ref 04/13A

British West Sichuan Martin Scott with Geoff Cohen, Dick Isherwood and Bill Thurston. April-May 2004
The objective of this team was Haizi Shan (5833m) which lies in an area of West Sichuan not previously visited by British climbers and never *officially* attempted by anyone. From Chengdu, their approach was by Landcruiser, first on a dual carriageway, but then on ever deteriorating surfaces. At base camp, they were surrounded by hoards of local people searching for 'worm grass' a sort of fungus reputed to have magical healing and aphrodisiac properties. After a few days' acclimatisation, they started climbing at the far left of the NW face, and established Camp 1 at 4405m. From here, their route led via a long ridge to the N summit (c5710m) which was reached by Cohen and Isherwood. Although much of the long traverse to the main summit was also climbed, it was slow going, time running out with 250m still to go and an estimated 4 to 6 hours needed to reach it and return. MEF Ref 04/33 (*See article 'King of Mountains', p 66.*)

British Qomo Lhari 2004 Julie-Ann Clyma with Roger Payne. April-May 2004
Qomo Lhari (7326m) in Yadong County, S Tibet (close to the Bhutan border) was first climbed in 1937 by F Spencer Chapman, but did not receive its second ascent until 1970 and its third in 1996. This husband and wife team's application for a permit to climb it was rejected in 2002, and although offered in 2003 was rescinded at the eleventh hour. But British expeditioners are very determined, which is a good thing, as it was third time lucky for this pair. Their plan was to make the first ascent of the NW ridge, and although they eventually found a safe way onto the route, they were forced to abandon it at 6000m due to extremely strong winds. However, in their few remaining days, they managed to make a very rapid ascent to the summit via the S ridge. This was the peak's first ascent in alpine style. MEF Ref 04/40

British Nganglong Kangri John Town with Derek Buckle, Toto Grönlund and Martin Scott. (August-September 2004)
Continuing the leader's exploration of remote areas of Tibet, this year's project took him and his companions from Kathmandu 1500km by road to Rutok County (Ngari Province) in the far west, where there are some 35

glaciers (two over 6km in length) and more than 40 peaks over 6000m. They were successful in making the first ascent of both summits of the highest mountain, Nganglong Kangri, by routes graded PD and F. Although the 'map height' of the highest is 6596m, they recorded two separate GPS readings of 6710m. MEF Ref 04/43 (*See article 'Nganglong: Walking on the Moon', page 71.*)

Big Walls of China John Arran with Anne Arran. July-August 2004
This husband and wife team were also attracted to the delights of Sichuan, their aim being to explore and make first ascents of big walls and rock spires in the Mt Siguniang National Park. Unfortunately, as they are now painfully aware, July and August are the wettest months of the year. Nevertheless, despite experiencing rain on two out of every three days, they were successful in making first ascents of two peaks – Niuxim Shan (or 'Heart of Cow') Peak (4942m) and Mi Mi Shan (5018m) – from the Suang Qiao Gou valley with technical climbing up to E4/5, 5c. Future parties planning to visit the area should be aware that the best months for rock climbing are March and October, with January the best for ice climbing. MEF Ref 04/51. (*See article 'Big Walls of China', page 80.*)
For further information see website: www.thefreeclimber.com

Hong Meigui Yunnan 2004 Hilary Greaves with Andrew Atkinson, Rich Bayfield, Duncan Collis, Simon Flower, Simon Froude, Rob Garrett, Rich Gerrish, Martin Hicks, Luis Hong, Chris Jewell, Martin Laverty, Martell Linsdell, Fleur Loveridge, Gavin Lowe, Lenik Amak Saymo, Andy Sewell and Pete Talling. July-August 2004
This was a continuation of a programme of cave exploration in Yunnan Province already supported in 2002 and 2003 (MEF Refs 02/48 & 03/49) and an unsupported expedition earlier in 2004. On this trip, the team attempted to find entrances at over 4000m that might connect with resurgences in the Yangtze Valley 2000m lower down. The hope was that they might find a system deeper than the current world record of 1800m. They covered a large area and logged 240 new entrances at heights up to 4400m but were unable to achieve any significant depths. MEF Ref 04/54

PAKISTAN

British Hispar Sar 2004 Simon Yates with Andy Parkin. September-October 2004
Hispar Sar (6400m) lies north of the Hispar glacier, and close to a very popular trekking route, so is relatively easy to access, yet remains unclimbed. This team attempted the steep Central Couloir of the SW face but a mishap with a karabiner in the dark from their bivouac point at the end of the first day on the route resulted in three stuff bags containing most of their food

and brewing kit sliding into the unknown. Despite limited rations, they continued climbing (up to ED IV) for a further three days until the summit was in sight, but then a storm blew up which they were unable to sit out due to the cold and wet combined with a lack of gas. A multi-abseil retreat from their high point of 6100m was followed by a disorientating meander down the Yutmaru glacier and a return home. Nevertheless, the pair had experienced an enjoyable and hassle-free expedition, which makes them recommend other climbers to return to the once popular mountains of the Karakoram. MEF Ref 04/14 (*See article 'Nought but Noodles on Hispar Sar', page 96.*)

CENTRAL ASIA AND THE FAR EAST

Scottish Kyzyl Asker 2004 Es Tresidder with Pete Benson, Matt Halls, Guy Robertson and Robin Thomas. August-September 2004
Following an unsuccessful trip to the Kokshaal Too area of Kyrgyzstan in 2002 [MEF Ref 02/41], this slightly changed team returned hoping that this time they would succeed in making the first ascent of the SE face of Kyzyl Asker (5842m), or 'Red Soldier' in the local language. However, an extreme thaw had virtually demolished the dramatic central ice line, making them think that it would probably be more appropriate to attempt it in winter than summer. They therefore turned their attention elsewhere. They were successful in climbing five new routes, including the second recorded ascent of Kyzyl Asker by a route on its N face (1200m with one pitch of Scottish VI) and first ascents of Great Walls of China (*Border Control*) and Ochre Walls (*Fire and Ice*), both 500m ED Scottish VII. MEF Ref 04/15

Zaalaiskiy Ridge Paul Hudson with Ian Arnold, Ken Findlay, Susan Jensen, Paul Lyons and William Parsons. July-August 2004
Once again, this leader selected a relatively unfrequented area for his exploratory expedition – the Zaalaiskiy range in the far south of Kyrgyzstan. They had originally planned to operate from the Nura glacier, but actually went to the even less visited western end of the range, close to the Tajikistan border, where they climbed 10 snow peaks up to 5513m and with grades ranging from F to AD and Scottish III. Although nothing was known about previous ascents, several summits were adorned with 'piles of stones that did not look natural', so probably only three were first ascents. MEF Ref 04/38

Kyrgystan - Djungart 2004 Ingrid Crossland with Graham Sutton. July-August 2004
With several previous visits to Kyrgyzstan behind her, this leader returned with possibly the first ever climbing expedition to visit the Djungart area of the Kokshaal Too range. Access to the area (very close to the Chinese border) has only recently become a realistic possibility with the establish-

ment of a seasonal helicopter base at Maida Adyr, accessible by 4WD vehicle. Base camp location was selected from a 1:200,000 map as it gave access to two separate valley systems. The weather was exceptionally warm for the time of year, with rain falling as high as 4000m. Both valleys were thoroughly explored but their base camp location turned out to be too far away from the mountains that they wished to climb; so although a good photographic record was obtained, no technical routes were undertaken and no new peaks were climbed. MEF Ref 04/39

MISCELLANEOUS

British Western Hajar Traverse 2003/4 Geoff Hornby with Susie Sammut, Mark Turnbull and David Wallis. December 2003-January 2004
Although small groups of British enthusiasts have been visiting the mountains of Oman since Sir Wilfred Thesiger's journeys in 1947, this was the first application for support submitted to the MEF. Encouraged by Sir Wilfred shortly before he died, this team planned to make a continuous SW to NW 600km traverse of the Western Hajar range from the base of the Wahiba Sands to Al Dawadi on the Indian Ocean by camel, foot and bicycle, climbing new routes on each of the major rock faces along the way. Wallis had to leave the team part way because of a family medical emergency, but despite continuous new rules imposed by Omani government officials and 'more foot blisters than you could throw a stick at', the other three managed to achieve this. En route they climbed five new routes between 300m and 500m in length and V+ to VI+ in grade. MEF Ref 04/07 (*See article 'Coast to Coast in Arabia', page 124.*)

Book Reviews

COMPILED BY GEOFFREY TEMPLEMAN

The Villain: the life of Don Whillans
Jim Perrin
Hutchinson, 2004, pp354, £18.99

This is an immensely enjoyable book. Jim Perrin is one of our finest mountaineering essayists whose writings illuminate the nature of our sport sensitively and without inhibition. His account of the life of Don Whillans displays all his narrative strengths and enthusiasms, though I do have some reservations about the way the book is composed.

The book touched many chords for me. My own (admittedly brief) rock-climbing days were the early sixties, in Snowdonia above all, when the feats of Brown and Whillans were relayed like news from the front line, and the myths about them were already multiplying. How we gazed at the lines they had put up, and reset our ambitions to encompass them. Snowdonia is Perrin's milieu and his love of the place shines through. His ability to find fresh and enticing adjectives to depict a succession of routes is breath-taking, and I could sense my fingers curling over the holds he described.

I enjoyed becoming reacquainted with Whillans through Perrin's writing. As a modest performer on rock, I had access to these gods through my work as a journalist, and naturally sought out commissions which would enable me to meet them. Thus I can say (just) that I climbed with Brown and Crew on Gogarth, at a time when the first lines on the crag were being established. I came to know Whillans when he was hired as a camera assistant to Chris Bonington during the *Eiger Direct* melodrama. I enjoyed his laconic talk, his quips that made perfect soundbites for the neophyte reporter that I was, and admired his determination to eat and drink his way through as much of the *Telegraph's* expenses budget as was humanly possible.

I had later encounters which revealed his dark side and his deepening alienation from his former comrades. Mick Burke told me of the occasion when Audrey Whillans remarked to her husband: 'Don, you know it's our wedding anniversary today, don't you?'

'Aye,' Whillans supposedly replied. 'Don't f——ing remind me.'

When I was canvassing opinions for a magazine profile about Chris Bonington, Whillans was deeply reluctant to help, on the grounds that, so he believed, it was Bonington himself who had suggested I write the article. I talked him round but it went deeply against the grain for Whillans to do anything to assist the man who had been his partner on so many important ascents. As Perrin relates, his alienation stemmed from a belief that Bonington had in some way 'sold out' to commercial pressures – when in fact, to most people, Bonington was exploring the possibilities of making a living from an activity which was at the core of his life.

I am gratified that my impressions of Whillans – the convivial drinking companion, the misogynist, the increasingly disgruntled fallen star – are at one with the character Perrin depicts. Perrin's research into his early life is meticulous, his cataloguing of the minutiae of Whillans' rock-climbing is detailed, bordering on obsessive. He provides an exhaustive account of a watershed era in British climbing, a time when both standards and the class basis of the sport were being irrevocably altered. This will appeal directly to a mountaineering readership, whom Perrin addresses without equivocation or the kind of compromises and interpolations a non-specialist audience might require. This strategy was an intriguing choice on Perrin's part, since his mountaineering obituaries in the *Guardian* are superb examples of how to write about our specialist subject in a way that appeals to insider and layperson alike.

At the same time Perrin examines the formation of the myths that enveloped both Whillans and Brown, so that his book becomes a deconstruction of the nature of heroism and the mythology of the sport. He accomplishes the same careful reporting and analysis of Brown's achievements in the Alps and the greater ranges. Because I had written about the dramas on the Annapurna south face in 1970, and had received first-hand accounts from friends such as Mick Burke, I felt I knew the outline of the story. Perrin adds a dimension to it with his account of the interplay of the characters, and where he does succumb to inference and judgment, they are absolutely to be respected.

The book is a genuine page-turner, luring you on with its detail and its love of climbing and mountains as Perrin constructs the distressing arc of Whillans' life, from high promise to pathetic loss of dignity. Perrin sustains suspense over his attitude towards Whillans and how it will play out. He accepts that Whillans had monumental faults but while he ultimately sides with him as a flawed hero, he provides enough data for readers to come to a different conclusion. Reading the book is an enriching experience that leaves you drained as you attempt to contend with your own conflicting emotions. It parallels his one previous book, *Menlove*, in broaching difficult themes, but the writing is far more graceful and confident.

My questions and reservations concern some of Perrin's decisions over narrative and structure. There are many extensive footnotes which he justifies by asserting that they provide context without interrupting the narrative flow. The problem is that some are so long that they do break the narrative if you pause to read them, but my feeling is that they are forgivable indulgences on the part of a commentator whose observations are always worth hearing.

Occasionally they exemplify another questionable characteristic of the book. There is a long and disturbing footnote describing an incident related by John Cleare. Whillans and his wife Audrey had stayed with Cleare and his family, who were also providing temporary refuge for a young woman friend who was in London to have an abortion. In the early hours, and despite the presence of his wife, Whillans had attempted to sexually assault the guest, who was outraged and distressed. Cleare's wife Viki demanded that Whillans leave the house at once, although the ever-hospitable Cleare insisted he be given breakfast first.

My own feeling is that such an incident was so central to the character Whillans had become that it should indeed have been integrated with the narrative, rather than relegated to footnote. It is as if Perrin, usually so authoritative, has suffered a loss of nerve over confronting the worst of Whillans' nature, for he never fully signposts the central issue of Whillans' repellent behaviour towards women, but introduces it diffidently, as if through a side door.

There is the same lacuna over Whillans' relationship with his long-suffering wife Audrey. Perrin tells how Audrey asked him to produce a 'warts and all' portrait. Yet Perrin justifies the fact that it took him 18 years to write by stating that he wanted to wait until Audrey died in case she was hurt by it. There is a further paradox, namely that Perrin hardly discusses the dynamics of the Whillans marriage at all, leaving you wondering how it functioned and what it meant to each partner, in view of the fact that – against all apparent odds – it survived. In the same way, Perrin does little to explore the nature of his two other most important relationships, those with Brown and Bonington, and what they represented to the respective partners.

There is one more gap in the narrative which I regret, namely that Perrin makes little attempt to explain why Whillans' life followed such a tragic course, or where his disfiguring misogyny, truculence and selfishness came from. I would like to have heard Perrin speculate on whether the wellsprings of Whillans' self-destruction were to be found in his childhood or upbringing, and whether some theory could be constructed to resolve why his flaws should become so overwhelming.

However, the book's readability and compassion far outweigh these caveats, and it establishes a marker for the standards that mountaineering biographers should aim for.

Peter Gillman

Whillans: a loyal friend with foibles
Dennis Gray

Jim Perrin's 'life of Don Whillans' is quite simply the best biography of a mountaineer that I have read. However its warts an' all approach, and in parts a lack of counterbalance may well annoy some of Don's friends. Anyone coming fresh to this subject, who never knew Whillans, might be forgiven after reading *The Villain* for concluding that he was a rotten little bugger without a single redeeming feature. This is far from the truth.

Perrin deserves plaudits for the amount of research and effort he has put into the project, but not for his tardiness in producing the book – his excuse being that he did not feel able to publish whilst Audrey, Don's widow, was still alive. Audrey originally approached me to write the Whillans story, and then a publisher suggested that Jim and I should combine and jointly write the saga. It quickly became obvious that this would have been a recipe for a disaster; I was over-committed working at the BMC and Perrin, understandably, wished to do the book on his own. I stood down, but I know that Audrey was willing to have a 'no holds barred' biography produced, and was subsequently upset by its non-appearance over many years. One can understand Jim's reticence, for *The Villain* is the story of an outstanding mountaineer destroyed by over-indulgence and excess, leading inexorably to a premature death, aged 52. But Audrey had no illusions and wanted the story to be told, for she suffered the most from Don's wayward behaviour.

The first part of the book is very well done, with fulsome coverage of Whillans's wartime childhood and adolescence in Salford. Being short, Don needed to stand up for himself from an early age in order to avoid being bullied. Occasionally this meant fisticuffs, standard practice in working class areas of the north in the 1940s.

Rambling in the countryside, first with family then with friends, led onto rock climbing, where he quickly emerged as an outstanding performer, and then the crucial meeting with Joe Brown at the Roaches in 1951. It was the beginning of a brilliant partnership. During the next few years, Whillans's feats on British rock, usually with Brown or other Rock and Ice members, earned him a legendary reputation for pioneering strenuous and/or extremely bold climbs at the highest standards of the day.

Yet it was his behaviour away from the crags that caused the most comment and the stories of his caustic wit and aggression began to build. Perrin has devoted a chapter to debunking some of these, including two stories, one ex Joe Brown and another from myself, concerning punch-ups with bus conductors. I stand by mine. It happened in February 1954 when I arrived to live in Manchester; the first half of the tale was common knowledge amongst the local climbing fraternity at that time and the second I had from Whillans himself. And I never knew him to exaggerate or misrepresent any event at which he was present. Surprisingly, after this debunking chapter Perrin then buttresses the Whillans legend with many stories confirming its potency.

Brown and Whillans's great alpine breakthrough in 1954 with the third ascent of the west face of the Dru and the first ascent of the west face of the Blaitière, are given their due prominence. But then the story begins to turn sour with Whillans supposedly envious of Brown's invitation to join the 1955 Kangchenjunga expedition. In the 30 years of our acquaintance I never heard Don say anything 'anti' against Joe personally, only against some of those who hung around with him at a later date. Jim makes the supposed bitterness of Don against Joe quite a theme in the book and if true it would be an indictment of his character. On the contrary, several times he told me that Brown was the best climber he had ever been with. Don might say something in jest, and he called me everything from 'a drink of water to a bloody little ta-ta!' But if anyone else had said that I am sure he would have reacted strongly in my defence.

Don's Himalayan climbing began with the 1957 Masherbrum expedition. It ended in disaster with the death of Bob Downes, and a near miss summit attempt by Whillans. Downes's death affected Don more than he let on. They had climbed quite a lot together including the first ascent of *Centurion* on Ben Nevis. It was during this trip he started smoking, after winning a raffle of 200 cigarettes on the boat to Karachi. And even more ominous for his future wellbeing he started drinking alcohol on a regular basis.

Whillans came to Gauri Sankar in 1964 on an expedition I organised. Expeditions then were hard work and we drove overland to save money. I left home in June 1964 and arrived back in January 1965. We very nearly climbed the mountain, and Don, I believe, put in his career best climbing performance. One can understand that being with a small group in such close proximity for so long strained relationships to the utmost, but we all remained good friends, albeit with one or two fractious arguments en route.

Throughout the late fifties and into the mid-sixties Whillans was without doubt 'the man', his reputation confirmed with climbs such as the Poincenot, the Central Tower of Paine and the Central Pillar of Frêney. I was Secretary of the Alpine Climbing Group and Don was the President for some of that time. He was the climber other British alpinists looked up to and he did not spare himself in encouraging others and handing down advice.

As to his fruitful partnership with Chris Bonington, initially Chris was the young acolyte, following in Don's footsteps, then things moved on and Bonington became 'Mr Big' and Don a team member. This was something Don found hard to swallow and here again Perrin highlights Don's sense of betrayal, particularly over the first British ascent of the *Eigerwand*.

Whillans greatest success was his 1970 ascent with Dougal Haston of the south face of Annapurna. But its genesis was misreported. When I returned from Gauri Sankar in January 1965, we planned to make Annapurna our next objective. We knew we could not go back to Gauri Sankar for the route we had opened up took us into Tibet. But the expedition had proved that a major technical face climb in the Himalaya was possible. After discussing objectives with Erwin Schneider, then engaged on mapping the Nepal Himalaya, I decided that the south face of Annapurna was the one most likely to yield a success. And I brought back a photograph of the face given to me by Jimmy Roberts. We started our planning; once again I was to be the organiser with Don as climbing leader. But then because of the Patterson incident Nepal was closed. When it re-opened for climbing in 1968/9, Chris Bonington wrote to me and asked if I thought it was feasible to get permission for Menlungste, I wrote back and said I did not think so but that the south face of Annapurna was a real possibility. He then expressed an interest and I sent him the photograph I still held because I could not go myself due to my changed circumstances. Thus Whillans knew all about the south face of Annapurna as an objective before Chris. And he believed, rightly or wrongly, that the project was as much his as Bonington's. One can make too much of such events, and Don's tragedy was that he could not let go and move on. If anyone slighted him then he held a grudge past all reasonable limits.

Perrin also touches on what he sees as Whillans' incipient racism and sexism, though in this he was not unlike other white working class men of his era. On one occasion when Audrey had kicked him out of their house I recall him living at my father's. He had turned up with a small battered suitcase containing a few possessions and my dad had taken him in. My father, a vaudeville and theatre artist all his life, a heavy drinker and smoker was nevertheless Old Labour, and no racist. Once in 1930s London he had been badly beaten by Mosley's black shirts, defending a fellow artist who was Jewish. He poked fun at Don mercilessly as he sat on his sofa holding forth about how lazy were the then recently arrived West Indian and Asian immigrants. 'They don't like hard work,' Don was complaining, but dad gave him short shrift. 'That's Bloody rich coming from you yer bugger, when did you last do a hard day's work?' And they both fell about laughing. I make no excuses for him; he was an unreconstructed male chauvinist, but he was a loyal friend and despite his foibles he and my father were good pals.

After his two trips to the south-west face of Everest, in 1971 and 1972, on both of which he was a star performer, it was downhill physically. Don was drinking and smoking heavily and although he continued on expeditions to Roraima, Huandoy, Patagonia, Tirich Mir and the Karakoram, his lack of fitness began to mean he was more and more becoming a climbing back number. The journeying also continued, with lecture tours to Australia and South Africa, a trip down the Amazon and to the Red Sea where he took up diving. He became ever more rotund and overweight but still outrageous in his behaviour as Perrin leaves one in no doubt. A famous run-in with the Lancashire Constabulary in 1975, for drunken driving, cost him dearly in the Birthday Honours List and how he avoided a custodial sentence is still a wonder.

Yet he remained the most popular climbers' climber in the country. If you went to a Whillans lecture it was always full of hardcore activists, and his wit and timing were widely appreciated and imitated. He also put something back into our sport, serving a full three years as a BMC vice-president. He was a prisoner of his times however and when I took him to the Leeds University wall to show him the new developments in rock climbing, Don came away shaking his head, 'There's no bleeding adventure on climbing walls,' he remarked. *The Villain* highlights this failure to adapt and change with the times.

Why was Whillans so popular? I guess because he remained what he was, a working-class climber totally without pretension. I was with him once when we met the Duke of Edinburgh at a function in the Mansion House. Don stood there in his flat cap, baggy trousers and desert boots looking just like Andy Capp. The sycophants about us were kowtowing, but when the Duke came over to us Whillans simply said ' Ah doo' which made the old fellow smile, and me too.

Whillans was the outstanding mountaineer of his generation and for almost 20 years a premier division climber. He should have stayed active much longer. If only he had kept himself in shape like, say, Brown or Bonington, he might still be with us, and probably climbing at a reasonable standard. But anyone familiar with the theory of the outsider will know this was just not a possibility. Such people are on a path to self-destruction and like Byron they're mad, bad and at times dangerous to know.

I liked Jim's concluding chapter, the calm after the storm set in the plantation in the Chew Valley where Don did his first climbs. It is poetic and worthy of the man. Climbers a half century from now will struggle with *Grond*, tiptoe up *Slanting Slab*, fight their way up *Goliath* or *Taurus*, arm bar in *Forked Lightning Crack* and fall off the *Cave Wall* at Froggat Edge, a route I was on with him when he made the first ascent. They will think, 'That bloody Don Whillans must have been one hell of a climber'. And so he was. *The Villain* is his story; it does not make for a genteel read, for it is unsettling, but it is a superb piece of work and I recommend all to read it.

Dennis Gray

Broad Peak
Richard Sale
Carreg, 2004, £22.50

First a quotation: 'My heart thumping like mad. But there are the last few rocks, the summit snow slope, just over there…and Marcus and Fritz…They had just finished taking their summit photographs and were on the point of starting down.'

So there we have it, the first ascent of Broad Peak in 1957. Marcus Schmuck and Fritz Wintersteller had reached the summit well ahead of

Kurt Diemberger – he of the thumping heart. Way behind was the fourth member of the Austrian team, Hermann Buhl.

The description comes from Diemberger's 1971 classic *Summits and Secrets* and leaves no doubt about the order of the ascents that day. Yet Richard Sale's contention in *Broad Peak* is that Diemberger has kept tight hold of the detail of the climb and has somehow rendered Schmuck and Wintersteller 'invisible'.

It is true that the two names that spring first to mind in association with Broad Peak are those of Buhl and Diemberger, but this could be explained without the nefariousness ascribed to Diemberger in this piece of relentless revisionism. Diemberger came back from the Karakoram with an attention-grabbing story: Buhl, remember, was already a legend after his gruelling solo ascent of Nanga Parbat. Diemberger had not only accompanied him to the summit of Broad Peak and photographed him there at sunset, but was on the ridge of Chogolisa when Buhl fell with a collapsing cornice to his death. Added to this, Diemberger was the only one of the summiters to have a book covering the ascent published in English. An account by Schmuck, the leader of the expedition, was never translated.

Sale has certainly brought Schmuck and Wintersteller back centre stage and in doing so has underlined the bold, pioneering nature of the Austrian expedition – the ascent of an 8000m peak without the aid of bottled oxygen or porter support high on the mountain. There is also a fascinating insight into the machinations of the Austrian Alpenverein as Schmuck was installed as leader in preference to Buhl, who was resisted by his own Innsbruck section of the Alpenverein as a troublemaker. Schmuck agreed to defer to Buhl's experience on the mountain; however the issue of leadership seems to have remained a running sore.

Sale has drawn on the diaries and testimonies of Schmuck and Wintersteller, who both appeared in rude health at the International Mountain Literature Festival in 2005, and on recently uncovered material by Buhl – reports sent back to his wife and a diary transcript. Buhl's diary has become a real bone of contention between the protagonists. Schmuck wrote in his own diary following Buhl's death: 'Kurt steals Hermann's diaries in which he is described.' Diemberger vehemently denies this, saying he kept them safe and returned the originals to Buhl's widow, Eugenie. In return, he accuses Sale of using the material without Mrs Buhl's permission. So too does Mrs Buhl, who is due to publish the diaries this autumn.

It all seems rather sad when set against the team's achievement. The diarists complain that Diemberger was not pulling his weight in breaking trail, neglected his duties as 'doctor', ordered the liaison officer about like a servant with personal requests, failed when called upon to act in his role as supposed 'ice specialist', revealed an 'increased truculence on the mountain' and attached himself to Buhl as a young acolyte, to Buhl's occasional annoyance. Towards the end of the trip, Schmuck boils over, calling Diemberger a 'lazy bastard' and 'self-centred egomaniac'.

Diemberger is, not surprisingly, exercised about the book, though his reaction to Schmuck's string of abuse was wonderfully laconic: 'What a bouquet of flowers!' The pity of it is that, after years of estrangement, the three old men of Broad Peak had patched things up sufficiently to co-operate on a reconstruction of their Camp II for the 'Call of the Mountains' exhibition in Salzburg five years ago. That fragile truce must be over.

Sale has invested a great deal in this book, not just in time but by paying for its production. But one wonders at his motivation. In 2000 he was ready to publish, with John Cleare, a history of climbing the 8000m peaks, *On Top of the World*. He had an agreement with Diemberger that his pictures could be used on the condition that Diemberger could see what was written about himself, with the offer to correct inaccuracies, but with responsibility for the final text remaining with the author. After page proofs had been checked by Sale, Diemberger contacted the publisher to withdraw permission for the pictures unless changes were made in the text. Pressed for time, the publisher, Collins, made the changes, with Sale remaining unaware until after the book was printed.

Schmuck and Wintersteller, who had allowed their diaries to be used, then wrote to the author to chastise him. Sale has set out to make amends and lift the pair from their unwarranted 'bit part' in the history of Broad Peak, as he sees it, to full acknowledgement as the first ascensionists. He has succeeded. However as the key facts are not actually at issue, the book's eyebrow-raising fascination is as a study in rivalry and resentment.

Stephen Goodwin

When the Alps Cast Their Spell
Mountaineers of the Alpine Golden Age
Trevor Braham
The In Pinn, 2004, pp314, £20

We have had a quite a few new books recently on our Victorian climbing ancestors. The trouble with these overviews is that they often tend towards the facile, regurgitating second-hand preconceptions, with the odd inaccuracy thrown in for good measure. So – what a joy to open Trevor Braham's treasure box of glittering surprises and correct some of my *own* preconceptions.

The first ascent of the Meije, in 1877, was made not by Coolidge, as I had thought, but by Emmanuel Bolleau, whose exploits merit a full chapter here, alongside our more familiar British pioneers, Wills, Tyndall, Stephen, Moore, Whymper and Mummery. Wordsworth and Coleridge, so often trumpeted as the instigators of a new romantic appreciation of mountain scenery, were actually beaten to it, many years earlier, by the Swiss scientist Albrecht von Haller whose poem, *Die Alpen*, extolled the glories of the Alps way back in 1732. And I never knew – or had forgotten – that Leslie

Stephen was the mentor responsible for getting into print Hardy's *Far From the Madding Crowd*. And the ever inconsistent Ruskin, for all his castigation of mountaineers' 'greasy pole' athleticism, was actually a closet adrenaline junky, confessing in a letter from Chamonix that 'if you go through with the danger ... you come out of the encounter a stronger and better man'.

That Ruskin letter is one of countless precious nuggets unearthed in this gloriously discursive book in which Braham celebrates the prodigious energy – physical and intellectual – of those Victorian pioneers. Stephen was a pillar of the literary establishment, who, like Tilman after him, scorned scientific 'adjuncts' to mountaineering. Tyndall, a friend of Faraday and Huxley, struggled to reconcile his scientific agnosticism with the inescapable spiritual sensations inspired by the mountains, writing that 'in the translucent glory of Nature I entirely forgot myself as a man'. Even Whymper, for all his brittle, pedantic egotism, had an insatiable curiosity and knew how to turn out fine prose.

And what about the actual climbing? Well, unlike some of the more pop dabblers in mountaineering history, Braham is a meticulous scholar who knows what he is talking about. His selection is based on a real appreciation of what was significant – Moore's futuristic ascent of the *Old Brenva*, Mummery's radical guideless pioneering, and so on – and he reminds us not only of how young these pioneers were (Bolleau was still only 20 when he climbed the Meije) but also how incredibly skilful. Mummery and his chamois-hunting friend Burgener climbed the Zmutt Ridge, on sight, in just nine hours, without the fixed aids now deemed necessary by the Swiss Alpine Club; his route on Dych Tau, done in eight-and-a-quarter hours, now normally requires an intermediate camp. And as for 25-year-old Whymper's campaign of pass crossings and first ascents in 1865 – who could match that record now?

The publishers have done Braham proud, resisting any editorial temptation to curb his eclecticism. I like, for instance, to be told in passing that Whymper's brother ran the Murree brewery in what is now Pakistan. The photo selection is good, with some spectacular comparisons of the 19th and 20th century Rhône glaciers to refute the flat-earth deniers of global warming. We are treated also to copious notes, an excellent table of first ascents and a proper index. And, in case anyone should think that Braham is merely peddling Golden Age nostalgia, he ends with a personal appraisal of some recent mountaineers who have impressed him. The fact that his choice includes Wilfrid Noyce, Peter Boardman and Pierre Béghin shows that he – and they – know what it is really all about.

Stephen Venables

This Mountain Life
The First Hundred Years of the Rucksack Club
Edited by John Beatty
Northern Light, 2003, pp114, £20

It all began when ramblers in Lancashire expressed regret that ramblers in Yorkshire had stolen a march and organised themselves into a club. The Yorkshire Ramblers was already founded and providing regular escape from the industrial north when two Mancunians, John Entwistle and Arthur Burns, responded to a leader in their local newspaper 'extolling the virtue of being out and about on mountain and moor'. They were keen walkers with a secret ambition to handle a rope and axe, who lamented that west of the Pennines there was no organisation where enthusiasts of the outdoors could fraternise. In 1902, from their initiative, the Rucksack Club was formed.

The first hundred years of the club's distinguished history are celebrated in *This Mountain Life*, a handsomely illustrated portrait, edited by John Beatty, spanning the century during which the Rucksack Club grew from an Edwardian society 'facilitating walking tours and initiating members into the science of rock climbing and snow craft' to its present respected place among the ranks of mountaineers, explorers, long-distance walkers and, as the founders described the membership, 'enthusiasts of like passions'.

Until local clubs were established, the strongest enthusiasm and passion had been directed at the grander mountain ranges and in Manchester a number of eminent mountaineers rallied to support the new club. Harold Dixon, professor of chemistry at Victoria University of Manchester and AC member, celebrated for his climbs in the Canadian Rockies, was the club's first president followed by Joseph Collier, a pioneer among rock climbers, and Charles Pilkington, former AC president and the first climber to prove that the Inaccessible Pinnacle was in fact accessible. Among the first members was J Rooke Corbett, first Englishman to complete the Munros and compiler of the list of Scottish mountains of between 2500 and 2999ft, now known as Corbetts. His other claim to fame was an ability to play several games of chess simultaneously.

The photographs show an exclusively male society, flat-capped and clinker-booted, swarming up the hills and rocks of Lancashire, North Wales and Scotland; in all, rather solemn-looking enthusiasts of like, perhaps narrowly focused, passions. A vote allowing women to become members did succeed by the narrowest of margins but not until 1990. As hill walkers, club members were formidable. Eustace Thomas in 1922 successfully attacked the Lakeland Fell Record, covering 25,500ft of ascent and descent over 66.5 miles within 24 hours. He also became the first British climber to scale all the 4000m peaks in the Alps. Other records fell to the redoubtable boots of Rucksack members.

On British crags club members were among those now recognised as being part of the forefront of British rock climbing, and here they are, pictured with their baggy breeches, Woolworth plimsolls and coils of hemp rope on fearsomely unprotected routes. As a new age dawns, the picture improves, members are seen well geared up and actually smiling as the club tigers take off to the distant summits of Nepal, the Hindu Kush, East Greenland and the scorched flanks of Yosemite.

But this is essentially the story of a club with great camaraderie dedicated to the simple end of enjoying mountains, wherever there are long paths to be trodden, rock to be climbed or rucksacks to be worn. Founding member John Entwistle, he of the resoundingly northern name, set an admirable example at the age of 82 by walking from Land's End to Manchester in time for the bowling season, later completing the ramble from John O'Groats to Manchester. A true Rucksacker.

Ronnie Faux

Between a Rock and a Hard Place
Aron Ralston
Simon and Schuster UK Ltd, 2004, pp354, £14.99

Mention of the name Aron Ralston will, I suspect, produce blank expressions on most faces. However, if I start talking about spring 2003 and a young American who amputates his own arm after becoming trapped by a boulder in a remote Utah canyon, there will probably be a good many ringing bells. At the time, the incident received huge global media attention and after all the hard-sell a book seemed inevitable. Would it be full of American hype? Would it be ghost written? Would it manage to convey anything like the real story? Was there even enough material to warrant a 350-page book?

By the time I reached page 23 the incident had already taken place. By the time I was half-way through the third chapter nearly all my questions had been answered. Despite his modest age of 28, Ralston is a remarkably articulate and perceptive writer. *Between a Rock and a Hard Place* is fast becoming an American Best Seller.

The story, for those not aware of it, is in essence quite simple. Ralston takes off from work in Aspen for a long weekend of solo mountain biking and canyoneering. He has no real fixed plans and therefore tells no one of his potential destinations. Driving his truck deep into remote Canyonlands National Park, he bikes a considerable distance to the head of Blue John Canyon, spends a night out and the following morning begins a descent of this narrow gorge 10 or more miles north towards his truck. Several hours later, while attempting to lower himself over a small drop in a narrow slot, the chockstone from which he is hanging cuts loose, slides down the constriction and pins his right hand against the canyon wall.

The whole incident, his eventual escape, and the simultaneous detective work by family, friends and the SAR team to discover his location, are fluently interwoven with the story of his youth and incidents from his relatively short but exciting mountaineering, skiing and adventuring career. OK, there is a section in the middle that is somewhat longwinded but thereafter it is gripping stuff.

This certainly isn't a book for the squeamish. Deciding at an early stage he would have to drink his own urine to survive, then subsequently try unsuccessfully to saw through his wrist with the ineffective blade of a Leatherman, will make even the most macho wince. Ralston confesses to a certain faith and feels it was divine intervention that led him to solve the problem of amputating his hand at the exact time that he did. Any earlier and he most likely would have bled to death before he got out of the canyon; any later and he probably wouldn't have had the strength to continue.

Two years on and he is climbing again (the front cover shows the ice axe prosthetic he uses on both rock and snow). He is training to be an American Mountain Guide and has just become the first to solo all the Colorado 14,000' peaks in winter. The book appears to be an inspiration to many American people, although the majority of Ralston's audience are more impressed by how he first gave up a promising engineering career with Intel, simply to go climbing: the '70s drop-out culture has long disappeared from the American technology industry, if indeed it was ever really present.

Although not on a par with *Touching the Void*, this is a remarkable story well told. I suspect it is not the last book we will see from this author.

Lindsay Griffin

Alpine Points of View
Kev Reynolds
Cicerone Press, 2004, pp237, £22

When Geoff Templeman asked me to review this book, the fact that (much to my surprise) Kev had dedicated it to me was not accepted as a reason for refusing. I'm bound to say that it's an excellent book: my praise is heart-felt and, believe it or not, entirely objective.

The book, 'a collection of images of the Alps', is a selection of one hundred splendid photographs, accompanied by appropriate comments, covering the Alps 'from end to end', from the Maritime Alps to the Julians. It presents an evocation of the Alps in all their aspects – peaks, valleys, glaciers, snow, ice and rock, mountain paths, villages, flowers, people and animals. (Kev will forgive me if I reveal that, among the people providing attractive foregrounds, I discern his wife Min, a steadfast companion and support on many of his alpine wanderings over nearly 40 years.) The book is a worthy companion volume to Kev's *Walking in the Alps*, reviewed in *AJ104*, 313, 1999.

According to the blurb, 'for some these views will reawaken old memories, for others they will inspire new dreams and ambitions'. For me they do both at once, even though in my case the dreams may have to remain dreams (one lifetime is just too short).

Kev Reynolds is a worthy successor to earlier great celebrants of the alpine scene such as Julius Kugy and Janet Adam Smith, and I am glad to see their classic books included in the list of recommended reading. But in addition to poetic evocations, his book gives practical advice on matters such as photography, and two points stressed by Kev seem to me particularly important. Firstly, he is no *Gipfelstürmer* who wants to look at the Alps only from the tops, nor (like John Ruskin) does he confine himself to peering up from the valleys. He believes in the mid-mountain vantage point, somewhere between valley bed and lofty summit, where you can 'look up and down in a single glance and absorb the best of both worlds' – what he calls 'alps upon the Alps'. And, secondly, he emphasises that, in the Alps which are considered by many to be nowadays overcrowded, spoiled and practically ruined, it is still perfectly possible to wander at length in solitude in regions that remain peaceful, undefiled and as delightful as ever. Of course he is wise enough to let readers discover these secret pleasures for themselves, but for those able to take a hint there is plenty of material in this wonderful book to stimulate their dreams and shape their plans for many years to come.

Ernst Sondheimer

The Joy of Climbing
Terry Gifford
Whittles Publishing, 2004, 174pp, £19.95

Terry Gifford would be a happy man indeed if this book sold half as well as the manual from which its playful title is derived – *The Joy of Sex*. It is intended as an antidote to the angst and morbidity school of mountain writing.

As if in homage to that earlier, and celebrated 'Joy of...' title, Gifford has liberally illustrated his book with rippling torsos, often his own. The cover photo sets the tone: Terry well-hung with a jangling rack that appears to be all he is wearing bar rock shoes and helmet as he laybacks some soaring sea cliff. Actually there are shorts hidden beneath that rack, though, like the helmet, they are of a certain vintage. How our holiday snaps give us away.

If this seems too much a case of judging a book by its cover, I call in aid Gifford's rhetorical question: 'Can the edges define the core experience?' He believes so. 'Some of the greatest fun has been going out climbing knowing the edges are going to be interesting.' And so he writes about the orchids, the peregrines, the jokes and the blisters. And ever the rock, the wine and the people; in Scotland, the Lakes, Wales, his adopted Peak, Europe and the USA. It is quite a pot-pourri.

The pieces about people, profiles of sorts, are among the most interesting – the author Anne Sauvy, Allen Steck, Gordon Stainforth, and the late William Heaton Cooper. The book is a compilation of Gifford's articles for magazines and journals over many years, but neither the organ nor the date of original publication is given. This could be irritating or intriguing.

Heaton Cooper died almost a decade ago and I guess this interview with the artist, still in fairly energetic old age, must be 15 years old. Yet some things are timeless. Heaton Cooper is ruminating on the imperative of climbers (in his day) not to attempt a route they were incapable of reversing. Then he observes: 'I think the art of climbing down is needed now, don't you, in world leaders for example?' Ah, there is wisdom at the edges of this book as well as joy, and, as you would expect from Terry, several piquant poems.

Stephen Goodwin

The Central Buttress of Scafell
edited by Graham Wilson
Millrace, 2004, pp184, £13.95

'What we really lack is the possibility of new ascents. They are all exhausted, and I think you must admit as much!'

'Not at all,' immediately returned the Old Stager. 'Have any of you noticed a bayonet-shaped crack descending from the skyline about midway between Moss Ghyll and Botterill's Slab on Scawfell? No? Has it never occurred to you that between these two climbs there is a stretch of nearly two hundred feet of unscaled rock?'

Thus in 1907 did Ashley Abraham imagine a conversation in 'An Hour in the Smoke Room at Wasdale'. Of course, he was playing the part of the Old Stager himself in writing this provocation in the *FRCC Journal*. In his story three parties rush up to the crack in the morning. 'After spending four futile hours thereabouts, they hastened down to Wasdale, intent upon slaying the Old Stager.' Twas ever thus. This little book charts the history of 'a project' in the words of the participants who produced ten articles between 1907 and Mabel Barker's reversing the climb with Jack Carswell in 1936. That project has come to be known simply by two letters: CB. There is a rich heritage of writing here that, when brought together, reveals a community sharing the gradual solving of entertaining problems in all its competitive detail. Graham Wilson adds provocative speculation in his linking commentary and concludes with a 2004 account by a young woman of the easiest ascent now possible (E1 5b) up the wall of the flake since the chockstone took a life in its flight from the crack in 1994.

In this small format, fine press, inspired book Abraham, Botterill, Herford, Sansom, Holland, Frankland, Beetham and Barker demonstrate what ought also to be true today: how questions of style, imagination and personality are resolved into the changing meaning of a climb and its reputation. Such historically appreciative initiatives as this little book deserve our support, which will be repaid by the entertaining interplay of writers teasing their peers in the manner of Ashley Abraham.

Terry Gifford

Millican Dalton: A Search for Romance and Freedom
Matthew Entwistle
Mountainmere Research,
69 Harwood Road, Rishton, Blackburn, Lancashire BB1 4DH

Millican Dalton, the self-styled Professor of Adventure, ranked as an extraordinary and eccentric character in a sport that produces its fair share of likely candidates. This biography by Matthew Entwistle is an affectionate tribute to the Borrowdale caveman and climbing guru who rejected convention and a stifling career as a fire insurance clerk and chose instead an al fresco life 'in search of romance and freedom'. Perhaps in an era of commercialised adventure, when 'opting out' for a year is a normal part of student progress, Millican Dalton was ahead of his time. His cave 'hotel' near the summit of Castle Crag in the Jaws of Borrowdale, where he spent many summer months, remains to this day a place of quiet interest for anyone intrigued by the Millican Dalton story.

Born in Nenthead in 1867 and brought up and educated in the Quaker tradition, Dalton was an able pupil with a strong streak of adventurous spirit and willingness to challenge convention, treating his life as 'a chemical experiment'. At the age of 35 the experiment became critical. His philosophy was so determinedly set along lines of pacifism and left wing socialism and his love of the outdoors was so great that he gave up an easy life in the City to become a true professor of adventure, 'free as the buzzard mewing by day or the owl hooting by night'.

He was among the early enthusiasts for rock climbing in the Lake District and a commercial guide long before there was any formal organisation. Although he showed little interest in being listed among the first to climb new routes in Borrowdale, it seems probable that a number of the more obvious lines were quietly pioneered by Dalton. He was regarded as a steady and safe pair of hands – even though publicity photographs of him peering unbelayed over the edge of a cliff, a loose coil of rope in one hand, might suggest otherwise.

A tall, goatee-bearded figure, Dalton moved with long strides among the hills and lived a Spartan existence. His appearance became his trade mark: rough, home-made clothes, clinker soled leather boots worn without socks and a Tyrolean hat sporting a feather held in place by what looked like a large ruby but which on close inspection proved to be no more than a red reflector from his bicycle. He, rather than Baden-Powell, is credited with introducing short trousers as a functional article of clothing and he was an ingenious designer of equipment useful for camping and the general outdoors. He would improvise, using anything he could find on the basis that one man's rubbish was another man's treasure.

Dalton never drank alcohol having signed the Band of Hope pledge at an early age, although he did smoke Woodbine cigarettes incessantly. His diet was simple, oats roasted in a pan and made with syrup into porridge. Wholemeal bread, which he baked himself, was washed down with strong coffee. Fruit and herbs that grew naturally in Borrowdale rounded off an austere but healthy diet prepared over an open fire, a Woodbine clasped between his toes to prevent ash falling into his food.

Dalton divided his time between Borrowdale and Epping Forest where he had a similarly outdoors lifestyle but closer to his family, whose address he used for his 'business'. He climbed with clients in the Lake District, Scotland and the Alps and was generally regarded as a man of very firm opinions, who could be argumentative though delightful, unselfish and intelligent company. He disliked crowds but there was nothing of the reclusive hermit in his nature. He mixed as easily with gypsies and vagabonds as with the well-educated fringes of intellectual society.

Although this account offers little evidence that Dalton had much interest in romance he was no misogynist and was at ease in female company. He dismissed Victorian protocol by organising mixed-sex expeditions and though occasionally pursued he remained a bachelor. Dalton introduced the redoubtable Mabel Barker to mountaineering. She was university educated, unconventional, one of 25 spirited young women from Essex known as the Walden Gypsies. She became the most accomplished rock climber of her generation and regarded Dalton as something of a Robinson Crusoe rather than a romantic hero, greatly impressed that the seat of his shorts had sewn into them a large patch of Willesden canvas to keep his rear end dry whilst seated. According to this account, there was about him a whiff of wood smoke and tobacco mingled with body odours that made standing up-wind a more congenial position.

Dalton's friendship with Mabel Barker lasted many years as he introduced probably thousands of newcomers to the notion of real adventure; rock climbing, rapid shooting and raft sailing – 'nature first hand and not merely in books' under the safe leadership of Millican Dalton otherwise known as Robinson Crusoe, Buffalo Bill, Peter Pan, Sinbad the Sailor, and the Wizard of the North.

Dalton retired as a mountain guide at the age of 75 and moved to High Heavens Camp in the Chiltern Hills as his winter quarters. His home was a wooden shed, which in 1947 burned down. Undaunted, Dalton moved into a tent that was poor protection for a 79-year-old against the historically severe weather that winter. He fell ill and died in hospital at Marlow after a life that well deserves this excellent tribute.

Ronnie Faux

With Friends in High Places
An anatomy of those who take to the hills
Malcolm Slesser
Mainstream, 2004, pp256, £15.99

I spotted the evocatively titled *With Friends in High Places* on the shelves of a local shop. Malcolm Slesser and I had both been members of the British North Greenland Expedition 1952-54. Near enough the same age as him, I guessed, not wholly correctly, that his book would recount the highlights of 60 years of mountain activity. I could hardly wait to read it and was about to buy a copy and share it with Mike Banks, another Greenland 'old hand', when the invitation came to review it.

After I had rushed through the first few chapters my first reaction was disappointment – over the inadequacy of the maps! I was aware that Slesser had done a lot in the Staunings Alps in East Greenland and, like him, I had seen this magnificent area from the air. I was keen to know more about his travels there, but the map was useless and without a magnifying glass it was impossible to decipher a single name. It was not until I had found, in *AJ* 1961-62, the map accompanying the account of John Hunt's expedition that I was able to appreciate the significant part that Slesser played in early explorations, namely: the exploration and ascent of some of the peaks surrounding the Bersaerker Braie, the first crossing of the southern Staunings from Alpefjord to the Schuichert valley and southward to Sud Kap on the shore of Scoresby Sound, the first crossing of Col Major from Gully Gletscher to the Bersaerker Brae and, as a member of John Hunt's expedition, the traverse of the Hjornespids from Col Major with Ian McNaught-Davis.

Reverting to an earlier chapter on the British North Greenland Expedition, the map to illustrate Slesser's arduous journey, from Queen Louise Land to Kap Rink and back in the dark after the sun had set for the winter, is inadequate. Also, there are a number of factual errors relating to this expedition. For instance, on page 43, it was in 1950, not 1949, that Jim Simpson first saw Queen Louise Land; on page 44, Sunderland flying boats did not land on Britannia Lake until the main expedition in 1952; on page 151, Buck Taylor was not an Army telegraphist but a naval Petty Officer. Also on page 62, James Wordie was not a member of Bruce's expedition but of Shackleton's *Endurance* expedition of 1914-1916. On page 157, a southerly blizzard becomes, four lines later, a northerly gale. These errors do not really affect the enjoyment of the reader and I mention them simply to make the point that the book is not history. Indeed, in his Introduction Slesser writes, 'It [the book] is not the story of my life as a mountain explorer, but of discovery with friends in high places.' And, I suspect, this discovery was not just of glaciers, peaks and passes but, amongst other things, of the truth that 'safety is awareness', a theme which runs through the book.

Slesser comes nearest to overstepping his own safety limits in a boat journey down the Greenland coast to reach a mountain described in a chapter with the apt title 'Pushing the Boat Out'. I imagine that most climbers would agree that, regardless of technical difficulty, they always want to be in control. Danger sets in when control is lost and they rely solely on good fortune. Taking a small boat down an inhospitable coast at the mercy of drifting pack ice seems to me to be perilously close to relying on good fortune – but oh for a map so that the reader can gain a better appreciation of the journey!

Despite these criticisms, the book is a good read. It reminded me of people and events now half-forgotten. Slesser expresses frank views about his companions, which may not be to everyone's taste though I have to admit I found the chapter 'The Tigers of Yesterday' most interesting. He also gives further accounts of high action, particularly in the ascent of the Peak of Communism, 24,584ft. I marvel at the perseverance and will-power that enabled his party, weak through insufficient food and upset stomachs, to carry their own loads and eventually to reach the top, especially when any pleasure must have been left behind at one of the lower camps.

The final chapters on skiing rough, expedition food, green issues and Crowberry Gully years later, are gentler, but no less enjoyable for that, as Slesser recounts and discusses some of the knowledge and wisdom accumulated from the mountain exeriences of a lifetime.

Richard Brooke

Oil, Sand and Politics.
Memoirs of a Middle East Doctor Mercenary and Mountaineer

Philip Horniblow
Hayloft Publishing Ltd, 2004, pp302, £25.00

The author is a regular attender of the Himalayan Club's annual dinner in London and a friend from several Himalayan expeditions but his book also reveals a completely different life of Buchanesque adventures from his days as a doctor in the Middle East. He alternates tales of intrigue in the Gulf States with periods of leave on expeditions to the mountains which will be of particular interest to readers of the *Alpine Journal.*

In 1959 Horniblow was recruited as expedition doctor on an army expedition to the Karakoram led by Tony Streather, near Haramosh, the site of the Oxford University tragedy two years before. He gives a frank account of personal relationships between the team members, which complements the *AJ* account rather well. Several 20,000ft peaks were climbed and it was a rather good show. Three years later he was back with another service team, this time going for Khinyang Chish with Jimmy Mills in charge. He was to witness the avalanche that took Mills and Dick Jones off the long ridge to their deaths. It is a poignant tale told plainly; the Army Mountaineering Association did not mount another Himalayan expedition until Tirich Mir in 1969. On that climb we used some of the equipment that came back from Khinyang Chish.

A few years later he went to the Simien mountains of Ethiopia for a month with the John Hunt Exploration Group. In the company of Tony Streather he went on to discover some ancient Christian churches hewed in the rock; and supervised the casualty evacuation of Joe Brown who had put his back out teaching some youngsters rock climbing.

The final expeditions he writes about, I was on too. He has some hilarious tales of life on the Army Everest Expedition 1976 that were not in the official report. He and Ronnie Faux from *The Times* were a breath of fresh air and gave us all a lift – not least by carrying loads through the icefall day after day. The contribution every member made comes through, which is not always the case in more heroic accounts. Brummie Stokes and Bronco Lane, who reached the top but suffered from snow blindness and frostbite leading to amputations, have Philip to thank for their treatment.

The final expedition he joined as Medical Officer was in 1978 with a team of Sappers to Trisul II in Garhwal. He writes that this expedition was a happy one. At the close Philip and three of the team took a diversion over the Ronti Saddle in the footsteps of Eric Shipton into the Rishi Ganga with the special aim of viewing Nanda Devi. They were delighted when they were successful; the photos were shown at the AC later in the year when the author lectured there.

There are 13 maps hand drawn by the author and 33 photos printed amongst the text. On several pages some lines of text have disappeared off the bottom of a page, sometimes popping up later in some other place which spoils an otherwise well turned out book.

Henry Day

The Alps of Tibet
Tamotsu Nakamura
Yamakei Publishers Co. Tokyo, 2005, 384pp

The many admirers of Tamotsu Nakamura's photographs from the borderlands of eastern Tibet and China are advised to take a look at this beautifully produced book – which I hope is in the AC library. I say 'take a look' because reading will be more difficult, except for members familiar with Japanese. Thankfully the all-important photo captions are in English as well as Japanese, and hopefully one day there will be a text in English too. Tamotsu's photographs of mountains, monasteries and people are superb and an inspiration to explore, particularly those peaks which he usefully marks as 'unclimbed'.

Stephen Goodwin

The Silent Traveller in Lakeland
Chiang Lee
With forward by Da Zhang
Mercat Press, 2004, pp82, £9.99
(first published in 1937 as *The Silent Traveller*)

As Herbert Read says in his preface, it is disconcerting when a Chinese artist turns his attention to a subject we know as ours, rather than a Chinese subject. It brings home that it is the vision and sensibility that counts, rather than the landscape; the ostensible subject. In this book we see that Chiang Lee's repertoire of marks is ready to deal with any subject including our beloved Lake District, and in this welcome re-publication of the original 1937 edition the illustrations are all there, but not quite as well reproduced, and not dispersed throughout the text as in the original.

On the plus side, however, there is a new and informative foreword by Da Zheng which is a useful addition, explaining just who Chiang was. Born in 1903 in Jiangxi Province at the foot of Mt. Lu, he trained as a chemist, served as a soldier as part of the Chinese Northern Expedition to fight the warlords, and following that was a magistrate, before leaving for England to study politics at the University of London in 1933.

After three years, weary of London, he went on a trip to North Wales, but he travelled as part of a group, thus being forced into conversation, which he did not like. The next year he decided to try the Lakes. It was not a warm welcome; he alighted from the train at Seascale at 8pm on a rainy August evening and had to somehow hire a car to drive to Wasdale Head where he was to lodge at Bowderdale Farm. His 'landlady' there, who was not expecting him that day, was the formidable Mrs Naylor, the mother of Joss the fell-runner.

Chiang spends the next few days wandering around Wasdale, where he paints the Screes, and the rain and mist, and he meets a keen fell-walker whom he asks permission to accompany up Scafell. Still in ordinary town clothes, Chiang gets a third of the way up and is content. He has a near-visionary experience on the way down, looking over the lake at the clearing mist. This prompts him to talk about the Chinese phrase *ling lueh*, which he says is a good one for expressing one's reaction if one is trying to analyse one's enjoyment of nature. *Ling* means to perceive or to receive an impression, and *Lueh* means a sketch. These two words together have the arbitrary meaning 'to accept into the understanding'.

The last time I was at Wasdale I tried to imagine how it all looked to Chiang. In the paintings he seems to use generic mountains and lakes from his stock of stereotypes, and it is only when reading the caption that one knows the topography. The small green fields with high walls did begin to look like paddy fields, from some angles.

After three days he decides to go to Keswick. He walks over Sty Head Pass to Borrowdale, aware of the surprised looks of walkers he encounters, admires Taylor Ghyll Force on the other side and catches the bus to Keswick, where, following some people, he comes across Friar's Crag. He returns there several times, making a painting of the whole panorama which has some sharply observed and recognisable mountain profiles.

All the time he thinks about the news of the Spanish Civil War which has just started, and of the Sino-Japanese War, because his homeland has been invaded and his family have had to flee from the Japanese. He says that he tries to paint the nature in his mind, not the nature in nature, not an exact resemblance.

In Keswick he meets another Chinaman in the street and has the first real conversation of his trip. They wander around together, causing a stir at the boat-landing by rowing out into the lake the 'wrong' way round, but Chiang prefers it that way as he can see where he is going. They are shocked at the profusion of 'private' signs on pieces of land. In China he says everyone has free access to scenery. He is very impressed with Lodore Falls and goes there twice, doing a painting of it which, disappointingly, is not reproduced.

After a coach trip (in the rain) to Bowness, he stays a night in Ambleside and walks to Grasmere, where he visits Dove Cottage and is deeply sceptical of the tourist's impression of Wordsworth, though an admirer himself. He quotes De Quincey's words that: 'Wordsworth came to his love of nature through physical activity in the fells, angling, snaring, swimming, hunting, so the growth of his thoughts combined with his eye and ear.' Chiang himself prefers to read the writings and look at the surroundings, which he constantly compares to commonplace scenes in the Yangtze Valley, though he misses China's dykes, bridges, and ornamental pavilions.

The original book had Chiang's poems in Chinese script on the same page as the pictures; this points up how closely related script and image are compared to the Western equivalent. A traditional painter in China is trained to use and memorize hundreds of slightly different inflexions of the brush which give subtly variant takes on whatever is being depicted. It is like learning an alphabet and then the words of a language. They pre-exist to a certain extent in a unitary form and it is a matter of selecting the right stroke at the appropriate time for whatever is being dealt with. There is an attitude that expects maximum integrity and visibility to the constitutive strokes of the brush, being the work of the brush in 'real time' and an extension of the painter's own body.

Chinese painting's value is in its 'facture', and touch, the marks of the brush-in-hand. The aim is not to do something particularly original or new but to follow the appropriate path that brings out the subjective mood of the painter towards the scene itself, not imposing a stringent law on representation. As Chinese painting became more sophisticated the view of it changed from a picture of something else to being an object for aesthetic contemplation in itself.

This attitude is now familiar to us in the West but like a lot of things it happened earlier in China. Rocks, mountain-peaks, streams, and waterfalls everywhere have a common character, a melancholy strangeness, and this is brought to a supreme level in Fan K'uan's painting *Travellers among Streams and Mountains* painted around 1000 AD. I think there is something evocative and rather timely about the centuries-old Chinese concern with depicting 'mountains and rivers without end'.

This is a delightfully written book, in which I rate the writing higher than the paintings. But the paintings do show what could be done with the familiar Lake District landscape by means of a certain shift of perception and way of working; a lesson that I am learning from Chinese painting myself.

Julian Cooper

Taking Leave
Roger Hubank
The Ernest Press, 2004, pp269, £10

The prescience of the Larkin lines which preface the first chapter of *Taking Leave* will be wryly acknowledged by all those in the autumn of their lives:

> It is too late to start
> For destinations not of the heart.

Anthony Hardwick, eminent university lecturer in English literature, is weary of the 'cleverness' which has built him his reputation and imprisoned him in his unfulfilling job. He flees to the open skies of a Derbyshire moor, deserting his job and his stricken marriage to starve the sour cynicism which has so firmly and finally closed the door to self-realisation.

The lyrical evocations of place urge on the reader a sense of a living presence, akin to the omnipresent landscape in the work of Thomas Hardy and, by turn, crushing and reviving those who live in its environs:

> Under that sloping light the dark moor resembled a hazy upland desert:
> a baked,brown waste of shadowy folds and glowing copper hollows.

This entity then, is both benign and malevolent: just as it begins to heal Hardwick's wounds it annihilates those who wander in it unprepared or unaware, whether friend or foe, native or stranger.

The Ashe family, local farmers with whom Hardwick strikes up a shy aquaintance, are victims of this sometimes brutal duality. They have farmed for generations, developing an intimacy with the land which Hardwick envies but are also at its mercy, unprotected despite their arcane knowledge. Sheep are lost in huge and crippling numbers in severe winters and the modern plague of foot and mouth disease trails financial ruin and incarceration in the sterility of town life in its vicious wake. The family's feral child, Tommy, inheritor of his grandfather's primal and instinctive empathy with the land, is claimed by a brutal storm as he runs desperately from the trials of his new existence: a telling dichotomy.

All is not entirely lost – the Ashe family may have taken enforced leave but Hubank, winner of the Boardman Tasker Award with *Hazard's Way* (2001), allows a continuity built on necessity and respect for the land. The farm survives under a new stewardship – altered, but with the capacity to renew the acquaintance with the natural energies which sustain the rural community.

And so Hardwick is not alone in taking leave, though his flight is chosen, not forced – as it is for the Ashe family. His wife Elizabeth has also slipped from the maelstrom of suffering inflicted by the hammer-blows of her repeated miscarriages and the couple's eventual childlessness. She envelops herself in her work – ironically in the field of psychotherapy – freezing the memories of the foetal deaths until they have iced over her ability to resume the perilous task of living again with her estranged husband.

Hubank gives us hope: the Hardwicks' marriage takes its first tentative steps towards revival; the past provides illumination as well as despair and the human spirit survives despite the griefs and bereavements: in the words of St. Augustine: 'a dim glimmering of light yet un-put-out in men.'

Val Randall

Prealpi Bresciane
Fausto Camerini
CAI-TCI 2004 463pp 36.50 Euros

The last in the CAI guides co-ordinated by our late member Gino Buscaini, the Bresciane is the area west of Lake Garda, between Brescia and Trento. Here the mountains are more for the summer and winter walker, and never too far from a road. They will also be unknown to the huge number of climbers who annually flock to the World famous crags of Arco in the valley below. However, hidden up in the hills are some impressive limestone faces such as the Cima Capi, where there are routes up to 750m in height, giving nearly 1000m of climbing up to UIAA VIII–. Under winter conditions the 2064m Dosso Alto has couloirs up to TD– in standard.

Lindsay Griffin

Life and Limb
Jamie Andrew
Portrait, 2003, 306pp, £17.99

A Test of Will
Warren Macdonald
Greystone Books, 2004, 198pp, $14.95 US

Climbing for Seasoned Gentlefolk
Norman Croucher
St Ives Painting and Publishing Co, 2004, 84pp £9

You can't keep good men down; like the Black Knight in *Monty Python and the Holy Grail*, loss of limbs is no deterrent. Reading these books – three further examples of the triumph of the human spirit – inspires us all to get up and do what we all know our bodies can still do if the effort is made. These stories are especially instructive for those of us who, like me, have worn out our knees and had them replaced with steel and plastic. There's no excuse for getting maudlin. Check out *Life and Limb* and the photo of author Jamie Andrew on page 210 climbing *Christmas Curry* without hands or feet. However does he do it?

Jamie is very much the regular, committed mountaineer in the early part of this book, conveying with conviction all the ups and downs, fear and excitement of alpine climbing. All committed alpinists will readily identify with the preparations for his climb on Les Droites north face with Jamie Fisher: the 'electric charge of apprehension was building inside me…I suffered it before every major route…until the moment I first swung my ice axe…then the electricity would discharge and all that nervous energy would flow out and drive me up the mountain.'

The pair achieve their climb, finishing in bad weather that only gets worse, turning into a major, prolonged and fearfully cold storm. The book grips your emotions as Jamie tells of their remorseless deterioration and the eventual death of his companion. It is told with a powerful honesty, the slow awakening in hospital to the awful nature of his injuries and an agonised self-questioning – did they make basic mistakes, why did he survive and not the other Jamie? I recognised this; it was just how I felt when Nick Estcourt was avalanched on K2. Why the hell hadn't I gone down with him? It was the only time I have ever had a rope break.

There is a parallel here with Warren Macdonald's story – Warren had both legs amputated after having them trapped beneath a giant boulder – in that both men come to accept that what happened to them was, in effect, an act of nature. As Warren says: 'I was simply in the wrong place at the wrong time.' I don't know why it is important, but it is interesting that both needed to feel that for their own peace of mind.

Warren, an activist in the environmental movement in Australia, was out scrambling on Mount Bowen on Hinchinbrook Island off the North Queensland coast. He and his friend were exploring a streambed, Warren wanted a pee, and, being an environmentalist, starting scrambling away from the watercourse. That's when the boulder slipped, trapping him across the thighs.

Another parallel in Jamie and Warren's stories is the emotional first meetings with friends and family and the support and love as they rebuild their lives – Jamie with Anna, his girlfriend at the time of the accident, and Warren with Margot, whom he meets at a party in Banff. Jamie's first visits in the Chamonix hospital from Stu' Fisher (Jamie Fisher's father) and Anna are perhaps the most moving episodes in *Life and Limb*. The equivalent in *A Test of Will* is the concern and care of Warren's father, wheeling his son out of the ward. 'It must be 30 years since he pushed me like this in a stroller,' says Warren.

Like Jamie, Warren continued his life in the outdoors and in 2003 reached the summit of Kilimanjaro. Both men are an inspiration, and there are others of course; I think of Norman Croucher, David Lim, John Hawkridge and Paul Pritchard. Our hearts go out to them. And you know you just don't want to go through what they've gone through. Whilst they are not pushing at the frontiers of mountaineering, Jamie, Warren and Norman (who climbed Cho Oyu on his tin legs) are our equivalent of para-Olympians, pushing at mental barriers, their courage revealing the extraordinary capacity of the human spirit. *Climbing for Seasoned Gentlefolk* is a kind of 'how to do it' book for the elderly, halt and lame. In all Norman's writing his impish sense of humour shines through, such as his observation that there are now 475 climbing walls in Britain, then adding: 'As I said in 1973, "They won't catch on".'

These three books deserve to be read widely, inspire us all and earn their authors a lot of money. However, I have in mind a comment by Arthur Lees from Bristol who, though severely handicapped by cerebral palsy, walked all the way to Makalu base camp. Paralysed down one side, he arrived late every night. We were sitting round the fire discussing other disabled climbers when I mention how well Norman Croucher had done, achieving many good routes on his tin legs. Arthur agreed, then added: 'Aye, but he's gone commercial, writing and lecturing about it.' Whatever our infirmities, we're all the same with our prejudices and ethical dichotomies.

Doug Scott

Emilius - Rosa dei Banchi
Giulio Berutto and Lino Forelli
CAI-TCI 2005 415pp 36.50 Euros

The area of wild mountains south-east of Aosta and east of the Gran Paradiso National Park Boundary provide little technical Alpine climbing but no shortage of interesting walking, scrambling and ski-mountaineering. Most well-known is Mt Emilius, a 3559m magnificent rocky pyramid that dominates the town of Aosta and famous for its truly splendid panorama of the Alps from Mt Blanc to Monte Rosa (and on a clear day the Maritime Alps). The rock is generally poor but there are some big faces that would provide mixed climbing under the right conditions. However, to date there has been little development of winter climbing. Several classic ridge scrambles have recently been equipped and the area is well-served by a series of rifugios and bivouac huts.

Lindsay Griffin

Nanda Devi: A Journey to the Last Sanctuary
Hugh Thomson
Weidenfeld & Nicolson, 2004, ppxviii+126, £18.99

The story of Shipton's and Tilman's expedition through the Rishi Ganges gorge and their attainment of the Inner Sanctuary of Nanda Devi in 1934 is well known; as is the subsequent first ascent of the mountain two years later by Tilman and Noel Odell, in a team which included Charles Houston and T Graham Brown. A number of successful ascents followed, by the French, Indians, Japanese and Americans, but which also included some shady 'goings-on' in which nuclear-powered spying devices were apparently placed near the top of Nanda Devi and Nanda Kot. It was surely no coincidence that when these were publicised in 1978, the Sanctuary was closed shortly afterwards by the Indian Government, although the reason given was environmental.

The Sanctuary has remained almost inviolate but, in 2000, permission was given for a party led by 'Bull' Kumar and John Shipton to go throught the Gorge and into the Sanctuary with the aim of producing a report on the feasibility of its reopening. This book is a report on the trek through the gorge and back, but it is made very readable by the author's easy style and by the fact that it is also a history of the mountain, together with character studies of many of the members of the party which included Ian McNaught-Davis, George Band and Steve Berry. The photographs, both historical and of the trek itself, are excellent and the author finishes by saying:

Ian McNaught-Davis produced a report for the International Mountaineering and Climbing Federation, recommending that the Sanctuary be opened under strict controls for a few limited expeditions. A small official Indian team visited it in 2001 on behalf of the Indian Mountaineering Federation, and reported likewise. At the time of writing, the Sanctuary is still closed and the Indian Government shows no desire to open it. Personally I am only too happy if it remains closed. But then I've been there.

Geoffrey Templeman

Casimiro Ferrari
L'ultimo Re della Patagonia
Alberto Benini
Baldini Castoldi Dalai 2004 220pp

This is the long awaited biography of a legendary Italian climber, the most prolific Patagonia activist of all time and perhaps most famous for being the first to stand on the summit of Cerro Torre. Ferrari's determination was renowned, as was his difficult personality and complete inability to get on with most of his climbing partners. He was diagnosed with stomach cancer in 1983 and given between three and six months to live. Instead he went to the Patagonian ice cap, chain-smoked his way through weeks of bad weather while sat in an ice cave below Cerro Murallon, before finally making a very bold first ascent via a technical line. This is a book that surely should be translated to English but in the meantime can be ordered at www.ibs.it

Lindsay Griffin

In the Ghost Country. A Lifetime Spent on the Edge
Peter Hillary and John E Elder
Mainstream, 2004, pp (8)+344, £15.99

This book recounts Peter Hillary's three-month-long expedition skiing across Antarctica to the South Pole with two companions – companions with whom he became increasingly disenchanted, ending in an acrimonious dispute which continued after the expedition had finished. Partly because of this, Hillary found himself alone with his own thoughts for much of the journey, and the book therefore turns into more of an autobiography, as he recalls family life, travels with his father, the death of his mother and sister, two ascents of Everest, K2, the North Pole and other travels. The basic narrative is written by the Australian journalist John Elder, interpersed throughout by the personal thoughts of Peter Hillary.

Federation, Australia's Adventure Peak
Kevin Doran
Desdichado Publishing, 2004, pp128, $15.00

Our member Dr Kevin Doran emigrated with his family to Tasmania over 30 years ago. In his early years he had been introduced to climbing whilst in the Scouts, and then continued in the London Hospital Ski and Mountaineering Club, walking and climbing all over Britain, before spending three years in the Navy. After emigrating, he made six trips to the Himalaya, including being MO to the AC's Annapurna Circuit meet in 1981. (See *AJ* 1982)

Since being in Tasmania, however, the author's love affair has been with Federation Peak. First climbed by John Bechervise and party only in 1949, this 1225m peak lies in the south of the island, due south-west of Hobart, and is the highest point of the Arthur Range, with a very Chamonix Aiguille-like summit. The author has now reached the summit a record 21 times, and describes in detail the many attempts and ascents he has made, together with the bush trekking that is involved. 32 pages of colour plates complete a fascinating description of this little-known area.

The Pyrenees
The High Pyrenees from the Cirque de Lescun to the Carlit Massif
Kev Reynolds
Cicerone, 2004, pp464, £18.00

This is the first in a proposed 'World Mountain Ranges' series by Cicerone Press. The author, Kev Reynolds, is a well-known guidebook writer and an acknowledged expert on the Pyrenees. His *Walks and Climbs in the Pyrenees*, published more than 25 years ago, has been the major source of information in English to the area – until now. This book packs into its 464 pages all you could wish to know for walking and climbing in the High Pyrenees, and it is copiously illustrated throughout. A bit heavy to carry about with you, but a must for anyone with an interest in the area.

Norway: The Northern Playground
W Cecil Slingsby
Ripping Yarns, 2003, pp 234

From the Himalaya to Skye
J Norman Collie
Ripping Yarns, 2003, pp 186

Let's Go Climbing
Colin Kirkus
Ripping Yarns, 2004, pp 164

Ripping Yarns.com was established by Ian Robertson in 2002 to publish out of print adventure books on the internet, with the more popular ones being republished in soft-back book form. These are the first three titles, the Collie being originally published in 1902 as *Climbing in the Himalaya and other Mountain Ranges*. Each volume has brief additional material; Kirkus's book has an introduction by Steve Dean, and the Slingsby has one by Tony Howard and a chapter on mountaineering in Norway today by David Durkan.

In Memoriam

COMPILED BY GEOFFREY TEMPLEMAN

The Alpine Club Obituary	**Year of Election**
Jeremy Richard Naish	1974
Fosco Maraini	1960
Charles Serby 'Jules' Cartwright	ACG 2001
Adolf Alexander Verrijn-Stuart	1974

This year's In Memoriam list is, mercifully, short, only four members having died since the 2004 *Alpine Journal* was published. An obituary for each of these is included here, plus John Sumner and Sir William Wade from last year. One or two other obituaries from last year are 'in the pipeline', and will hopefully be included next year.

Jules Cartwright 1974-2004

I knew that, so far, our generation of British alpinists had been relatively lucky. I also knew that luck would not last; the mountains don't play by luck. What came as a real shock though was that it was Jules, so steady and so strong, whom we lost while he was guiding on Piz Badile. Only 29, Jules had already managed to squeeze in a lifetime's worth of mountaineering. Almost a permanent resident of Chamonix, his numerous alpine ascents included the second winter ascent of the *Lesueur* route on the Dru and new routes on the Grand Pilier d'Angle and the Aiguille Sans Nom. Trips to Alaska and Yosemite were appetizers for his greatest love, the Himalaya, to which he returned year after year. A natural in the mountains (his family are keen climbers and had sown the seeds with trips to the hills shortly after he started to walk) he exuded confidence and skill. His performance in the mountains was matched only by that in the bar, where it was normal for him to be the last one standing in the early hours and then first up for some early alpine or Scottish start for the hills. His ambition for the most futuristic projects in the mountains coupled with this boozing black belt led me to dub him the Alex MacIntyre of our generation.

These characteristics attracted not only the most talented partners amongst the British alpine scene (Nick Bullock, Sam Chinnery, Rich Cross, Matt Dickenson, Simon Yates, etc) but also the best amongst the world's alpine elite. Jules had climbed the Droites with Valerie Babanov, a training route basically done to check each other out for an attempt on Meru's Sharksfin. However, Valerie was still deep into his solo phase and so went alone; nevertheless the pair had deep mutual respect for each other. In Alaska last summer Valerie pried for hints as to where Jules's secret future projects might be. Typical of Jules was that despite being an alpine purist he did not follow the fashionable criticism of Babanov's tactics, rather judged the man he had actually met. Jules was good at cutting through the bullshit; he always enjoyed ribbing me when I'd got over-excited with some journalistic hyperbole.

When Slovenia's top alpinists visited Scotland it was natural for Jules to team up with their leading light, Marko Prezelj. They had met on ENSA-organised international gatherings in Chamonix where, despite not climbing together, bar sessions convinced each other they were on the same wavelength. Once in Scotland they made up for lost alpine opportunities, tearing through repeats of the likes of *Citadel, Shield Direct, The Fiddler's Nose* and the *West Buttress Directissima*. The pair stole the show at the international winter meets, not just for the fact that these climbs were usually second ascents or rare repeats but for the way these back-to-back routes were sandwiched between monster bar sessions. The Scottish visits had a profound affect on Prezelj, revitalising his own mountaineering and forging the pair's friendship. They were all set to go on their Himalayan expedition together last autumn, but it was not to be. Jules and his client Julie Colverd fell to their deaths on 30 June while heading for the Cassin route on the Badile's north-east face.

Brought up mainly in Gloucestershire, Jules gained a BA Hons in Design and Manufacturing at De Montfort University, Leicester. However, he dedicated his life not to industry but the mountains. He was sailing through his guide's scheme, had bought a house in Chamonix and had his sights set on the hardest, most outrageous routes in the Himalaya. Twice nominated for the Piolet d'Or, his stand-out route must be his 11-day alpine-style ascent, with Rich Cross, of the enormous and supremely committing north-west ridge of Ama Dablam in 2001. It was a line that had seen almost a dozen previous attempts, including a bolted siege by an eight-person Dutch team. The Brits opted for a pure and simple alpine ascent, trimming their gear to an absolute minimum; the ice rack consisted of only two ice screws and a snow-stake. I say simple ascent but the terrain was far from that, with over 4000m of twisting, gendarmed ridge sucking them in like a trap. One 60m horizontal section took a full day to navigate and their eight days of already scant rations were stretched ever thinner until the food ran out with the final snow buttress still to climb. At the time, I described it as 'probably the most significant British ascent in the mountains in the last decade'. Since then that assessment hasn't diminished and the north-west ridge sits alongside the likes of Renshaw's and Tasker's Dunagiri climb, or the Shisha Pangma ascent by Baxter-Jones, MacIntyre and Scott, at the pinnacle of British alpine-style Himalayan climbing.

I was lucky enough to climb with Jules on my first big trip to the mountains. A real greenhorn when Jules suggested a trip to Alaska, I jumped at the chance. The fact that he had planned a new route on the Moonflower Buttress of Mt Hunter (at that time hallowed ground and the test-bed of American alpinism) did not phase me as Jules emanated so much confidence he made it seem like the sort of thing anyone would try. We met Mark Twight who told us you couldn't afford to fall in the mountains. It soon became clear that Jules was trying something really special when he took more than half a dozen falls. One pitch, which took two days to climb and saw repeated lobs, Jules graded A2. When I protested he finally consented to the mysterious A2++! Four days into the climb a close encounter with a plummeting snow mushroom left me with two broken ribs and our effort looked as if it would be in vain. We had a difficult decision to make: up or down? At this point I saw another side of Jules's personality as he fixed me with a penetrating stare. Without a need for words I knew which way we were going. From then on Jules took over and towed me for a further three days climbing, including a 36-hour storm during which we were battered by avalanches.

When we eventually began descending one morning, Jules had that glint in his eyes again, except this time it was focused on a different objective. Methodically he sped us down the 35-plus abseils, dragging me into camp that evening and then immediately wandering over to the last remaining bush plane on the glacial airstrip. Next thing I knew, by some cunning Jules had arranged a fly-out for the weekend for 50 bucks and within an hour we were celebrating in the Fairview Inn.

That to me sums up Jules; his drive on what became one of the hardest routes of its type, his generosity in schooling me in the dark alpine arts and most importantly his ability not only to climb seriously but to seriously have fun. Amongst the alpine fraternity Jules will long be remembered, not just for his amazing climbs but for that glint in his eye that was able to persuade friends, close and new, to take on challenges greater than they'd normally dare, whether in the mountains or at the bar.

Ian Parnell

Jeremy Richard Naish 1930-2004

Jeremy Naish, who was born on 20 August 1930, died in 2004 aged 74. He established his reputation as an audacious climber when, as President of the Oxford University Mountaineering Club, he made the first ascent of Christ Church's Tom Tower with an American Rhodes Scholar Jim Murray, having surmounted the crux by using the clock's minute hand as an aid. He followed this up with a solo ascent of the Radcliffe Camera, leaving his shirt flying from the top as proof positive. When seconding Jeremy's inexplicably delayed application to join the Alpine Club in 1973, a future President and Oxford don David Cox could still recall the youthful feats of this 'extremely nice man'.

After leaving Gordonstoun, Jeremy, as befitted a distinguished admiral's son, did his National Service as a midshipman in the Royal Navy before going up to Oxford to read law at New College in 1951. Already blooded by two Cairngorm winter seasons at Gordonstoun, he launched himself into OUMC mountaineering with characteristic enthusiasm and during his university years notched up the equivalent of six months' climbing, mainly on OUMC meets in Wales, the Lakes, Scotland and the Alps. At the 1953 OUMC meet at Saas Fee he climbed with Alan Blackshaw and John Hobhouse amongst others, then spent another three weeks at Chamonix with Jim Murray, his Tom Tower partner. His routes that summer included the Dom's north-west arête, traverses of both the Jägigrat and Portjengrat, the Aiguille du Plan's east ridge, the Dent du Requin's Voie des Plaques and the north-north-east ridge of the Aiguille de l'M.

After going down from Oxford in 1954 Jeremy joined the Elder Dempster Line in Liverpool but found the work somewhat prosaic. His 1955 Alpine season in the Dolomites with Robert Bruce, Richard Adrian and John Hobhouse included a grade V climb on the Cinque Torre and, having by now left Elder's, he then spent four months as an Outward Bound instructor at Ullswater. The following year he joined the Colonial Service as a District Officer in Zanzibar, later serving as ADC to the Governor. Here he met his future wife Gillian who was then working as an assistant to Professor Louis Leakey, the eminent anthropologist.

Local leaves from Zanzibar offered scope for mountaineering in the then still exotic snow mountains of East Africa. In 1958 Jeremy undertook a remarkable three-week expedition to the Ruwenzori accompanied by nine porters and their headman Sadekia. From Ibanda their route to the heart of that magical range wound through bamboo junge, the Jabberwocky forest of tree-sized heathers and the infamous Bigo bog to the groves of giant groundsel that surround the Bujuku hut. Jeremy climbed Mt Speke on his second attempt supported by the valiant Sadekia clad in gym shoes bound with sacking. He then soloed Edward Peak on Mt Baker and finally Moebius on the Stanley Plateau. Before leaving Zanzibar, he and Gillian climbed Kilimanjaro by the Ratzel glacier route.

By the early 1960s the Colonial Service offered no long-term career prospects, so in 1962 Jeremy and Gillian reluctantly returned to England where he embarked on the daunting task of qualifying as a solicitor. After spells with Carlisle and Cambridge law firms he joined Morrell, Peel & Gamlen in his beloved Oxford and eventually became its senior partner. In 1962 he undertook the last serious Alpine season of his youth, attending the joint AC/CC meet at Pontresina for climbs in the Bernina and Bregaglia followed by a Zermatt fortnight with Anthony Rawlinson, John Emery and others doing routes which included the Dent Blanche (Ferpècle) and Rimpfischhorn traverse.

The professional and domestic demands of re-building his career and bringing up a young family meant that for over 10 years from 1962 Jeremy did little mountaineering. However, in 1973 he joined a trekking party I organised to cross the Cambrian mountans and after his election to the Club in 1974 began a mid-term mountaineering career with customary brio. His emphasis now was on classic Alpine routes and overseas expeditions including one to the Nanda Devi region in 1981 and another to the then virtually unknown Tien Shan in 1988. Many of his climbing companions during this period were members of the Gorphwysfan Club, an informal group of friends who had once made full use of the old Pen y Pass hostel.

But most particularly he climbed with our member John Rowlinson who has warm recollections of their happy days together on the Mönch, Jungfrau, Grandes Jorasses and many other mountains. I am indebted to John for his memoir of epics such as their 21-hour day on the Weisshorn in difficult conditions; or Jeremy's crevasse rescue on the Aletsch glacier by John and his wife Nancy; or the occasion when a near-fatal lightning bolt on the Gross Grünhorn summit struck John and knocked Jeremy unconscious. John's tribute *'We all have had occasion to be thankful that there was someone of his physical and moral strength on the other end of the rope'* is a measure of the man.

Jeremy made light of the heart condition which afflicted his latter years but he never really got over the untimely death of his charming wife Gillian two years before his own. His family, friends and climbing companions will always remember his resolution, integrity and courage in good times and in bad and the warm hospitality that he and Gillian dispensed from their lovely 17th century house at Charlbury.

J G R Harding

In compiling this obituary I am indebted to John Rowlinson, Jeremy's lifeong friend Ian Smart and the Editor of the New College Record *for their generous assistance.*

Fosco Maraini 1912-2004

Early in 2004 I received a card from Florence with kind words from Fosco Maraini on my becoming editor of the *Alpine Journal*. He pointed out that he had at his house a full run of *AJs* from 1863, plus the two forerunner issues of *Peaks, Passes and Glaciers* – a rare and valuable collection indeed. Sadly I will not now be able to take up his invitation to visit him in Florence and admire his library.

Maraini was an alpinist in the classic European gentlemanly mould, urbane and witty; the mountains a different venue for social engagement and intellectual inquiry as well as fun and physical challenge. His list of climbs in the Dolomites and the western Alps from 1929 to 1937 is impressive. He was elected to the Alpine Club in 1960 and remained a member to his death.

While most of Maraini's climbs were done guideless, he made several excursions onto the spires of the Dolomites with the Trieste ace Emilio Comici, notably two ascents of the *Dülfer* route (V+) on the Cima Grande di Laveredo and the committing *Preuss Crack* (V) on the Cima Piccolissima. Maraini kept fine company. Against one climb on the Torre del Diavolo, on his record is written: 'with E Comici and King of Belgium'.

This phase of activity came to an end when he travelled East; to Tibet in 1937 and later to Japan where he taught in the University of Kyoto from 1941 until he was interned in 1943. Opposed to fascism, Maraini and his young family remained incarcerated at a camp at Nagoya until the war's end in August 1945. In happier times, he had climbed Mt Fuji and made several ski ascents of peaks in Hokkaido.

A lifelong student of Oriental ethnology, Maraini's academic life began with teaching Italian to the Japanese and ended teaching Japanese to Italians, as a lecturer at the University of Florence, the city where he was born and died.

In 1958, Maraini's knowledge of Asia and facility with languages made him a useful member of the successful Italian expedition, led by Riccardo Cassin, to Gasherbrum IV (7925m), the 'Matterhorn of the Baltoro glacier'. Maraini secured the all-important peak permit in Karachi, and later reached 7200m on the mountain. A year later he led a team from the Rome section of the Italian Alpine Club to Saraghrar Peak in the Hindu Kush. Four climbers gained the 7367m summit. Looking back on this trip he delighted in the contrast between the mountaineers' enjoyment of 'the ruder pleasures of nature' and a sophisticated Rome where 'the last descendants of feudal lords mingle with monsignori and abbots', coupled with the 'rather scandalous aura' of politics and cinema stars.

Maraini recorded these adventures in *Karakoram, Ascent of Gasherbrum IV* (1961) and *Where Four Worlds Meet: Hindu Kush 1959* (1964), accompanied by superb photographs. He had earlier written the highly regarded *Meeting with Japan* (1959), and concluded his *oeuvre* in 1999 with a sort of autobiography *Case, Amori, Universi* (Houses, Loves, Universes.)

But, for me, his most enduring work is *Secret Tibet* (1952), an account of two visits in 1937 and 1948 in the company of the Orientalist Giuseppe Tucci – 'the great master' as Maraini called him, though politically the two were poles apart. Tucci was a Mussolini supporter who lectured at the dictator's behest in Japan on racial purity, while Maraini's philosophy was summed up in advice to one of his daughters: 'Remember always that races do not exist; only cultures exist.'

Secret Tibet is by turns intimate and scholarly as he and Tucci visit villages and monasteries on a route from Sikkim to Lhasa. Maraini couldn't know it at the time, but many of the statues and wall paintings he photographed with his Leica and described so elegantly, would be destroyed in Mao's Cultural Revolution – a term he regarded as horribly ironic, describing 1966 to 1977 as 'those years of fire and shit'. The photographs in *Secret Tibet* became the only record of the treasures of places like 1,000-year-old Kyangphu monastery, reduced to rubble. Five years ago, a new edition of *Secret Tibet* was published, augmented with fresh reflections (dated 1998) by Maraini on his travels, Buddhism and the future of Tibet. When he recalled Kyangphu, he did so, he said, 'with tears in my eyes'.

Stephen Goodwin

Sir William Wade 1918-2004

Sir William Wade, QC, Master of Conville and Caius College, was born in 1918 and died on 12 March 2004. As a jurist he was the foremost scholar of administrative law in the United Kingdom; indeed, he was at the heart of what Lord Diplock described as 'the greatest achievement of the English Courts in my judicial lifetime'. At his memorial service in Great St Mary's there were four addresses: by Lord Woolf, the Lord Chief Justice; by Sir Jack Beatson, formerly Rouse Ball Professor of English Law; by the Rt Hon Sir Martin Nourse, High Court Judge and past Treasurer of Lincoln's Inn; and by his son Dr Michael Wade who read a charming extract from an article his father had written on climbing Mt Kenya. These four addresses summed up Bill Wade's unique qualities: immense academic distinction and influence nationally and internationally, coupled with a deep and long-lasting devotion to mountains. He reminded me of two other distinguished members of the Club from a different age, Lord Bryce and Lord Schuster, also men of national distinction for whom an active love of mountains was, one feels, the foundation of their lives.

Bill Wade joined the Club in his mid-forties in 1964. He was proposed and supported by a bevvy of Cambridge dons (or ex-dons): A M Binnie, Sir Claude Elliott, Professor J R M Butler and Michael Vyvyan. In his proposal form, his list of 'expeditions', as we used to call them, runs to two full pages covering a period of 10 years or so. He had climbed in the classic Alpine areas, but also in the Pyrenees and the United States. And he carried on climbing wherever he happened to be. His academic reputation was such that he was much in demand for advising the UK Government, as well as the new governments of the rapidly expanding Commonwealth and other new nations, and at conferences on legal and constitutional matters. He also found the time to write engaging articles in *Country Life* with accompanying photographs, as he was also an accomplished photographer. His varied subjects included the Tetons (1968), Morocco (1970), the Canadian Rockies (1973) and East Africa (1975). We also find him trekking in the Karakoram in his 72nd year. None of his climbs was spectacular, nor did they include notable first ascents or indeed 'epics'. Although after a family traverse of the Zinal Rothorn, when they were caught in bad weather and had to bivouac, his wife, waiting anxiously in Zermatt, vowed that she would not accompany any more climbing expeditions.

On another occasion, in 1967, he recorded that he crossed from Austria to the Italian Brenta, living in Italian huts for a whole week without being aware of the one-hour time difference. Judging from his diary notes, the range of his climbing was extensive. In addition to the areas already mentioned, he had climbed in the Dolomites, Corsica, Norway, New Zealand and Japan.

Bill was educated at Shrewsbury and at Caius, Cambridge. His academic career began with a fellowship at Trinity from 1946. He then had 15 years at Oxford as Professor of English Law and fellow of St Johns, returning to Caius as Master from1976 to 1985 and as Rouse Ball Professor of English Law from 1978 to 1982. During this time he guided the Fellows towards their decision to admit women. His reputation in academic law was recognised by a knighthood in 1985. To this honour should be added his Honorary Benchership at Lincoln's Inn, Fellowship of the British Academy – the list of academic and legal awards is lengthy. His memorial is perhaps his book *Administrative Law*. When it first appeared in 1961 it was a mere 300 pages. Today, in its eighth edition, it runs to well over 1,000 larger pages. Prior to this, he had already made a name when he co-authored, with Sir Robert Megary, their *Law of Real Property* which is now in its seventh edition. This brief resumé merely scratches the surface of a remarkable range of public activities.

I first met Bill at Oxford, I think in connection with the University Press, and then, subsequently, I also being a Caian, at College feasts. He was good company, easy to get on with, good humoured, witty (without too much donnishness), and always interested in what was going on in the mountaineering world. For my part, I don't think I was then aware of his academic and public distinction, because he did not remotely parade it. But one was certainly aware that this apparently easygoing and straightforward don was clearly a somebody and, at the same time, devoted to mountains.

Roger Chorley

J G R Harding writes:

When our paths first crossed at Cambridge, where Bill was both my tutor and Director of Studies at Trinity, he had recently returned to the hills. At that time the law exerted considerably less appeal to me than did mountaineering but had I known that we shared at least one common interest, my student path might have run smoother. Later, after meeting Bill again at the Alpine Club, we became the firmest friends: exchanging news and views, staying at each other's houses and walking together. Sadly, I never climbed with Bill but came to appreciate that under a detached exterior there lurked a sharp wit and a generous heart .

As a 19-year-old in 1937 he had climbed the Wildspitze – his only guided ascent. Thereafter, the war, marriage, the upbringing of his two sons and pressures of work delayed his mountaineering career until 1953 when, at the age of 35, he took to rock climbing in the Lake District, Skye and the North-west Highlands. Curiously, he postponed his entry to serious alpinism until his forties.

After leaving Trinity for Oxford in 1961, Bill's outstanding academic and administrative abilities led inexorably to his Oxford Professorship of English Law, his Mastership of Caius and a knighthood. Throughout, he always maintained his zest for mountain travel which ran in concert with his ever-expanding legal horizons. Not content with Oxbridge lecturing, tutoring, academic research and authorship, his early career was characterised by intellectual exploration overseas including British Council lectureships in Scandinavia (1958) and Turkey (1959); service on the Kampala Commission to review the constitutional crisis between the Kabaka of Buganda and the Ugandan Government (1961) and lectureships at Michigan University (1961), New Delhi (1971 and 1982) and Madras (1974). These variegated experiences prepared him for subsequent weightier missions as the leading constitutional guru advising sovereign states old and new. Refreshingly, Bill was not simply an academic lawyer but had his commercial feet securely grounded, as I discovered when my own law firm instructed him to advise on a delicate constitutional issue involving the Sultanate of Brunei. His single-page opinion, sent by return, was both unequivocal and unchallengeable.

A natural athlete and a keen oarsman in his youth, Bill took on mountain challenges in whatever country he visited, though his preferences were
for less trodden ways and classic Alpine routes which he still enjoyed into
his sixties. Almost his first and his best-beloved mountains were the Pyrenees
where, in 1958, 1963 and 1964, he climbed 17 of its major peaks, mainly
with his old Trinity colleague A M Binnie. He particularly prized his photograph of the Vignemale's north face, delineating his route up the famous
Arête de Gaube. And it was as much to his enthusiasm that I owe my own
interest in those enchanted mountains which he cherished not only for
their ambience but also for that rare green and yellow distillation that he
considered a rival to Chartreuse.

Anthony Snodgrass writes:
One small gap in Roger Chorley's excellent account concerns the 'autumn
flowering' of Bill Wade's climbing record. In 1978, when he was already
60, he asked me to join him as a younger climbing companion, much as he
had done with the 17-years-older A M Binnie in earlier seasons. Bill's Alpine
experience was greater than mine, as were many of his skills. Although I
led on the climbs of these years, I would not have got up some of them
without his encouragement and advice on the rope below. He was still a
very steady goer uphill.

At Arolla in August 1978 we enjoyed perfect weather – 12 successive
fine days – and good snow, for a series of ascents that included Mt Collon
by its west ridge and the Dent Blanche by the standard route. In June/July
1979 we turned to the Dolomites where mixed conditions drove us off some
routes, but we had a perfect day for our climb of the Cima Grande di
Lavaredo by the south face. In the Pyrenees at similar dates in 1980 we
again met with variable weather but got up five of the less taxing rock peaks.
As Roger Chorley says, nothing spectacular and no 'epics', but quite good
going for someone in his sixties.

Bill left me vivid meories of his likes – he had an encyclopædic knowledge
of Alpine wild flowers – and his dislikes, which ranged from minestrone
and salami (awkward in Italy) to talk after lights-out in the huts and flabby
young people who had used mechanised means to reach the same points
as we did.

John Sumner 1936-2004

Historically, British rock climbing has been influenced by individuals whose
vision and activities have exerted a disproportionate effect on the climbing
development of a particular region. Well known examples include Tom
Patey's affinity with the North-west Highlands of Scotland in the 1960s, or
Arthur Andrews' pioneering exploration of Cornish sea-cliffs in the 1920s.
After the early 1970s however, the incidence of such climbing 'auteurs'

declined markedly. A huge rise in the climbing population, better communications and the advent of mass car ownership meant that intense competition for new routes nationwide evolved amongst leading climbers. These developments largely spelled the end for the phenomenon of the regionally dominant climber. John 'Fritz' Sumner, however, was one of the few that bucked this trend. In his chosen domain of mid-Wales, he remained without compare as an exploratory climber. His peers would come to acknowledge that without his exceptional energy and enthusiasm, rock climbing on the remote crags and cliff-faces south of central Snowdonia would never have been developed so thoroughly or so effectively. Even more outstanding was the longevity of his climbing campaign, which was spread over the best part of half a century. Starting with cutting-edge routes pioneered in the mid-Fifties, the evergreen Sumner continued to generate a steady stream of exciting new climbs right into the new millennium, when he was still climbing 'Extreme' lines.

Born in Blackburn in 1936, John Sumner moved to Stafford in his youth to take up a job as a draughtsman with the English Electric company – a post he would retain with the firm's successor companies for the rest of his working life. It was here that he joined the town's vibrant Mountain Club. Attracted to the nearby Peak District, his initial impact on the world of outdoor pursuits came not with climbing, but with what might be termed 'extreme fell walking'. Sumner and fellow Mountain Clubber Ronald Lambe's 37-hour, 60-mile circumnavigation of the Peak's gritstone moorlands in 1953 remains one of the most arduous challenge walks undertaken in the region. Their effort was especially impressive given that it was done mainly in rain and low cloud, requiring compass navigation for much of the way. Despite the discouragement of one of their friends, Red Mayes, who claimed that 'Not even the army would make you carry on in this', the duo gritted their teeth and pressed on into the night. Towards the end there was a telling sign of Sumner's nascent enthusiasm for rock. The pair, both dead beat, arrived at the gritstone outcrop of Froggat Edge. Lambe recalled that Sumner 'brightened up and began to take an interest in the various boulder problems that line the pathway – this in spite of the fact that he had difficulty with his vision, for his eyes refused to stay open.'

Sumner's first forays into serious pioneering rock climbing followed shortly afterwards with what would later become much sought-after routes in the Peak such as *The Thorn* (HVS) at Beeston Tor. Not long after this 'Fritz' Sumner acquired his Germanic nickname from no less a luminary than Don Whillans. Sumner had become briefly interested in difficult aid climbing and, with Ron Moseley and others, succeeded in overcoming the brutally strenuous *Main Overhang* at Kilnsey Crag in 1957. Whillans, unimpressed by the young climber's use of pitons and etriers, but recognising his skill and courage, likened his efforts to the pre-war death-or-glory Austrian and German climbers on the Eiger Nordwand. His ironic nickname for Sumner, 'Fritz', stuck.

Around this time Sumner began pioneering climbs in the area that he would make his own; the mountainous parts of Merionydd and adjoining counties. Using the basecamp of the Stafford Mountain Club's newly acquired hut below the brooding cliffs of Craig Cywarch east of Dolgellau, Sumner would end up being principally responsible for the creation of over 150 routes in the area. Many of them were of an extreme degree of difficulty such as *Pardon Me for Breathing* in the Berwyns, or *Little Red Rooster* on Craig Cywarch, but others were of a less technically difficult nature, reflecting Sumner's range and zest for climbing in general – and for the company of others. 'Fritz was prepared to climb with anyone, anywhere,' recalled his good friend Peter Benson. 'He was a great bloke to be with on the hill - he always felt it was important to see others enjoying themselves.'

A reflection of this inclusive nature is perhaps seen in one of his most famous and popular creations, the easy classic climb *Will-o'-the-Wisp* (V.Diff) on Craig Cywarch. Sumner's much vaunted enthusiasm was very much to the fore during the production of this route which required not just athletic skill to ascend its intricate airy traverses, but also sheer physical graft to initially excavate the rock holds from beneath a mantle of moss and heather. 'An intensive cleaning programme began, mainly on cold, rainy winter days', he wrote. 'The blood and sweat came from me and the tears from [Sumner's wife] Jill as she went numb with cold holding my rope (a hazard from which all my seconds suffer).'

Sumner was also prescient in perceiving the potential that mid-Wales held for ice climbing. Most climbers had previously disregarded the pastoral green folds of rural Merionydd as unpromising winter terrain but in 1979 Sumner and his friends pulled off a multitude of icy climbs. Among these were two of the most impressive and enjoyable pure ice routes in the United Kingdom. Sumner's and Glen Kirkham's discovery of the frozen *Maesglasau Falls* (IV) produced a magnificent 120m route up a great cascade of tumbling ice that is almost unique in this country. That same winter the pair, along with John Codling, created another great route in the area much sought-after by ice-climbing *aficionados*: *Trojan* (Grade V) on Cader Idris. '*Trojan's* streak of near-perpendicular ice beckoned siren-like and sinuous', Sumner later wrote. '[It] called to every "ice-man" worthy of the name to come and climb.' It was perhaps telling that none had been found sufficiently worthy before Sumner coaxed his team down to unfashionable Cader – and probably with good reason. The route required hair-raising climbing on splintering, brittle ice, and a 'mind-blowing pendulum' on a rope strung from a poor piton to reach a stance part way up, before it succumbed. Only someone used to testing their limits on unknown terrain was likely to succeed in such a situation. But despite Sumner's predilection for mid-Wales, his climbing vision extended far beyond the parochial. He climbed extensively in Canada and the Alps, where he had an excellent record, including several first ascents and first British ascents of testing routes in the high mountains, such as the difficult *Cassin Route* on the Dolomite's Cima Ovest. He joined the Alpine Climbing Group in 1972.

All this activity was achieved, remarkably, despite the time constraints of family life and a full-time job. Indeed, Sumner's talents were such that his employers were reluctant to let him retire early, and he continued in post until the age of 65. Age, however, hardly appeared to weary him. Every autumn would see Sumner undertaking the arduous 40-mile Derwent Watershed Walk across some of the most calf-sapping terrain in the Pennines in order to test his fitness. He had also become an increasingly keen practitioner of the especially tough and serious activity of winter alpinism at an age when most climbers would be thinking of giving it up. Sumner also continued rock climbing to a very high standard to the end of his life. During the 1990s he struck up a climbing partnership with the leading (and considerably younger) south-west climber Martin Crocker and together they pioneered many new extreme rock routes in the Rhinogs and elsewhere. 'He was always out in front', recalled Crocker, who is renowned for his own strength and stamina. 'It was simply impossible to keep up with the guy's energy and enthusiasm.' Still physically extraordinarily fit, it seemed, therefore, both unlikely and shocking when Sumner succumbed to a heart attack. His death ends a remarkable era in Welsh climbing, and a climbing life always lived to the fullest.

Colin Wells

This obituary first appeared in The Independent.

Adolf Alexander Verrijn Stuart 1923 - 2004

'Xander' Verrijn Stuart started mountain climbing with his parents in the Austrian Alps. When, in 1931, he made his first guided climb he very proudly marked in the *Gipfelbuch* not only his name but his age as well. These early experiences made him very familiar with the mountain landscape and terrain.

After graduation at the University of Amsterdam, Xander obtained a PhD in physics at the University of Ann Arbor in Michigan, USA, and joined Shell. At this time he made his first guideless climbs in the Alps. But in a period when climbing in the Mont Blanc massif was fashionable, he turned his efforts to areas more remote and demanding with respect to orientation and endurance. He made climbs such as Sonnighorn near the Almageller Alp, Cherbadung in the Binntal, Monte Leone above Simplon and the Breitlaubgrat of the Fletschhorn. All these enterprises involved wild camping, a way of mountaineering he remained devoted to all his life.

Physically, Xander was a very strong man. He never shrank from a heavy rucksack, a steep path or a thunderstorm. He was a very keen lover of outdoor skating. No less than six times he finished the famous Dutch *Elfstedentocht*, an almost 200km long skating tour.

117. Adolf Alexander Verrijn Stuart 1923-2004

After a stay of several years with Shell in Iran and in the UK he returned to the Netherlands in 1969 when he was appointed the first Professor of Informatics at the University of Leiden. He became active in Dutch mountaineering and in 1971 succeeded Jan Saltet as editor of *De Berggids*, the journal of the KNAV. He was a very productive author, contributing numerous articles. Notable are his articles on climbing holidays in Wales and in the Lake District, on his backpacking adventures in the Alps and on camping and photo equipment. He was elected to the Alpine Club in 1974.

Around that time Xander was asked to become leader of an expedition to the Nepal Himalaya. For the first time in history a Dutch team took up the challenge to climb an 8000m peak, Annapurna I. One of the Dutch members and one of the Sherpas reached the summit on 13 October 1977, the fourth ascent of the mountain. To reach the upper slopes a safe but technically demanding new route was opened along the 'prominent rib' which later became known as the 'Dutch rib'.

Not long after, Xander was asked to organise and conduct an expedition to Mount Everest. Permission was granted to approach the mountain from the north, at that time (1982) relatively unknown ground. The expedition was not successful for several reasons. Weather conditions were very unfavourable and an avalanche below the North Col caused serious injuries to one of the members. The team also suffered internal friction, and as a result of modern communications those frictions became immediately known at home. Xander deeply regretted the consequences for the team's reputation.

In the following years Xander remained faithful to his enthusiasm for backpacking in the Alps as well as in Scotland, Scandinavia and the Pyrenees. He became an honorary member of the KNAV in 1984.

He never suffered the drawbacks of old age, remaining fully active in his profession as well as socially till he passed away in his sleep. Xander will be deeply missed by his wife, his two sons and their families. Among Dutch mountaineers he will be remembered through his many articles and his books on the two Himalayan expeditions.

Charles Dufour

Alpine Club Notes

OFFICERS AND COMMITTEE FOR 2005

PRESIDENT	S Venables
VICE PRESIDENTS	R F Morgan
	R Turnbull
HONORARY SECRETARY	R M Scott
HONORARY TREASURER	I Appuhamy
HONORARY LIBRARIAN	D J Lovatt
HONORARY EDITOR OF THE *ALPINE JOURNAL*	S J Goodwin
HONORARY GUIDEBOOKS COMMISSIONING EDITOR	L N Griffin
COMMITTEE ELECTIVE MEMBERS	D R Buckle
	T J Clarke
	R Eastwood
	T A Grönlund
	P Mallalieu
	A E Scowcroft
	W G Thurston
	P Wickens

OFFICE BEARERS

LIBRARIAN EMERITUS	R Lawford
HONORARY ARCHIVIST	P T Berg
HONORARY KEEPER OF THE CLUB'S PICTURES	P Mallalieu
HONORARY KEEPER OF THE CLUB'S ARTEFACTS	D J Lovatt
HONORARY KEEPER OF THE CLUB'S MONUMENTS	W A C Newsom
CHAIRMAN OF THE FINANCE COMMITTEE	R F Morgan
CHAIRMAN OF THE HOUSE COMMITTEE	
CHAIRMAN OF THE ALPINE CLUB LIBRARY COUNCIL	H R Lloyd
CHAIRMAN OF THE MEMBERSHIP COMMITTEE	W G Thurston
CHAIRMAN OF THE GUIDEBOOKS EDITORIAL AND PRODUCTION BOARD	L N Griffin
GUIDEBOOKS PRODUCTION MANAGER	J N Slee-Smith
ASSISTANT EDITORS OF THE *Alpine Journal*	P Knott
	G W Templeman
PRODUCTION EDITOR OF THE *Alpine Journal*	J Merz
NEWSLETTER EDITOR	R Turnbull
WEBSITE EDITOR	P Wickens

ASSISTANT HONORARY SECRETARIES:
ANNUAL WINTER DINNER .... W A C Newsom
LECTURES .... M W H Day
MEETS .... T A Grönlund
MEMBERSHIP .... W G Thurston
BMC LIAISON .... D D Gray
TRUSTEES .... M F Baker
                                                                              J G R Harding
                                                                              S N Beare
AUDITORS .... PKF

ALPINE CLIMBING GROUP

PRESIDENT .... D Wilkinson
HONORARY SECRETARY .... R A Ruddle

GENERAL, INFORMAL, AND CLIMBING MEETINGS 2004

13 January	General Meeting: Lieut Col Nick Arding and Warrant Officer 2 Dave Pearce, Royal Marines, described the Royal Navy Everest North Ridge 2003 Expedition.
27 January	Members' Evening
13-14 February	Scottish Meet, Laggan
18 February	Northern Lecture: John Arran, *Venezuelan Big Wall Climbing*
24 February	General Meeting: Alun Hubbard, *Sailing and Climbing down South*
9 March	General Meeting: Kathryn Bridge, *On Phyllis & Don Munday*
23 March	Members' slide night
2-3 April	North Wales Meet, Betws
4 April	General Meeting: Brig David Nichols, *British Schools Exploring Society expedition to Chile, the Falkland Islands and South Georgia.*
27 April	Informal Meeting
7 8 May	Pcak District Meet, Stoney Middleton
10 May	General Meeting: Dr R Gibson, *2003 Kyrgyz-Kuili Expedition*
25 May	Informal Meeting
8 June	General Meeting: Julie-Ann Clyma, *New Routing in Sichuan*
22 June	Informal Meeting: Dave Nicholls, *Chile, Falklands & South Georgia*
27 June	Ski Mountaineering Symposium
10-24 July	Alpine Meet (with ABMSAC & CC): Meiringen, Switzerland
11-25 July	Alpine Meet (with ABMSAC & CC): Zermatt

23 July-10 Aug   AC Canada Meet, Mt Waddington
24 July-7 Aug   Alpine Meet, Grindelwald
4-11 September   Alpine Meet (with ABMSAC & CC): Maritime Alps
14 September   General Meeting
24-25 September   Lakes Meet
28 September   Informal Meeting: Jim Curran Exhibition Private View
8 October   Boardman Tasker Memorial Award ceremony
14 October   General Meeting
13-21 October   Alpine Meet, Mt St Victoire
20 October   Northern Lecture: John Porter, *Wild, Stylish & Innovative*
26 October   Informal Meeting: Jerry Gore, *Peaks and Personalities*
9 November   General Meeting: Kenton Cool, *Annapurna III SW Ridge*
                  Julian Cooper exhibition, 'Cliffs of Fall'
17 November   Northern Lecture: Nick Colton, *Super Alpinism*
27 November   Symposium, South America
                  AC Annual Dinner at Shap Wells
7 December   AGM and President's Valedictory Address

ALPINE CLUB SYMPOSIUM ON SOUTH AMERICA

Held at the Shap Wells Hotel, Cumbria on 27 November, the Club's 2004 symposium was a most enjoyable day featuring a good mix of pictures from all over South America, though concentrating mainly on the Andes of course. The speakers talked in a diversity of styles about everything from the desperate and dangerous ice faces in Peru and the difficult spray soaked big walls near Angel Falls to the sun-kissed rock climbing in Rio and the remote volcanoes of Bolivia's south-western desert. Routes ranged from the ridiculously accessible climbing just five metres from the road in Brazil to the challenges of Tierra del Fuego, where a friend with a 15m ocean-going yacht is more or less a necessity to get to the mountains.

A common theme was the influence of global warming on the future viability of routes, a very relevant theme after the events in the Alps of summer 2003. Many of the speakers mentioned the disappearing glaciers in the Andes and talked of the way in which formerly easy trade routes are generally becoming harder and the more challenging steep faces in Peru are generally becoming more dangerous.

After a brief introduction by incoming president Stephen Venables, my job was to give an overview of the whole of the Andes; a difficult task indeed to cover about 7000km of mountains featuring at least 20-30 sub-ranges in just 45 minutes. After a relatively leisurely stroll from Venezuela south to the Puna de Atacama I had to sprint though Patagonia to Cape IIorn! In particular my photos of ski-mountaineering in Chile seemed to awaken interest in the audience, at least judging by the feedback I got later in the day.

Nick Bullock followed with an excellent talk on some of the extreme climbing he has done in Peru, very much espousing the modern tactic of going fast and light, although it appeared from his successful three day ascent of the south face of Quitaraju with Al Powell that they set off a bit too light and found the going not quite fast enough for comfort.

Jose Camarlinghi, a guest from Bolivia, gave an informative talk on the four main mountain ranges in Bolivia including the remote volcanic peaks of the Lipez, which I knew very little about until then.

After lunch Anne Arran took us away from the Andes to the big walls she and husband John have climbed in the Roraima area of Venezuela, including several attempts to free an aid line that very closely follows the line of Angel Falls. [They succeeded in 2005.] This was another area of South America I have never visited but her talk fairly whetted my appetite and I may be visiting soon, though only if I can find some rock climbing at a more realistic grade for myself.

Carlos Buhler had the mid-afternoon slot and gave an informative and very professional talk on the mountains of Peru, covering the main ranges of the Vilcabamba, Vilcanota, and Cordillera Blanca and spanning several decades of climbing experience. In contrast to Nick, he was proud to represent the 'old guard' who still like to climb carrying enough food and fuel to enjoy a comfortable bivouac when it inevitably comes about. Carlos also described some of the hard climbs he has done on the South face of Aconcagua and Cerro Torre.

The day was rounded off by Simon Yates, who described two expeditions in to the eastern end of the Cordillera Darwin on Tierra del Fuego. Simon opened his talk with a very lively and amusing account of his sailing lessons on Ullswater as training for taking a 15m ocean going yacht around Cape Horn and up the Beagle Channel. The audience was once again captivated and thoroughly enjoyed the rest of his talk.

As one of the 'experts' on the Andes I particularly enjoyed the day and would like to offer my personal thanks to the organisers, Bill and Derek, all of the other speakers, and to Stephen Venables for the very difficult job of keeping the show running on time.

The symposium was followed by the annual dinner, well attended and convivial into the wee small hours. Guest of honour was Yvonne Chouinard, continuing, in a way, the South America theme. Not only is the company he founded called 'Patagonia', the Yosemite legend is now involved in buying up thousands of acres at the tip of the continent to conserve as wilderness.

John Biggar

KANGCHENJUNGA:
IMAGING A HIMALAYAN MOUNTAIN

One of the many pleasures of the Kangchenjunga 50th party at the AC on 6 June 2005 was not only the good company and liberal flow of alcohol but the fact that all around on the Club House walls were some of the finest images of the mountain ever painted or caught on camera.

The paintings, prints and photographs were brought together by Simon Pierse, a lecturer at the School of Art, University of Wales, Abersystwyth, and now an AC associate member. Accompanying the exhibition was an anthology of word and image surveying the differing ways Kangchenjunga has been seen and interpreted over two centuries.

Simon contends that Kangchenjunga is a much more alluring mountain than Everest. While Everest is jostled by rival 8000ers, Kangchenjunga stands free, dominating the skyline from Darjeeling. The argument seems unassailable backed up by the paintings of, among others, Somervell, Edward Lear and Nicholas Roerich, and the photographs of Vittorio Sella.

To call this work a 'catalogue' hardly does it justice. Getting up a lot closer than the panorama from Darjeeling, there are splendidly reproduced photographs from the 1955 ascent and Doug Scott's north-west face climb in 1979 with Boardman and Tasker. The most recent painting featured is a powerful oil on canvas of the north face by Julian Cooper (2005).

A full review of *Kangchenjunga: Imaging a Himalayan Mountain* will appear in the 2006 *AJ*. Copies of the 124-anthology are available from Simon at a reduced price of £10, plus £2 p&p, for AJ members (£14.99 retail). Contact him on email srp@aber.ac.uk or telephone 01970 622460.

SG

MALLORY'S 1922 ICE AXE

The ice axe used by George Mallory on the 1922 Everest expedition last year emerged from years of obscurity to be donated to the Mountain Heritage Trust and added to the Mallory-Irvine display at the National Mountaineering Exhibition, Rheged Centre, Cumbria. Mallory put the axe to good effect on 21 May 1922, saving his own life and those of Somervell, Norton and Morshead who were sliding from the north ridge towards the glacier 1000m below. The axe passed from Ruth Mallory to another Pinnacle Club sister, Nancy Carpenter, who, late in life, gave it to William Threlkeld, a young neighbour at Matterdale End, Cumbria, with an eye on winter climbing. William died in a motorcycle crash 20 years ago. His parents, Stan and Dot, kept the axe safe until on visiting the mountaineering exhibition they realised they had found it an appropriate home.

SG

118.   Returning the Everest marker flag. *Left to right:* Ernst Hofstetter, Bruno Spinner (Swiss Ambassador), Jacques Asper, George Lowe, George Band.

EVEREST MARKER FLAG RETURNED TO THE SWISS AFTER 52 YEARS

During the British Everest Expedition in 1953, George Lowe souvenired the only Swiss marker flag seen, which was one of those used by the Swiss in 1952. On 24 March 2004 Ernst Hofstetter, aged 93 years, and Jacques Asper, aged 78, came to the Swiss Embassy in London for the handover of the 'petit fanion'. George Lowe, in the presence of George Band and Michael Ward, performed the simple but moving ceremony organised by the Swiss Ambassador, Bruno Spinner. On 8 May 2004 George Lowe travelled to Geneva for the informal presentation of the marker flag to Anselm Zurfluh, Director of the Museum of the Swiss Abroad, in the Chateau de Penthes. At the museum this significant artefact is the stimulus for recording Swiss climbing outside of Switzerland and especially the Everest expedition of 1952. In the spring of 1952 the group of climbers from Geneva, the Androcase Club, were the first full-scale expedition (after the Everest Reconnaissance of 1951 led by Eric Shipton) to the south side of the mountain. Raymond Lambert and Tenzing Norgay reached 8595m before very severe weather drove them back.

For more information about the Museum of the Swiss Abroad and its alpine garden visit www.penthes.ch

George Lowe

THE BOARDMAN TASKER PRIZE FOR
MOUNTAIN LITERATURE 2004

The winner of the 2004 Boardman Tasker Prize was announced at an Alpine Club reception on Friday 8 October by the chair of judges, former London and New York book publisher Eric Major. In his adjudication, Major observed how mountaineering continued to produce the best in sports literature while golf and cricket had dwindled to the quickie biography. There had been a particularly diverse entry this year of 21 titles ranging from poetry, drama, history, fiction, travelogue, survival and expedition narrative.

From a shortlist of five the winner emerged as Swiss-based octogenarian Trevor Braham for his epic work of reference, *When the Alps Cast Their Spell: Mountaineers of the Alpine Golden Age*, published by the In Pinn. The judges praised Braham's deep understanding not just of the British pioneers – Stephen, Mummery, Tyndall, Moore, Whymper – but of the local guides who were often more skilful than their employers, in a story not only of great summits, but also of the way that cols were crossed linking Alpine regions together.

In his response, Trevor Braham expressed his particular gratification as a former friend of Peter Boardman, and noted that while last July 'a talented Swiss tennis player carried off the Wimbledon trophy in a sport that the English introduced over a century ago, it is encouraging that British mountaineers still count among the leaders in a sport that they introduced over a century and a half ago.'

Eric Major revealed that the decision on the winner had been a damned close run thing, the debate raging via telephone, emails and letters over two to three days with his fellow judges Steve Dean and Ian Mitchell. The four other shortlisted authors were: Jamie Andrew for *Life and Limb: a true story of tragedy and survival against the odds* (Portrait Books), an extraordinary story of endurance and courage told with a laid back modesty by the survivor of a five-night blizzard on the north face of Les Droites; Richard Askwith for *Feet in the Clouds: a tale of fell-running and obsession* (Aurum Press), an account of how, in his own words, an effete, overweight, cigarette-smoking southerner became hooked on fell-running and achieved the Blue Riband of the sport, the Bob Graham Round; Malcolm Slesser for *With Friends in High Places: An Anatomy of those who take to the Hills* (Mainstream), a distillation of 64 years of worldwide climbing, mountain exploration and walking; and Hugh Thomson for *Nanda Devi: A Journey to the Last Sanctuary* (Weidenfeld & Nicolson), recalling the topography, culture and history – both local and climbing – of one of the world's great places.

For further details of the award see www.boardmantaskcr.com. Judges for the 2005 Award will be Steve Dean (chair), Ian Mitchell and Chris FitzHugh.

Margaret Body, Honorary Secretary

18TH INTERNATIONAL FESTIVAL OF
MOUNTAINEERING LITERATURE

Listening to a succession of speakers at Bretton Hall telling us how it really was – you know, *really* was – on K2, Broad Peak, Yosemite or in the Brown-Whillans hey-day in the Peak and North Wales, I kept thinking of an old friend, Khalid Hasan, and the title of a book of Urdu short stories he had edited, *Versions of Truth*. That is what we, an attentive full-house of an audience, were getting, new versions, or at least a different perspective, on mountain exploits we had thought we had the measure of.

Thus Richard Sale, author of *Broad Peak* (Carreg 2004) adjusted the spotlight away from Kurt Diemberger and Herman Buhl and on to their comrades on the 1957 Austrian expedition, Marcus Schmuck and Fritz Wintersteller, who were actually the first to the top of the mountain. (Schmuck and Wintersteller were present to hear their reputations burnished, and to receive a standing ovation.) And Australian Robert Marshall rubbished Ardito Desio's 'official' account of the Italian first ascent of K2 in furtherance of his campaign to untangle a 'web of deceit' that has blighted the life of Walter Bonatti.

Bretton impresario Terry Gifford had set the theme of the festival as 'Whose History?' It worked well, so much so that one was left thinking that everybody's account of anything should be qualified by an 'it is alleged' or a 'claimed'. Chris Jones highlighted the unsung part played by Europeans in North American climbing history while Matthew Entwhistle upgraded Millican Dalton, the eccentric Borrowdale caveman and 'professor of adventure', to a more serious educationalist with unspecified new routes to his credit. (*Millican Dalton: a Search for Romance and Freedom* Mountain-mere Research 2004)

Given the age and pedigree of much of regular lit' fest' audience, it was no surprise that the keenest interest was in Jim Perrin's readings from *The Villain: the life of Don Whillans* (Hutchinson 2004). Several of the audience had climbed with Whillans and more had an acquaintance. Perrin though is a smooth and engaging performer and dealt with a disarming frankness when questioned by a panel, notably Gordon Stainforth, about a possible lack of candour over Whillans's excesses and treatment of his wife Audrey.

The Villain was an attempt to achieve a realistic portrait that would do Whillans credit, Perrin said. 'Obviously there is material I didn't include in the book and there is material of which I had a suspicion but I couldn't actually get it. It is quite difficult this. I do know things that have happened and I deliberately left them out.

'When you attempt any portrait, the matter of shading is crucial. And the shading is as I wanted it to be.'

Perhaps Khalid Hasan could have called his book 'A Matter of Shading'. *Versions of Truth* was dedicated to Zulfikar Ali Bhutto, the deposed and hanged president of Pakistan, for whom Hasan had worked as a press officer.

Writing from his death cell, Bhutto had wondered whether his name would be bracketed with criminals or heroes.

Climbing, of course, is neither as serious nor as risky as central Asian politics, but as Bretton showed, its practitioners are every bit as touchy about their reputations. Many thanks to Terry Gifford for exposing our conceit.

Stephen Goodwin

FIRST KENDAL MOUNTAIN BOOK FESTIVAL

November 2004 saw the launch of the first Kendal Mountain Book Festival, running in conjunction with the well-established film festival. Sponsored by Jennings Brewery and Ottaker's book shop, the festival offered an excellent opportunity to update on the current mountain writing scene in close proximity to the ever-busy programme of the film fest' itself. The eight book events were held in a variety of locations close to the Brewery Arts Centre and attracted encouragingly large public support, especially given the rather low-key and short-notice launch.

The festival commenced on the 13th with the broadcaster Eric Robson fronting a panel including Ken Wilson, Maria Coffey, Bernadette MacDonald (of the Banff festival), Bernard Newman (*Climber*) and myself, discussing 'Inspiring the Imagination: Mountains in Print'. This resulted in a lively debate with a witty and well informed audience and plenty of laughter.

The second event featured Malcolm Slesser and Jamie Andrew discussing their respective books, *With Friends in High Places* and *Life and Limb*, and engaging with a responsive audience in a lively discussion about risk-taking in the mountains and as a philosophy more generally.

A presentation of Cumbrian Mountain Literature was held on the Thursday night leading into the main festival weekend. Speakers included Langdale farmer and photographer Bill Birkett, Eric Robson (talking warmly about the work of Alfred Wainwright), Roger Hubank, author of *Hazard's Way* set in Wasdale, and Simon Yates, who lives and writes in the Eden valley. A large number of people attended this event which turned into an excellent social occasion well lubricated by the sponsor's fine beer – Cumbrian-brewed of course.

Friday featured a fascinating discussion between Julie Summers, great niece of Sandy Irvine and author of *Fearless on Everest*, and Audrey Salkeld, exploring Audrey's remarkable involvement with climbing literature over 40 years. In the afternoon, Maria Coffey gave a thought-provoking talk on her book *When the Mountain Casts its Shadow*, which led to an interesting discussion on the pressures on family life imposed by dangerous activities. Later, the group Woman Mountain Words provided a real contrast with readings, comic interludes, stimulating imagery and audience participation, resulting in the creation of a poem in a matter of minutes!

Saturday lunchtime saw the action shift to Kendal Town Hall with a talk and reading by Dermot Somers from his recently published *Collected Short Stories*. Always entertaining and thought provoking, Dermot is a wonderful reader of his own superbly diverse material, by turns tinged with sadness and laconic humour. The festival concluded on Sunday lunchtime with a well-attended event at the Riverside Hotel dedicated to the distinctly Cumbrian activity of fell running. It began with Eric Robson's film about the Wasdale runner Joss Naylor *60 at 60* and moved on to a reading by Richard Askwith from his book *Feet in the Clouds*. Revealing the pains and pleasures of fell running, Askwith's book came very close to winning the Boardman Tasker Award in 2004 and is highly recommended. For me personally, the highlight of the whole festival was hearing Joss Naylor's words of great kindness complimenting Richard on his book on behalf of the fell community whose story he had told – a wonderful moment.

Full marks to Julie Tait and her team for staging a really enjoyable and varied series of events, bringing into focus a wide range of writing. As with the film festival – once again a roaring success – it was an ideal opportunity to meet all the usual suspects, writers and would-be writers. In all, an auspicious beginning for an event that deserves to become a fully established date on the mountain culture calendar.

Steve Dean

ALPINE CLUB LIBRARY ANNUAL REPORT 2004

This has been a year in which the frustrations seem to have significantly outweighed the benefits, owing to events largely outside our control. We have been battling to make better use of our space, but ending up the year with the prospect of occupying less than at the beginning.

The Club's decision to take an additional 800 sq ft on the top floor for use as a Committee and Members' Room proved to be ill founded, because a 30% drop in commercial rents plus unexpectedly heavy building maintenance costs incurred during the year meant that it could no longer afford to forego the equivalent rental income. It was decided to give up the space in mid-year so that the whole of the top two floors could be rented out which was fortunately achieved without a void period. This consequently left the Club without a dedicated Committee room and the Library was therefore asked to vacate the space that it had only recently been allocated for our growing Photo Library, which is now actually earning useful income for the Club and the Library. Where could it go? The Basement is considered an unacceptable working environment for paid employees. Attempts to make better utilisation of the ground floor Lecture Room and Bar also as a Committee Room, or alternatively hiring a room at a nearby pub, have only been partly successful. In the end, we have reluctantly agreed to try to accommodate both the Archivist and the Photo

Library in the Archives Room. This entails moving our most valuable books from the Archives Room (specially protected by a fire wall) down into the already congested basement, which is supposed to be a dedicated Library area. Since much of the congestion is created by the Club's 1000 surplus *Alpine Journals*, cards, stationery and other items, these are now being moved elsewhere first, in an unproductive merry-go-round, which is unlikely to be completed before early 2005. The opportunity is being taken to review the Library's holdings and whether to dispose of some of the less attractive stock, such as the more ancient foreign language annuals.

The Club President's Future Policy Committee has also been considering various laudable options to make more funds available to support 'active' mountaineering. While on the one hand, Club members are generally keen to safeguard the Club's heritage, this Committee has wondered whether one option might be for the Library to be amalgamated in some 'British Mountaineering Library' perhaps centrally located within the UK in a lower cost area. While such options are being debated, it is not sensible to commit some £30,000 for installation of rolling stacks for more efficient storage of books and paintings in the basement. In March 2004 a 'pre-application' was made to the Heritage Lottery Fund to support this project, but at a subsequent 'Grants Surgery' in May, the HLF indicated its preference for a more general application, encouraging greater community involvement and increased public access, which was hardly appropriate in the present circumstances, so a full application has been deferred.

To help the Club with capital funds, a small collection of the more valuable duplicated or non-core books was sent for auction at Bloomsbury on 21 October, and raised a useful one-off £50,000. Bob Lawford has continued his sales of lower value duplicated books, which income is agreed to be retained by the Library. Over 20 years he has raised £123,000 in this way. This year the Library has greatly appreciated bequests of books from the estates of Oliver Turnbull and Peter Lloyd.

Five Council meetings were held during the year. At the AGM in May, Luke Hughes and Chris Fitzhugh asked to stand down as trustees and we thank them sincerely for their contributions. The RGS nominee Michael Westmacott also agreed to stand down, but in the absence of any response from the RGS has agreed to continue for another year. To replace the first two AC nominees, the ACL has proposed Barbara Grigor-Taylor, herself a specialist bookseller, and Kimball Morrison who has considerable Photo Library experience. The other trustees are Jerry Lovatt, Hon Librarian; Peter Berg, Hon Archivist; Richard Coatsworth, Hon Treasurer (BMC nominee), myself, and Margaret Clennett as Hon Secretary.

On the professional side, our Librarian Yvonne Sibbald has now completed her first year and settled in very well. The Photo Library has seen further changes. After only 14 months, Kate Miller sadly had to resign when her husband's job took them to Newcastle. Rachael Swann, equally experienced and enthusiastic, replaced her in June and has recently returned from honeymoon. The Photo Library is now listed in the Stock Index UK and participated in the BAPLA Picture Buyers' Fair in May, which has helped to enlarge our circle of contracts and generate new business. Over 2900 images have now been scanned and additional back-up computer storage created. We are now keen to add more recent high quality images from Club members to complement the predominantly historic collection. Volunteers from NADFAS continue to help with photo conservation which is now more than half completed. One would like to be able to include both the Library and Photo Library catalogues on the Club's website, but in our present deficit situation this is not an expense we can easily justify, although Kimball is working out how it might be done more cheaply.

One unexpected event was the appearance on the market of three portfolios of fine, mostly captioned, mountaineering photographs from the period 1926-1939 taken by Basil Goodfellow, a well respected Hon Secretary of the Club 1950-1954 during the Everest years. As we already possessed a post-war collection of his photos, we felt we should not miss the opportunity to acquire them. We are most grateful to several members of the Club who have generously contributed to their cost.

In late 2003, our endowment fund managers J P Morgan Private Bank gave notice that they wished to increase their minimum fee substantially, so in March we made a successful switch to Rathbones who welcomed our business, together with managing the portfolios of the Club and the MEF.

We are delighted to record that this year's Boardman Tasker Award was won by our member Trevor Braham for *When the Alps Cast Their Spell*, a book about mountaineers of the Alpine Golden Age. In gratitude for the research facilities and photographs provided by the Library, he made a most welcome extra donation. A legacy from the estate of John Byam-Grounds was also much appreciated. Without such serendipitous contributions, the Library would not be able to fulfil its obligations to the Club.

It is disappointing that the Custodial Agreement, intended to redefine the relationships between the Club and the Library, completed in May 2003 by a special working party set up in March 2002, under the chairmanship of former Vice President Patrick Fagan, was no longer felt to be necessary or desirable by the present AC Committee, so it has been shelved.

Looking ahead, the year 2007 marks the 150th Anniversary of the Club, the oldest such club in the world. After the success of the Chairman's 50th Anniversary Everest book (to be published also in paperback in April 2005) HarperCollins have agreed to publish a history of the Club and, perhaps without fully realising what he has taken on, he has agreed to write it for publication in October 2006. At least the advance will bring additional revenue to the Club and the Photo Library.

As always, my sincere thanks to all our employees and volunteers for their dedicated work through out the year.

George Band
Chairman, Alpine Club Library Council

Contributors

ANNE ARRAN has climbed in more than 20 countries around the world, particularly relishing UK sea cliff routes such as The Cad and the adventure of making big-wall first ascents in Asia and South America – taking part in the recent free-climb of the 1000m back wall of Angel Falls. She was BMC Youth and Training Officer 1998-200, a British team member for 10 years, and is now President of the UIAA Youth Commission. Early this year she enjoyed an assignment on Out of Country Voting for the Iraqi elections in Turkey.

BEN AYERS is the founder of Porters' Progress - a Nepali NGO dedicated to improving the lives of mountain porters. Under his guidance, Porters' Progress has lightened the burdens of tens of thousands of porters. When not drinking *chang* in the Everest region, he works as a logger in the North-eastern US practising sustainable forestry and saving up for his next extended adventure in Nepal.

ALAN BLACKSHAW OBE joined the AC aged 21 and contributed to the revival of British alpinism in the 1950s with first British ascents of the N Faces the Badile, the Triolet and the Col du Pain de Sucre. He wrote the definitive textbook *Mountaineering in Britain* in 1965. He led the first British ski traverse of the Alps and a N-S traverse of Scandinavia. As President of the BMC he moved the office to Manchester in the 1970s. An Honorary Member of the AC, he has recently been President. He is currently President of the UIAA and represents them on the UN's Global Mountain Partnership.

ANTONIO GÓMEZ BOHÓRQUEZ lives in Murcia, Spain. A librarian and documentalist (information scientist), he specialises in ascents in the north Peruvian ranges. He has written two books: *La Cordillera Blanca de los Andes* and *Cordillera Blanca, Escaladas*, Parte Norte. He has climbed since 1967, with first ascents including *Spanish Direct* on the north face of Cima Grande di Lavaredo, Italia (1977), Pilar del Cantábrico del Naranjo de Bulnes, Spain (1980), east face of Cerro Parón (La Esfinge, 5325m), Peru (1985) and the south-east face (1988).

JOHN BRACEY, at 27, is one of a very strong group of alpinists who served their apprentiship in the Leeds University mountaineering club in the mid 1990s. In 2001, along with Al Powell, he made the first ascent of the daunting 900m north face of Tupilak in Greenland whilst battling against temperatures as low as minus 30C. He is training to become a British Mountain Guide but is still as enthusiastic as ever about his own climbing. This autumn he hopes to have a look at the Emperor face of Mt Robson.

NICK BULLOCK was a PE instructor for the Prison Service until he turned full-time climber in 2003. He discovered climbing in 1991 on a work-related course at Plas y Brenin since when he has established himself as one of Britain's leading alpinists. He has put up new routes in the Alps, Nepal and Peru, notably *Fear and Loathing* on Jirischanca in 2003. This year's itinerary includes a return to India to attempt a new line on Changabang.

KELLY CORDES lives in Estes Park, Colorado, where the granite of Lumpy Ridge and Rocky Mountain National Park continually distract him from his work as assistant editor of the *American Alpine Journal*. After a dozen expeditions to various ice and mixed destinations, he'd convinced himself that an alpine rock trip would prove far less sketchy, far more fun, and entail minimal suffering.

RICHARD DAVY is a retired journalist. He was a foreign correspondent and leader writer for *The Times* and a leader writer for *The Independent*. A keen skier and mountain walker, he visited Zermatt many times and came to know Ulrich Inderbinen while translating his biography.

DEREK FORDHAM, when not dreaming of the Arctic, practises as an architect and runs an Arctic photographic library. He is secretary of the Arctic Club and has led 21 expeditions to the Canadian Arctic, Greenland and Svalbard to ski, climb or share the life of the Inuit.

STEPHEN GOODWIN renounced daily newspaper journalism on *The Independent* for a freelance existence in Cumbria, mixing writing and climbing. A precarious balance was maintained until 2003 when he was persuaded to take on the editorship of the *Alpine Journal* and 'getting out' became elusive again.

LINDSAY GRIFFIN is currently serving what he hopes will be only a temporary sentence as an armchair mountaineer. However, he is still keeping up to speed on international affairs through his work with Mountain INFO and as chairman of the MEF Screening and BMC International Committees.

JERRY GORE has climbed abroad on an expedition every year since 1977, often in pure alpine style and up to 8000m, with major new routes on every continent except Antarctica to his credit. Following a commission in the Royal Marines, and 15 years in the UK outdoor equipment industry, Jerry now lives with his family in the French Alps where they run AlpBase.com offering self-catering chalets and mountain courses in the Ecrins Massif.

DAVID HAMILTON earns a precarious living organising trekking, mountaineering and ski touring expeditions to the greater ranges. He spends a good deal of his time in northern Pakistan, leading expeditions in the Karakoram, Hindu Kush and Pamirs. These, often unpredictable, projects – increasingly on skis – help satisfy his enthusiasm for exploration and adventure. Recent trips to Iran, Turkey, Tibet, Greenland, South America and Antarctica ensure that David is seldom at home.

JOHN HARLIN III moved to Switzerland after his youthful Chamonix summer, and lived there until his father died on the Eiger in 1966. The climbing bug hit hard in college and hasn't left. John is the editor of the *American Alpine Journal*, a former editor of *Backpacker* and *Summit* magazines, and the author of *The Climber's Guide to North America*. His first route with Mark Jenkins was the first ascent of the real south face of Mt Waddington, accomplished from the sea in a wilderness adventure that was as true to North America as Mont Blanc's huts and gondolas are to the Alps.

HEINRICH HARRER was born in Carinthia, Austria, in 1912. One of the four climbers who made the first ascent of the north face of the Eiger in 1938, he told the story in *The White Spider*. Interned in India the following year, he escaped to Lhasa where he became a confidant of the Dalai Lama, describing the adventure in *Seven Years in Tibet*. The mementos of his life as a mountaineer, traveller, author and photographer are on display at Hüttenberg, close to his birthplace.

ALAN HINKES is a British Mountain Guide (UIAGM) who, in 1997, having climbed nine eight-thousanders, resolved to embark on his 'Challenge 8000' and climb the lot. In spring this year, with 13 summits in the bag, he tackled the last on his list – Kangchenjunga.

GEOFF HORNBY is a consulting engineer now resident in the Italian Dolomites. He has made over 250 first ascents in the mountains outside of the UK and is looking forward to 250 more, inshallah.

TONY HOWARD was a 1960s contributor to Gritstone and Limestone Peak District guidebooks. He was on the first ascent of Norway's Troll Wall in 1965 and wrote the now classic guide to Climbs in Romsdal. A founder of Troll climbing equipment, he has opened new routes in Arctic Norway, Greenland, Canada and across North Africa and the Middle East. He discovered Wadi Rum in Jordan in 1984 and wrote the guide to it. He has recently been involved in trekking explorations in Nagaland.

DICK ISHERWOOD has been a member of the Alpine Club since 1970. His climbing record includes various buildings in Cambridge, lots of old-fashioned routes on Cloggy, a number of obscure Himalayan peaks, and a new route on the Piz Badile (in 1968). He now follows Tilman's dictum about old men on high mountains and limits his efforts to summits just a little under 20,000 feet.

JOHN JACKSON was born in Lancashire and started climbing on gritstone 72 years ago. He first climbed in the Himalaya in 1944 after completing operational flying duties in Burma. Later he was a reserve member of the 1953 Everest team and one of the team that made the first ascent of Kangchenjunga in 1955. The Director of Plas y Brenin for 16 years, John led expeditions in the Garhwal, Kashmir and Nepal and travelled in Greenland, Africa, Peru and Canada. He died on 2 July 2005.

HARISH KAPADIA has climbed in the Himalaya since 1960, with ascents up to 6800m. He is Hon Editor of both the *Himalayan Journal* and the *HC Newsletter*. In 1993 he was awarded the IMF's Gold Medal and in 1996 was made an Hon Member of the Alpine Club. He has written several books including *High Himalaya Unknown Valleys*, *Spiti: Adventures in the Trans-Himalaya* and, with Soli Mehta, *Exploring the Hidden Himalaya*. In 2003 he was awarded the Patron's Gold Medal by the Royal Geographical Society.

KEVIN KELLY has been an active climber for 13 years. Probably best described as an all rounder, he has made first ascents in Scotland, Norway and the greater ranges. These include a 1997 first ascent of *The Throne*, Himachal Pradesh, and in 2002, two kilometres of new ice routes up to WI VI in less than 10 days in the Settesdal, Norway. A tree surgeon and IT engineer, he has been enjoying a bit of a renaissance in his rock climbing of late.

PAUL KNOTT is a lecturer in business strategy at the University of Canterbury, New Zealand. He previously lived in the UK and briefly in Morocco. Since 1990 he has undertaken nine exploratory climbing trips to Russia, Central Asia and the St Elias Range in Alaska/Yukon. He climbs regularly in the Southern Alps and has an undiminished yearning for exploration.

GRAHAM LITTLE works as a senior manager in the Ordnance Survey and balances his career with family life and a passion for climbing. He has climbed hundreds of new routes in Scotland and been on 14 expeditions to the greater ranges, including first ascents of several Himalayan peaks by challenging lines.

JIM LOWTHER is a land manager and developer. His first ascents in the greater ranges include 45 in east and south Greenland and an ice cap crossing; in India, Suitilla (Kumaon), Rangrik Rang (Spiti) and the north face of the Kulu Eiger (Himachal Pradesh). He has also attempted Arganglas (Ladakh) and Sepu Kangri (Tibet).

ROBERT MARSHALL is an Australian surgeon. He is not a mountaineer, but is a dedicated skier and hiker who has skied and trekked all over the world for many years. His fascination with mountains and mountaineers led him to take a particular interest in the life and times of Walter Bonatti, especially in relation to the prolonged K2 controversy. He lives in Melbourne.

JOHANNA MERZ qualified for membership of the Alpine Club in 1988 and subsequently devoted most of her energies to the *Alpine Journal*, first as Assistant Editor, then as Honorary Editor from 1992 to 1998, and currently as Production Editor.

ADE MILLER currently lives, climbs and sometimes works in Redmond, Washington. He has visited and climbed in numerous mountain ranges but has spent the last few years climbing in Washington, British Columbia, the Yukon Territories and Alaska.

ERIK MONASTERIO is a Bolivian/New Zealand psychiatrist and climber, currently living and working in NZ. He has climbed all over the world, but specialises in the Andes, where he has achieved more than 30 new alpine routes over ice, rock and mixed ground. He is engaged on research into personality characteristics and accidents to climbers.

JOHN McM MOORE is a geologist and academic by profession, a regular climber and alpine mountaineer on foot and ski for the last 42 years with a few excursions to the greater ranges; Ruwenzori, Nepal Himalaya etc. for work and pleasure. He has a penchant for Italy and the Teutonic world, has been an AC member since South Audley Street days and has served several lengthy sentences as Eagle Ski Club, Alpine Ski Club and Fell and Rock committee member, to mention but a few.

TAMOTSU NAKAMURA was born in Tokyo in 1934 and has been climbing new routes in the greater ranges since his first successes on technical peaks in the Cordillera Blanca of Peru in 1961. He has lived in Pakistan, Mexico, New Zealand and Hong Kong and in the last 15 years has made 27 trips to the Hengduan mountains of Yunnan, Sichuan and South-east Tibet. He is currently editor of the *Japanese Alpine News* and a councillor of the JAC.

SKIP NOVAK, an American based in the UK, has for the last 15 years been leading combined 'sailing to climb' expeditions from his vessel *Pelagic* to far-flung destinations like the Antarctic Peninsula, the island of South Georgia and Tierra del Fuego. In 2003 he built a successor, a 23m sloop *Pelagic Australis* that is now plying Arctic waters in the northern summer, forever in search of unclimbed summits accessible from the sea.

IAN PARNELL is based in Sheffield and divides his time between his work as a freelance photographer and as *Climb* magazine's alpine editor. After several years learning his alpine craft with lightweight first and second ascents in Alaska he's recently concentrated his energies in the Himalaya.

SIMON RICHARDSON is a petroleum engineer based in Aberdeen. Experience gained in the Alps, Andes, Patagonia, Canada, Himalaya and Alaska is put to good use most winter weekends whilst exploring and climbing in the Scottish Highlands.

ROYAL ROBBINS' list of accomplishments as a climber is long and remarkable, including first ascents of the north-west face of Half Dome and of the three great faces of El Capitan. A prime mover in the change from pitons towards less destructive gear such as chocks, he founded, with his wife Liz, the clothing company that bears his name, and sold the business in 2001.

C A RUSSELL, who formerly worked with a City bank, devotes much of his time to mountaineering and related activities. He has climbed in many regions of the Alps, in the Pyrenees, East Africa, North America and the Himalaya.

BILL RUTHVEN has been Hon Secretary of the Mount Everest Foundation since 1985 and welcomes this opportunity to put something back into the sport that gave him so much pleasure over fifty-odd years of active mountaineering. Now confined to a wheelchair, he considers himself the 'complete social climber', attending indoor events such as conferences, symposia, film festivals etc. For his MEF work, Bill has been made an Honorary Member of the Alpine Club.

DAVID SEDDON is a physician in Nottingham. He has walked, climbed and skied in a number of unusual places often in the company of John Harding or Derek Fordham. On a good day he has even been known to get to the top of a mountain. He was editor of the Eagle Ski Club Year Book from 1997-2003.

CHRIS SMITH was MP for Islington South and Finsbury from 1983 to 2005, and Secretary of State for Culture, Media and Sport from 1997 to 2001. Made a peer this year, he runs the Clore Leadership Programme in the cultural field. He is President of the Ramblers' Association, has climbed all the Scottish Munros, and has climbed in the Pyrenees, the Picos de Europa, and the Austrian Alps. Since 2002 he has been the Chairman of the Wordsworth Trust.

GEOFFREY TEMPLEMAN, a retired chartered surveyor, has greatly enjoyed being an Assistant Editor of the *Alpine Journal* for the past 30 years. A love of mountain literature is coupled with excursions into the hills, which are becoming less and less energetic.

MIRELLA TENDERINI lives in the Italian Alps with her husband, a mountain guide. She works in publishing, specializing in art books, and has also edited more than 100 books on mountaineering, travel and adventure. She is the author of several books including biographies of American mountaineer Gary Hemming and the Duke of the Abruzzi, which have been published also in English.

JOHN TOWN is Registrar and Secretary at Loughborough University. He has climbed in the Alps, Caucasus, Altai, Andes, Turkey and Kamchatka, and explored little known mountain areas of Mongolia, Yunnan and Tibet. He is old enough to remember the days without GPS and satellite phones.

DAVE WILKINSON, a university teacher, has been climbing for 41 years. During the 1970s and 80s he was very active in the Alps, repeating classics such as the Walker Spur and north face of the Matterhorn and putting up new routes on the Mönch and Fiescherwand. He has made 22 expeditions to the greater ranges, notably the Karakoram and Andes, specialising in low-key, alpine-style first ascents.

SIMON YATES has, over the last 20 years, climbed and travelled from Alaska in the west to Australia in the east, from the Canadian Arctic in the north to the tip of South America. He is the author of two books, *Against The Wall* and *The Flame of Adventure*. As well as writing, Simon runs his own commercial expedition company (www.mountaindream.co.uk) and lectures about his adventures.

Index 2005

NOTES FOR CONTRIBUTORS

The *Alpine Journal* records all aspects of mountains and mountaineering, including expeditions, adventure, art, literature, geography, history, geology, medicine, ethics and the mountain environment.

Articles Contributions in English are invited. They should be sent to the Hon Editor, Stephen Goodwin, 1 Ivy Cottages, Edenhall, Penrith, Cumbria CA11 8SN (E-mail: sg@stephengoodwin.demon.co.uk). Articles should preferably be sent on a disk with accompanying hard copy or as an e-mail attachment (in Word) with hard copy sent separately by post. They will also be accepted as plain typed copy. Their length should not exceed 3000 words without prior approval of the Editor **and may be edited or shortened at his discretion.** It is regretted that the *Alpine Journal* is unable to offer a fee for articles published, but authors receive a complimentary copy of the issue of the *Alpine Journal* in which their article appears.

Articles and book reviews should not have been published in substantially the same form by any other publication.

Maps These should be well researched, accurate, and finished ready for printing. They should show the most important place-names mentioned in the text. It is the authors' responsibility to get their maps redrawn if necessary. This can be arranged through the Production Editor if required.

Photographs Colour transparencies are preferable. These should be originals (not copies) in 35mm format or larger. Prints (any size) should be numbered (in pencil) on the back and accompanied by captions on a separate sheet (see below). Images on CD are acceptable but must have been scanned at high resolution and must be accompanied by numbered captions that match the serial numbers on the CD.

Captions Please list these **on a separate sheet** and give title and author of the article to which they refer.

Copyright It is the author's responsibility to obtain copyright clearance for text, photographs and maps, to pay any fees involved and to ensure that acknowledgements are in the form required by the copyright owner.

Summaries A brief summary, helpful to researchers, may be included with 'expedition' articles.

Biographies Authors are asked to provide a short biography, in about 60 words, listing the most noteworthy items in their climbing career and anything else they wish to mention.

Deadline: copy and photographs should reach the Editor by 1 January of the year of publication.